AN INNOCENT ABROAD

David M. Addison

Other Books by David M. Addison

An Italian Journey

A Meander in Menorca

Sometime in Sorrento

Bananas about La Palma

Misadventures in Tuscany

Confessions of a Banffshire Loon

The Cuban Missus Crisis

AN INNOCENT ABROAD

The Misadventures of an Exchange Teacher in Montana

Award-Winner's Edition

David M. Addison

An Innocent Abroad: The Misadventures of an Exchange Teacher in Montana: Award Winner's Edition by David M. Addison

First revised edition published in Great Britain in 2015 by Extremis Publishing Ltd., Suite 218, Castle House, 1 Baker Street, Stirling, FK8 1AL, United Kingdom.
www.extremispublishing.com

Extremis Publishing is a Private Limited Company registered in Scotland (SC509983) whose Registered Office is 51 Horsemarket, Kelso, Roxburghshire, TD5 7AA, United Kingdom.

Copyright © David M. Addison, 2015.

Previously published in another format as *An Innocent Abroad: The Misadventures of an Exchange Teacher in Montana* in 2011 by AuthorHouse UK Ltd.

David M. Addison has asserted the moral right under the Copyright, Designs and Patents Act 1988 to be identified as the author of this work.

The views expressed in this work are solely those of the author, and do not necessarily reflect those of the publisher. The publisher hereby disclaims any responsibility for them.

This book is a work of non-fiction. Unless otherwise noted, the author and the publisher make no explicit guarantees as to the accuracy of the information included in this book and, in some cases, the names of people, places and organisations have been altered to protect their privacy.

This book may include references to organisations, feature films, television programmes, popular songs, musical bands, novels, reference books, and other creative works, the titles of which are trademarks and/or registered trademarks, and which are the intellectual properties of their respective copyright holders.

All rights reserved. No part of this publication may be reproduced, stored in a retrieval system, or transmitted, in any form or by any means, electronic, mechanical, photocopying, recording or otherwise, without the prior permission in writing of the publisher.

This book is sold subject to the condition that it shall not, by way of trade or otherwise, be lent, re-sold or hired out, or otherwise circulated without the publisher's prior consent in any form of binding or cover other than that in which it is published and without a similar condition including this condition being imposed on the subsequent purchaser.

A CIP catalogue record for this book is available from the British Library.

ISBN: 978-0-9934932-0-1

Typeset in Goudy Bookletter 1911, designed by The League of Moveable Type.
Printed and bound in Great Britain by IngramSpark, Chapter House, Pitfield, Kiln Farm, Milton Keynes, MK11 3LW, United Kingdom.

Cover artwork and stock images are Copyright © Shutterstock Inc.
Cover design and book design is Copyright © Thomas A. Christie.
Author image and internal images are Copyright © David M. Addison and Fiona J. Addison.
Internal map designs are Copyright © Richard Addison.

To all my friends and even my foes in
Missoula, both living and dead.

The State of Montana and the United States of America

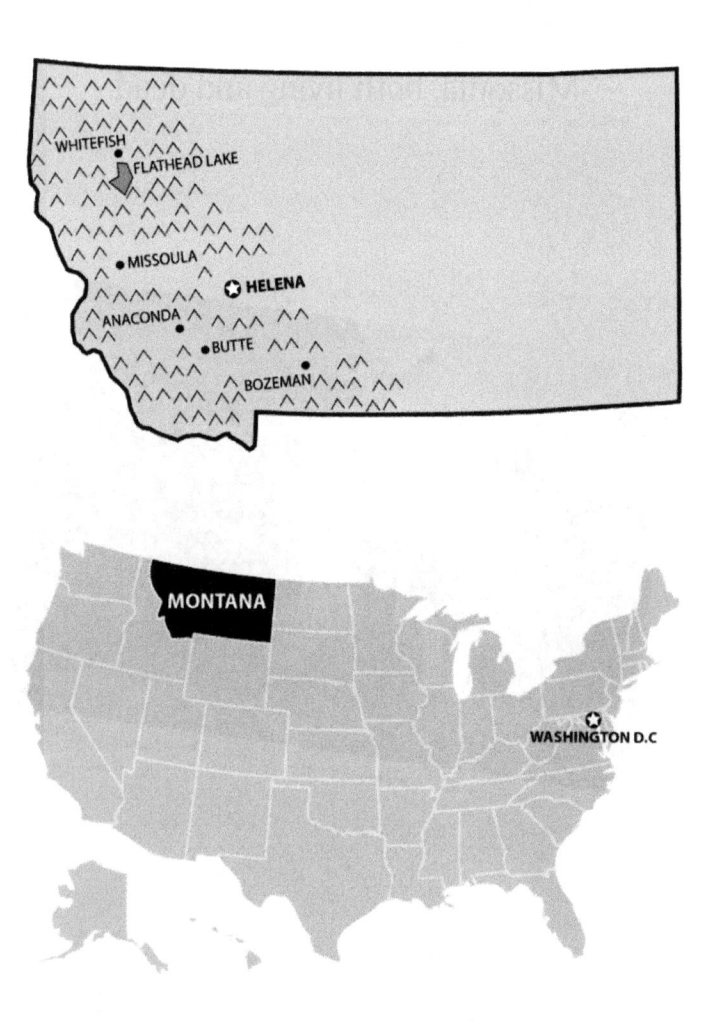

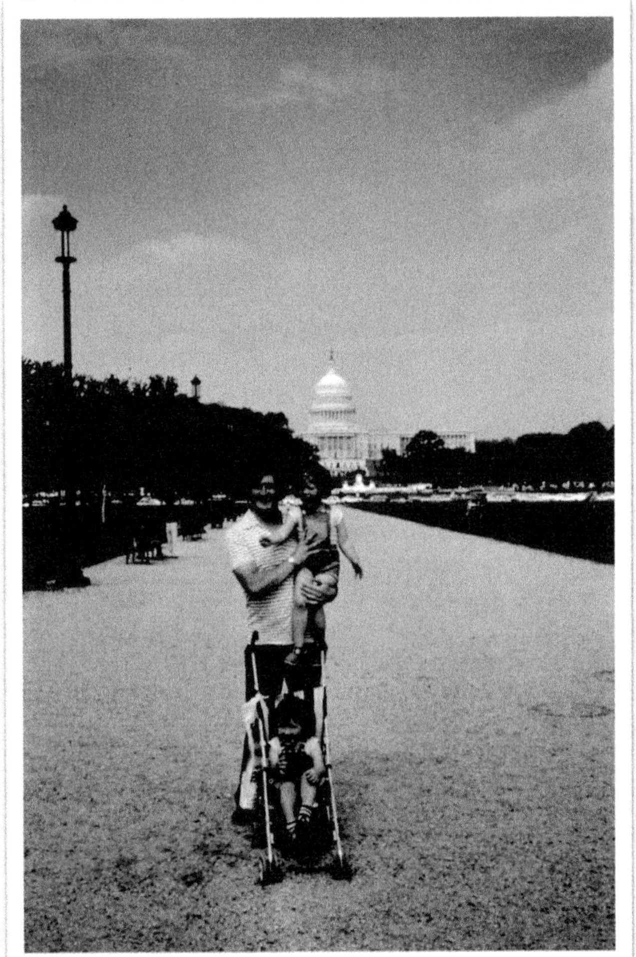

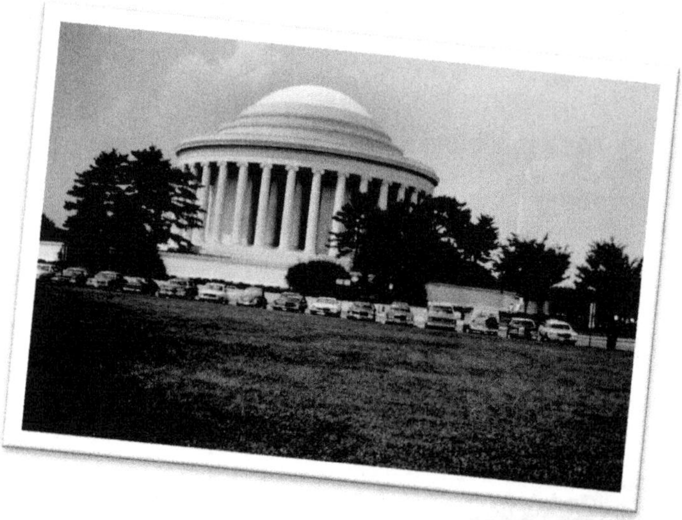

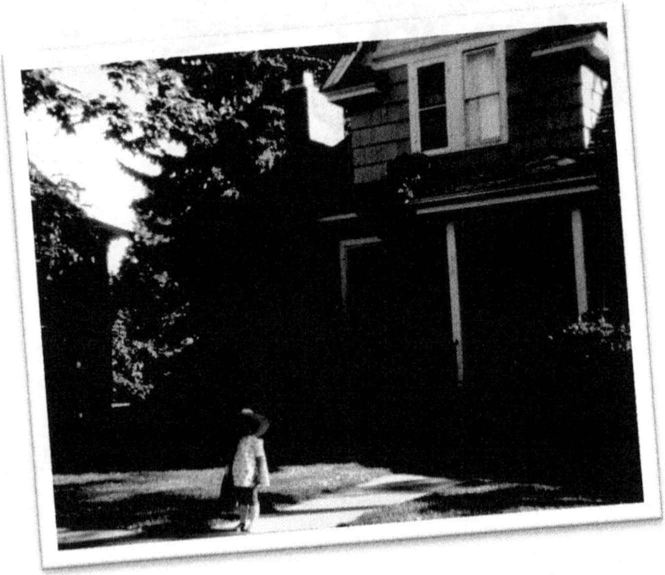

Prologue

The unrefulgent disc of the sun, although it is late June, cannot penetrate the miasma that is peculiar to Grangemouth in central Scotland. I am lying on my back looking at it and not even squinting and my nostrils have long since been accustomed to the smell.

Here I am in the sports stadium for the good of my health. I have just completed two laps of the curiously spongy track and have thrown myself on the grass verge, chest heaving and gulping in lungfuls of air with God knows what chemical additives. In a moment of madness, (I don't know what came over me – I am not remotely addicted to exercise) I had agreed to accompany my colleague Kenny in our lunch hour to this latter-day arena of competitive combat. It is empty now apart from us, so thankfully, there is no-one to laugh at my pathetic efforts to get fit.

Right now I am fit for nothing except to wonder by how much I have shortened my life by the lung-bursting deep breaths of chemically contaminated air I have sucked in. Only time will tell, but maybe I'll be run down by a bus or die in an air disaster before my natural time anyway.

The latter seems a more plausible possibility, for shortly we are to take off on the greatest adventure of our lives. Not much of a big deal for George who is only 16 months old and for whom every day brings a new experience and possibly not for Hélène either who at this brief stage in her life is twice as old as her younger brother. That makes it sound as if Iona and I had left a respectable distance between their births, as if we knew what caused children and had planned accordingly, instead of George arriving unexpectedly like a rabbit out of a magician's hat.

We are innocents, but we don't yet realise just how innocent. They say that travelling broadens the mind, and for our ages, and as far as our meagre funds have allowed, Iona and I are pretty well-travelled compared to our friends, having embarked on camping trips all over Europe. Yet neither of us has been across the Atlantic before, let alone lived in a foreign country for a year, so for us it is a great step into the unknown, the sort of step that only innocents would dare undertake because they have no conception of the hazards and pitfalls that lie in wait. But as I lie supine in the grass in this late day in June 1978 breathing in my last toxins of the summer, I am impatient for the adventure to begin.

I had applied to the Central Bureau for Educational Visits and Exchanges for a year's teaching exchange to the USA, stipulating that if successful, I should prefer to go to the eastern seaboard. The reason for this was purely financial and nothing to do with parsimony but everything to do with impecuniousness. As the exchange teacher, my fare is being paid by the Bureau, but I have to find the fares for the family myself. George goes free but does not get a seat. Hélène goes half price while Iona, naturally, is full fare. If we were placed in the east, then I would not have to find the funds for what could be a costly transcontinental journey.

Which is why, I suppose, we ended up being selected for Missoula, Montana, nestling in the foothills of the Rockies which is just about as far west as you can get in the United

States, give a few hundred miles to the Pacific Ocean. I have been posted to Emerson School in District # 7 and been matched with Mrs Marnie Charbonneau, a forty-something divorcée with three children.

We have been in correspondence. We are exchanging houses and jobs, but on the advice of the Bureau, not cars. That means her detached three-bedroomed house, which from the photograph, looks as big as a mansion, for our humble semi-detached (two bedrooms and a box room); her job as sole teacher of Language Arts to 7th and 8th grade students and mine as principal teacher of English to M3 and M4 pupils, the equivalent of the first two years of secondary school. We are teaching kids of roughly the same age but that is where the similarity seems to stop.

By the looks of it, I am going to have the easier passage as my classes are twice as big as hers and they don't seem to be expected to write half as much as my pupils either. It is not in my nature to be too optimistic however. Too much optimism results too often in bitter disappointment. Better by far to expect the worst, and when it doesn't happen, you get a nice sense of relief. So, while Marnie has my assistant, Judy, to help her, I will be on my own, though Marnie tells me her good friend, Art Moore, a 6th grade teacher, will help me out if necessary.

It was March when I had first heard that I had been successfully matched but warned that the exchange could still fall apart at the last moment and on this late day in June with all the arrangements made – medical, personal and travel – I am impatient to be gone, relishing the idea of the Wild West and the notion of exchanging the surreal pipes and cooling towers of Grangemouth's BP petrochemical industry for the snow-clad peaks of the Rockies where the air is pure.

The dream is taking more tangible shape daily, as necessary and sometimes tedious arrangements are made, as well as worrying about such things as are our cases big enough for our luggage and what do you pack for a year anyway, apart from nearly everything? It seems the younger you are, the more luggage you need. The kids have much more baggage than us and George, who is the youngest of all, has the most. Nappies mostly. Not disposable. The good old-fashioned type that you fasten with a safety pin.

"You know, I envy you, Dave," says Kenny, as if reading my thoughts. "You are getting out of the rut. But just look at me, what have I got to look forward to?"

Since he asked me to, I do look at him. His name may be Little but he is certainly not by nature. We have given up the jogging and are now in the shower and I can't help but notice despite the sporran of soapy suds, he has a dong that would not disgrace a donkey. He's older than me, has never been married and lives with his mother, which no doubt accounts for it not having been worn away by constant use.

There's not much I can say to console him. After all it is true. I had been in Grangemouth only two years, exchanging Galloway in the scenic southwest for the industrial central belt in the interests of promotion and already I felt that that was exactly what I was in – a rut. Part of it was due to the school system. Grangemouth had, uniquely in Scotland, introduced a middle school arrangement whereby the top two classes of the primary and the bottom two of the secondary were taught in the same building. This meant that I was teaching nothing but first and second year pupils and I was beginning to feel the limitations of the curriculum. It was all getting a bit repetitive and boring.

But at least I had a life outside school and a family and although I was severely short of money, the good thing was that it gave me enough problems to keep boredom at bay as I wondered how I was going to pay the mortgage every month as well as meet all the other bills. It also sparked off a hobby: making my own wine. I was too poor to buy anything remotely alcoholic. It was all I could do to keep my family in milk.

But what about Kenny? Being a bachelor, he was bound to have more money than me. He probably didn't even have a mortgage as he was living with his mother.

But who wants to live with their mother when they're forty?

Chapter One

In which the adventure begins and I meet my exchange partner.

It is 4 pm and we have just landed in Washington DC. According to the pilot, it is 90°F out there. From the plane window, I can see parked cars shimmering in the heat but it's their gargantuan size that I notice most – not a single little one or medium-sized one in sight.

Into sight lumbers a bus which by some sort of hydraulic wizardry rises from its axles and clamps on to the plane door so that all we have to do is walk down the aisle and into the bus. All aboard and the bus shrinks back to its original size before transporting us to the terminal building. I've heard it said that the Americans are lazy, that they complain about there not being a lift – "elevator" I should say – in such structures as the Leaning Tower of Pisa. But this seems to convey a different and indeed literal meaning to the expression "terminally lazy". I am impressed, nevertheless, by the gadgetry.

Whilst I try to identify and hoist our six suitcases from the carousel, Iona goes in search of a trolley and eventually we pass through customs and immigration without a hitch. It is only when we pass out of the terminal building that we get our first experience of the Washington climate as the bus-that-grew and the terminal building were both air-conditioned. This is our first breath of natural American air. Within a minute we are perspiring and our sweat glands leaking like sieves. I discovered later that Washington was built on a swamp – which is why it is not just the heat that strikes us, like the blast of air from a furnace, but the humidity.

The bus transports us through leafy countryside and it's not long before I get my first glimpse of the Potomac. Its shores are heavily wooded, not with the dark coniferous green so familiar in Scotland, but with light and variegated deciduous greens which uplift the spirits. It is wide and it is vast and it brings to mind what the vehicles on the road have already intimated to me – that I am on a different continent. In the distance I can see some rapids and already I can imagine Indians in former times skilfully negotiating them in their bark canoes.

We arrive at American University which is to be our home for the next four nights while we are briefed about life in America and educational matters. After registration, we are shown to our room. Room 602. First impressions are it must be a storeroom. There are windows but no curtains and a damp smell that turns out to be a leak in the air-conditioning unit which doesn't work. It's no use opening the window to let out the smell as that just lets in warm, moist air. We prefer the trapped, moist fuggy air to the heat of that outside so I shut the window again.

There is a cot for George though and there are cupboards and wardrobes scattered about the place in an apparently random formation. We are in fact in a student dormitory and this seemingly haphazard arrangement of furniture is designed to offer some privacy to the occupants, should they be smitten with an overwhelming desire to do some studying, or more likely, entertain a guest in their room.

The cord carpet is brown and maybe the glass is tinted in the same sort of shade, for the view outside looks distinctly gloomy and depressing, even cold, which we know not to be the case. Perhaps it is because we are tired. After all, it was 9 pm our time when we landed and then the time spent at the airport and then the bus journey followed by the registration at the university and we are pretty tired and hungry. Long past my bedtime, to say nothing of the kids'. Our hosts have laid on a meal in the Mary Grayson Center so we head off there as the first step in the addressing of one of these problems and we reckon if the kids let us get some sleep, we'll feel a whole lot better in the morning.

The Mary Grayson Center turns out to be a huge refectory. People are busying about like bees for here are not only all the British teachers with their spouses, but the American teachers and their spouses, not to mention the children of those that have them. The air is alive with the sound of chatter and the chink of crockery and it is apparent that some teachers have already met their exchanges. Somewhere in this human maelstrom, I presume, are Marnie and her brood. Please let her not discover us until the morning, I pray, when hopefully I will have a bit more energy.

The food is better than the average mass-produced variety or perhaps we are just so hungry that the sole of an old boot would have tasted good, but in any case there are mountains of it which even the vast hordes seem unable to make a dent in and even more amazing, at least to me, is there are what Enid Blyton would have called "lashings" of soft drinks. There is no ginger beer, the preferred beverage of the *Famous Five*, (maybe root beer would be the closest substitute) but from machines dotted around this vast hangar of a place, in an apparently unstoppable flow comes: Coca-Cola, Fanta, Pepsi, milk, skimmed milk, chocolate milk... My God, this must be costing the American Government an absolute fortune! It is hard for me to come to terms with this lavishness, to see what is regarded as a treat by my family, treated here as if it were as commonplace as water. I have to blink hard, and not just because my eyes are tired. Surely this must be Canaan. All that is needed is the honey to go with the milk lake.

So fed, and our stomachs bloated with Coca-Cola bubbles, we make our weary way to our depressing-looking dorm. The blinds don't work but if we want to preserve our modesty when preparing for bed, we can always hide behind a cupboard. Anyway, the kids couldn't care less and are getting fractious with tiredness, though they had slept on the plane. We had been lucky to have been allocated three seats together in the centre and to our delight, two empty ones in the same row which meant we could unburden our laps of George and let him stretch out and sleep at least for part of the flight. Hélène, however, did not sleep until we were practically at Washington.

Iona and I are relishing the thought of laying down our weary bones to sleep when there is a tap at the door. We freeze and look at each other in dismay. We both know without any shadow of doubt who it is. Whilst we stand silent and unmoving and wondering if we can get away with pretending we are out or out for the count, the tap at the door comes again, a second time, but not so much a tap as a knock saying: "We know you are in there!"

I look at Iona sorrowfully, shrug my shoulders in a gesture of resignation and step towards the door.

She is lean and dark and swarthy with coils of shoulder-length black curls. She could be Italian, or Spanish, or even Greek. This country is the melting pot of nations after all, and all her surname tells me about her background is that at some time in the past, her husband's ancestors were almost certainly French, or French-Canadian.

"Hi!" she says apologetically. "I hope you don't mind. I know you must be tired, but we just couldn't wait to see you!"

"No, of course not, come right in."

They troop in. There are only four of them, but it seems like an invasion.

"Gee, what's that awful smell?" says the bigger of the two boys. Despite the bacon and baked beans I had consumed at the Mary Grayson, I know my conscience is clear. I explain about the air conditioning.

"Sure stinks. I wouldn't like to sleep in this room."

Marnie ignores his forthright comments, leaving me unsure whether that is because this is the candid way in which her firstborn normally speaks and she doesn't mind, or whether she is ignoring them to avoid a scene.

"This is Lewis and this," indicating the smaller boy, "is Harvey, and this is Beth."

Beth is dark, like her mother, while the boys are fair.

"Lewis is 11, Beth is 9 and Harvey is 6."

I introduce my family. Lewis and Beth show an interest in George and Hélène and whilst we sit on a bed and talk, they take charge of them, leaving Harvey a roaming commission to explore our room and our things. Marnie doesn't seem to notice, or at least, doesn't seem to mind him picking them up and looking at them. I am too polite to say anything, but my concentration on what Marnie is saying is somewhat impaired by watching him to see what he's going to do next. For her part, Iona is keeping an eye on Lewis as he seems to be treating Hélène rather roughly. She is wriggling with tiredness and really just wants to be left alone to go to sleep. Don't we all?

At last Marnie interrupts our conversation to suggest mildly to Lewis that Hélène wants to be left alone to which Lewis says that she doesn't, to which Marnie responds in the same sort of tone as before, that Hélène *is* tired. Lewis repeats that she isn't and I intervene by pointing out that we've had a long flight and a long day, that for us it is already five hours later than the present time, and finally Lewis sulkily surrenders his charge and Hélène is tucked into bed.

But George seems to be enjoying being cooed over by Beth, so Lewis muscles in on that instead. I'm sure I wasn't interested in kids and babies when I was his age. I don't think I even knew where they came from and certainly couldn't have cared less, but I wouldn't be surprised if Lewis knew all the details already.

Meanwhile, Marnie and I talk of generalities. We don't talk of school at all. Marnie says how glad she is to have got the exchange and how she is the first ever to get an exchange from school district # 7 and how she is looking forward to going to Scotland rather than England and I say that I am really glad to be going to Montana instead of the east. Marnie agrees. She is a Bostonian by birth and has never regretted moving out west.

"It's totally different out there," she says. "Just you wait until you get there. The people are so neat."

I know that "neat" has nothing to do with dress sense or personal grooming. It just means "nice". I wish I could tell her the same things, but I can't. Furthermore, Marnie tells me that I am "neat" and that my family is "neat" and it is "neat" that we have got each other as exchanges as we are so well-matched. I don't know how she can tell all these things so quickly, but I wholeheartedly agree and Marnie takes her leave, saying that we'll meet again tomorrow and talk business. I tell her we certainly must do that but do not add that it was because I could not read her writing in the letters we had exchanged once we had heard we were matched. Nor do I mention that what is worrying me most are the house arrangements.

If I had known what she had to tell me about that, exhaustion or no exhaustion, I probably would not have slept at all that night...

Chapter Two

In which we are fêted at the British Embassy and I start to worry.

After a breakfast of pancakes and waffles and maple syrup and doughnuts (no wonder there are so many fat Americans) it is time for me to begin my 'work'. Meetings. First a welcome meeting, then an overview of American education by some geezer called Trump who has written a book about it. He tells us how good his book is but that is about all I get from his exposition. I ask a question about the PTA system as I had heard that parents exert a great deal of influence on American education, at least at local level and he spins off onto what, in his view, it *should* be. At least I had shown an interest, but I wish I hadn't as we could have been finished half an hour earlier. Are those daggers I feel in my back or is it just prickly heat?

At last we are released into the oven that is Washington. Marnie is at a meeting on British culture so we can't get together. I muse on what sort of culture she is likely to meet in Grangemouth. A culture shock from its absence, I should imagine, unless it is the sort of low life you find in a Petri dish. Anyway, tomorrow morning is scheduled for an official get-together, so Iona and I decide we'll take the pushchair, I mean stroller, put George in it, and we will go for a stroll.

The sun is sweltering but the humidity is horrendous. Within only five minutes we are dripping with perspiration. We come across a fire hydrant, colourfully painted like a golliwog with stars-and-stripes trousers and I wonder if that is not considered a bit rude and insulting in a city where 75% of the population is black. Anyway, even if it were turned on and sprayed us to death, we could not possibly be any wetter than we are now and so we decide, ironically, to go back to Room 602 and have a shower. As I stand under that gentle, balming spray, (actually there are a number of sprays you can choose from, from soft as silk to hard as nails) I cannot help but reflect that if George Orwell reckoned that the worst thing in the world is in Room 101, the worst thing in Room 602 is not being able to open the window to let the smell of the carpet out.

And while I am reflecting on this, it dawns on me that this must be a male dormitory. It's nothing to do with the smell reminding me of sweaty socks in a boys' changing room. No, the smell is definitely due to the leaking air conditioning. My epiphany is due to something much more subtle. Whilst our accommodation may run to unlimited drinks of the kind that does not inebriate, in the matter of mirrors it is sadly lacking. The only kind of reflecting that goes on here is in the mind, and the notion that four young women could spend an entire academic year in here without a full-length mirror is inconceivable.

* * *

I feel slightly important as we step into the august surroundings of the British Embassy. I don't suppose I'll ever be invited to it, or any other embassy again, but it is a reminder that my fellow exchanges and I are, in a small sense, ambassadors for our countries and I feel a small frisson of excitement to think that here I am, a Banff-born boy, a by-product of the boondocks, here, in these splendiferous surroundings, a guest at the British Embassy in Washington. Incredible!

But not for us a meeting with the ambassador or even any minor bigwigs. We are merely occupying the premises. It's an informal affair with wine and canapés and a chance to meet some of our fellow exchanges on a similar mission.

Chance places us beside a New Zealand couple, Will and Nelly Bennett, and a Canadian couple, Bob and Vicky Lee. I am struck dumb by Nelly. She has a voice and an accent that could cut through metal like bolt cutters, but it is her face that is truly amazing. It is a china doll's face from which she has removed her natural eyebrows and drawn them higher up with thin black arches, while below, on the bottom of the eye socket, she has painted thin lines like the petals of a daisy, meant to represent eyelashes I presume.

Whilst these have a startling effect on me, they have the effect of giving *her* a permanently startled expression. And that's not all. To complete this doll-like effect, she has rouged her cheeks in such a way they look like polished red apples, while her mouth is a bright red gash. If she were to sit on Will's knee, (a place where she would not look in the least out of place as she is so petite) she might easily be mistaken for a ventriloquist's dummy. What's more, this would give Will a chance to control what came out of Nelly's mouth for a change as it only takes me about five seconds to realise that she loves to talk and who the dominant partner in this relationship is.

By contrast, the Canadian couple are very quiet. Bob is Chinese, from Vancouver, and has that polite and deferential manner that I associate with that race but I can't help wonder why he would want an exchange to the States. Surely it can't be all that different? The educational system perhaps, but not the culture, surely? But then maybe he is more interested in American education than the culture.

It is very interesting to learn what Nelly tells me about the education system in New Zealand and it feels like she is telling the rest of the room too as heads swivel to look at us. By the time she is finished, I know more about the system in New Zealand than I do about the United States, despite my background reading and the lecture this morning. Maybe it's the way Nelly tells it, maybe it's because she has my undivided attention as I can neither avoid hearing her, nor take my eyes off her face. I still can't quite believe she is real.

From what she says, I should not like to be a teacher in New Zealand, especially if I were going for promotion. It seems that all teachers are colour-coded and promotion involves rigorous testing. Nelly is an infant mistress and a yellow, which involved a two-week, two-inspector visit plus an interview with the headmaster to get from the first rung on the ladder, which is green, to the second.

Sounds like too much stress for me. I would have stayed a green. Especially about the gills if I were in the same school as Nelly.

* * *

The next morning I meet Marnie to talk about our schools and jobs. I begin by showing her my typewritten syllabus and scheme of work as well as a range of examples of the work pupils have produced. As for what she has to do, she doesn't need to worry. It is all cut and dried, all written down. All she needs to do is follow the course, get the kids to do the reading and then the writing and if in doubt, ask Judy, my assistant. Simple really. Admittedly, it's going to be a lot of work having to familiarise herself with no less than six novels. I use a setting system and the novels in the upper classes, I have to admit, are pretty lengthy. That's just for starters. Worse still will be all the correction she is going to have to keep abreast of, from six different classes with about thirty pupils in each.

Marnie has nothing to show me but assures me she has left lots of handwritten notes. Whilst that is good to hear, I hope she has left the key to the cipher as well. She talks endlessly about "programs" but they mainly go over my head, though some go in one ear and out the other. Try as hard as I can, I cannot make sense of what she is telling me. It's too abstract. What I want to hear is chapter and verse (such as I have provided) as to what I am actually expected to *do* with her students. Maybe it will click into place when I get there, but at the moment I feel overwhelmed by too many things I don't understand and completely unprepared for the actual confrontation at the chalk face.

She tells me about some of her colleagues and warns me that they will probably play a trick on me, but I am not to let on that she told me. I take this to be a sign that she has warmed to me, otherwise she would have vicariously joined in the fun from a distance. The plan seems to be that they are going to pretend that a TV crew is coming to film one of my lessons. Thanks, Marnie, but there is no way that I would have fallen for such a stupid one as that anyway.

After our morning together, we part with me, at least, feeling rather depressed. She may be a nice person, a very neat person indeed, but organisation, it is becoming patently obvious, whatever other skills Marnie may possess, is not one of them, particularly with regard to the domestic arrangements.

For a start, it seems that there has been someone living in her house since she left, and most worrying of all is that for that reason she did not have the utilities read before she left. She says not to worry, she'll write to Terri about it and get Terri to tell her guest, Lindy, to pay them. Terri is her friend and neighbour and has been designated to help us, to show us the ropes, to be a friend in need until we find our feet and make our own friends. We had done the same thing, nominated a friend at our end, just as the Bureau had instructed.

This solution does not inspire me with confidence. That letter would be from Scotland, when Marnie found the time; when she recovers from the culture shock; when she has read all the books she must do to keep ahead of the pupils; when she is on top of her correction; when she remembers she had promised to send that letter; when Terri can decipher it. No wonder I am worried. Why hadn't she sorted all this out before she left? Why had she not instructed Lindy to make sure she had the utilities read when *she* left? That would have been so much simpler.

I suspect Marnie thinks I am being too particular, too precise and pedantic, not to say a bit mean, worrying about paying for other people's utility bills in this way. But if that was my second culture shock (the first being the non-stop flow of free soft drinks) it might shock her to know just how little I earn compared to her. It transpires that she is being paid twice as much as me, the equivalent of my headmaster in fact and presumably with the alimony she is getting from her ex-husband, Perry, she doesn't have to worry about these sorts of things too much. By contrast, I *do* worry about such things because I have to because I have little or no money to spare by the end of the month and we don't exactly live like royalty in our little house.

And that's not the only thing that is worrying me.

As well as having the utilities read prior to our departure, I had also, as the Bureau recommended, been to a lawyer and drawn up an inventory and a lease, according to the terms of which, Marnie has to pay a deposit. The only thing I did not do was to change the telephone to Marnie's name as that would have involved a charge and another to change it back after we came home.

Marnie had agreed she would do the same, but when I look at the document which she now produces for my inspection, she confesses that she did not have time to read it before she left and this is her first reading of it too. Clause 1 states how much I have to pay a month. It gets worse from there and it is clear that not only had Marnie left it to the last minute, but she had not properly briefed her lawyer on the nature of the exchange either.

It is not an encouraging start. Still, in spite of these setbacks, we get on very well, maybe because I have not let Marnie see the extent of my anxieties. For her part, Marnie seems to have none at all and I can see why that is. It's not just due to my super-organisation or a tendency on her part to be laid back: it just hasn't dawned on her yet just how small our house is and how hard she is going to find the teaching, especially at the beginning. But I can just see Lewis's nose wrinkling as he steps over the door before pronouncing: "Gee this place sure is tiny!" and I suspect that may give her some problems too.

We arrange to go to the Smithsonian that evening. Marnie arranges a taxi and pays for it. Lewis is fanatical about the Second World War and drags me off to look at that exhibition. He bores me to death telling me all about it and in the end the only thing to do is to tell him I am more interested in the space section and I leave him to his own devices and wander off to have a look at that.

They have a model, or maybe it is the real thing, of a moon-landing vehicle and there are space capsules too, the Apollo XIV, and the very first, those flown by Al Shepherd and John Glenn. I marvel at how tiny and cramped the cockpit is, admire the guts it must have taken to crawl into what would have been, at least as far as I was concerned, this tiny claustrophobic cabin with thousands of gallons of liquid fuel about to be ignited beneath my bottom, not to mention the mind-concentrating thought that should I survive that conflagration, on re-entry, I might end up as tiny cinders scattered all over the globe.

From the ceiling hangs the tiny and fragile Wright Brothers' *Flyer* and Lindberg's *The Spirit of St Louis*. Incredible to think what massive developments occurred in flight technology in less than 60 years: from Kitty Hawk to the moon – a fact I had pointed out to my pupils many, many times in my science fiction unit and here I am looking at these actual vehicles now! What a privilege! I still can hardly credit it.

And there's a lesson for me too. Have I too not embarked on a journey of discovery?

It is then that I have my second epiphany of the day, throwing my own personal journey into perspective and which makes me realise what an absolute wimp I am. There are bound to be difficulties, trials even, as I come face to face with new situations, but whatever they turn out to be, they are hardly likely to be life-threatening. What's more, had I not gone into this with my eyes open? Did I not choose and desire to get out of the safe and secure rut I was in? Would I rather stay safe and secure like Kenny? Most definitely not! These unknown experiences therefore, however testing they may prove to be, should be seen as life-affirming.

Just look at how far I have already come out of the rut! On the way back we passed The White House (which looked much smaller than I'd seen on TV) and some nondescript office buildings which our taxi driver pointed out as being the infamous Watergate Buildings, still a fresh wound in American politics. I had also been to the British Embassy in Washington and I had met Nelly, the most unforgettable New Zealander on the planet. Elephants, it is said, have long memories, but as a mere man, I know that I'll never forget her as long as I live.

In my childhood, there was a song played constantly on *Children's Favourites* called *Nellie the Elephant*. From now on, whenever I hear the word "Nelly" or see an elephant, I will always think of her. And she will always be as she was then, as if preserved in aspic. For me at least, she has discovered the secret of eternal youth.

So I gave myself a severe talking to: "What those astronauts did was truly a giant step, a leap into the unknown, so stop shivering in fear you timid little cretin – you're not doing anything like half as brave, so just get on with it and make the most of the experience."

But just like my kids in school, I wasn't really listening to these words of wisdom at all.

Chapter Three

In which I explore the nation's capital, say farewells but make a new friend in adversity.

It is the last day, at least as far as the course is concerned. I have to say I have not found it very useful or informative, and I dare say that is my fault, but the food is good and the soft drinks still flow as from a fountain. Our reward for attending all these lectures on the American educational system is a sightseeing tour of the nation's capital. I am all for this.

It is a blistering hot day but the bus, is of course, air-conditioned. In spite of this, George, who is on my knee, is wriggling and squirming. His hair is plastered to his head and he is sweating so profusely he's as slippery as an eel. He's not interested in the Capitol or the Lincoln and Jefferson memorials; he'd rather have a drink but due to our lack of inexperience of travelling in hot and humid climates, we have not brought one.

I adore the neoclassicism of the architecture and appreciate just what an incredible privilege it is to actually be here and even better to think that it is all at the expense of Uncle Sam! It's a great thing to go travelling but it is a greater thing to do it at someone else's expense.

I follow Abe's impassive gaze from the Lincoln Memorial down the length of the Reflecting Pool and it sounds mad to say it, but for the first time I really feel that the adventure is actually happening. Here I am in the capital of the United States! I never imagined that I would ever be here, let alone in this country for a whole year or more!

Now we are at the Washington Monument and George stretches out a podgy, sweaty arm towards it. He thinks it is a bottle of some life-restorative liquid and wriggles and lifts his voice in protest when he can't have it. He couldn't care less that it is built from stones from every state of the Union and is a different colour a third of the way up, the Civil War having interrupted the building. Hélène is prancing about, holding her mother's hand. She's too young to appreciate where she is. She's in her own world but we are in the nation's capital and I wonder how many Americans in this vast country have never visited it, like Marnie for example, until today. But I suppose the distance from Missoula to Washington must be about the same as from Edinburgh to Vienna and I have never been there, yet here I am in Washington DC, all the way from Banff. Thank you Uncle Sam!

* * *

In the evening we go to The Tavern, the pub on the campus. Lewis is in charge of all the children, but I trust Beth more. Marnie orders a pitcher of beer. Instead of getting a round of pints or whatever measure they have here, you get a big glass jug and the required number of glasses and get drinking. Good idea. It saves waiting while the pints are poured and even better, short unassuming guys like me who have been trying to attract the attention of the bar staff for five minutes are not humiliated by the sight of taller, more assertive guys being served the moment they arrive – if you get the pitcher.

We are joined by our friends from the Embassy, Nelly and Will and Bob and Vicky. This is the last time we shall all be together for Marnie is being picked up early in the morning and the others are off betimes also. But not us. We have to stay on another day because our flight to Missoula, via Salt Lake City, is not for another day yet. We have to amuse ourselves in Washington for another day.

But that is tomorrow. For the moment Scots, Americans, Canadians and New Zealanders enjoy each other's company. Let us drink and be merry but at last that sad time comes when we must part. We say fond farewells and hug and kiss each other goodbye and wish each other luck. We exchange addresses but that is just a way of making the present parting less sorrowful, but deep down we know that our paths are never likely to cross again.

It's going to be too early in the morning for us to say goodbye to Marnie, so we make our farewells now. It won't be forever of course, as we will be in touch by letter or phone. We wish each other luck and embrace for one last time and as we go our separate ways, I stop at the corner and look back. Instinctively, Marnie has stopped too. We wave goodbye.

I couldn't know of course that that would be the last time I would ever see her. Ironically, we had spent hardly any time in each other's company and yet we were to have a profound influence on each other's lives. That was especially true in her case.

* * *

Sunday morning and the campus is like a ghost town. The first exodus had been on Friday and the remainder yesterday. Only a few desultory stragglers are left, looking as glum as

The Free Church of Scotland congregation on a wet Sunday afternoon. Only it is morning and already warmer than the hottest day of a Scottish summer.

We stroll down to the refectory to discover that the land of milk and honey has also gone. The buzz and the chatter which made this place so full of life has been replaced with an empty, echoing chamber, the few occupants rattling around in it like the brains in the heads of some of my less cerebral pupils. The Coca-Cola fountain has dried up and it's a case of get and pay for your own breakfast. We eat a meagre breakfast for the first time since our arrival. It's good for us not to have the waffles and bacon and maple syrup and the pancakes with blueberry syrup. Much healthier to have a bowl of cornflakes and share an orange juice.

I have to make my own arrangements to get to the airport with all our worldly goods. I have been told that what I have to do is to get a taxi to the Chevy Chase Inn and then get a bus to Dulles International. But where is this Chevy Chase Inn? How far away is it? How often do these buses run? Will we be able to take our mountain of luggage on the bus? And not least, how much is it all going to cost?

There is no-one to ask; no-one to give any guidance; no-one who could have made a couple of quick phone calls and got it all sorted out. The admin team from the Bureau has gone, as have their American counterparts. Although she is a stranger in these parts, I expect Marnie could have helped, but she will be somewhere over the Atlantic by now.

I should have got this sorted out earlier, but somehow there just didn't seem to be the time. I am feeling very lonely and have a sinking feeling in the pit of my stomach. Those who had left earlier had been given free transfers to the airport. Why could that not have been us? It would have saved so much stress. But then not everyone is going to the back of beyond, to Missoula, Montana. Someone I'd met, an American, had expressed sympathy when I had told him where I was going. He made me feel as if I had drawn the short straw, scraped the bottom of the barrel.

And back at our room there is another, more pressing problem. We have been robbed. Well not exactly, as it was not ours in the first place. But someone has been to our room and taken George's cot away. As far as we can tell, that is all that appears to be missing.

So it is down to reception to report the loss and try to get it returned. Sounds easy but I am prepared for problems. That sinking feeling I had in the pit of my stomach has turned into a lead weight.

"Em... excuse me, I'm from Room 602. Our cot is missing."

"Pardon me?"

"The baby's cot in 602," I repeat. "Someone has taken it away." Then just in case they have a different word for it over here, I put it another way. "You know the thing where a baby sleeps so it doesn't fall out of bed? Well, ours is gone. It was there this morning but now it is gone. Where's my baby going to sleep tonight?"

Right away I can see I've got off on the wrong foot with her. I can read the message in her eyes: "I know what a cot is, you sarcastic pig." She removes her Medusa-like stare from my face and transfers it to a sheet of papers. "Addison. Room 602," she reads. "Right. I'll see that it is returned right away."

I breathe a sigh of relief. "Thanks."

My joy is short-lived as the Gorgon speaks again. "That will be $27. 50."

"Pardon?"

She sighs heavily, not bothering to conceal her exasperation. "For the use of the room," she explains crisply.

"But I am with the Teacher Exchange programme."

"Yes, I know that (moron) but the conference stopped on Saturday and you're responsible for the extra day."

"But no-one told us about this!"

But even as I protest, I know it is useless. She's only the messenger, not the one who makes the decisions. I tell her I had not come prepared for this development and will have to return later with some of my ever-dwindling supply of dollars.

And although I know I am wasting my time, I ask her about getting to the airport, tell her what I have heard about getting the bus from Chevy Chase but she just shrugs her shoulders and shifts her gum to the other side of her mouth. She doesn't know anything about that. Well, does she know how much it would cost to get a taxi to the Chevy Chase? She doesn't. Well, no reason why she should really, but it is her couldn't-care-less attitude that strikes a chill in my heart. Here we are in this huge continent with very little money and where no-one knows us or gives a damn. I feel small, insignificant, isolated, the lecture I had given myself in the Smithsonian already forgotten. What if Missoula and Emerson School should turn out to be one big ghastly mistake? There's no turning back now and a year could seem like an eternity.

My heart is in my boots as I turn to go.

"Excuse me!" The voice is cultured and English. I had vaguely noticed the speaker standing next to me at the desk. "I heard what you said about getting to Chevy Chase and I've been told the same thing too, but nobody seems to know anything about it."

Although he is English, he has a Scottish surname and an Irish forename – Patrick Campbell. We fall into step as we head back to the dorms. He thought he was doing a smart thing, saving money by organising his own flight to Texas instead of that arranged by the Bureau but, like me, has now found that he has had to pay for accommodation and transfers. Actually, he is more glum than me and with good reason. He says he had $100 stolen from his wallet in the refectory and his exchange partner had had some money stolen too. I would have wept if that had happened to me. He also said that there had been some camera thefts.

So here we are, stuck on this campus in the muggy heat, feeling miserable, with nothing to do or any idea of what we are going to do next. Patrick suggests we team up and go to the zoo which boasts a pair of pandas. "It's free," he adds and I am persuaded, especially when he says that the public transport is cheap. It will fill in some time until the next depressing event.

So three buses and almost as many hours later, finds the Addisons and the Campbells strolling around the zoo. We are in no hurry and do not make directly for the panda enclosure. It's sunny and it's muggy, but it always is in Washington, so we are unsuspecting and unprepared for what was shortly about to happen.

For me the flora in the zoological gardens is as much an attraction as the fauna. It is Hélène's first zoo and George's too of course, and Iona enjoys showing them the animals, especially the elephant which came within a trunk-tip of hoovering up her hair. Well, she didn't exactly enjoy that but the rest of us did. We all thought it was hilarious. And of course I couldn't but help but think of Nelly from New Zealand.

We are in the reptile house when it happens. There is a flash and a sizzle and an amazingly loud crack right over our heads. Simultaneously and in unison, the kids begin crying. I can tell they are crying because of the expressions on their faces and they way they are cowering, terrified, but I can't hear them because all of a sudden, rain is drumming on the roof like bullets. Another flash and this time the sky turns green. Another crack and we can hear the sizzle short-circuiting through the air. I have never been scared of lightning before but I am now. A line from *Holy Willie's Prayer* springs into my mind: "But Thou remembers we are dust" and I think it's quite likely that's what we could be reduced to any minute – little black heaps of dust with smoke spiralling from all that remains of us.

It's the sound of that sizzling, like bacon in a frying pan, that reminds me how awesome is the power of Nature and how powerless we would be to prevent it should it decide to fry us. The rain is unrelenting and the noise so deafening it is beginning to hurt my ears. Even George, who is profoundly deaf, can hear this. Speech is impossible. We try to calm the children and I try to look brave. Surely this cannot go on for much longer, not at this rate? There can't be that amount of water in the sky, can there? But there is. The reptile house, already muggy to accommodate its reptilian inhabitants who thrive in this sort of temperature, is becoming increasingly hot and humid and if it's like paradise for them, it's hell for us.

Like a fish out of water, I feel out of my environment and I don't like the way that that evil-looking python is uncoiling himself and flexing his muscles as if something in the air has stimulated his appetite. It's as if time has slowed down as he lethargically uncoils himself. There are yards of him and I wouldn't mind betting his name is Cassius, for he hath a lean and hungry look and I don't like the look he is giving me. I wish we had gone to the pandas first because then I could I have seen one before I die.

Once again George's hair is plastered to his head and in his discomfiture, he is squirming around in his stroller. Now Hélène wants to go to the toilet. Not surprising with the rivulets of water streaming down the glass walls. It's enough autosuggestion to make us all cross our legs. But where can we take her? And to go out into THAT! I'd rather wet my pants. But at least no one would be able to tell if I did.

And still it goes on. Will it *never* cease? But finally it does seem to ease off enough to let us hear ourselves speak as long as we raise our voices sufficiently, but by this time George has fallen asleep through exhaustion while Hélène is thoroughly miserable and girning. Normally we would not consider for a moment venturing out in this downpour in our light summer clothes, but it's getting really airless and claustrophobic in this snake pit and God knows how long we would have to wait until it decided to totally dry up. We decide to make a dash for it and reckon if we all share a taxi it shouldn't be *that* much and it certainly beats hanging around here, our ears being pounded to pulp by raindrops the size of Pandrops while we slowly die of asphyxiation.

To venture into that wetness is as satisfying as relieving a bursting bladder. So what if we are soaking right through within a couple of minutes? I would rather anything than stay in that reptilian hothouse a moment longer. In fact, there is a perverse sort of delight in splashing through the waterlogged paths and being pounded by the rain. It's warm rain after all, and being accustomed only to the cold, *dreich* Scottish variety, I reflect it's actually no different to being in a vigorous shower except for the unpleasant clinginess of my clothes hugging my skin like a scuba diver's outfit. Hélène's feet are so wet she takes her shoes off and walks barefoot. Why not? I would like to take off all my clothes and walk naked except Debbie, Patrick's wife, (not to mention Iona) would probably prefer if I didn't and besides, I wouldn't want to make the donkeys jealous.

When we get outside the zoo gates, I wonder what sort of sorry spectacle we must present with our hair plastered to our heads and our saturated clothes. Surely taxi drivers will not want us swamping their cabs? But the first one that comes along doesn't seem to mind. Like all the taxi drivers I have seen (and bus drivers for that matter), he is black, and neither the weather nor our sodden state seems to worry him one whit for he seems to have a naturally sunny disposition. We could certainly do with some heat because the air conditioning in his cab is blowing out a cold draught and chilling us to the bone.

He is interested in my accent so I tell him where I am from and why I am here and then I ask him how much it would cost to get from the university to Dulles airport. $20. It sounds like the first number that came into his head and while I am wondering if it is a good price or not and wondering whether I should phone round some taxi firms when I get back, Patrick pipes up.

"Can we book you for tomorrow?"

"Yes, suh? What time you wanna be at the airport?"

So Patrick books him and I think what a hassle it could be phoning around and comparing prices. Maybe Patrick has researched it and knows it is a good price and that is why he jumped right in there. I am starting to shiver and I just want to get back to our musty, smelly dorm and get out of these wet clothes. I want it done and dusted, goodbye to care and to hell with the cost. For the peace of mind, I book him too.

***

Having settled our dues (extra for the cot), just time to write a postcard to Mum before we leave for the airport. I put a quarter in the machine that dispenses stamps. It's 21 cents to send a postcard but all I get is a 20 cent stamp. The rapacious machine charges 5 cents commission on each stamp, so I still don't have enough money to send the card. I post it anyway.

The taxi comes to pick up the Campbells so that is a good sign. The driver would appear to be reliable. Their flight is long before ours. We have come to see them off and as I watch the taxi bear them away, I feel a vast sadness and more alone than ever. It seems we are absolutely the last to go. Now it's just Iona and me with the children in this huge land of 350 million people where no-one knows us.

I hate this place now. It's like hanging about a morgue waiting for a slab except the dead have the advantage over me in that they don't realise what they are doing. I wish I had gone to the airport with the Campbells. Hanging about airports may be the pits, but at least they contain life. I am desperate to get out of here; it's giving me bad vibes.

A year and a fortnight from now I will be back here for the debriefing. What events, good and bad, will I have experienced by then? Whatever they may be, I just wish they would begin. This hanging around waiting for something to happen is worse than anything my imagination can come up with.

Or so I thought.

Chapter Four

In which I narrowly avoid a religious conversion, meet my first Missoulians and finally arrive in Missoula, Montana.

When the taxi driver arrives, I feel like hugging him. Not only is he the person who is taking me away from this hated place, but he is the person I know best in the whole of Washington DC – no, the whole country even! An alarming thought and I don't even know his name. Once again I feel incredibly small and helpless in this vast land where everything seems so much bigger than I am accustomed to and as we head for the airport, that unwelcome thought comes unbidden again – just how wise a decision was it to take this enormous leap into the unknown? Would it not have been better to have remained safe in our boring but ordered lives in Scotland?

Our luggage is whisked away by a porter, whether we want one or not. The kids are enough to cope with, so believe it or not, I am happy to pay for this service. He picks up the cases as if they were made of polystyrene and I can't help but notice as he does so, that his fingernails seem to grow *down* all the way to the first knuckle though they are short at the ends. Unaccustomed as I am to tipping, I give him a couple of dollars and he seems happy enough with that, as am I, not to have to manhandle the luggage.

The flight is delayed by an hour as the plane has to be sprayed against some sort of Japanese beetle and as we had to be at the airport an hour prior to departure anyway, that makes two hours or more we have to fill in. But there is a buzz about the airport that is a nice contrast to the funereal atmosphere of the university, and it is air-conditioned. Hopefully, we have had our last sweat in the capital, both of the cold and the hot varieties.

* * *

The plane is a DC8 and in my limited experience of planes, the best I have been on. A very good meal, 6 channel radio, free soft drinks and games to keep the kids occupied. Better still, I am grateful to be sitting where I am and not across the aisle. Had I been, I might have been converted to Mormonism before we landed, like the poor passenger sitting next to a well-dressed young man in a well-pressed suit – the uniform of a Mormon missionary.

Had I had any doubts, I would then have known for certain that I was on the right plane. We are indubitably bound for Salt Lake City, the capital of Utah and Mormonism. I had noticed this individual earlier and had surreptitiously pointed him out to Iona so she could observe the phenomenon. He was poring over two Bibles and annotating one of them. Maybe he was preparing a lecture or doing his homework, but now the unfortunate passenger next to him is getting the benefit of his studies and the full Ancient Mariner treatment.

As he looks across the aisle at me, his face looks as stricken as if he were having a heart attack. I give him a helpless smile of sympathy. If I were a Christian I would change places with him. But I am not. Instead I mouth, "Tell him you are a Roman Catholic." I've heard that works. But he can't make out what I am saying so I make the sign of a cross on my chest but he remains uncomprehending. I expect he mistakes me for a zealot too or assumes I am scared of flying – which I'm not. It's the sky pilots who strike fear into my soul.

So there he is, a hostage to misfortune, and Mormonism, for three hours. On a plane, you can't slam the door in their faces, or pretend to be out, or hide behind the sofa or under the table. You are well and truly captive. Poor devil. Why doesn't he go to the toilet? But maybe that's worse than being Mormonised. Three hours into a flight, it might just be.

At this point, by which time the passenger across the aisle is looking catatonic, I am aware of a pain in my ribs. It is not a heart attack, only Iona, who is sitting by the window seat, her elbows as sharp as bodkins, nudging me to draw my attention to a grid pattern of buildings far below. We are about to land in Salt Lake City.

During the flight across the Atlantic, I had visited the cockpit. I saw Labrador spread before me like a monstrous raisin, folds after folds of brown rock rippling into the distance, as far as the eye could see. It was the setting for Hammond Innes's *The Land God Gave to Cain*, most of which I read under the desk whilst my English teacher was banging on about something much more worthy and it was a thrill to see for myself why Innes gave Labrador such an apposite name. And only from the air can you truly appreciate the true barrenness, the amazing scale of the inhospitable landscape. That was staggering and I am scarcely less impressed as I look down into the cauldron of which Salt Lake City forms the core and where the peaks, snow-capped, even at this time of year, form the rim.

As we soar over the city like an eagle, I feel my spirits lifted. We are about to land in another place, a famous place that I never dreamt I would ever see, even if it is only from the air. And if the passenger opposite is anything to go by, I reckon that must definitely be the best vantage point, the safest place to be with all those predatory Mormons lurking about below.

* * *

When we land we discover there is a problem. There have been high winds in Denver and the flight we were to catch from there has not even taken off yet and no-one knows when it will. It is all compounded by the fact that North West Airlines, which should have been our carrier, is on strike, has been for months and everyone, but everyone, is travelling with Pioneer Airways. It sounds like an experimental sort of airline but if you do get a seat on a flight, you should consider yourself lucky. Fortunately for us, some far-sighted person at the Bureau had switched our tickets to Pioneer some time ago, and when the plane does eventually get in from Denver, we should be on it.

In the departure lounge, I get into conversation with a man from Missoula who came off the previous Denver flight but missed his connection and has been put on standby for ours. He has been told that there are two seats available but there are three of them. I offer to take Hélène on my knee so he could have her seat but he seems hugely unimpressed by this friendly gesture. Likewise, it has to be said, I am not impressed with his son. He has a perpetual scowl on his face – enough to turn milk sour and he keeps drumming, drumming his fingers on his chair until I want to strangle him. He has a leg encased in plaster and I wish fervently it were both arms. It's just as well my offer has been rejected if he was going to keep that up during the entire flight. God forbid he should turn out to be one of my pupils. He looks about the right age.

This, my first encounter with Missoulians, leaves me with a horrible thought. What if these people are typical? On the law of averages, I am more likely to meet the most common types before the exceptions. The father works on the railways and there is a rough-and-ready look about him and his wife, which I know from experience (for have I not met scores of them before in Scotland?) means that education is not high on their list of priorities. I have them down as not being amongst the most supportive of parents and I sincerely hope they are not mine, for although percussion appears to be the boy's hobby, drumming education into the little darling's head would seem as fruitless as Sisyphus rolling that boulder up the mountain.

Time passes. Slowly. There is not much to do at Salt Lake Airport except dodge the proselytising Mormons. Actually I can't see any, but there are notices that warn: "WE APOLOGISE FOR THE PRESENCE OF RELIGIOUS GROUPS WHO MAY SOLICIT PASSENGERS." Underneath is an addendum: "UNDER FEDERAL LAW, THEY HAVE A RIGHT TO DO SO."

So, this is America where one man's right is another man's invasion of privacy. In the land of the free, why *shouldn't* they have the right to invade your privacy? They are only trying save your immortal soul after all. Their intentions are good; they are merely misunderstood. But I keep a sharp lookout for them all the same. Those sharp suits are a dead giveaway.

We do see a big ice cream parlor and the prices, even for an airport, seem much cheaper than those back home, so we spend some more of the rapidly diminishing dollars and a great deal of time there. Money well spent if it gets me away from the Little Drummer Boy who looks as if he could keep it up till Christmas. We find somewhere else to sit when we leave and yes, he is still at it.

George is nodding. His eyes are heavy, not to mention his body, so I put him down on the floor where he continues to sleep. Nor does he stir when our flight is called (not that he would hear it of course) or when I pick him up and we take our seats on the plane.

We make a brief touchdown in Bozeman and half an hour later, the lights of Missoula are beneath us. From the air, it looks an immense sprawl. Somewhere down there is our home for the next year and Emerson School, but most importantly, in the arrivals lounge, Al and Terri Hertz whom Marnie has delegated to pick us up.

There is a bump and a roaring sound as the engines go into reverse but George does not even blink. Not for the first time I envy his imperturbability. Whatever is waiting for us out there in the course of the next year remains to be seen but he is oblivious to it all.

I swallow hard for whatever it is, it is just about to begin.

Chapter Five

In which we finally arrive at our house in Missoula and find a nasty shock awaiting us.

It is 1.15 am Mountain Time and we have not slept in ages, Iona and I. To make matters worse, the handle of one of the cases is hanging off and Terri and Al are not here either. There's no excuse for that as the plane is half an hour late, which is to say, half an hour later than the two hours it is already late. They should have been here by now and cursing *us* for keeping them out of their beds. Questions, in a rising tide of panic, start welling up in my head. When will they show up? Will they show up? What will we do if they don't? Why the hell didn't Marnie choose someone more reliable? I know that at the other end, my mother-in-law will have made a point of meeting Marnie on time.

I'm desperately tired and all I want to do is collapse into a bed. I don't care if it's a bed of nails; I just want to be horizontal for a change. But it looks as if bed is going to be postponed for a while. I envy Hélène and George who are dead to the world, free of all cares and worries.

I take in my surroundings. From where I am standing, I can take in the whole terminal. Missoula airport is just the sort of airport you would expect in the Wild West, a pioneer sort of place and I see where the airline got the inspiration for its name. Our fellow passengers have departed and once they have gone, the place settles down to the sort of depressing silence that has something of the grave about it.

There is plainly nothing else to do in Missoula airport at 1.15 am, when you don't know if your contact is going to show up or not, so I may as well complain about the damage to the suitcase. I hope they are going to be reasonable and apologetic as I am too tired for a fight.

I'm sure I must resemble a chimpanzee with haemorrhoids as I make my way towards the Pioneer desk, but it's difficult to walk normally when you're lugging a ton-and-a-half suitcase by its broken handle and when your legs have been like a half-shut penknife for the past couple of hours. The good news is there no-one watching this exhibition of simian locomotion since we're the only living things in the place apart from the Pioneer employee behind the desk.

"Excuse me, I'd like to report damage to my suitcase."

"What?"

"Well, my suitcase seems to be damaged." I indicate the damaged article. "It was OK in Washington DC."

"You wanna make a claim?"

"Well, yes, I suppose I do."

The friendly face of Pioneer airways doesn't even glance at the damaged article but brings up a flimsy bit of paper from below the desk without looking for that either.

"Fill that in. Bring it back tomorrow." Up till now her attitude has been dishearteningly negative but now she presents me with two positively plump posteriors and I realise I have been summarily dismissed. Welcome to Missoula! Is this the real face of Pioneer Airways I'm looking at now? She's bending down to pick up something from a shelf behind her, probably Pioneer's manual on *How To Treat Customers Making A Complaint,* just to make sure she hasn't been too encouraging.

I am not of the slightest interest to her. Not even my soft Scottish brogue ignites a spark of interest. Surely there are not that number of Scottish exiles who drift into Missoula airport at 1.15 am, or any time? I don't have much hope of recompense but at least I'm spared verbal fisticuffs at what is for me, 3.15 in the morning. Another day I'll be fitter for the fray.

To my relief, when I next catch sight of Iona and the kids, she is in conversation with two people, one male, one female. Could it possibly be that my luck is beginning to change, that this is Al and Terri? To my immense relief, it is.

Terri is plump and friendly. She gives us a bear hug and says, "Welcome to Missoula, Montana!" Al's biceps are as thick as my thighs. He crushes my hand in his fist. I show my manliness by not yelling in pain and trying not to let it register on my face. He wears spectacles and has the sort of moustache which, if you could shave off in one piece and glue to a stick, would be pretty useful as a toilet brush. He has a swarthy complexion and his face is pitted with pockmarks.

"This your luggage?" he drawls, nodding at our six cases. There is something about his tone which gives my heart that sinking feeling again. I feel another problem coming on. "No way, man." Then, so there should be no room for misunderstanding, (unlike the room for our luggage) he repeats, "No way, man. We ain't gonna get all that stuff in the trunk. What cases you wanna bring? I can only take three. We'll get the rest tomorrow."

I try not to show my deep and utter despondency. Not only does it mean more money unnecessarily spent on left-luggage lockers, but as my eyes sweep round the entire terminal, I can take in at a glance that the situation is even worse than I had supposed. Apparently left-luggage lockers have not yet made their pioneering way this far west. For the small price of a locker fee, or three, I might have secured and saved half my worldly goods, at least as far as this continent is concerned. Such a cost would have been a small price to pay against such a loss.

And it is this possible loss that is exercising my mind. It worries me so much that if I had had the strength left in my body, I would have carried these cases myself rather than leave them here, unprotected like this. But I haven't. I feel as weak as Samson, shorn. Besides, I don't even know where I am going or how far it is. From what I had seen of Missoula from the air, it looks as if it could be miles.

Iona and I look at each other helplessly. Has she a better idea than me of what each case contains? She may have, but I can see she is closer to complete exhaustion than I am. Her eyes are pleading: "I don't know. You choose. I'm too tired to think."

This could be a vital decision. We could be looking for what may be the last time at those possessions which must sustain us throughout this year. I indicate the three largest cases. Since the kids have much more luggage than we do, I've probably chosen piles of nappies and short frocks.

Inwardly, I'm cursing Marnie. Just another example of her lack of organisational skills. Why couldn't she have sent someone more reliable, or someone with a car big enough to collect all our luggage? Surely, from the amount of her own luggage, she could have at least warned Al and Terri that there would be a lot of it? My mother-in-law had had to have a roof rack fitted on her small Vauxhall to take us and our luggage to the airport and that would have remained in place in order to transport all Marnie's goods and chattels back to

Haygate Avenue. She will have landed on her feet. Why, oh why, couldn't we?

That feeling that I've made a mistake, possibly the worst of my life, is recurring so often that it is beginning to haunt me. What is a poor teacher and his family from the north east of Scotland doing in the north west of the USA? I can't suppress the feeling that I am so far out of my natural environment that it was never meant, in the grand scheme of things, that I should be here. Otherwise, why, in this land of gas-guzzlers had we been unfortunate enough to end up with probably the only family in Missoula with a small car?

As if they were feathers, Al picks up the rejected luggage (including the damaged case – I reckoned it would be harder to steal) and stows them in a corner of the lounge.

"Will they be OK?"

"Yeah, sure," Al grunts and I have to trust him. After all, he is a cop and he should know what the crime rates are.

We carry kids and Al carries luggage out to the car.

"Is this your car?" I ask him in amazement.

It is my first close encounter with the T-Bird immortalised in the *Beach Boys* classic. Plenty of room, you would have thought, for two small kids, two little Scottish people and six suitcases.

Al mistakes my tone for admiration and his 44-inch chest swells out another two inches, belying his nonchalant, "Yup."

It soon becomes clear why there is not enough room for our luggage. Most of the boot space is filled with a big red box with a white lid and a tap at the side.

"What the hell is that doing there?" my mind says. "Why, in the name of the wee man, could he not have taken that out before he came to pick us up?" But my voice actually croaks, "What's that?"

"That's a cooler," says Al as he fits two of the cases around it. He takes the lid off. There must be two dozen cans of beer in there, nestling amongst cubes of ice. "Here, you wanna beer?"

"No you great big plonker, I definitely do not want a beer. I just want all my cases in the car. It's nearly four o' clock in the morning as far as we are concerned and if you had taken out that bloody big box before you came to pick us up, like a normal person with half a brain, then maybe I could have got another case, maybe two, in the car and then perhaps I would have something else to wear for school other than a nappy and a frock which will come down as far as my nipples if I am lucky. And, by the way, why would you want a cold beer at this time of night, I mean morning, anyway? And you didn't even get here on time," I add rather petulantly.

But Al is too busy cracking open a beer for himself to read the rant written in my face. Apparently carrying these heavy cases to the car has worked up a thirst.

We're in the car now. In the back, Iona and I have a child on each lap with a case between us. Plenty of room to have stacked the other cases beside us as well but I can't raise the energy or courage or lack of politeness to point this out.

Al slugs his beer as we make our way out of the airport and swing towards the lights of Missoula, while Terri swivels round and talks. "What kinda trip you have? Did you meet Marnie? She's neat, huh? What d'you think of the kids? They're really neat kids, aren't they? You lookin' forward to teachin' in Emerson?"

I make what's meant to sound like encouraging noises. I have Dramatic Arts in my degree, have trod the boards in amateur productions, even produced plays myself, but I'm not trained to RADA standard and I doubt very much if I'm producing the right amount of enthusiastic sounds now. It is hard to do so when your heart is in your boots and your eyes are mere slits and all the energy you have left is concentrated in a superhuman effort to keep them open that far.

"We're gonna show you the town," Al interrupts Terri's monologue. "Show you the school."

You don't argue with a cop, especially with one who's got biceps like a road roller. Besides, he might be a bit insulted if the first thing we do is throw this kindly gesture of friendship in his face.

"Em, thanks," I hear myself say and dimly I can hear Iona making "Gee, that's really kind of you noises" but we look at each other in the dim interior of the car in wordless despair.

Terri points out landmarks, shops and streets. Al points out bars. Now we are passing an austere red brick building with lots of windows and wire-mesh fencing. I don't need anyone to tell me that this is Emerson School. I'll see plenty of that later. I didn't particularly want to see it now. In fact I definitely do NOT want to see it now but I hypocritically express what's meant to sound like sounds of interest and heartfelt thanks for taking us miles out of the way and keeping us out of our beds even longer. The kids have been mainly sleeping since Salt Lake City and I know, and Iona dreads, that in three hours if we're lucky to get even that long, they'll be up and clamouring for food and attention.

But finally we are turning into journey's end – Lincoln Street, though I was soon to realise that the Americans don't bother with "street" and "avenue" and "crescent". The severe grid pattern doesn't allow anything as sexy and curvaceous as a crescent, so they wouldn't say that anyway, though whimsically they say things like "Paris, France" or "Rome, Italy" just in case, understandably, you might confuse it with some two-horse town of the same name in some state or other.

"So here we are guys! Home! 914 Lincoln!" chirrups Terri as Al pulls up outside a house. The rest of the houses in the street are in darkness but this house, our house, is brilliantly illuminated, like Leonard Mead's house in Ray Bradbury's *The Pedestrian*.

"Oh, my God," I mutter inwardly in a mixture of panic and despair. "How long have these lights been on?" As if I don't have enough problems already without paying the bill for this, never mind Lindy's! This is not so much a sign but a burning beacon telling me that coming here was one big mistake.

Terri promises to call round tomorrow with our missing luggage. I hope that she does and that it's not "missing" in the irretrievably lost sense of the word, but I'm not entirely hopeful. They carry in the remaining luggage we do have and dump it in the hall, bid us good night and we're left alone in the house that is to be our home for the next year. We're too tired to look around and the first thing must be to get the kids off to bed, followed by us, just as soon as we can make it.

But before I do that, I have an even greater priority. I switch off every light in sight as fast as I can, before joining Iona upstairs to help get the kids into bed. They whimper and waken momentarily as we get them into their sleeping suits, but they are asleep on their feet and so, practically, are we.

"What the hell possessed them to light the house up like that?" I grumble as I bend George's arm halfway up his back into his sleeping suit. Fortunately for him, he appears to be double-jointed.

"I expect it was meant to make us feel welcome."

"Hmm."

She's right of course. They weren't to know how worried I am about Marnie not having the utilities paid before she left, not to mention having someone here burning electricity through the entire night, for all I know.

It would have been depressing, I suppose, to have come to a totally dark house. But Al and Terri just didn't realise how much more depressing it was for me to come to one which was lit up like a Christmas tree in early August.

Chapter Six

In which we explore our new home, find some bizarre objects d'art *and further problems come to light.*

It must be morning. The bedroom is light and there is not a light on. Iona is standing over me. There are tears in her eyes. No, it's worse than that; they are positively running down her cheeks. I am drugged with sleep but already my heart is thumping in alarm. Has one of the kids died of exhaustion during the night and Iona has just discovered it?

"You've got to get up," she says. "I've been up for *hours* and you've just got to come downstairs. I can't stand it!" Her voice chokes and she hurries off again and in a soporific state of panic I wonder what can possibly be wrong. A glance at my adjusted wristwatch is enough to tell me it's too soon to start worrying about the luggage. It must be something else.

I swing my legs onto a bare wooden floor, make my way along a bare wooden corridor and down the bare wooden stairs. Our luggage is still in the hall where we had left it last night. Through a square arch without a door, there is a room ahead of me which Marnie had described as the "family room". That leads to the kitchen, also without a door, where I can hear the kids gurgling and Iona sniffling. I am really worried by now. It's far too soon for homesickness surely to God, so what can it possibly be that is upsetting her so much? Obviously the kids aren't dead which makes me worry all the more and of all the panic I've experienced since I arrived on this continent, this is by far the worst.

I make my way into the kitchen where it is difficult for my eyes to pierce the Stygian gloom. This house, which was a bright beacon of welcome last night, is as dark and gloomy now as it was light last night and about as welcoming as the grave.

George and Hélène, still in their sleeping suits, are pinned behind a big, dark-oak table so they can't fall out, their eyes as wide as owls at this hellish time in the morning.

I let my adjusted-to-the-gloom eyes wander around the room. There is a monstrous brown fridge, a cooker, a sink, and above it, the only window in the room, a very small one. Outside it, the branches of a huge fir tree, so close that they are practically touching the panes, effectively cut off any light from penetrating the interior. The window may as well give up the struggle. That small aperture is never going to compete against what must be, by the height and density of it, a tree that must be at least a century old.

On the table, to counter the effects of the dark, there is a small Anglepoise lamp directing its feeble beam six inches ahead onto the table's surface, while the rest of the room remains in gloom. When I pick up the head to adjust it, it flops back like a drunk's and a shower of sparks at the base briefly provides a pyrotechnic display that lights up the room. George flaps his arms in amusement and makes noises that mean: "Do that again daddy! Do it again!"

"Jesus! Why are you using this? It's bloody dangerous! Why don't you use the main light?"

"Because it doesn't bloody work, that's why!" Iona snarls.

Her self-pity has given way to anger at me. Which is only fair as it is my fault that we are in this mess in the first place. Why did I ever want to leave our cosy, semi-detached, fully carpeted, well-lit, miniscule house in Brightons for this dark mansion in Missoula, Montana, halfway around the globe, away from friends and family, where our only points of contact were Al and Terri who couldn't even turn up on time, couldn't take all our luggage and couldn't understand that all we wanted to do, with two small children, was to crawl off to our beds, not have a guided tour of Missoula when our eyes needed to be propped open with matchsticks and to cap it all to find that the house was aglow, lit up with electricity I couldn't afford to burn?

I must have been mad to exchange that for this. I feel like weeping myself. Why couldn't I have been content? What hell is this I have brought my family to? But there's no going back. We are here for a year now, like it or lump it.

What Iona said about the light is true. Click as I might, there is no response from the switch on the wall. The kitchen remains as dark as my mood.

"And just look at this place!" Iona says.

From the gesture which accompanies her tone of despair, I deduce she means the kitchen rather than the house in general. The tears, at least, have dried up, but look in imminent danger of bursting out again. And here I have to confess that if there is one thing I really don't know how to handle, it is a crying woman. I think I know how to handle a happy woman or handle a woman to make her happy, but a tearful woman I just don't know what to do with.

The gloom of the kitchen is heightened by black linoleum on the floor and as one lifts one's gaze to the wall decorations, the depressing mood is carried on to the walls. Nailed to thick and uneven planks of grey, weathered and apparently ancient pieces of wood, are what appear to be, at first glance, medieval torture instruments. There is an assortment of knives, some without handles and the blades have been whetted down to slivers of steel, though Sheffield stainless they are not – for they are all covered with a patina of rust or could it even be blood? There are also metal shapes, with sharp edges, in different patterns, some round, some square, some star-shaped but all bearing as much rust as my (t)rusty lady's bicycle back home, which I use to get to school when Iona needs the car.

"What the hell are they?" I ask, somewhat ingenuously, wondering why you would ever want to attach these things to boards which look riddled with woodworm anyway.

"Baking things. For cutting out dough."

"God! Wonder who last died of food poisoning from them."

"I think they are meant to be ornaments. And just look at this."

Leaving the kids to thrust their tiny fists into the trough of their Pelican Bibs whence have fallen regurgitated and missed-the-mouth morsels, I follow Iona back into the family room. Hanging on the red-striped wallpaper by a piece of red wool is a yoke, painted red, the sort of thing milkmaids wore in the olden days. Only it's not a complete yoke – the ends are missing from it, the bits where the milkmaid would have slung her pails. Pretty important bits I would have thought. You can see the white wood showing through the splintered ends where they have been snapped off.

I study this exhibit as if looking at the *Mona Lisa*, not sure what to say. I've never been that impressed with the *Mona Lisa*, can't understand what all the fuss is about, but I know that to admit that would be tantamount to admitting I am a boor, an idiot, a person without any culture. So just how *do* you interpret *Yoke on the Wall* by what looks to me like the work of that lesser-known, not to say, positively obscure Korean artist, Pi Sa Junk?

Personally, I think Marnie must be mad, first of all for buying this and secondly for hanging it up on the wall to show how she has been conned into buying this piece of wood with the ends missing – probably calculated to make its provenance appear more ancient and authentic. That's what it looks like to me; but if I wanted to impress, I could say, after deep and meaningful reflection: "This yoke, painted red, represents the yoke of the Communist regime, while its splintered ends symbolically represent both the anguish of the people's suffering and how they will eventually break free, but not before the rivers run red with blood, represented by the red wool."

But before I can say anything, Iona directs me to the other side of the room. On the windowsill, in front of which is a red couch, there is an array of old bottles. Some of them are Coca-Cola bottles, the original ones with the iconic curvaceous shape but these have rusty tops and the contents have long since gone. Clearly Marnie has a fetish for rust. I remember her telling me how much she loved her house and that she collected "antiques".

There is a big black fireplace, though it is made of red brick, and a mantelpiece which is a repository for more rusty bottles and other unidentifiable objects, though amongst them, I do recognise the jawbone of a creature that probably belonged in life, to a rat. It must have been to the rat dentist when it was alive as it has had some extractions and since the remaining teeth haven't any fillings, I deduce it was a poor rat who elected to have extractions rather than pay for the much more expensive fillings. Not surprising in this country where everyone has to have private health insurance. Still, one wonders, why would you put such a thing on your mantelpiece? Unless you wanted to collect some dust in it I suppose. It's good for that as I can see.

In a corner is what looks like a butter churn. My aunt Janet used to have one of these, but not in the living room. As one might expect, its handle is seized up with rust. It hasn't churned butter in an aeon. But there is something else in the room that does churn something and that something is my stomach and the object which causes it to churn is the chair which takes up a dominant position before the fireplace. Neither of us has seen anything like it in our lives before. It is a rocker but not the spindly thing you think of when you think of a rocking chair. This is a solid piece of furniture with intricate carvings on the supports of the broad arms. But what makes us both gasp in incredulity is the seat and the high back.

It has been upholstered in what looks like the pelt of a woolly mammoth but probably is actually genuine and dirty-looking, Old English sheepdog. It is repellent but at the same time fascinating. I shudder to think what manner of insect life crawls in their shoals and thousands amongst its matted and knotted hairs. Surely, in a previous life, before Marnie was conned out of more of her dollars in some "antique" shop, it must have belonged to some Viking chief who from that very throne had ordered the next rape and pillage. It would not look out of place in a longhouse where the smoke from the fire might fumigate it, but here it just looks plain unhygienic and ugly. Yet, drawn by a kind of awful fatalism, I *have* to sit in it. Now I know how the sailors on the Rhine must have felt when they passed the Lorelei.

This room is dark too, because, although the window is quite large, it is screened with net curtains and in place of a tree this time, a massive bush obscures the bottom third. Our original fascination with the *objets d'art* is beginning to be displaced with depression as this second room, despite its bright red wallpaper, exudes a gloomy atmosphere with its associations of death when you think of the jawbone of a rat and the beast which gave up its life so that hideous chair could be created.

I realise all too well why Iona had to get me up. The archway to the dungeon of doom where Hélène and George are contentedly breakfasting faces the window. We pop in to see they are all right. They seem blissfully unaware of their surroundings. We must find out what the rest of the house is like. Better to get it over with all at once, like ripping off Elastoplast in one movement of exquisite torture rather than the agonising hair-by-hair method that wimps prefer.

Out to the hallway again. This is the nicest room in the house so far, but how can we live for a year in the hall? There is a bookcase from floor to ceiling which looks interesting. I believe you can tell people's characters from the books they read. I expect to find books entitled *The Lust of Rust* and *How to Create your own Dungeon* but that will have to be for later. The only bad thing about the hall is there is a huge rug made of rags covering the wooden floorboards and our abandoned cases remind me that we only have half our luggage. The rest is probably heading out of state at this very minute.

Aah ha! There actually *is* an internal door downstairs. There is one ahead of us now and it is shut. What fresh horrors lie behind it? If the kitchen is the dungeon, maybe this is the torture chamber. But it's not. To our surprise, it is a large and airy room. There is a window which is unobstructed by any foliage whatsoever although it does boast the dreaded netted curtains. There is a comfy-looking, honey-coloured sofa and, wonders to behold, there is a carpet on the floor! There is even a piano. Doesn't mean anything to me, but Iona, who can tickle the ivories, is bucked up. Typically, there is not a door into the next room which turns out to be the dining room if the table and chairs are anything to go by, but there is a window at the far end and wonders of wonders, it also is totally devoid of vegetation.

Iona and I don't need to speak. We know that this will be where we will live. This will be our nest. We can close that door and forget the great hairy chair and the kitchen. Well, not really, as that is where Iona will have to cook, but we know there is an escape from the Adams' family room with the great hairy monstrosity and the yoke that wasn't a yoke and the empty rusty bottles and the jawbone of the rat. The butter churn I could live with.

And so, Iona and I, feeling slightly uplifted, make our way back from the world of light and sanity to the world of gloom and madness where we'd abandoned the poor innocents. Had we known then that actually we were to spend most of our winter months in the family room, I think, at that moment, we *would* have gone mad with despair or Iona would have grabbed the children and gone back to mother.

There is still the rest of the house to explore. A basement, downstairs, naturally, and three bedrooms and a bathroom, upstairs. The bathroom is at the end of a long corridor, very good for skating and breaking your neck on. There is a shower over the bath which is a luxury for us, as we don't have one.

As we wander from bedroom to bedroom, each of which is bigger than the biggest room in our house, I notice that for some reason, Hélène's is the only one with a carpet. For a moment I entertain the mad thought that we might move in here, but a single bed is too narrow for both of us and instead, I reflect on the likely culture shock Marnie is experiencing at 20, Haygate Avenue, Brightons, Falkirk with her brood of three pre-adolescents. From what I had seen of them, the boys would be likely to be vociferous in their protests. No shower, no dishwasher, no bare floors, no basement, no "antiques" but above all, no space. No doubt after they had made their exploration of the house (it wouldn't have taken them long) they too sat down in dismay and wondered how they could last an entire year living on top of each other like this. Did Marnie too, have misgivings about how she was ever going to cope, all on her own with three children? And then it hits me how brave she was to undertake this expedition – unless desperation made her bold of course.

Whatever Marnie's children thought of their new abode, our infants, by contrast, couldn't yet express a vocal opinion, at least in what passed for intelligible English. Well, that's actually not quite fair. George, being 18 months old, could hardly be expected to be a lexicon, even if he had not been profoundly deaf. Hélène, now three months short of her third birthday, was a reluctant talker at first. And when she did finally utter her first word, long after the books on child development said she should, she eschewed the conventional "da da" for "cock" which, to a non-poultry orientated person like myself, but the father of what I was certain would be an increasingly irresistible daughter as she grew up, filled me with alarm and made me think of taking an immediate course in moat construction.

What happened was that Iona's mother, exasperated at her first grandchild's lack of communication skills, (and as an infant teacher, she knew only too well how far Hélène was lagging behind in the speech development stakes) made up her mind to do something about it. So, whilst she was baby-sitting for us one night in her house in Paisley, she made up her mind to make that baby talk. Goodness knows how many objects she had presented to the infant before, finally, she held her before the grandfather clock which stood in the hall and drummed into the child: "clock, clock, clock." Her perseverance only partly paid off. She got "cock" instead. There may be an "l" of a difference, but Iona's mother was satisfied.

There's only the basement left to explore. To get to that, I have to go back through hell's kitchen and down some stairs at the end of a passage which leads to the back door. Iona stays to administer to the children who have apparently finished their second course from the trough of the Pelican Bib and are clamouring to be set free.

I must explore the basement on my own. What delights lie in wait for me down there I shudder to think.

Chapter Seven

*In which the exploration of the
house of horrors continues.*

The door creaks open ominously. There is a light switch on my left and a flight of wooden steps. The light scarcely penetrates the gloom which doesn't altogether surprise me, but one thing quickly becomes apparent, if the kitchen ornaments are rusty, then this is dusty. Dust everywhere. Dust on boxes, dust on bookcases, dust on the books in the bookcases. Dust on the walls, on the floor, on the beams of the ceiling. Motes of dust, disturbed by my presence, create a miasma, seeking somewhere else to settle. And then suddenly, comes the alarming thought: *This is just the sort of place where Norman Bates kept his mother.* What could be lurking behind that bookcase? It wouldn't surprise me to find her there, in her rocking chair. My God, it could even be the twin of the one upstairs, rocking, gently rocking with its horrific occupant ensconced or even worse – empty, which means she must be somewhere close at hand, ready to pounce...

My eyes are now becoming adjusted to the half light (if only we had this much in hell's kitchen.) The light is enough to show a shadow, a shape, which I was just beginning to make out. I feel the hackles on my neck rise, and those lines from *Macbeth* suddenly spring to mind:

Why do I yield to that suggestion

Whose horrid image doth unfix my hair
And make my seated heart knock at my ribs...

Exactly how I am feeling, Will. My heart is beating again after its momentary seizure and seems to be making up for lost time by beating twice as fast as I stand transfixed by a huge shadow on the far wall – a huge, thick, flaccid tentacle as if some giant octopus or squid or some unknown creature of the deep is lying in wait to reach out and grab me.

My throat is dry, (no wonder with all this dust) but logic dictates that this obscene shape cannot really be what it seems, so I make my way, shuffling through a carpet of dust, towards the awesome shadow on the wall and relief flows through me as I realise what it is. It is merely what I now call an "electricity eater" because of the cost to run it. I am referring of course to nothing more sinister than a tumble dryer with its elephant trunk of an outlet hose. But instead of being given an outlet outside, as it should, the end of this hose is lying languidly over some boxes so that instead of spraying its *oos,* as we say in Scotland, into the wider world, here it is destined to spread more and more fluff and dust in this place forever until, in the fullness of time, it must surely resemble the pile of the Golden Dustman in *Our Mutual Friend.*

Anyway, it certainly explains why there is so much dust down here. But there won't be any more dust added *this* year, I resolve with all the assuredness of a man who thinks he is the boss of the house, but has yet to discover, after only six years of marriage, that he is merely the pawn. Surely to God, if we can manage to dry our clothes in Scotland's damp climate, we must be able to dry them here without this contraption! I make an executive decision not to tell Iona about it. I know I have only to say I saw a rat down here and she will never set foot on even the first step and I will save a packet.

As I climb back up the stairs and put out the light, I reflect that it nevertheless seems a good place to keep your mother if your name is Norman Bates. It also makes me wonder why we don't have basements back home. It seems such a waste of space in our crowded little island and it would be ideal for storing all my homemade wine – a real cellar. But maybe it has something to do with the water table. In any case, it is a great pity we don't have them.

When I get back and report to Iona that there is nothing down there but junk and possibly some rats and probably Norman Bates' mother, she trumps me. She has been exploring herself and has a discovery to report. She tells me she has discovered something in the cupboard under the stairs. She is far too calm for it to have been a body, but had I found her hysterical, I would have known instantly who had put it there.

It's only a Hoover and it is at least as old as me. In fact it looks like a prototype. *Hoover erectus* by the look of it, but I am not an authority on domestic cleansing equipment, so I could be a hundred years out, give and take.

"Have you tried it? Does it work?" I am wondering if this is a functional piece of equipment or if it is an *objet d'art*.

"Does it *look* as if it works?" Iona replies scathingly.

I plug it in at the nearest point and it emits a feeble beam from the glass panel at the front. I click the ON switch and a hellish roar and a vibration suddenly assaults my senses and makes me start. From the casing of the machine, a fountain of sparks lights up the gloom of the family room. I hastily switch it off but the air is filled with the acrid smell of an electrical fire.

"This house is a death trap!" Iona is near to tears again. She stomps off to get the kids washed and dressed.

I'd better get dressed too in case Terri arrives with the cases. I put the body of *Hoover erectus* back into its mausoleum and am just about to climb the stairs when I notice a piece of paper lying next to the telephone.

It's addressed to me, from Lindy, Marnie's friend from up north, in Whitefish. She says she has paid the papers and August's garbage removal, but she owes me for four phone calls. No mention of what worries me most – the electricity bill. Perhaps her note is meant to sound like *a quid pro quo,* that the papers and the garbage are intended to cancel out the electricity. At least I don't have to worry about the gas bill – there was enough light in the kitchen to notice that this is an all-electric mansion and however else it may get us, it won't gas us to death.

Once upon a time, I had an arrangement with the local Post Office and Newsagents to reserve a copy of *The Glasgow Herald* but, as often as not, when I went to collect it, it had been already sold. I didn't need this additional stress in my life, so I severed my relationship with the Post Office/Newsagent's. As a result, Marnie need not buy a paper unless she wants to but it looks like I am saddled with Marnie's *Missoulian.* I could always stop it I suppose, but it's just another example of Marnie's lack of foresightedness and she should have cancelled it before she left or asked me if I wanted to continue it. Perhaps she had, only I couldn't decipher her writing.

But the garbage bill is not something I *can* stop nor was prepared for. It had not occurred to Marnie, apparently, to inform me about this and it's not something that in Scotland she will have to stump up for either – it's already taken care of by my prepaid rates. It seems to me that in this house, I could die a death from a thousand financial blows unless it was by electrocution of course, which seems increasingly likely.

As regards phone calls, I knew from my chat with Marnie that local calls were free but out of town calls were not and were horrendously expensive. That sounded good news to me, as apart from the occasional call home we might make, all our calls *would* be local. But where had Lindy been phoning? Whitefish probably. God knows, that is probably far enough. Her note also invites us there sometime, so she will surely pay for the electricity she has used for the past four weeks or so, won't she? But since it doesn't seem to have occurred to her to offer, it would be embarrassing beyond words to have to ask.

Meanwhile, in the bathroom, Iona is getting the kids out of their sleeping suits preparatory to getting them washed and dressed.

"David!"

I know by the tone of her voice that this is more than just wanting help with the kids' ablutions. What has gone wrong now?

Before I get there however, I can hear the sound of running water. Not a trickle, but a torrent. Iona points to the WC. We have the Horseshoe Falls in miniature in the bowl and it is filling up rapidly.

"Oh, my God!" I am a bit of a technophobe. In fact, I am worse than that. I am the most untechnically minded person on the planet and I've got to get this Niagara stopped and by the looks of it, I don't have long to do it and if I can't get it stopped here, I haven't a clue where the stop cock is to cut off the supply from the mains. We're going to have water flowing down the stairs in a minute unless I get this sorted out – and fast!

I whip off the lid of the cistern and wrestle with the ballcock. Miraculously, the water stops. The sound of rushing water, silenced, is the best sound in the world and even better, the tide that was threatening to engulf us is actually retreating. I replace the lid on the cistern. Simple really, when you know how. I hope Iona is impressed with my masterly technical skills and how I manfully came to the rescue and solved the crisis in seconds. I start to walk nonchalantly away to get dressed, as if it's the sort of thing I do a hundred times a day. But Iona halts me in my tracks.

"Will it work the next time?"

Damn! She's right of course. And if it doesn't and if I can't fix it this time... Thoughts of another inundation torment me as I reach for the handle of the flush, but as I reach for it, even I can see that it is not going to work. The handle is in the depressed position and I come out in sympathy. I mutter curses under my breath, but not low enough apparently, for these new sounds seem very attractive to Hélène's young ears.

"Ugga! Ugga! Ugga!" she chants, picking up the refrain as she hears it and in her delight, tries to skip around the room in her sleeping suit, which is a bit like running in a potato sack.

At the bottom of the rusty, filthy, disgustingly discoloured cistern, I can see an S-shaped piece of wire that looks as if it may have been made out of a coat hanger. I can see what its function is and it looks exactly like the Heath Robinson sort of repair I would have made. With horror, I realise I am going to have to put my hand in there. I'd rather put it into a tank of piranhas, but there is nothing else for it. I am up to my elbow and fishing about for the stupid bit of wire, but it's like guddling for a minnow blindfold because, just to make things more difficult, I can't see what I'm doing.

Eventually I capture it and get the whole thing back together. Now for the testing moment. I flush. The bowl empties obediently and starts to fill up. So far, so good. But will it stop? It starts to slow down, becomes a trickle and... continues trickling. But it's only a little trickle and we'll just have to come up from time to time to time to flush it if it doesn't stop. I am not going to tempt fate by meddling any further. That's good enough for me at the moment.

"There you are!" I say to Iona as if I knew what I had been doing all along.

I make my way along the dim and long passage to the bedrooms. I am going at a normal, sedate pace. At least, I start off like that, but suddenly I find am taking off at the rate of knots. Furthermore, I realise, to my horror, that I am about to do the splits, which I suspect will be as painful as the time, that unforgettable time, in my schooldays, when standing on the pedals to get better purchase on a particularly steep hill, the chain slipped and I came down on the bar of my bicycle. I think that was the most excruciating and exquisite pain I have ever experienced in my life. The bruises were spectacular, but wasted, as no-one saw them but that is now why I ride a lady's bicycle and I don't give a toss about the conclusions some people might draw from that.

To keep my balance, to prevent that awful calamity, my arms are flailing like a manic semaphore messenger. To keep upright, I have to make my little legs work harder, like when you're going down a mountain and if you first start to run to keep your balance, you can't stop running or else you *will* fall. I manage to stay upright until I come to a halt by crashing against the wall at the end of the passage. Thank God there was not a window there or else I might easily have gone through it in a shower of glass, like a fugitive in the movies making his last-ditch attempt at escape.

Iona comes out of the bathroom to see what all the noise is about. Apparently I have been screaming as I careered along the corridor.

"It's these bloody rugs!" I shout at her as if she were personally responsible for putting them there with malice aforethought to collect the life insurance. "It's not the first time that I've nearly slipped on one of these things. That does it!"

In a temper, I go about the house picking up all the death-inducing rag rugs, no doubt lovingly fashioned by Marnie's fair hands. In any case, I can't stand the sight of them. Apart from harbouring wild life I can only conjecture at, they are an eyesore. I fling them into the cupboard at the bottom of the stairs, right at the back and that is the last we see of them for a year, when we have to restore the house to its original condition, for Marnie's return.

Once I am clothed, it is time to inspect the outside of the house. First the front. It is a wooden, clapboard house, painted pale green with an angular, pitched roof. I recognise the bush in front of the family room window, and there at the side, is the massive fir outside the kitchen window. Our bedroom window is above the kitchen, but it's not quite so dark in there as the branches are a bit thinner. There is a porch reached by a flight of half a dozen wooden steps to the front door which is protected by a flyscreen whose rusty springs (what a surprise!) creak protestingly like arthritic joints do, I am sure, if we had the ears to hear them, yet these springs are strong enough to shut the door with quite some force.

I see all this, and I see another gloomy couple of trees at the other, non-kitchen side of the house and it dawns on me that this *is* the house from *Psycho* and the brief glimpse I had seen of it in silhouette last night must have been subliminally imprinted on my mind and when I made that first, exploratory descent into the dusty basement, the image of Norman Bates' mother hadn't just been due to the spookiness of the interior. And now I am struck by another sudden thought: is it safe to have a shower, even if it is not an electric one? It is enough to give you the creeps and bad dreams into the bargain but you have to hand it to Marnie – she has certainly created a gloomy, spooky, interior to match the grim exterior.

And so through the house again, through hell's kitchen to the back door, to examine the rear of the house. There is a big garden with a hexagonal child's climbing frame and grass that is, by anyone's definition, long enough to be called a meadow. Marnie, or Lindy, might have cut this before they left. In fact, it is more of an orchard than a back garden, with half a dozen trees. I'm not too much up on trees when they are not bearing fruit, but I wouldn't mind betting these are apples, pears and plums, and amazingly, there are even some vines growing. I have to remind myself that Montana's border with Canada, on the 49th parallel, actually places us on the same latitude as Switzerland.

But how is one man, me, going to mow this meadow? By the back door there is a mower, which I am disappointed to see, is a manual pusher. I am familiar with this. After all, I have one like it back home. It's all I need as my "lawn" is so small, that if you could pick it up, it would be just about big enough to blow your nose on. But to tackle all this with that!

It seems hopelessly inadequate for the task and will take hours. On closer inspection however, I realise that I won't be cutting any grass with this for the blades are coated in rust and have not cut a blade of grass in decades.

"How the hell am I going to cut all this grass?" I bemoan to Iona. "Even if it worked, it'd take me all day to cut all this with that! It's as bad as that bloody Hoover inside. How the hell does Marnie manage?"

But Iona isn't listening. It's not her problem after all. She has gone round the side of the house and has discovered something else.

"Come and see this!"

I go round the corner and if this had been a horror film, there would have been a crescendo of screeching violins and some camera effects, probably rapid zooming in and out and someone would have screamed. But we didn't scream; we were becoming hardened to Marnie's sense of décor. For there, hanging on the wall, is a complete skull. Not human: probably something bovine judging by the horns, maybe a buffalo given this location, but probably just a cow and weathered white. For an exquisite finishing touch, the skull has been framed by the hoop from a barrel. The hoop itself, of course, is finished in an attractive shade of rust, which sets off the contrasting white of the bone to perfection.

"My God! I bet Norman Bates' mother *really* is down in that basement. I'm locking the basement door anyway!"

So that was it. 914 Lincoln and our home for the next year – if Mrs Bates doesn't get us first. Or the house electrocutes us.

Chapter Eight

In which my fears and despondency increase.

The doorbell rings. A tall, bearded man is standing on the step. He introduces himself as Perry.

I invite him in. So this is Marnie's ex. If it had not been for his extracurricular activities with one of his clients, I would not be sitting here now and he could still have unlimited access to the Viking chair where he is sitting now, stroking the arms with fond familiarity. He must be curious to meet the person who is responsible for transferring Marnie and his children halfway round the globe. He is our first visitor and I had hoped when the doorbell rang it would be Terri with our luggage.

"What d'you think of the house? Pretty neat, huh?" His eyes dwell lovingly on *Yoke on the Wall* by Pi Sa Junk and the butter churn in the corner. Maybe he is thinking: *Have I made a mistake leaving Marnie and Yoke on the Wall and the butter churn and the jawbone of a rat and the rusty Coca-Cola bottles and the rusty lawnmower outside and the skull on the wall and the Thing in the basement – all that for a younger model?* And if he'd had eyes in his behind, Perry would probably be looking at that lasciviously too but perhaps his buttocks are appreciating its hairy warmth.

I am polite, an ambassador and a diplomat. Or, to put it another way, I am a liar. I take a deep breath.

"Yeah!" I inject as much enthusiasm into my voice as I can, but feeling the inadequacy of the monosyllable will betray me, I plunge on. "It's much bigger than ours."

"Yeah, that will be good for Marnie, give her a chance to bond with the kids." Then, as if he feels his is just as inadequate a reply as mine, he adds what sounds to me suspiciously like a non sequitur: "Say, wanna go for a ride, see the town?"

I leap at the chance. To get out of this mausoleum would be brilliant. The thought of exploring the town in daylight intrigues me. After all, the house is incidental: it would have been nice if it had been nice, but it could be worse (I suppose) and what I am really here for is the land and the people, oh, and to experience the educational experience of course.

We all pile into Perry's beat-up station wagon which gives me the opportunity to say that this is the very sort of vehicle I have in mind to purchase (only not so beat-up). I tell him that apart from requiring a set of wheels to get around the town and explore the immediate area, my plan is to drive back east after the school year is done and I need something big enough to carry all our luggage and us. Which makes me remember my cases still at the airport and suppressing another anxiety attack, I add that the plan would be to camp and maybe two of us could sleep in the vehicle.

"Right, we'll take in some car lots," says Perry.

As we head out of Lincoln onto South Higgins, there is a mountain ahead of us, and about a third of the way up is a huge letter M, painted white, with a zigzag track leading up to it. It's obviously a popular walk. Perry says that's what schools and colleges do here, paint big letters on the mountain, but he doesn't say why, as if it's a perfectly normal thing to do. I don't ask in case it's like asking why people climb them, which, as everyone knows, is because they are there, as George Mallory once remarked and about Mt Everest in particular. And by "school" of course, I have enough knowledge of the American educational system to know that Perry means university.

"That's Mount Sentinel," he says. "Mount Jumbo, on the other side of town, has an L on it."

What an unimaginative name for a mountain – Jumbo. Apparently it was named after P.T. Barnham's favourite elephant and supposedly the largest pachyderm on earth, to which the early settlers thought Mt Sentinel bore a startling resemblance. They could be right about that – I'll decide for myself later, but the extinct volcano known as Arthur's Seat that dominates the Edinburgh skyline would be hard to beat as far as a resemblance to an elephant is concerned.

I have to confess that I am a bit disappointed in the mountains as a whole. Mt Sentinel may be big, and Jumbo suggests it may be big too, but Sentinel is not my idea of a Rocky. When I first heard I was going to the Rockies, I was excited by visions of craggy, snowy peaks, but these don't look any higher than the hills back home. In fact, they look a good deal less impressive than some of our more dramatic Munros. At over 5000 feet, Sentinel easily outstrips Ben Nevis, Scotland's and the United Kingdom's highest mountain, by 1500 feet, but it doesn't look anything like as high. That's because Missoula, at an elevation of more than 3000 feet, gives Sentinel a head start. Even someone as unfit as me could climb it in a couple of hours, I suppose, at least to the M. I make a mental note to do that sometime and impress the folks back home with tales of how I scaled a Rocky. I wouldn't tell them of course, about its rounded shape, that it is covered in brown grass and even has trees growing most of the way up.

We are travelling north on S. Higgins and presently we come to a bridge over the river. Perry tells us it's the Clark Fork and we're now in the downtown area of Missoula. This is the oldest part, and here, in the main street, the buildings are substantial stone-built edifices. One is a sort of mini skyscraper which Perry informs us is the Wilma building. Not long after, we turn right onto a street called Broadway which certainly lives up to its name. I have already been impressed by how wide the streets are, but this is certainly broader than any of the others. God knows how you would get across it as a pedestrian though. There are no traffic islands and the flow of traffic is relentless. I wouldn't care to try it.

We turn right again and I know I have been here before, only a few hours ago, though it seems a lot longer. This is none other than Emerson School. Everyone seems to think I am desperate to see it, but to tell the truth, I am a bit nervous about starting there and prefer to keep it at the back of my mind. Actually, it doesn't look that intimidating. It's not exceptionally large, built of red brick with large, aluminium windows and, what's more, they all appear to be intact. And in another good sign, there doesn't appear to be any graffiti scrawled on the walls either. I hope that doesn't mean that the pupils still have to learn to write.

I still have two weeks before school starts, time to get adjusted a bit, and time to get a car. Poor Marnie has even less time than that to acclimatise, but she has landed lucky as far as getting to school is concerned as one of my colleagues lives in the same street and will give her a lift to school until she gets herself sorted out. More than ever, that is one of my priorities as it now transpires it is a fair walk to the school and if I don't want to get up at the crack of dawn, which I don't, I'll need some transport – and soon. So far, I have only noticed one garage – H.O. Bell's, and I point out this severe lack of car shops to Perry.

"Yeah, they're all on the south side of town, mainly. We're gonna go there now."

We head over the Clark Fork again, this time over a different bridge to the east. Presently we come to the university campus which is on our left and then turn right again. Perry says that we should get some good help with George at the university. Seemingly it has a bit of a reputation for being in the forefront of deaf research.

From what I have seen, I am favourably impressed with Missoula. It looks like an oasis. There are avenues of trees on every street, with broad pavements and charming white clapboard houses, and not one the same - so unlike our serried rows of identical houses, lined up like soldiers in some 19th century battle formation. It's not what I thought it would be like at all: it's got none of the brashness, the glitziness, the vulgarity of American cities that I had seen on TV. But Missoula's nickname is "The Garden City" and already I can see why.

Perry tells us we are heading for the main drag. It's called Brooks but it's also Highway 93, leading down the Bitterroot Valley to Stevensville and Hamilton. The bitterroot is the state flower. But any flowers here have long since been buried under concrete, brick and asphalt. Here there are no trees; they have long since been replaced with forests of signs and billboards.

As we drive down the valley (or Brooks) with cars to the left of us, cars to the right of us, cars ahead of us and cars behind us, I understand that north of the river, Missoula is a different city. Here the senses are bombarded by a plethora of signs of every shape, colour and variety. There are the golden arches of McDonald's and Pizza Hut and Burger King. All these we know and do not love, but there are scores more – no, maybe even hundreds, as I can see many, many more along the intersections at which we have to stop every so often when the lights are against us. Restaurant after restaurant, mainly providing fare along the hamburger and pizza line, and other restaurants boasting every culinary taste that you could care to think of, (except Indian it seems) and obviously not franchises like the others. And supermarket after supermarket and bar after bar and astonishingly, gun shop after gun shop, though perhaps I should not have been so taken aback by this as this is the West after all and you don't just slough off a century of gunslinging tradition just like that.

It's not lit up just now but at night this place is going to look just as bright and brassy as those TV cities. I am disappointed: The Garden City blooms not flowers but neon at night, just like the rest of them.

And there are second-hand car salesrooms by the score. You can't avoid seeing them, decked out in bunting, all advertising the best deal in town but the curious thing, I notice, is that there are not any prices on any of the cars. Obviously the only thing to is ask a salesman and that, I fear, means the big hard sell. I am overwhelmed, shell-shocked, feel as if I am drowning in a sea of choice. I am not yet ready for this, I tell Perry.

That feeling of utter hopelessness and helplessness comes over me again. Where am I going to begin? And how am I going to get here? And getting from one dealer to the next will be no easy feat either as they are so far apart: I can't see how I can possibly do it without a car.

I feel defeated by the extent of the task. Perhaps, even at this late stage, it is not too late to turn tail and flee. But I know that is not really an option and I've got to stick it out somehow. By the time we turn into Lincoln and the house from *Psycho* looms into sight, my spirits are at a very low ebb indeed.

Missoula may be at 3000 feet but I feel as if I were in the shadow of the Valley of Death.

Chapter Nine

*In which I take to driving on this continent
for the first time.*

This time when the doorbell rings it *is* Terri and even better, Terri with luggage. And she has a surprise for me. It is already parked outside. It's her Beetle Volkswagen. To my utter amazement at her kindness, not to say wonderment at her foolhardiness, she tells me I can use it until I find a car of my own. I bless her for bringing the luggage and I bless her again for the use of the car. I don't think I would have offered my car to someone I'd only met for five minutes. Now I will be able to get down to Brooks and check out a few dealers. I don't remembering uttering a prayer but this looks like the answer to one.

Terri asks if there is anything else we want and Iona says she needs to go to the supermarket. "No problem," Terri tells us. "We can kill two birds with one stone; Iona can shop and you can drive the VW." She is going to come with us and show us how to get to Albertsons.

There's just one slight matter that's bothering me.

"Am I insured to drive the VW?"

Apparently I have just said something very amusing, for Terri chuckles with laughter and appears to be wiping away a tear from behind her glasses. "Oh, we don't bother about things like that!" she says, flapping her hands in a dismissive manner and in the sort of tone which makes it sound such a trivial detail that it wasn't worth wasting breath on.

The engine groans throatily into life. The whole body shakes as if suffering from convulsions. Terri laughs. "This is a car of character," she says. "It's got its characteristics but I love it to bits."

There is nothing more calculated to make a driver more nervous than he already is, in a strange car, in a strange land and driving on the "wrong" side of the road, than to tell him you are driving their pride and joy, especially when you have the proud owner sitting beside you, so close that you are actually rubbing shoulders. It is like sitting my driving test all over again – and it was bad enough the other two times. I pray this supermarket isn't far. (Well, you never know, there might be a God.)

As soon as I back the car out of the drive, I know that something is wrong, seriously wrong with this car. The steering is extremely heavy and it wants to drive on the pavement. If it could vote, it would be extremely left wing. I have to keep pulling it over to the right all the time, just to make it go in a straight line.

I haven't much time to get used to this as, apart from a doctor's surgery, we are the last house on Lincoln and before I know it, it is time to apply the brakes as Terri tells me we are going to take a right on Higgins. But when I press the pedal, to my horror, it goes right to the floor. I'm not travelling at much more than walking speed, fortunately, and I pump the brakes frantically, at the same time hauling back on the steering wheel like the reins of a horse. Sweat starts to bead my brow as the car shows no sign of stopping, then it does – suddenly. I have just made an emergency stop causing us to lurch forward violently in our seats. I grin apologetically at Terri but I am thinking: *Why the hell did you not warn me that the brakes are spongy and the whole damned thing pulls to the left?* Unless you did – those are the "characteristics" you were talking about.

It's bad enough driving this death trap, but without any insurance as well, it is just plain madness. And the funny thing is that Terri's husband is a cop and she should know that. And why would she put her life into the hands of a Scotsman whose driving skills she knows absolutely nothing about? Unless she imagines that having his wife and children on board is insurance enough against reckless driving. Which would normally be the case – but in this car...

Mercifully, at the junction, all I have to do is turn right into the flow of traffic. I don't know how good this car is at accelerating; not very, I suppose, so I want to leave plenty of space between oncoming vehicles. It doesn't take long however before I realise I am never going to get the sort of space I would have liked for safety and I'm going to have to either take a chance or put down roots.

I see a gap. There's not a chequered flag, but there might just as well have been, the way I take off. The G force slaps us back against our seats and to my alarm, I find us bolting much faster than I expected, not to the right, but *across* the road. We are flung against the side of the car as I overcorrect by wrenching the wheel too far to the right. It's no use braking, so I take my foot off the accelerator and our necks jerk forwards as the car suddenly slows to a dawdle while I wrestle with the wheel, struggling to make the car go in a straight line. Now I have it under control and we are moving down Higgins, but as I go up through the gears, I make a solemn vow to myself that if ever I get this car back in one piece, I will never use it again.

Iona, in the back with the kids, is silent, probably struck dumb with terror. I can't see her face because, for the first time, I notice that there is no rear-view mirror, which minor deficiency and I would have thought, legal requirement, even in Montana, I point out to Terri. She says she knows. It fell off a while ago and she just uses the wing mirrors.

"Oh!" she adds, as if she has just remembered, "the lights don't work, so if you are using the car at night, be careful!" She chuckles again in that infectious way she has and I look at her in amazement to see if she is completely crazy or just mildly mad.

I apologise for the way I have been driving, and ever the diplomat, blame myself and my unfamiliarity with the car for treating her baby so roughly. "That's OK!" Terri laughs.

I wonder if anything ever flaps her. Just to test her, I think about saying: "You know, this is the first time I have ever driven a car and it's rather fun. How fast does this thing go anyway?" but I am in too much in a state of nervous panic for any levity, so what I actually say is: "Where is Albertsons by the way?"

"It's on Brooks."

Gulp! I might have known that was where we were headed – I was going to what Perry had called "Malfunction Junction". He had said, with a sort of pride in his voice, that this was the busiest junction in Missoula. In fact, it was the busiest junction in Montana and you had to go 500 hundred miles west to Seattle before you would see more cars passing through a junction in an hour. Great! And I have to negotiate it in this wreck, which in Scotland would never be allowed within a million miles of a road – and without any insurance. The horror of it makes me want to close my eyes so I won't see all the traffic I'll have to deal with.

Eventually we get to Albertsons. My throat is dry when I bring the car to a halt by the preferred method of pumping the brakes rather than colliding with something. When I get out and stand up, I can feel my legs trembling. We have made it, the car still intact and the little money I have in the bank too. I know what a litigious land America is and I don't suppose Missoula will be any different if you cause an accident.

"You can drive back," I tell Terri, pressing the keys into her hand. "Saves having to give me instructions."

As the song nearly has it, *she* can drive her baby back home.

Chapter Ten

In which I become an expert on my national drink.

"Hey, Dave! You gotta come over an' see this hot sauce I'm makin'."

It is Al on the telephone. When Terri left, after driving us back from Albertsons, she had invited us round for a meal so we could meet the rest of the family, but now, in a tone which brooked no argument, Al was inviting me round to *look* at a hot sauce. Oh well, I thought, why not?

The Hertz house is the next house but one along, on the same side of the street, but while we are 419, they are 429, according to the big black numbers screwed to the doorframe. It is an imposing two-storey white house with the windows and shutters picked out in red. It looks very nice; why couldn't Marnie have lived in something like this?

I don't need to ring as the door is actually open with only the flyscreen door shut and Al must have seen me, for as soon as I arrive, he shouts, "C'mon in, Dave!"

There is a flight of stairs on the left and the first thing that strikes me is that the banister could do with a good lick of paint. Paper is hanging from the wall and there are great bare patches where it has come off altogether. Perhaps they are in the process of decorating. Like Marnie's house, there is an absence of doors. Whilst we like our rooms to be self-contained, the Americans it seems, prefer open plan.

I can see Al at the end of the corridor in the kitchen and to my right, there is a long room in which the dominant feature is a massive fireplace and although it is mid-August, a good fire of logs is burning merrily as if it were Yule. Two small kids are running around shrieking and perhaps the heavily built woman who is with them is deaf because the noise they are making would get on my nerves but it doesn't seem to bother her at all. I don't have time to notice anything else, except I am standing on a hairy carpet which looks as if it could have come from the Viking chair's big brother.

Al is rolling sausage meat in his massive fists. He is making meatballs. A mountain of them at his elbow already, he keeps on making more and more, but breaks off to thrust a spoonful of red liquid at me.

"Here, you gotta try this hot sauce," he says. So he did want me to come over, not just to see, but taste his hot sauce! But surely I would have tasted it at the meal anyway?

Tentatively, I try a little sip. Suddenly, I am gasping for air and my eyes are watering.

Al flings back his head and roars with laughter. It looks like this was the desired and expected reaction and I have passed the wimp test with flying colours. He takes the spoon from me and swallows the lot without even blinking. Having shown me who is the alpha male around here, he next shows me a jar and explains that these are jalapeno chillies, the very hottest and that is what forms the basis of his sauce. He explains that he is Italian and he likes hot sauce and Italian food. I didn't know that Italian food was spicy before, but I had studied German in school and knew that his surname, Hertz, was as Italian as liver sausage and lederhosen. Ever the diplomat, I nod in understanding. Anyway, my vocal cords are on fire.

"Have a beer," he commands and opens the biggest fridge I have ever seen, even bigger than Marnie's and that is saying something. One half of it dispenses ice and iced drinks and the other half seems to be filled with cans of beer. I am grateful for the chilled beer to soothe my throat but when Al offers me a Scotch, I refuse.

Al is horrified, blinks at me owlishly in disbelief. "Aw shit! You gotta have a Scotch, man. You're Scotch!"

To my amazement, he hauls a bottle out of the fridge, so big it has a handle. It's an American gallon, which is smaller than our gallon admittedly, but it's still a lot of whisky. I have never heard of the brand before – *Monarch of the Glen* – and I look at it dubiously.

"That good whisky?" Al wants to know. I am beginning to wonder if this is the real reason for my early summons.

I tell him I don't know because I have never heard of that brand before, though it does say *Produce of Scotland* on the label, sure enough. Al is studying my face intently. He is plainly disappointed.

"You gotta try it an' tell me what it's like," and he pours me out a big slug. He does the same for himself, and without ceremony, knocks half of it back, then looks at me, expectant and impatient for my verdict.

I realise that Al thinks that because I come from Scotland I must know all there is to know about whisky, and so I should, coming from Banffshire, the heart of the whisky industry. There was even one distillery a mile away from where I lived in Ternemny, but all I knew about it was that the Clydesdale which pulled the dray was called Charlie and the ungrateful brute just about bit my finger in two when I gave him a lump of sugar. Actually, it was not Charlie's fault: I didn't know that you were supposed to hold your palm flat...

But I was only ten then; now I am older and wiser and an ambassador for Scotland and I have to do better.

Al watches me as I sniff the contents of the glass; he gapes as I hold it up to the light then sniff it again. My face becomes thoughtful. At last I permit a small amount to pass my lips. I swill it around in my mouth, become even more pensive, swallow, look Al in the eye, take a larger sip and swallow that straight. I wait for that to go down and make a big play of rolling my tongue about. By this time I can see Al is desperate for the verdict. He's forgotten his meatballs and even the whisky in his own glass.

"Well," I pronounce with a great degree of gravitas, "this is a blend of course, not a single malt." This is about where my knowledge of whisky starts and stops, so from now on, I am flying by the seat of my pants and I only knew it was a blend because it said so on the label. "It's smooth enough, quite peaty but not overpowering, just enough to make it interesting. There are underlying heather and honey aromas, but it has a tanginess and a slightly salty aftertaste which leads me to conclude that probably it's formed mainly from whiskies close to the sea which would rule out Speyside or the Highlands. It's probably from one of the islands, probably Islay. But I wouldn't like you to quote me on that," I add with a hasty caveat for effect.

Al blinks at me behind his specs. "Well, no shit," he says. "Hey, Terri, Rob, Cassie, somebody get Pops, you gotta hear what Dave says about this goddamn whisky!"

The rest of the family troops into the kitchen with little degree of enthusiasm. I presume Cassie is the mother of the two kids who, for the want of any introductions to anybody, I'll call Cain and Abel. Rob, the youngest, looks about fifteen or sixteen. I thought that must be all the family but actually it turned out to be only a representative sample. In fact, not everyone who *is* in the house is even in the kitchen yet, much to Al's annoyance.

"Where the hell's Pops, goddamn it?" He raises his voice a dozen more decibels. "Hey, Pops you gotta come in here! Goddamn it!" and he gives a sigh of long-suffering exasperation.

Presently, a bewildered-looking old man shuffles into the kitchen. He has a walking stick in one arthritic hand and a faded green baseball hat on his head. I notice he also has a hearing aid. He looks incredibly ancient. This, evidently, is Al's father and he appears the complete antithesis of his son: short as Al is tall; pale as Al is swarthy; slightly built, as Al is sturdy; quiet and unassuming and gentle, as Al is not.

"Where y' bin for Chris' sake? Dave's gonna tell us about this here whisky."

I wonder if my audience is as reluctant to hear all this as I am to say it. It seems very possible. What exactly did I say anyway? I didn't expect to have to repeat it. If I had, I would have paid more attention to what I was saying. Anyway, they politely hear me out and I must have done all right as Al seems satisfied. In fact, he seems delighted to be in the company of such a knowledgeable person, while the rest of the family, the show over, melts away. They seem to have no more interest in me as if they had seen me every day of their lives, as if Scotsmen were in the habit of popping in every day of the week.

I have scored a big hit with Al though. We have a mutual interest in whisky, or so he thinks, and that makes us buddies. I cement our budding relationship when I tell him about the Dewar's I have as my duty-free allowance and I promise I'll take a bottle over this evening and let him have a taste.

He presses me to finish my drink and pours himself another one. I do after a time and then I say I've got to be going. I refuse another drink and say again, I've got to be going. Al pours himself another whisky and begins adding more meatballs to the mountain in front of him. Stage left, I can hear Cain and Abel still running riot.

I don't see anyone as I let myself out.

Chapter Eleven

In which I meet another member of the Hertz family and experience a couple of further shocks.

It is some time later. The four of us are heading towards a rendezvous with hot sauce with some trepidation. I have warned Iona about it and I am clutching my own brand of firewater, the unopened litre of Dewar's as tribute. On the street outside stands a red-and-white truck that hadn't been there before. As we get closer, we can see that the number plate reads "Big Al". It only increases my sense of unease. I can't think why, but somehow it conjures up pictures of men in black shirts, sharp suits and fedoras with submachine guns as accessories.

For the first time I am actually in the room with the huge fireplace (which is still burning merrily) and have set foot on the hairy carpet. At the other end of the room, a massive table is groaning with food. Abel and Cain are fighting, as usual; their mother, Cassie, is oblivious to them, as usual, languidly smoking a cigarette on the settee. Grandpa is nodding in an upright chair by the table. Al and Terri are in the kitchen but she comes out to make a big fuss of the kids. She says that her daughter, Sandi, has a girl about Hélène's age called Amy and it will be neat for them to be friends. Sandi has another kid, a boy called Ron after his father, but they call him Daniel for short. I don't ask and I'm not told.

Al, in the meantime, makes a big fuss of the bottle of Dewar's and wants a tasting right now. I don't know how I get that impression unless it is because he is asking me if this is the Scotch I took from Scotland and produces a couple of glasses as he speaks. I hope I don't have to go through the tasting notes again as I take the hint and unseal the bottle. Al smacks it around his lips and pronounces it the best Scotch he has ever tasted and sets his empty glass down, by coincidence, next to the bottle.

"Hey, Rob, Cassie, Pops, you gotta taste this Scotch Dave has brought from Scotland!" He doesn't need to shout on Terri as she is right there. He is already splashing generous measures into glasses as the family materialises in answer to the patriarch's summons.

"Goddamn it! What's he doin'? Hey, Pops, you gotta come here and taste this Scotch Dave brought from Scotland!"

Al looks at me apologetically. I think he's about to say sorry for doling out my whisky to everybody, whether they want it or not, but what he actually says is: "He's deaf. He don't hear too good."

Then, as if someone had switched a light on in his brain, he realises he has committed a grave error of hospitality. He has not poured a glass for Iona.

"Gee, Eeeona, you wan' some?"

He is not to know that he has not insulted Iona in the slightest as she can't stand the sight, smell or taste of whisky. The entire kitchen is reeking of it – quite enough to make her feel sick without having to face the additional torment of tasting so much as a drop. Everyone unenthusiastically pronounces it very good, except Pops who sips his and says nothing at all.

Duty done, they all drift away.

"That *is* good whisky," avers Al in the sort of tone that leaves me in absolutely no doubt that that was just a sample as far as he was concerned.

It had been my intention over the year, especially at Hogmanay and New Year, to proffer this to colleagues and friends as a little taste of Scotland. I tell him to help himself and as he does so, my heart sinks commensurately with the level of liquid in the bottle.

The meal is pronounced ready. We sit around the massive table. This is one of Al's celebrated dinners and he is in his element. There is salad and bread to go with the meatball mountain and there is enough spaghetti to knit a blanket. I am relieved to discover that the hot sauce is an optional extra. To wash this down, there is red wine that doesn't come out of a bottle, but, like Al's whisky, comes out of a gallon flagon. The food is actually very good and despite Abel raising Cain and Cassie and Rob ignoring me, and everybody ignoring Pops, it is a very convivial and lively occasion. Al is a good host and the wine glass is not allowed to be empty and more meatballs and spaghetti are constantly pressed upon us.

I make some conversation with Pops. It's a bit hard to make him out, but it seems he was in Europe in the First World War and he is a lover of pre-Second World War cars. He was an electrician and when I tell him about the lamp in the kitchen and *Hoover erectus*, he says he'll come round and have a look at them. I thank him and he says he'll bring some prodoos with him.

"Prodoos?" I ask.

"Yeah," he says. "Do you have prodoos back home?"

"Well, er, em... Prodoos?" I repeat blankly.

I am glad I am having this conversation with Al Senior and not Big Al. Pops is patience personified. "Yeah, prodoos," he repeats. "Corn, squash, zucchinis..."

In a flash of illumination, I realise that "prodoos" must be "produce". I know that corn is maize, but I've never heard of the other two, so it is safe to say that no, I don't have any garden produce. I don't ask what the other two are as Pops says he's going to bring some round so I'll find out then.

At that moment the outside door opens, the flyscreen door slams and a buxom girl of about eighteen erupts into the room. Her breasts are half-hanging out of her top. A slim young man with long hair follows her. He is carrying a small child in his arms and there is a little girl, about Hélène's age, whom Terri swoops upon, sweeps up and lifts aloft.

"God, I hate kids!" says the girl with feeling. "I'm gonna run away into the mountains!"

I am deeply shocked. Imagine saying that in front of your own children! The infant is too young to understand, but the little girl certainly is. Has she understood? I anxiously scan her face for signs of rejection. Probably not, as Terri is making such a fuss of her, thank God.

At this point the girl catches sight of me. "We're not married!" she says, with a nod in the direction of the man holding the infant.

I can feel the blood draining from my face. Worse and worse! It is one thing to announce to your kids' faces that you hate them, but another thing completely to announce with your very first words to perfect strangers, that you are not even married to their father. God knows if she registered the shock and horror on my face, but it was there for all to see as I was totally incapable of covering it up.

That sinking feeling I had at the airport is sweeping over me again. I look at Cain and Abel, at the snotty little girl on Terri's lap, at the dirty infant in the arms of the man whom I take to be the father. I look at Cassie and Rob whose faces are expressionless. Pops is struggling with his spaghetti; Al is pouring more wine. What have we come to? In despair, I throw a glance at Iona, but to my surprise she doesn't seem to be in the least shocked and seems to be taking this recent revelation totally in her stride.

The reluctant mother bends over the table to get a piece of garlic bread and I am inadvertently treated to an even fuller view of her cleavage.

"Hey, Debs," says Al. "You gotta try this Scotch that Dave has brought from Scotland." He goes back into the kitchen to get the bottle. I don't know why, but at that moment I have a Damascene moment and feel a wave of relief rush over me like a cold spray. Why the hell does nobody ever introduce anybody in this family? It now dawns on me belatedly, as it must have become apparent to Iona straight away, that while the man holding the baby is its father, the girl with the bosoms is not the children's mother but their aunt. She'd obviously had enough of looking after her sister's kids all day and her announcement was simply to stop us forming the wrong impression. Well, that backfired spectacularly in my case. So, the little girl must be Amy, whose mother is Sandi, but this is Debs. Right, got it at last.

When Al comes back with my New Year's bottle, I positively feel light-headed with relief that things aren't quite as bad as they seem and I don't mind at all when Al decides he may as well have another slug of the Dewar's to keep Debbie company. Mind you, he does offer me some of my own whisky too, but I refuse as I have already had a couple of glasses of wine and I may not know much but I do know that you don't mix the grape and the grain and I've already probably had a treble of the latter anyway the way Al pours them.

Eventually, we say our farewells. We thank Al and Terri for an absolutely great time and I tell Al how great his meatballs are. By this time, the Dewar's has evaporated to such an extent that it is not worth taking home. Home. The house from *Psycho*.

Thus endeth our first whole day in Missoula. Only one day! There had been enough shocks, both of the cultural and electrical, to resuscitate a corpse. But there was one more left for us that day, as we were just about to find out.

We get the kids ready for bed and mercifully, in the bathroom, Niagara does not erupt again. And it is only when we retire ourselves that we realise that the only bedroom that has any curtains at all is Hélène's room. All we have for a curtain is the fir tree outside and I reckon that's not enough to stop us from a visit from the vice squad. It's going to have to be in the dark from now on.

Just as well I don't need to read the manual.

Chapter Twelve

In which the Great Car Hunt begins, I meet my new boss and see my classroom for the first time.

In the land of the automobile and the land of the free, I can't be free until I get a set of wheels. My priority therefore is to get a car. You really need a car, just to get to the other side of the street in this place. The only place you see pedestrians is in the centre of downtown and you don't see a lot of them either as they are mostly down at the big stores and food franchises at the other side of town. The problem is I don't know where to start and I'm scared to drive Terri's VW. But there's nothing else for it, so we all pile into the death wagon and head off for Malfunction Junction which we negotiate safely. By now I am a bit more used to the VW's senile eccentricities, or maybe I'm just less nervous without Terri in the car.

The garage we have come to, like all the rest, is decked out with bunting flapping gaily in a stiff breeze. The bunting is saying: "Come into my parlour innocent little Scottish people, where we will tell you we have the most wonderful car in the world and we've been saving it just for you as we think you will be the only mugs in this whole town who will buy it." There are hundreds of cars to choose from but not a single price displayed on any of the windscreens. There's no chance of seeing a car that we like at a price we can afford and walk away if there isn't. Iona and I peer into the interiors as best as we can, trying to read the mileages and as we do so, I notice that every single one is an automatic.

"Hello there, can I help you?"

The speaker is a young man with short-cropped hair and a short-sleeved shirt and tie to match. It only comes down to the third button, à la Nigel Molesworth school of contempt for such unnecessary fripperies. This is the first tie I have seen since Washington DC but I hadn't seen it coming. Its wearer seems to have popped up out of nowhere, but we must have been under observation all the time. Unwittingly we must have tripped his invisible wires and he has scuttled out of his lair with his gleaming $1000 dentistry on full display.

"Yes. I want a big car with a big boot, lots of space, low mileage for about $600 to $900." It sounds like a lot of car for not a lot of money and I wouldn't blame him if he laughed but he doesn't and of course I didn't have to say "boot" for him to know that we weren't natives. He wants to know where we're from and when I tell him he says it's always been an express desire of his to go to Scotland because the country is so beautiful and he's heard that the people are so friendly.

His name is Don and when I tell him my name is David, he calls me Dave and says I have such a lovely wife it's not surprising we have such beautiful children since their parents are such fine-looking people. Well, he didn't actually say that, but that's the impression I got. He could have been St Nicholas himself, the fuss he made over the kids. We are invited into his lair for a cup of coffee while the kids can have some juice. As we follow him, Iona and I look at each other askance. We know we are in for the hard sell, but what perturbs me most is the thought that if I have to go through this routine every single time I go car shopping, I'll never get one before Christmas.

Don does his best to make us feel at home and heaps so much more praise on us, and our country, I think his real name must be Uriah. It seems we are very lucky to have come to him as his is a company in which we can put an absolute trust, (not like some of the other outfits "out there") and his prices, I am amazed to hear, are the most competitive in the whole town. I can't believe my luck. Of all the car joints in all Missoula, I have just happened to stroll into the very best! And not just that, but would you believe, he just happens to have the very vehicle, which he is convinced, will fulfil our requirements! Before our eyes finally glaze over and our smiles freeze into rictus, he finally goes off to get the car of our dreams.

Right away I can tell it is nothing like that at all. Obviously Don is straight out of shark school and hasn't listened to a word I'd said about wanting a station wagon for about $900. Instead he brings us a two-door Dodge Monaco priced at $1300. Dodge is the operative word. To spare his sensibilities, though there's no reason why I should, I pretend to be mildly interested in the car and then tell him I'd be daft to buy the first car I've seen without shopping about a bit.

His evangelical smile fades and his voice has a hard edge as he tells me that I am making a big mistake and he hopes I won't live to regret it. Maybe he didn't actually articulate the last bit at all; but the atmosphere is certainly not as sunny as it was when he first clapped eyes on us. Why does he have to take it as a personal insult, just because he couldn't sell me his lousy car? If only he had listened to what I wanted to buy rather than what he wanted to sell, he might have been in business.

But who would buy a car from a firm called Robin Steele Inc. anyway?

***

The doorbell resonates. When I go to the door, there is a sandy-haired individual standing on the doorstep. He has brown brogues, spectacles and is casually dressed in a smart sort of way in muted colours. It has taken me about ten seconds flat to realise he is conservative with a capital C in a country where they don't have a political party that rejoices under that name. He clears his throat and swallows before he speaks. He seems very nervous.

"Hi, Dave. Pleased to meet you. I'm Matt Olsen," he says, extending his hand.

So this is Matt, my principal, my boss, about whom Marnie had less than a ringing endorsement, but of course I don't let on that I know anything about that, just as I hope Marnie keeps what I said about "Wally", my headmaster, to herself. Perhaps it is the fate of all who are promoted over their peers to be criticised by them. It's part of the price you pay for the higher salary. For my part, it's part of the culture shock to be called Dave. I'm not called that at home, even by my friends, let alone by my boss whom I've just met, but I've been warned to expect greater informality, especially in the classroom.

I invite him in to meet Iona and the kids. He looks decidedly uncomfortable and asks how we are settling in. I don't tell him, don't ask him: "Well, how would you like to live in the house from *Psycho*?" but I notice he prefers to stand, rather than sit in the place of honour, the hairy Viking chair. I lie and tell him, we're doing just great. After that there is an awkward silence. Matt shifts his brogues an inch and clears his throat. I realise this means he's about to speak.

"Say, Dave," he says, as if he's just thought of it, "would you like to go an' see the school?"

I haven't the heart to tell him that this is not my heart's desire, but I act as if it is. He and I pile into his truck and as we drive to the school, Matt tells me what an honour and a privilege it is for him to have a Scotsman in the school. It is a real feather in the cap of School District #7 as his school, Emerson, is the first in the district to have an exchange teacher. I am a bit puzzled by this as I know there is a teacher, somewhere in Missoula, from Hellgate High School actually, who had an exchange just last year.

Lesson number one in the Missoula education system. The secondary and primary schools, or elementary as they call it here, are entirely different and run by two separate Superintendents or Directors of Education, as we would call them. Although I am secondary trained, I am attached to the elementary sector. Emerson takes kids from K through, as they say it, and "thru" as they spell it, 8. "K" stands for kindergarten and "8" stands for the eighth-graders, who, with the seventh, will be my charges. This system is not unique in the USA and I might have ended up anywhere, whereas my school is practically unique in Scotland, there being only one other middle school in the entire country, also in Grangemouth.

In addition to this, Matt says, they have a Special Ed school for handicapped kids.

"We're lucky to have them," he continues. "They learn shop."

"Shop?" Would that be lessons in retail? More likely a class in everyday life skills.

"Yeah. Workin' with wood."

"Oh, I see."

"We've also got a Hearing Impaired Unit. Maybe we can get George fixed up in there," he says, his jaw jutting forward like Superman's but what might only be a nervous tic.

I doubt it. George is only 18 months old and in nappies.

Matt takes me up to my room. I can't believe my eyes. It is vast – double the size of two normal classrooms and clearly it could function as two classrooms if desired, as about the middle, there is a room divider concertinaed against the two longest walls. After the size, what I notice next and to my complete astonishment, is the green wall-to-wall carpet. Actually, I wasn't particular about the colour – it could have been dog poo brown for all I cared – and I can't help but reflect on the eccentricity of the Americans who carpet their classrooms but keep the floors of their houses bare. A big, black clock hangs on the wall of each half. I'm not sure if it's principally for the teacher or the pupils, (I mean students) but anyway, both can see the amount of tedium remaining.

There are only about 20 desks in the room just like the ones in *Snoopy* cartoons. Just in case you can't picture them, this means the seat and the desk form a single unit and the desks are deep enough to accommodate all the students' books and stationery. I like the way they are arranged, but a Scottish schools inspector would throw a fit because they are in rows. Group teaching is the new method, the benefits of which are obvious: half the class have their backs to the teacher and the blackboard, an arrangement which also allows the pupils to speak to each other much more easily and therefore avoid the necessity of having to pass notes to each other. Or as the inspectors put it, they can "interact and learn from each other."

As I had already realised anyway, this puts beyond doubt that I have a much better deal than Marnie. For a start, I have half the number of kids, plus I have a nicer room to teach them in: a room with a view, through the trees, of the big white M on Mount Sentinel. In Grangemouth I have no view at all. My room is in an old Victorian building with high windows and all you can see are the branches of the trees and a patch of sky in winter. The weather is always a surprise when you get outside. Those architects knew something about not letting children's attentions go wandering, though it has to be said my students here won't be able to admire any view either as they will have their backs to it.

I tell Matt how fine it is and for the first time, I think, since I came to Missoula, I do not speak with forked tongue. I wander over to my desk to the right of the door and spot a sheet of paper written in Marnie's illegible scrawl. It's hard for me to scan it and decipher it at the same time, but Matt is practically wetting himself, desperate to know what it says, but doesn't know how to get it from me. At last he clears his throat.

"Em... ahrrum, could I see that a moment, Dave?" His hand is already hovering over it.

He scans it, but like me, he can't read it, familiar as he is with American handwriting. It's not long before he gives up the struggle. "I'll just take this down to the office and photocopy it." And with that I am left alone in the room that is to be my workplace for the next year. What sights and sounds will it witness I wonder?

But why is Matt showing such an interest in these notes? Unless... he thinks that Marnie has written something about *him*.

While he is away, I have a look in the cupboards. They don't hold a lot of materials. Compared to this, my bookstore in Abbotsgrange is like Aladdin's cave. I am pleased to see however, that there is one book I recognise – *The Pigman* by Paul Zindel. In fact, I use that with my M4s and I have brought some material on that with me as exemplars, so if I'm stuck, I can always use this until I find my feet.

Ah, here is the handbook that Marnie told me about with the boring grammatical exercises. What she didn't tell me is there is a teacher's copy as well, with the answers written in blue in the spaces where the students' responses are meant to be!

I find another book of exercises of stencils, which they call "dittoed sheets". These can be run off on a spirit machine and all the pupil has to do is to write one-word answers, as in the handbook, except they are sometimes required to write as much as a phrase there. To my horror and utter disbelief, there is a poetry section in which the grade to be awarded depends upon how much they *write*!

My heart sinks as I survey what appear to be my materials. There is no indication of when I should use what, of any structure, of any curriculum they should be following, or what they should be expected to cover. Am I expected to dip in to this book like a Woolworth's' Pick 'n' Mix? And apart from that, there seems to be no opportunity for extended writing, of using different writing techniques, of oral work, of studying literature. In fact, all there seems to be are grammatical exercises of brain-numbing boredom.

If this is all they are expected to do, I am going to have the easiest time of my life because the correction is just going to consist of ticking correct answers and the classes are so small, this is going to take no time at all. Can it really be this simple? Can it really be that bad? Could I, in all conscience, go through a year just doing that? I doubted if I could. I might have to fall back on my own materials which I'd brought with me as I had been warned by the Bureau that most likely I'd be asked to give a talk about what I did in Scotland.

If I am suffering some angst, I reckon it will be nothing compared to what poor Marnie is feeling. If I were her, I'd be on the first plane home. If this is all she is used to, her new workload must seem insurmountable, but at least she would not be in any doubt as to what was expected of her: one novel per term per class, plus project work, plus oral work. Three classes per year group and each practically double the size she is used to. Six novels to read and get to know. The marking alone would be enough to strike terror into her heart with an extended essay due every fortnight from every pupil in every class, not counting the correction of the worksheets on the novels. Some difference to ticking dittoed sheets! But at least she knew what she had to get through – which was more than I did.

Maybe that *was* it; I didn't have to do much. It certainly didn't look like it anyway. Even if they were to do everything my pupils in Scotland did, it would still be a holiday for me, due to the much smaller class sizes. Poor Marnie! I could see her now chain-smoking her way through a mountain of correction, yelling at Lewis and Harvey to shut up and being unable in our miniscule little house, to escape from them. Somehow, because we speak the same language, almost, I didn't expect there to be this much culture shock but our work and our houses were worlds apart and of the two, I know whose shoes I'd prefer to be in.

Matt comes back with the Marnie original, looking a bit more relaxed. I wonder if he has had time to read it and seen that it does not say anything derogatory about him. He asks me if I've seen enough and I say I have. I pick up the books and the book of stencilled sheets. Maybe there will be something in them or in Marnie's notes, which will give me some hope or guidance.

But when I study them later in the house from *Psycho*, they just increase the gloom as if the depressing ambience of the surroundings, by some sort of osmosis, has permeated the pages.

Chapter Thirteen

In which I have a very embarrassing experience and come across an incredible coincidence.

Al has promised me he'll help me with the car purchasing. He takes me to see a friend of his called Martin Fleischman who sells used cars at H.O. Bell's which is just on the other side of the river. Al tells Martin that I am his friend from Scotland and that I'm a teacher over on exchange for a year and one of my priorities is to get a car and what I don't know about Scotch is not worth knowing.

Martin acts interested, or maybe he is really, and shows me a car which I say I am not in the slightest interested in as I'd prefer a station wagon as I could sleep in it when we go off on our transcontinental trip at the end of the teaching year. He shows me a huge blue 1972 Chrysler Plymouth station wagon. It is on offer: was $1695 now $1000, a bit more than I was expecting to pay, but it looks more like the sort of thing I am looking for.

It's automatic of course, with power-assisted steering, cruise control, radio with twin speakers, electric rear window, headlight delay (so it can light the way to your front door) and Martin showed me how the tailgate could be opened horizontally so you could sit on it or use it as a picnic table or something. When I sit behind the wheel, the bonnet looks like a vast expanse of blue ocean and the bench seat is so wide three people could sit side by side and unless they were very large, never rub shoulders. I reckon we could all sleep in this if we had to, never mind just two of us. The engine is as quiet as an Indian in moccasins. I'm not in love with it exactly, even if it does happen to be made in the same year as we were married, but I think this could be the car for me.

Martin says I can take it home and give it a test drive and see what my wife thinks about it. It is the first time I have driven an automatic car with power-assisted brakes and I am not used to the gentle way you have to apply them. I brake like I do with my Morris Marina back home and practically catapult myself through the windscreen as the car comes to a sudden stop and rocks on its springs. Al and Martin smile indulgently as I wave them a flustered goodbye.

I have only gone a few yards when I notice that the fuel tank is empty and an orange light is blinking at me urgently. "Gimme gas! Gimme gas!" I don't know how much gas (I'm already becoming American) is left, but I think I'd better get some fast. I know there is an Exxon on Broadway, near the school, so although it is the wrong direction, I turn left so I can go round the block and head for it. The grid system may be boring, but it is practical.

I make it to the Exxon without having to push. I don't know what side the filler is, but I slide into the nearest available space and hope the hose will stretch if I guess wrong. I locate the petrol cap easily but I can't get it open. I push it and I bang it and I break my fingernails trying to prise it open. In the meantime, the man in the kiosk is looking at me, wondering what the hell I am playing at and giving me very odd looks indeed. Now a motorist has drawn up behind and is looking daggers at me through the windscreen. I can't believe it! What could be simpler than filling up your tank? But I just can't get the bloody thing to open. I become increasingly flustered as the damned thing refuses to budge and in the meantime, someone else draws up behind the car behind me.

By this time, the man in the kiosk is giving me some very frosty looks indeed as he serves other customers. Meanwhile, the man behind me is drumming his fingers on the wheel and his moustache is beginning to quiver. The motorist at the other side of the pump is placidly chewing gum as he fills his tank. Desperation makes me accost him, throw myself at his mercy.

"Em, excuse me, but I can't get my filler cap to open. I wonder if you could help?"

The stranger looks at me with limpid blue eyes. "You talkin' to me bud?" His tone is lazy, disinterested, but at least not hostile, so I feel emboldened to repeat my request. I don't know if he's heard or not. He barely inclines his head, lowers his eyelids so imperceptibly I can't be sure if he did, nor what it might mean... and goes on filling his tank. The man behind me has stuck his head out the window now and the man in the kiosk has stopped serving customers and is looking hard at me. Who would believe that a visit to the petrol station could turn into a nightmare like this? I desperately prise at the filler cap again, at least to show that I am trying to do something about the problem.

But it's useless. The thing still refuses to budge. Just as I decide that it would be a far, far better thing to flee and run out of petrol as long as it is out of sight of this garage, my acquaintance from the other side of the pump leisurely hangs up his hose and strolls round to my side. He glances at my filler cap, opens the driver's door, leans inside, and next second, as if by magic, the filler cap pops open. I am stunned. I look at it in disbelief. Our cars back home don't have this degree of sophistication, at least, not the ones I can afford. I feel like a total idiot and blabber my thanks to my new friend who inclines his head a fraction of an inch and strolls off again without saying a word.

I put in two dollars' worth of petrol. You can go quite far for two dollars in this country and besides, I didn't even know if I was going to buy the thing.

When I go to pay, the man behind the desk gives me a sulphurous look. "That'll be two dollars," he says in a voice loud enough so everyone in the place can suspend what they are doing to look at the freak who has only bought two dollars' worth of petrol and created a queue of irate customers. But mainly he is voicelessly saying: "What kinda nut are you, for Chris' sake?"

It could have been worse. I am supremely relieved that I happened to have this amount of money with me. I never carry a wallet and haven't done so since I was about seventeen. Never had enough money to make it worthwhile buying one. Any money I have, I just stuff in my pockets and I never know at any given time how much I have, or even if I have any at all.

As I hand over the money, I feel as if I want to say that I'm sorry, that I was new to the place, that I didn't know about remote petrol cap levers, if that is what they are called, and I was only trying out the car, that it wasn't mine, but embarrassment keeps me silent. Besides, an inner voice was telling me I had to protect my nationality from scorn and derision.

His eyes are still boring into me as I turn to leave. I can't see, but I can feel that everyone else in the place is doing likewise. He is still staring at me as I climb into the car. The man in the car behind me is looking slightly more mollified, but I am still smarting from shame and can't wait to get out of there fast enough. My haste makes me start off too fast. In alarm, I stomp on the brakes and the car comes to a shuddering stop, rocking on its springs again. These brakes really are fierce, so different from those on Terri's VW. The attendant is still staring at me. I vow that I will never, ever, in my whole year in Missoula, ever visit this filling station again, not even if it's the cheapest in the whole town by a mile.

The blush of utter humiliation that has suffused my whole body has just begun to leave my neck when, on checking the dials on the dashboard, I realise something is seriously wrong with the car. The thermostat is showing red hot although I've hardly gone much more than a mile. It should, if anything, be cold, not pointing to the other extreme.

I can't believe it! I've literally left one crisis behind and another has loomed up right away. Why couldn't I be more like Iona? Once, in our first car, the Wolseley, she had driven all day with the ignition light burning like a red, satanic eye, commanding her to stop, but which she had ignored as she didn't know what it meant. In fact, she regarded it as such a trivial matter that she didn't even mention it when she got home and it was only the next day when I went to use the car that I noticed the light. When I lifted the bonnet, I saw to my horror that there was no fan belt. I couldn't believe that she had driven as far as she did without the engine seizing up.

As for me, I knew I should stop, but I didn't want to. I just hoped I could make it to Lincoln where I could examine what was wrong without the whole of Missoula watching me make an exhibition of myself. But some hopes of that! By the time I cross the river and head on to South Higgins, there is an ominous trail of steam escaping from the bonnet; by the time I pass Hellgate High, anyone would have been forgiven for thinking that I had indeed come from the gates of Hades itself and by the time I turn into Lincoln, the blue station wagon is smoking like Stephenson's *Rocket* and leaving a trail so thick I can't see anything out the back window. I was never so glad to see the house from *Psycho*.

I open the bonnet and an enormous cloud of white steam is whipped away by the wind, while from the engine compartment, a geyser of steam continues to erupt. I leave the bonnet open and go and report to Iona. The plan had been to see what she thought of the car, but that scarcely mattered now. I had to get it back to H.O. Bell's. I let it cool off a bit, and as I pour in the water, I could see it pouring straight out the water pump. I hope two gallons will be enough and start the engine.

The gauge says normal but as I proceed, the needle creeps closer to the danger red part of the dial. I will it to stay where it is and eventually make it to the garage without looking as if I were behind the wheel of a traction engine. Naturally, I have no intention of buying this car. I have just come to dump it and glad to be rid of it but Martin swears he'll fix the pump and I can come back tomorrow and try the car again. I should say: "Do you think I'm mad? A car with a faulty water pump and not enough petrol to go a hundred yards, and that could just be for starters." But instead I think: *Well, I haven't signed a contract yet and if they fix the pump, maybe the car will be OK and it certainly shouldn't need another water pump and besides, there's nearly two dollars worth of petrol in it.* I hear myself tell Martin that if he fixes the pump, I'll come back tomorrow and give it another try.

So, here I am downtown with no transport and therefore I have to do that most un-American activity of all – walk home, but whilst I'm in the business district, I decide I may as well go into a bank and open an account. My salary has to have a home, so the sooner I do this the better. I've been focussing on cars recently, but there is another life beyond cars, though from what I've seen of American society so far, you wouldn't think so.

The first one I come to is called, appropriately, The First Bank of Missoula, so I enter what turns out to be a vast marble area filled with potted palms and other plants. In my bank at home, I am used to a rabbit run of space where the customers stand, fenced off from the tellers by floor-to-ceiling glass which might even be bulletproof for all I know. And yet, here in the land of the gun, anybody could just stroll in and speak face to face with the employees without any apparent security measures at all.

There is a desk which has "Enquiries" written on it and behind the desk there is an attractive brunette. I need no further enticement.

"How can I help you?" she smiles pleasantly.

I tell her that I've just moved into town and I need to set up a bank account for my salary to be paid into.

"Where you from?"

"Scotland."

"Yeah, I know, but what part?"

I am surprised at her interest, but I tell her I'm from the North East, near Aberdeen, knowing she will never have heard of it, but impressed with her customer-relation skills. I think I will definitely open an account at this bank if they show such an interest in me. So what if they do pay half-a-percent interest rate less than the others? (I hope they don't.) In any case, my salary is so meagre it wouldn't make that amount of difference.

She is not to be satisfied with this vague answer. "How near Aberdeen?"

I think she is carrying customer friendliness a bit far, but she is easy to look at and I'm not in any particular hurry, so I make my customary joke when people ask where I'm from.

"Oh, I'm just a bit round the bend," I say. "A place you'll never have heard of. A wee place called Banff."

"So you're a Bumffer!" she exclaims.

Knock me down with a feather all right! Not only has she apparently heard of Banff, Scotland, not to be confused with that Canadian upstart in the Rockies, but she knows how to pronounce it just like a native. My jaw must be hanging somewhere about my navel as she gives a chuckle.

"I'm from Elgin," she explains.

My jaw drops a further foot, if that were possible. Elgin is about thirty miles from the place of my nativity. I used to go there in the days of my youth to try to ensnare women at a sort of upmarket cattle market dancing venue called the *Two Red Shoes.* And at Elgin Town Hall, we in the boondocks could see celebrated bands of the Sixties such as the Kinks and the Searchers and on one memorable occasion, I actually met the Swinging Blue Jeans. But that is another story.

When I've recovered a bit, I say: "Fit are ee deein' here? Yir an afae lang wye frae hame an' ye dinnae spik as if ye came frae Elgin." She obviously can understand the Doric, but like my French and German, understands it better than she can speak it, for in American, she explains that she came to the States in 1958, where, in due course, she met her husband and has been States-side ever since, though not all of it in Montana. Twenty years has certainly removed all trace of her origins.

We get to talking. She wants to know why a Bumffer is in Missoula, Montana of all places, so I explain about the teacher exchange programme and how I'm engaged at the moment in buying a car.

When I tell her about the Plymouth station wagon, she suppresses a cry of horror. "Don't go to H.O. Bell's whatever you do! They're a bunch of crooks!"

"Are they?" I ask, swallowing her words like a lump of lead.

"Don't go near them!" she cautions earnestly. "Here, I've got a friend who's got a car business." She takes a scrap of paper and writes that I am a friend of hers, a fellow Scot and he's got to give me a good deal. This could be my lucky day. The North East mafia strikes again.

Since the Demarios garage is on this side of the river, I decide I'll walk over. It can't do any harm. But when I get there, the boss is not in and a salesman takes me in hand. We get in a car and he takes me to another car lot and I drive a Chevrolet. As we are driving along Broadway, towards the hospital, we come across a cop car pulled across the middle of the road with all its lights flashing.

"What's going on?"

"Helicopter for St Pat's, probably," the salesman replies nonchalantly.

And sure enough, there is a great clattering overhead and a helicopter lands in front of us. There is a blur of white coats around the machine and a patient is wheeled out and away. The helicopter clatters into the sky again and the cop car drives off. It has only taken a couple of minutes. I've hardly ever seen a helicopter in my life, let alone one land in the middle of the street just yards away from me.

"Does this happen often?" I want to know.

The salesman shrugs. He's not so impressed as me. "From time to time," he says.

When we get back to the first garage, the boss is still not there, but his brother is. I show him the note from my new friend but it impresses him as much as the salesman was with the helicopter. He tells me I can have the Chevrolet I was driving for $1300. I tell him that I don't have that much to spend and leave.

Somehow I don't think I'll go back and see his brother. When it comes to business, why should he give me a good deal on the strength of coming from the same place, nearly, as a friend of his? I don't think he will. It seems such a tenuous link, I decide not to go back.

And I didn't. Which might just have been the biggest mistake I had made since I decided to come here in the first place.

Chapter Fourteen

*In which the Great Car Hunt continues
and the past comes to haunt us.*

Perry comes the next day and the Great Car Hunt resumes again. It's really kind of him to help me like this. For a start, it means I don't have to drive the VW and for another, he is good moral support. I feel that in his company, I'm not so likely to be ripped off.

We drive to a few lots and I try some more cars. Meanwhile, the kids are getting fractious, so Perry takes Iona and the kids home. I take one for a drive then bargain over the price. They want $1900 but I am prepared to pay only $1300 which I think is a bit ironic as I had said yesterday that I didn't have that much money to spend on a car. The salesman won't budge on the price and after that, there is nothing more to talk about because once the negotiations break down, the salesman doesn't try to sell me another car. Maybe that one was the cheapest he had, or maybe he is thinking: *I'll never make a profit out of a Scotsman. I'll just save my breath.* In any case, his earlier bonhomie has evaporated like snow off a dyke at the first sign of sunshine.

Normally one would just walk away at this point and it gets increasingly embarrassing waiting for Perry to return. To me it seems interminable, but at last he does come back and takes me to another garage where I drive an Oldsmobile. Whoever thought of calling a car a stupid name like that? Makes it sound like an invalid carriage. A car for the elderly presumably – though how they would have the strength to turn the wheel I don't know because I hardly can and I am young and relatively fit. It has no power steering.

We look at another. It looks good but this salesman has not been to lying school yet as he tells us that it has a hole in the petrol tank. I decide not to buy it for some reason, despite of the salesman's honesty. Instead we move on to T&W Chevrolet on the outskirts of town where we see an immaculate Chevy. It is two-tone, in red and white, Aberdeen's colours, so perhaps it is meant for me. What's more, it has only done 44,000 miles but it is old: 1967, so it was already 11 years old and I decide not to even bother driving it. Besides, all this research has at least decided me by now that I want a station wagon, so Perry drives me to H.O. Bell's. The Plymouth is in a fenced-in lot, so we can't get closer to look at it. It looks as if it has never been moved since I took it back and it doesn't look as if it is going to get fixed that day either, but Perry says it looks OK for the price and drives me home.

By the time we get back, it is 3 pm and neither of us has had any lunch. Iona, like Queen Victoria, is not amused, especially when I tell her the results of our researches and we are as far away as ever from getting a car. I wonder if Perry's new wife, Karen, is fizzing. But that is Perry's problem and he's a lawyer, so if he's anything like the famous fictional lawyer of the same name, I'm sure he'll be able to sort it out.

* * *

The *Missoulian* tells us that there is a Scottish Heritage Society show on – pipers from British Columbia, so we decide to get a touch of home and go and see them. Are we feeling homesick already? We would never have considered it, had we been at home.

But our preparations are interrupted by a ring at the doorbell. It is the Burdens. They are an even closer reminder of home than that. They were our neighbours once, until Colin got a job lecturing at McGill University, Montreal. His subject is engineering and so we have nothing in common really, apart from living next door to each other and both being in the education business, although of course, I was in a much more lowly position than his. They had phoned yesterday to say they would be coming – sometime. And now they have arrived and what's more, they are bearing gifts, extravagant gifts for the kids – a plastic trike for George and a talking doll for Hélène – things I could never afford.

I take it this is a sign they are faring better financially since we saw them last. If I hadn't known any better, I would have said theirs was a house of the long-term unemployed, living below the bread line. Although a detached house, therefore more costly than our inferior semi-detached, they had no carpets in the living room/dining room and such furniture as there was, was shabby and rickety and obviously second-hand.

One night, when I, not Iona, for some reason, was baby-sitting for their only daughter, Christine, my curiosity got the better of me and I did a very bad thing. Intrigued by the apparent poverty, curious to see how they had furnished upstairs, indeed if there was any at all, but persuading myself that I was really checking that Christine was all right, I went upstairs.

Their bedroom door was open and I couldn't resist sticking my head in. I saw there was a bed, not just a mattress on the floor though unsurprisingly, there was no carpet but what did amaze me was to see that on the inside of the door there was a massive black bolt, such as you would expect to find on a garden shed. Talk about lack of finesse! If it was intended to allow them privacy in which they could try to create a sibling for Christine (and what other reason could there be?) it was a mighty deterrent indeed. Or was it simply that Colin was even less of a handyman than me? That hardly seemed possible, for if there's one thing about Colin you should know, it is that he knows everything - apart from, hopefully, that I ever snooped about his house. And the answer to that I presume, is he does not, as he has brought the kids such nice (and embarrassingly expensive) presents.

Acquaintances rather than friends, nevertheless good manners and politeness dictate we make them welcome. They are a link with home, even if they are not Scots and it is more than a year since we saw them last, so hopefully, there will be plenty to talk about and no long embarrassing silences.

Colin's plump and jolly wife, Pam, whom I rather like, takes Iona and the kids to Albertsons for some shopping in their car, while Colin and I do the much more manly thing of going to the pub in the VW. We end up in a pub called The Squires. I am a bit ashamed to come halfway round the world only to go to an English pub, but there is a good reason for it. I had noticed during my car shopping that they have what they call a "Happy Hour", where the beer, already cheap at 75 cents a glass, is only 50 cents. And it's not just for an hour either, but two!

Over the beers, I tell Colin of my favourable impressions so far of the transatlantic way of life but Colin sets me right and points out where I am going wrong. It seems there is nothing good about it. The North Americans are "shallow" and "consumer-driven". For "Canada" read

"America" – for they are all tarred with the same brush of capitalism.

For the first time it occurs to me that Colin may be a communist. Perhaps that explains why he furnished his house in that minimalist way, feeling guilty for having joined the property-owning classes. It's a weak defence for the capitalists, but I point out that at least the Happy Hour is a good idea and I wish we had it back home, for all the poor people like me who had to make their own alcohol, but Colin doesn't think so and launches into a thesis about why it is not. I am not really listening, at least when I can't follow the argument any more, and instead I get to wondering: *How long are you planning to stay?*

I tell him about the Plymouth station wagon and take him up to see it. It is still in precisely the same place as where Perry and I saw it yesterday. On the way, Colin gives me the low down about Missoula. After all, he has been here a couple of hours now and has had time to suss it out and advises me of the pitfalls I can expect to run up against. Since he is such a fount, I can hardly wait to hear his verdict on the car.

"It'll be fine," he says. "At that price you can't go wrong. Those engines are so big they go on forever. You'll only get scrap value for it back east though."

At teatime, the talk is of the old days mainly, the year before last year, and the neighbours, but since they had even less to do with them than me, especially Colin, who regarded me as being his closest intellectual inferior, the conversation soon peters out and after a while my brain can't absorb any new things I should know about transatlantic life and it shuts down too.

Pam contributes the information that she finds the people in Montreal standoffish and unfriendly. I wonder if it could possibly have something to do with her know-all, seen-it-all, done-it-all and even-what-I-haven't-done, I-know-it-all, husband.

But then I don't really know anything, so I could be completely wrong.

* * *

They leave in the afternoon of the following day. When they are gone, I feel strangely empty, despite the not entirely successful evening. They may not be our closest friends, but they are a link with home. I suspect I am beginning to feel the first vestiges of homesickness, another layer upon the nagging base of unease that I can't suppress, that like a balloon held under water, insists on bobbing up to the surface.

But maybe it has more to do with Colin's negative attitude to transatlantic life which he has left behind hanging, invisible, intangible, like a miasma in the air. What if he's right? He's had a year across the Atlantic and obviously isn't that enamoured with it. What if I end up feeling the same way? What if this year turns out to be a nightmare? Nervousness begins gnawing at my entrails like a rat.

However, the Burdens leave behind something more tangible than a memory as a reminder of their visit. Each of them has left a memento which we only discover one by one, so we don't get too much pleasure all at once. Pam has been the least subtle. She has had a shower. In the house from *Psycho,* you expect horrible things in such a place and there is: a matted mass of long black hairs in the plug. But that wasn't the problem; the curtain had been drawn across the outside of the bath instead of the inside. The floor is so wet, she *must* have noticed the mess, but obviously had made no attempt to wipe it up or even confess.

Christine has left a purse bulging with Canadian coins and by the time we have found the third and mercifully the last of their mementoes, any feeling of sadness I'd had at their departure has turned into grumpiness, tinged with relief. The best was kept till last and contributed by Colin, naturally – a pair of heavy brogues that weigh much more than the purse. It is going to cost a fortune to send them to Montreal.

Thank you, Colin, Christine and Pam. Burdens by name and burdens by nature.

Chapter Fifteen

In which, amongst others, I meet some of my future colleagues and make an unpleasant discovery.

We are invited to the Hertz household for four o'clock. They are holding a party in my honour so I can meet some people, especially my prospective colleagues, in order to facilitate my start at school. It's really kind and thoughtful of them, above and beyond the call of duty. I can't imagine Marnie receiving the same treatment in Scotland, though I hope she is. We Scots are much more reserved than Americans appear to be. You can live for twenty years in a place and still be considered an "incomer" at the end of it. It's not that we're unfriendly: it's just we've got to suss you out first and that takes time.

But maybe what we've experienced is not the norm here either: perhaps we've just landed lucky. Just look at what Al and Terri have done for us: had us over for a meal, taken us shopping, helped with buying a car – even lent us a car, for God's sake and now this! But maybe they are just typical of what Marie was talking about back east, about the friendliness of the westerners.

I'm feeling nervous about meeting so many new people all at once, but it certainly beats boredom and routine and every minute I've spent in this country has certainly lived up to that. Out of the rut, I most certainly am.

Marnie's special friend, Art Moore is there. Marnie had told me that he would look after me at school if I needed any help or advice. He's a sixth grade teacher so maybe he has some idea of what they are meant to be doing in seventh grade. Hopefully I'll get a chance to speak to him later, show him the books and ask him what I'm meant to do with them. I'm not quite sure what the relationship is between him and Marnie. By the sound of it, they seem to spend a lot of time together and he seems to be her confidant but I'm not sure if it goes any further than that. His welcome is very effusive and I get the feeling that I could easily approach him with my worries about school.

The school librarian and her husband are present too. Her name is Millie Fergusson and she is Canadian by birth. She seems very nice and I'm sure she'd be helpful too if I need any help in tracking down some sources. Her husband is also very friendly and says he's got a boat on Flathead Lake and he must take us out in it sometime. Flathead Lake is a hundred miles and more to the north but they think nothing of travelling that sort of distance or more for the weekend or a day even. At the orientation we had been told this was likely to happen, that we could expect all sorts of invitations like this. Americans' standard of living being so much higher than that in the UK, it was not uncommon for them to have boats or holiday cabins out of town somewhere and they'd be keen to invite us to share them.

There is another teacher there, Art's friend, Sam White. His face is almost entirely hidden by a bushy black beard and a pair of large spectacles. I notice he has a limp and I later discover he only has one leg and wears a prosthesis. He smiles broadly and shakes my hand warmly.

"Well, hello, David!" he drawls. "What d' you think of Missoula?" He is the only person since I got here who has called me by my proper name. He chuckles. "Don't you think it's just such a *neat* place?" I assure him that I think it is very neat indeed.

I am hustled off to meet other people. The house is swarming with guests. Most noticeable is a portly man wearing a cardinal-red blazer, an appropriate, if not somewhat pretentious choice of colour, for he turns out to be Al and Terri's priest. He is the epitome of the merry cleric. His voice is loud and booming and his meaty fist seems to have a symbiotic relationship with food and drink, for it is never empty. He never moves more than a few feet from the table where the food and the beer and the wine are laid out.

Grandpa is sitting beside the table with a shot glass in his hand. His eyes are half closed and he is nodding to himself. Other members of the Hertz clan are there too. Cassie is not moving about much. She is sitting on the couch smoking a cigarette, as usual. There is no sign of Cain and Abel.

Al is hugging a girl with an olive complexion, full lips and very dark frizzy hair.

"This is my Italian daughter, Sandi."

So this is the mother of Amy and Daniel, as dark as Debbie is fair. Al is so proud of his Italian blood that I imagine that this is as good as saying that Sandi is his favourite daughter. Sandi certainly seems to appreciate the compliment and admits that she is only an eighth Italian but as the Italian genes dominate, she regards herself as Italian and if anyone asks what her nationality is, that's what she says, she tells me.

Non-Italian Debbie has, however, a boyfriend. "This is Ben," she tells me, and not pausing for breath, adds, "He works down the sewers."

A brain surgeon you might boast about, but not this. I take it in my stride, I think. I hope I have kept my face expressionless, but Debbie, from the instant I met her, has a way of verbally hitting me in the solar plexus. Ben is pasty-faced and shy. From his complexion, it looks as if he does indeed spend a great deal of his time in subterranean tunnels. I give him a nod of acknowledgement, not deeming it necessary to shake hands. But before Ben has the opportunity to invite me on a guided tour, which rather disappoints me, as I imagine not many Missoulians get such a chance to inspect the bowels of their city, Al materialises to bear me off to meet someone else.

"This is my best friend, Chris Mendez. He's a hair bender."

"A hair bender?"

Al is delighted at my puzzlement. He makes a pantomime of Chris cutting people's hair with an extremely limp wrist. The bender's hair is very short and neat and tidy (who cuts his?) and he has a white stripe in his forelock which I suspect is not a natural Mallen streak. He has a close-cut beard, a gold necklace, and as he holds his hand out for me to shake, I can't help but notice a gold chain round his wrist and that his fingers are dripping with gold rings. If I hadn't been told he was a hair bender, I might have concluded he was a jeweller so dedicated to his work that he had taken it home with him. In earlier times, with an earring, it would have been easy to imagine him as a Spanish grandee. Clearly, there is money in the hair bending game. I don't think Chris is just an ordinary bender of hair though and if he's a friend of Al's, I imagine he's as heterosexual as a bull. Al confirms both of my suspicions at a stroke.

"He's got his own shop," he says. "Bends the hair of all the rich dames in town. Not just the hair on their head either!" He throws back his head in laughter and Chris's laugh is ready chorus. "Not bad for a wetback! You know what a wetback is, Dave?"

I have to confess I don't.

"He's a Mex," Al explains. "Swam across the Rio Grande. That's why his back is wet!" and he roars with laughter again and once again, Chris reprises his stooge act, while I feel rather foolish, not being able to join in the joke.

A lot more people are milling about and I forget their names almost as soon as I hear them. They are friends of Al and Terri and I don't suppose I'm likely to meet them again anyway.

It's not really the place or the time for kids. They are getting increasingly restless and difficult to amuse.

"Is it all right if the kids go outside and play in the garden?" Iona asks Terri.

"Oh, no, don't let them anywhere near the garden!" For once, Terri, the unflappable, looks horrified.

It was only a question asked out of politeness after all and we are astounded by her answer. What could it possibly be about such a modest proposal to provoke such an animated response, and from Terri of all people? I can see now where Debbie gets her knockout verbal punches. We are still visibly gasping when Terri fills our sails with some much-needed air. "They can play in the yard, certainly," she adds hastily, "but please keep them out of the garden. The garden is where we grow our prodoos."

Sometime later, and after having expended some of their energy in the yard under Iona's supervision, who made sure they did not uproot any zucchini or squash, I take the kids back and put them to bed.

By the time Iona relieves me and I go back to the party, things have livened up a good deal. Sam White is sitting behind the breakfast bar cradling a Budweiser. Beside him is his girlfriend, Margaret Brown. She seems very quiet and the way Sam looks at people, me included, and then makes sotto voce remarks to Margaret, makes me feel rather nervous, as if I were an insect under the microscope. Sam is evidently like Chaucer, the sort of bloke who prefers to sit on the sidelines observing people rather than make things happen. Actually, I'm a bit like that myself.

"Say, David, would you like to go rafting?"

Before I ever came to Montana, I'd made up my mind that I wasn't going to refuse anything, especially any invitations that came my way that year. When Sam drawls on about how it's white water in some places and we have to wait till the weather got really hot, into the nineties, as there was every chance I'd be thrown into the river, I try to act unfazed, like I wasn't scared of drowning. He probably doesn't really mean it anyway; he was just being friendly. We are heading into Autumn and the low eighties or high seventies we've been experiencing recently feels plenty warm to me and it seems pretty unlikely as we nudge into October, that it'll get warmer. I reckon I've got no need to worry, at least not for the moment.

The conversation turns to what I've been doing since I came to Missoula. The Great Car Hunt takes up a lot of the time and I tell him about my travels with Perry.

"Perry!" Sam snorts. "Perry is an asshole! That right, Margaret? Perry is a number one asshole!" He takes another slug of Bud as if rinsing his mouth out.

I am shocked. He has been pretty obliging to me, and apart from having a weird taste in furniture and not being scared of his wife, like most normal men, I have not detected a fault in him, unless, of course, you call leaving Marnie for a younger woman, a fault.

It seems this is what Sam has in mind. He says he was a right "asshole" to Marnie, living with Karen but coming round all the time to see Marnie.

"Perhaps he was coming round to see the kids, rather than Marnie," I suggest in a placatory fashion, as I can see Sam is getting a bit worked up.

"Naw! He was screwin' her up and probably screwin' her as well. As well as Karen. I mean even *after* he married Karen. Boy, was Marnie screwed up! That's why she went on the exchange."

I had thought as much from what Marnie had said in her preliminary letters and our meeting in Washington, D.C. Not for the first time I reflected on the irony that out of this whole exchange, the person I was going to know least was Marnie. My friends and colleagues back home were going to know her a lot better than me. I was going to find out more about her, like this, little by little, from snippets dropped in conversation, just as she would find out more about me. And interestingly, she might find out things about me that I probably didn't even know myself.

Sam asks me what I think of the house. If it had been Art, I would have said it was neat, but I tell Sam that it's a lot bigger than ours and a bit dark and a bit of a shock to find so few doors and carpets, though I refrain from mentioning the more literal shocks it is likely to give us. But perhaps because I'm on my second Budweiser since I rejoined the party, I tell him that I was a bit disappointed to find that the house had not been left ready for us to walk into, like ours was for Marnie, and there was the matter of some bills which Lindy had left unpaid.

"Lindy's husband is an asshole! That right, Margaret?"

Margaret, as usual, makes no comment.

"Lindy's husband?"

"Yeah, they come down every year, when school gets out. Lindy's gotta make some credits."

"They?" I'll worry about "credits" later. This sounds more worrying.

"Yeah, Lindy an' her husband an' their kids an' her dog."

"You mean they were all there, in Marnie's house?" If I sound incredulous, it's because it sounds like an invasion. Not what Marnie had led me to believe at all.

"Yeah, they were all here this summer, as usual. Lindy's husband though, David, he's a real asshole."

I have no way of knowing if Lindy's husband is a "real asshole" or not. I might be able to judge for myself if ever I go to Whitefish, but Sam's revelation about the house comes as a shock since Marnie had only ever referred to Lindy being in the house. It wasn't any concern of mine really, what Marnie did with her house before the exchange took place, except while I had been particular to have everything ready and all the meters read, it now appears Marnie had had a whole menagerie living there all summer who had just abandoned it like the *Mary Celeste* or the lighthouse on Flannan Isle – and left me to pick up the tab. That sinking feeling starts gnawing at the bottom of my stomach again and it's all I can do to refocus my mind when Sam asks me if I have seen the school yet. I tell him about Matt taking me up there, about him photocopying the note from Marnie. He is scandalised.

"What a dildo! God, did you hear that Margaret? Gee, what a dildo!"

He launches forth on a diatribe about what a weak personality Matt has and how he's terrified to make a decision, and once he's made one, he'll change it back again if you feel strongly enough to protest about it. It seems that I was right, that Matt *was* scared Marnie had written something about him. To me it's a miracle that he agreed to the exchange at all. He must have been worried sick what Marnie would tell me about him at the orientation in Washington. Maybe that was why he seemed so nervous when he met me; maybe it wasn't just down to shyness at all.

Chapter Sixteen

In which I make some observations on American life and culture and some light is shed in the kitchen.

The next day we putter to H.O. Bell's in Terri's VW but the car is still precisely where I had left it on Friday. I don't want to look too keen to buy it, so I go instead to the Triple A, the American Automobile Association, where I find out that it would only be $35 dollars for both Iona and me to join. And for "thus much moneys", as Shylock put it, in addition to the breakdown service, we will receive route maps and handbooks of any state I want, free of charge. These handbooks tell you about campsites and charges as well as providing thumbnail sketches on each and every town along the way and where there is a site or a town of special significance, it goes into a considerable amount of detail. Since the plan is to drive from coast to coast once the school year is over, that sounds to me like the bargain of the millennium and even although I don't have a car yet, I join at once.

What the helpful man advises me to do very strongly is to get a garage to check the car over before I buy it, and especially to get a compression check done. He gives me the address of a garage that will do this and out of all the garages in the length and breadth of Missoula, which one does he pick but the Exxon garage on Broadway!

"Em... em... is there another garage you could give me?" I ask lamely.

The assistant's forehead furrows as he gives me a queer look.

"Em... em... I just thought I'd shop around a bit," I bluster. It doesn't sound convincing to me and it doesn't convince the AAA man either.

"They're all the same," he says. "This one is the closest an' easiest for you to get to."

He's absolutely right. He may know my address from the application form but what he doesn't know is I could leave the car there while I am at school so it's even more convenient than he realises.

"Oh, I see. Well... em... that's fine then. Thanks," is what I manage to burble, but what I am actually thinking is: *Damn! Maybe Al or Perry can recommend another garage, or maybe I'll see an advert in the Missoulian.* Yes, that would be better, lest, for sport, the gods made them recommend the Exxon garage as the best in town.

* * *

I have been here nearly a week now and never been in that temple of American consumerism, the supermarket. I had been shopping at Albertsons but that only sold food and I have been to plenty of second-hand car lots, but not a single proper supermarket. Now the time has come.

For my initiation, we choose K-Mart as Marnie had said it was cheap. As supermarkets go, it is massive by our standards. I buy some film – K-Mart's own brand. Kodak is still a lot cheaper than we would pay back home but this is a great deal cheaper than that. I just hope the quality is all right as I don't want this record of my stay ruined by grainy prints where the colours aren't quite right. I reckon it won't do any harm to try a couple of rolls and see how they turn out.

George needs shoes but above all, we need some plastic plates. He and Hélène have been testing Marnie's china for bouncability on the kitchen floor. Since there is no carpet, not a single one has survived the experiment. I hope to God that they were not what Marnie classed as "antiques". The patterns certainly look bad enough to meet her criteria as priceless examples of the potter's art, and as not a single one matches another, it's pretty likely she picked them up at junk shops around the State, if not the country.

The Bureau had told us before we left, if there was anything that would cause us heartbreak if it were broken, to put it away. I hope Marnie had done this, but since she has not, for example, put the jawbone of the rat away for safekeeping, I worry that she is going to be upset about the plates. Furthermore, since she doesn't appear to have done any of the other things recommended by the Bureau, it's a pretty safe bet that she hasn't done this either.

Iona picks some cheery cherry-red plates that will brighten up the stygian gloom of the kitchen. And as well as preserving what I hope is not Marnie's priceless china collection, they will also be useful when we go camping at the end of the year.

The other thing we could do with is a kettle. If we want hot water, we have to heat it up in a pan, on the hob. There is every electrical gadget imaginable in this vast emporium, but no matter how hard we search, we fail to uncover the slightest sign of a kettle. It's incredible to think that we are in the most advanced nation, technologically speaking, on the planet – the country that can put a man on the moon but doesn't yet have the most basic kitchen appliance with which to boil water efficiently!

Finally I buttonhole an assistant who explains that since Americans are a coffee-drinking nation, as opposed to a tea-drinking one like "you English" and since they have machines to make the coffee, why would they need such a thing as a kettle? I don't bother to point out that in our house we don't drink much tea, not because we are not English, but because Iona hates it and we use the kettle all the time to make coffee, for washing the dishes and a host of other uses and that it is probably the most indispensable appliance in the home.

It's another example of cultural shock. We can live without the kettle, but Marnie's shock must be so much greater. The only gadget they've got in the entire house is a measly little electric kettle that doesn't seem to have any practical purpose. How will she manage without the coffeemaker, the quintessential requirement for the American home? As for the dishwasher, I can just imagine the squabbling and the fighting as Marnie's kids moan about chores having to be done that they have never had to do back home. I can also see poor Beth being the one who ends up doing the dishes.

***

It crosses my mind that today's the day Marnie goes to school, begins work. She may be there now, or will it all be over by now? The time difference is too complicated for my feeble, arithmetically challenged brain to work out, but here I am, still on holiday, sitting in Marnie's back garden, writing a letter, the sun beaming its pleasant warmth upon me and a beer gently effervescing at my elbow. Life would be perfect if it were like this all the time but there are two black clouds on the horizon: the car and what I'm going to do at school.

The letter written, I turn from writer to reader and learn in the *Missoulian* that electricity is cheaper at night, so our new regime will start tonight. We'll switch it off during the day and put it on all night, and if we need more hot water or heating, then we'll just have to switch it on. I hope Lindy knew to do that.

I also learn there are plenty of places where I could get the compression check done, if only I had the slightest clue in this sprawling city where these garages are. I am beginning to think it is maybe not such a bad thing after all that we have inherited, albeit by default, the *Missoulian*, because it contains a supplement called *The Entertainer* which, amongst local cultural events, also lists the TV programmes.

Marnie's TV is black and white and as you might expect from appliances in this house, it belongs to one of the first generations of televisions. Now that is the one thing which I think Marnie's kids *will* think is good about our house, and Scotland. We may not have a dishwasher and only a small fridge but we do have colour TV which might go some way to persuading them that Scotland is not so primitive as they think and the house has one redeeming feature at least. Naturally I can't take any credit for the superior quality of the programmes. We may have a more restricted choice, but what's the point of greater choice if the only choice is between degrees of rubbish? And God bless the BBC which is completely free from adverts. Here you can't avoid them at all.

According to *The Entertainer*, there are numerous channels and because we are on the border between the

Mountain and Pacific time zones, it's possible to catch the same programme an hour later. It lists the programmes for both, presumably for people like me who can't do the arithmetic. Except Marnie's TV doesn't seem able to receive Pacific time, something that does not worry me much at all, just like I am not too disappointed to discover it doesn't seem to be able to receive half of the channels we are supposed to get either. Maybe it's something to do with the aerial but what it tells me most is that Marnie is not the most dedicated television viewer in Montana. But don't the kids feel deprived?

I have to confess I have been watching a bit of TV. They show a lot of old shows like *Sergeant Bilko*, (which Marnie's TV shows in original monochrome) and a favourite of mine, *M*A*S*H*, which is many episodes ahead of us, naturally, and one of the unforeseen benefits of this exchange is that I can see, long before the rest of our nation, the character who replaces the sadly-missed Frank. On the other hand, the American version has canned laughter so you know when someone has said something funny and when to laugh. It drives me so mad that it's all I can do to watch an episode to the end, which would have been a lot sooner, had it not been for the adverts which interrupt the show every eight minutes. I know because I made a particular point of timing them. Thus an intelligent show that runs the gamut from comedy to pathos, sometimes in a matter of moments, is completely ruined.

One thing that does intrigue me however, is that there are two television companies just for the town of Missoula itself. Marnie had told me that they might want to do an interview with me and I'd heard it mentioned at the orientation meeting, that we might be asked to go on TV but

I had thought that pretty unlikely. But now I could see that on a poor day for news, one of the local channels may be driven to interviewing an exchange teacher from Scotland about the education system in Missoula. I hope that if that happens, it's not before I can find something flattering to say.

After I finish my letter, I take the kids and Iona to see my room in the school. She likes it a lot better than the house from *Psycho* because it has carpets and curtains like a normal house and it is bright and airy. The public library is just a stone's throw from the school so we go along to join but are rejected on the grounds that we have no ID. Why should it matter what name we register under? In fact, you might positively *want* to use an alias if your intention is to take out *The Story of O* or *Fanny Hill* or *The Tropic of Cancer* or even *Lady Chatterley's Lover* for that matter, should they stock them in the first place. In Scotland, unless you take the Mick by calling yourself Adolf Hitler or Attila the Hun, they are inclined to take your word for it that you are who you say you are.

When we get back, Grandpa Hertz arrives armed with a screwdriver and some "prodoos". His hands shake so much and it's so dark in the kitchen, I can't work out how he can see to do anything or fix anything, but miracle of miracles, a few minutes later, we have a light in the kitchen. At least one that you can shine on the table and see what's on it. But the surrounding gloom seems to have intensified, as if the darkness from the table had shrunk back in fear and crowded into the corners.

I give Grandpa a whisky from the other, and last remaining bottle, of duty-free Dewar's and try to make conversation with him although it is difficult as he can't hear me very well and probably is struggling with my accent anyway. Not for the first time, I find it difficult to imagine that this sweet, timid, gentle old man is Al's father. Maybe he just slowed down a bit. Maybe he was a real hell-raiser when he was young. But I can't see it somehow.

Whilst we are chatting, or rather I am talking and Grandpa is nodding, the phone rings. It's Martin Fleischman to tell me the car is ready. I, however, am not. I tell him I'll pick it up sometime tomorrow. I am not just playing hard to get: I have to arrange for a compression test somewhere. With less than two dollars' worth of petrol in the tank and not knowing how far that would get me, I can't afford to go chasing all over the town. And I don't want to put in any more petrol because I might not be buying the car anyway, especially if it gets a bad report.

There is only one choice left open to me. With a bit of luck, it wouldn't be the petrol pump attendant's shift and even if it were, he would have nothing to do with the compression testing anyway. I decide to act like a man, not a mouse, and phone the Exxon garage.

Chapter Seventeen

In which I make another amazing chance encounter and the Great Car Hunt comes to an end.

We take Terri's VW to the Bell garage, where Martin is especially pleased to see me. He wants me to settle an argument. One of his colleagues has been counting up the foreign countries he has been to and there is a dispute between them because he says he has been to Wales and to England which counts as two, but his mates say that that only counts as one, that it's the same country.

I am the arbiter, the fount of knowledge on this arcane subject, the judge and the jury. But what to say? It *is* the same country but it isn't. What kind of an answer is that? I have to be definitive. I say that you don't need a passport, but yes, it is a different country, with its own football team and rugby team, though we share the same sovereign and Parliament. I don't consider myself as English, though I might admit to being British, but I consider myself to be a Scot first and foremost.

I am just about to expound that the same principle applies to Wales and England but Martin's colleague isn't listening any more. He turns to the others in glee. "See, what did I tell y'all? That'll be ten bucks, guys!"

I've made a tactical error. I could easily have said we were all part of the one United Kingdom and Martin would have been saved from stumping up. It might just be a bit harder to get a good deal now. I wonder if it would be possible to swap salesmen.

As I drive up to the Exxon garage, I scan the forecourt to see if the petrol attendant is in attendance. It looks as if it may be the same guy but he is too busy to see me pull in, pass the pumps and drive up to the garage proper. We are told to come back in an hour, so we go back to the library and having the requisite ID, are duly admitted as members then we go to a coffee shop on Higgins to while away the time. I am not a coffee addict but Iona is and besides, we can't go trailing around because although we have a pushchair for George, Hélène's short legs aren't up to an hour's pavement pounding.

Iona and I have a coffee each and the kids have two small cokes. After a while, the waitress comes round and fills up our cups again before I can stop her. Curses! If I had been on my own, I wouldn't have had any coffee at all. Now I'm going to have to pay for four. I make up my mind to be more alert the next time. The waitress seems to have got this dodge down to a fine art as she is like a bee gathering nectar from flower to flower, except in her case, she is dispensing coffee as soon as she spots an almost empty cup, materialising behind the unsuspecting customer's shoulder and pouring the black liquid before they have time to protest.

But when the bill comes, there must be some mistake. It only comes to 75 cents! Four coffees and two cokes and there's change left out of a dollar! It is my first introduction to the bottomless cup of coffee. I could have had six cups or more for the same price. Unbelievable! I can't help thinking again of Marnie and what her reaction is going to be the first time she goes into a café and expects her cup to be filled up again for free, to say nothing of the price of her first and only.

As we come out of the coffee shop and stroll up the street, we nearly bump into a slightly-built man with a moustache who is unchaining a bicycle from a lamppost.

"Sorry!" I say automatically, but it's actually his fault as he is backing into us, unaware, with his bike. That is a very British thing to do, apologise when it is not your fault, but his response absolutely stuns me.

"Are you the Addison family?"

By what alchemy had this perfect stranger known my name, from just one word? Surely his deductive powers must be superior to even that of Sherlock Holmes's brother, Mycroft, brighter than Sherlock, but lazy. However, like conjuring tricks, which, after they have been explained, seem banal and leave you with a feeling of disappointment, or even foolishness that you've been tricked so easily – so the stranger's explanation is similarly simple and ordinary, for seeing my amazement, he smiles and points to the pushchair.

"It's the stroller," he says. "You don't see too many of them around here and I've just got back from England and saw them all the time."

It's true. I had been vaguely aware of passers-by giving us odd looks. I had wondered if it was something to do with the clothes that we were wearing, or even not wearing. Iona, for instance is wearing a skirt, and I, who have a passing interest in the opposite sex, had not spotted a single female who was not in jeans or trousers of some description. "Pants" as they call them. As for me, I was hatless which also made me an oddity, for practically every male was wearing a baseball cap, or, and this I must admit, gave me a small frisson of excitement, a Stetson or a cowboy hat, like in the Westerns I used to watch as a boy. It made me feel as if I really were not only in a foreign land, but in the wild and woolly West.

But the pushchair, although it might identify us as being English, God forbid, (as opposed to Scottish) could not reveal our name, not unless we had left the luggage label on it from the flight. But for this, Mycroft would have to have had eyes like a hawk to read our name from such a distance without appearing to pay it any attention. Besides, there wasn't any label anyway. So how did he do it?

He explains that he was in fact an exchange teacher himself, that he'd just got back and that his exchange partner, in their correspondence, had told him that there was a Scottish teacher called Addison coming to school district Number 7. You see, it is simple when you know, and rather disappointing. The mystery seems better.

He tells me he didn't like his school in Colchester very much. He had asked to go there as he was actually born there and having left as a small child, wanted to see the land of his birth. His name is Bill Kennedy and he teaches English at Hellgate High. He says he'll give me a call and we must get together.

Still musing on the coincidences I keep having in this sprawling town, we stroll into the bookshop outside which this brief encounter had taken place. We still have half an hour or so to wait and there I have another shock. We are not well off for bookshops in Falkirk, not even Stirling, which is bigger and fifteen miles away. You have to go to Edinburgh to find anything decent, yet here, in this town of 35,000 souls, The Little Professor Bookshop was as good as Thins in Edinburgh.

When I lived in Edinburgh, my lodgings in Portobello were with the manager of Thins and although I had not thought of that previous life for years, I think of it now as I stroll around this Aladdin's cave of literary works. I suppose it is due to its being a university town that it boasts a bookshop as good as this. Amazingly, the population of Montana, which is the fourth largest state in size, has one of the smallest populations, only 800,000 people, or to put it another way, the same as the population of Edinburgh, Scotland's second largest city.

Missoula is not the capital of Montana; that falls to Helena, but Missoula is the hub of the State. Like Rome, all roads lead to it, nestled as it is, at the junction of five valleys. In fact, in a sort of reverse parallel, another similarity with Edinburgh crosses my mind, for although Edinburgh may be the capital of Scotland, Glasgow is really the city which is at the hub of the nation.

Although I could spend many an hour in The Little Professor and certainly will do in the future, it is time to go and collect the car. Like the curate's egg, the news is both good and bad. The good news is that the car is in pretty good shape overall, but the compression check showed that one cylinder was hardly working at all due to a burnt-out valve. So much for Colin's remark about the engine. The brakes would need doing soon and the wheel alignment and the torsion bar, whatever that is, need adjustment too. So, should I buy it? Try as I might, the man at the garage would not commit himself as to whether it was a good deal or not.

Fortunately Al is in when we get back to Lincoln and he knows of a place that would fix the valves, so we drive round there and the man says it would cost $250 to fix and I should get that price taken off the car. Next I phone Perry and he says he'll help me fix the brakes, so that'll save me a bit of money too. He still doesn't sound like an asshole to me.

It's time to see Martin. I tell him about the faults the car has and he says he'll fix the valve at cost.

"How much will that be?"

He picks up the phone. "$250," he says after a conversation with an invisible voice at the other end of the line.

"No thanks," I tell him. "I can get it done for that price somewhere else. What I want is $250 off the price." What I don't tell him is if I get it done at the other place then I am pretty sure it would be done, whereas here, how could I really be sure? It's not as if, like God, I could look at it and see that it was good. Apart from that, there is a ringing in my ears. I don't have to answer to know that it is my friend from Elgin on the line.

Martin looks aghast. "Aw, come on, Dave, if I took 250 bucks off it, I'd be giving it to you for half price."

"Sounds good to me. I've not got $1250 to spend, let alone what it's going to cost me to get the brakes and all the rest of it done. I just can't afford it."

Martin looks at me and I look back at him unblinkingly. I'm serious and I hope he'll climb down as I don't want to have to go through this rigmarole every time I am serious about a car.

"All right. You can have the car as it stands for $900."

It's not as much off as I would have liked. It means he is only coming down by $100 but there is something much more attractive-sounding about three figures rather than four. I reckon this is as much a concession as I'm going to get. After all, he's still got his ten bucks to make up, thanks to me. And the original price was supposedly $1695, so I think it sounds a pretty good deal, especially when I translate that into sterling and consider how much more car you get here for your money. It won't be very economical as far as fuel is concerned, but since they practically give that away over here, it scarcely matters. It will probably still cost far less to drive per mile than my own car back home. Poor Marnie! That's another couple of nasty shocks lying in wait for her if she has not already found out – the price of cars and the cost of petrol. But then she is earning twice as much as me, so it all balances out in the end.

I can't give Martin any money for the car until I've got things sorted out at the bank, but we sign the contract and I phone Iona to tell her that the deed has been done and the quest is finally over, for better or worse, like a marriage.

I drop into the bank on the way home to talk to my friend. I hope she won't mind me not taking her advice, on two counts: buying from Bell's and not seeing her friend Demarios. But she doesn't seem to mind when I tell her the whole story and from somewhere under her desk, she fishes out a fat little blue book.

"What year and model is it?"

"A 1972 Plymouth station wagon."

She licks her finger and flicks over the flimsy pages.

She is studying a column of densely-packed figures and running her finger down them. Plainly it is a book of used car prices.

I can't bear the suspense. Have I been well and truly ripped off? It won't be long now till I know. She looks up.

"'72 Plymouth station wagon you said?"

"Yes."

"And how much did you pay?"

God, why can't she remember! I'm scared to mention the figure again in case it brings forth a burst of uncontrolled derisory mirth.

"$900." My voice is a whisper, from a throat parched with fear.

She checks the figures again. "Well," she says, "I think you've got yourself a very good deal. It says here $1325 retail and $825 wholesale."

So I paid only $75 more than Bell's probably paid for it! That does sound good, but I have, of course, omitted to tell her that I've had to pay for a compression test, still have to fork out another $250 to have the valve fixed, not to mention however much it costs to fix the brakes and have the torsion bar (whatever that is) adjusted.

It's not half as good a deal as she thinks it is, and as I now realise myself. If only she had told me about the little blue book, I would have been in a much stronger negotiating position, but she hadn't and it's too late now.

But at last and at least, the Great Car Hunt is finally over. For better or worse, I have a set of wheels.

Chapter Eighteen

In which I am introduced to some bars and discover a darker side to Missoula.

Having bought the car, the next thing I have to do is register it. Al gives me a run to the city halls. At the moment I don't have a number plate because they don't come with the vehicle; they are removed after each sale and tax is paid on the license plate. At $40, it is a lot cheaper than the road tax back home. And you don't have to have the normal set of numbers either, you can call it what you want, up to a certain amount of letters. Al, whose truck is christened "BIG AL", wants me to spend another $20 and register the car as SCOTCH, but $20 is $20 and I would rather forego the vanity.

It's fun and it's free to read the names on other people's vehicles. I've not seen a BIG DICK yet, but I am sure there will be some conceited person out there somewhere with that plate but, strangely enough, I have seen a DOPEY, though it is hard to imagine why you would advertise your deficiency like that. Perhaps there's a SNOWWHITE and the whole gamut of dwarfs. Anyway, throughout the year, it is going to be a source of entertainment reading the license plates as we drive around town and the country.

Next, Al takes us to The Dairy. Apparently the woman who runs it is married to a Scotsman. The Scots are indeed everywhere, more living abroad than the 5 million resident in the homeland. Here we buy what's known as "raw milk" which means it's unpasteurised. I'm not exactly sure why we should want that, but that's where Marnie and Terri get their milk and so we feel it is only polite to buy some of the stuff since we are here. We buy three gallons which sounds as if it should last us for months, but a US gallon is a quart less than our gallon and Iona and the kids, especially, drink it like water.

After we've taken Iona and the kids back home, Al takes me to the guy who will grind my valves. He's working on BIG AL at the moment, so I have no qualms about leaving the station wagon in his tender care.

Having discussed what was needed and a date set, Al thinks it's time to celebrate and takes me to a bar that he thinks I'll like. It's called the Heidelhaus which, as its name suggests, is after the German manner. The waitresses are attired in gaily-coloured short skirts and black waistcoats with crisscrossed laces and puffy-sleeved white blouses with plunging necklines. There is a room called The Library which has masses of books stacked on their sides and crammed into shelves that run from floor to ceiling, all round the room. I imagine this is why Al thinks I would like it.

I am indeed impressed and let Al see my admiration. Although I can't read the titles from here and therefore can't tell if the shelves contain any works of literary merit, I can't help but notice the contents of the blouses of the pseudo-Frauleins as they lean forward to serve the beer and I consider how lucky I am to have a friend like Al who can introduce me to such exotic places. I might have spent a whole year in Missoula and never stumbled upon a bar with such an attractive theme.

Al introduces me to the boss. It's getting to be embarrassing because he goes through the routine of me being a whiz kid at the whisky, not realising what an impostor I actually am. Fortunately the boss looks underwhelmed and doesn't ask me any embarrassing questions on the subject, but he does buy us a drink.

The talk is of the latest scandal to hit Missoula and the boss thinks Al might have some information that maybe isn't in the papers. It has more than a passing interest to me too. It seems that a teacher has been tied up and raped and stabbed several times, then partially disembowelled.

"What? Here? Right here in Missoula?" I can hardly believe that a crime of such violence could be perpetrated in "The Garden City" and to a teacher too, for God's sake! Such things surely belonged to the big concrete jungles and they did not happen remotely near me in my humdrum little life.

"We got three unsolved murders right now," Al remarks in a matter-of-fact sort of way.

"Three!" Have I parachuted into the crime capital of the Wild West? Is the lawlessness that I thought belonged to the pages of history alive and well and flourishing in Missoula? It is enough to put you off your beer, never mind the contents of the blouses of the waitresses. "What are the others?"

"Well there's this three-year-old kid. Her mother's a hippy, sleeps around an' does all that drug stuff. This time she had a baby-sitter while she went hookin' at the bars, only the baby-sitter sent her home on her own an' some bastard picked her up, fooled around with her, stabbed her with a penknife an' threw her outta the car. After that some dogs gotta hold of her, looks like. But she died of exposure."

Al tells this in such a matter-of-fact way that the horror of it all seems to have passed over his head. I can hardly credit it on three counts: the mother, the baby-sitter and the killer. It is so horrific it seems beyond belief, the sort of thing that belongs in the pages of pulp fiction or in some vast seething metropolis. Not here.

"And the third?"

Al seems to relish this one. "A lawyer, found shot through the head. His brains were tricklin' into a dry martini he had in his hand."

It too sounds like a crime novel, so much like a crime novel that without too much imagination, I can picture the scene on the cover. It is a sobering thought that there are three unknown murderers roaming around this little town, two of whose crimes are particularly revolting. I don't know how many murders we have a year in Falkirk, approximately the same size, indeed, if we have any at all, but this does put a different complexion on Missoula, a darker side that I would never have dreamt existed.

Al thinks its time to move on to another bar, one of character, the one he normally drinks at and on the way there he boasts that we won't have to buy a drink because there will be all those people just desperate to throw their money at us. Of course it's just Al they will be throwing the money at as they don't know me from Adam.

We're in the Stockman's on Front, in the Downtown area – and nothing could be further from the Heidelhaus. It does not have the soft furnishings and the pervasive atmosphere of pampering of the Heidelhaus, nor any feminine soft touches. Here, the furniture, like the floor, is wooden and looks as old as anything could be said to be old, in this young State. It looks a man's sort of bar. Indeed, men are the only customers, wearing cowboy boots and cowboy hats and all appear to be drinking shorts, propped up against a long bar which is smoked a deep mahogany. In front of each man is a pile of peanuts in their shells, and at their feet, where they have dropped them on the floor, the empty husks. It only lacks the guns in their holsters at their hips to make me believe I had stepped into a time warp.

Al elicits a hearty hail of recognition as we approach the bar. An old-timer stands behind it whom Al introduces to me as the joint owner of the place. Does he know the owner of every bar in town? He tells him that I am his friend from Scotland and that I'm over here on an exchange for a year. To my relief, he omits the stuff about me being a whisky expert; maybe even he's getting tired of it.

He can't help it, but Al talks as if he's talking through a megaphone all the time. Now everyone in the place knows who I am, and to my huge astonishment, they actually seem to be mildly interested. They tip their heads at me and raise their glasses as if toasting my health. I smile and nod my head at the company like one of those irritating nodding dogs you sometimes see on the back shelf of some cars.

Just like Al said, the owner buys us a drink and it crosses my mind that perhaps I am the passport to these free drinks, since the natural friendliness of the Montanans prompts them to offer a stranger a drink, especially when the stranger comes from such a far-flung place as I do. But Al seems to be enormously popular and him a cop too! In Scotland, I am told, cops only have other cops as friends. A bit like teachers.

In front of us, as we sit on high stools at the bar, is a huge mirror and I reflect on the reflections it has cast in the past. This place doesn't look as if it has changed in a century – if it is as old as a century. Over the mirror is the legend: *Liquor up front, poker in the rear.* When I draw Al's attention to it, he bursts into embarrassingly loud laughter. I think it's mildly amusing myself, but hardly hilarious. What I really want to know is what does it mean, apart from the obvious?

Al makes a motion of his head in the direction of a room off to his left and behind him. "That's where they play poker."

Of course.

"Hey, Al, you gonna introduce us to your friend?"

The voice is unmistakably feminine from this haunt of the world of men. For the first time, I notice two comely women sitting at a table at the other side of the room.

Al greets them with abandon, throwing his arms around them and kissing them effusively on the cheeks.

"Dave, I wanna introduce you to Glenda and Lois. They're great pals of mine." He doesn't say how he comes to be such great pals with them, but I wouldn't mind having such curvaceous pals either, but Iona would never allow it. I feel my handshake is a bit understated after Al's bear hug but I've only just met them after all. Maybe I'll get to know them better as they ask us to sit down and have a drink. They are buying.

It turns out that Glenda is divorced and that Lois has just remarried and her parents are divorced. I had read that one in three marriages in the States ends up that way.

It doesn't surprise me when you look at Marnie's experience: done and dusted before you realise what you've done. From the time when she first found out about Perry's liaison with Karen, it took no longer than two weeks before she found herself divorced.

Chapter Nineteen

In which I go to work, in a manner of speaking, Iona has her first driving lesson, George has an accident, I admit to a secret passion and I see Missoula as most Missoulians never see it.

I have an early start in the morning. Matt had phoned when I got back from the Stockman's to say that he'd pick me up at 8.30 the following day to meet the Superintendent and other dignitaries. I grump at the uncivilised hour. After all, I am still on holiday, but I get ready for 8.15 in case Matt comes early. I don't want to create a bad impression by being late, even before I start.

When he finally does arrive at 8.40, I am resentful at all the minutes I could have been in bed but naturally I don't show it and Matt whisks me off to the education administration building where I am introduced to Joe Simpson, the Superintendent, Dan Gunn, Director of Personnel and Tammy Kinsella, Director of Reading, amongst others. They all seem very friendly and make me feel very welcome.

Dan talks about my health insurance. He says I could be put on the Blue Cross scheme. It's free for the teachers of District No 7, but I can be put on it for about $60 a month. It would only include me. I would have to take out insurance for Iona and the kids myself. The Bureau gives me $2000 of free health care, which is probably just about enough to cover me for an ingrowing toenail or something equally trivial (but painful). I point out that Marnie would be getting all her health insurance and health care absolutely free. That means all consultations with the doctor, all medicines and drugs, and should she or any of her kids, God forbid, need an operation, however major, it wouldn't cost her a cent.

Not only that, but it also includes free dental treatment and I express the opinion that if Marnie did not get her teeth checked out while she was over there, and all her children's, at the British tax payers' expense, then she should have her head examined at the same time, which would also be free. Personally, I think we are mad to offer free health care to all comers but I don't mention this to Dan, merely make the modest proposal that they should substitute my name for Marnie's as a quid pro quo.

It sounds very logical to me, but Dan looks doubtful. Perhaps he can't believe that it *is* really like that in Scotland, just like when we went to the Mary Grayson Center, I had to remind myself that I had not landed in Canaan. He says he'll try but his tone gives me no cause for optimism. So it's one up to Marnie at last! It's about time she had something in her favour for a change and free health and dental care for all of them for the year is, I would say, greater than all of my advantages put together.

Talking of insurance reminds me that I don't have any insurance for the car, yet I have been driving around quite legally, if not entirely complacently. Incredibly, there is no legal requirement to take out insurance here at all and what people who worry about such things do, is to take out a policy against being hit by an uninsured motorist. It seems to me a cack-handed way of going about things and an act of extreme folly not to have insurance in this notoriously litigious society, so unless I want to risk spending the rest of my life in the state penitentiary, I think the sooner I get some insurance the better.

When I get home, I try the number Dan gave me in this regard. It is going to cost $78 for 6 months, for what they call liability only, so I try the AAA next and they say it is going to be $12 a month. I phone Al and he says I won't get it any cheaper than that, so I agree to that and it now means that it's safer for me to let Iona get behind the wheel.

She's very nervous about trying this monster of a car and although I warn her about the power brakes, she just about breaks my neck and would have catapulted me and the kids in the back seat onto the floor had I not anticipated this and kept a firm grip on them. We drive round the block and Iona decides that's enough for her first try. She is discouraged. She thinks she'll never master it but I tell her it's really easy when you get used to it and you don't even have to be able to drive. With automatic transmission, all you need to do is point the beast in the direction you want to travel and when you get used to the fierceness of the brakes and the power-assisted steering which is so light that you could turn a corner with just one finger if you wanted to – she'll discover it's absolute child's play. The only problem may be parking, especially reversing into a parking space as the back window looks half a mile away and I'm not sure how much car there is after that.

But as far as I am concerned there is something enormously satisfying about sitting behind the wheel, gazing over that big blue bonnet and feeling that immense power respond to the slightest touch of the accelerator pedal as you are transported effortlessly to wherever you want to go without ever having to change gear at traffic lights or any other time you have to slow down or stop. And for all its enormous power, the engine is more silent than a whisper.

If Iona's test drive were not nerve-tingling enough, there's further drama as we enter the house from *Psycho*. Mrs

Bates exercises her evil influence on the youngest and most vulnerable member of the family by making George trip as he's going up the steps and blood gushes freely from his scalp. It is very frightening. There is so much blood everywhere it looks as if he's going to need stitches – and I haven't got round to arranging insurance for Iona and the kids yet. Although George is howling, it's nothing to the pain I'm going to feel when the medics hand in their bill. Oh, to be in Scotland, now that a crisis is here! Where are we going to take him anyway? St Pat's, where the helicopter landed? Where else? I don't know anywhere else. We keep staunching the wound and in the end, thankfully it stops.

Later, Terri tells us that scalp wounds always bleed profusely. George's vocal chords, full of sound and fury, signify little more than a slight cut. It is a timely reminder however, that I must not delay, must get the family insured and find a medical practice the sooner the better.

* * *

At 9 pm, I am watching a grainy black-and-white picture on the TV when suddenly the room is illuminated by a shaft of white light streaming in through the window. This cone of light is not still, but moves around the room cutting swathes through the family room like strobes from a lighthouse. Even the kitchen at the back gets the fright of its life as this all-invading beam penetrates its dusky remoteness.

"What the hell... ?" I leap to my feet and peer out the window, but can see nothing. All is blinding light. I am like a moth, transfixed through the thorax by this needle of light. The light moves about again, sweeping back and forward across the room. Suddenly a voice shatters the silence, a loud, booming voice as if amplified through a megaphone.

"Dave! You in there? C'mon outside!"

This time it *is* his voice through a megaphone, Al's voice, from his cop car. Brilliant! Now the whole street thinks I'm being arrested. I go out to find out what he wants. Typical Al, doing it in big style. Instead of just coming to the door and ringing the bell, why not arouse the whole neighbourhood, give me a bad reputation, wake up Hélène (George wouldn't hear it) and make me think I'm about to be abducted by aliens. But I don't let any of this show as I saunter down the path as if I'm accustomed to being summoned in this way from my house every night of the week.

"D'you want to come an' ride with us, Dave?" Al switches off the light which is attached to the pillar of the windscreen. He introduces me to his mate, who, like Al, is armed to the teeth. Bristling with their armoury and bulging biceps, I don't know what they do to the criminal fraternity, but they scare the hell out of me and I've nothing to be scared of. Have I?

"Ride with you? What do you mean? Right now?" Does my voice betray my nervousness? My conscience is clear, but I can't help search my mind for any infringements of the law I might have made. Am I being arrested, or is this an offer I *can* refuse?

"Yeah. D'you want to ride with us tonight on our shift?"

Al explains that every citizen has the right to go out on patrol with a police car. All you have to do is apply. But through my acquaintanceship with Al I can skip the queue – if there is a queue to be shot to death accompanying the police on their rounds, with three murderers at least, roaming the streets. This is one invitation I am definitely not going to turn down. What a privilege to see Missoula as most Missoulians probably have never seen it, and I've not been here much longer than a week! And much better than the sewers. I can hardly wait to get going. I hope it will be an exciting night, but not too exciting. No shootouts I hope.

Al is a Lieutenant which means his patch is the whole town. If he had been just an ordinary cop, he would have had to stick to a particular area, so it's more interesting for me he has this roving commission as we will be able to go where the action is hottest.

The hottest bit of action to begin with is a cup of coffee at Daphne's Diner on Broadway, not far from Emerson and the Exxon garage. This must be a regular haunt because Al is greeted warmly by the waitress and once again I am amazed that he doesn't have to pay for the coffees. Does he ever have to pay for anything when he is out and about? Like our Queen who carries a handbag but never any money because she never needs to pay for anything, (no wonder she's the richest woman in the UK) Al is like some visiting potentate upon whom his subjects shower love and gifts. Well, drinks anyway. Maybe love too. I don't know him that well yet, but this waitress and Glenda and Lois in the Stockman's seem to like him well enough.

Instead of sugar to sweeten the coffee, there are little jugs of honey. I have never tried this before and find it quite agreeable. We have two cups each and then we head off for the police station where Al introduces me to his colleagues and reprises my expertise in Scotch, telling them that I had brought with me the smoothest-tasting Scotch he has ever tasted.

In the station there is a commemorative plaque to a cop who had been shot dead whilst trying to arrest a gunman. Apparently it was a shootout in the street, like you see in the films, the cop taking what proved to be inadequate cover behind his vehicle. My God, it really still *is* the Wild West all right. How exciting would it be if we had to arrest one of the three murderers at large in the town (if they are still here) and he would have to sit right here beside me on the back seat! But I hoped it wouldn't come to a gun battle. That would be just a little bit too much excitement for a boy from the boondocks of Banff.

Our first bit of action concerns a drunk Indian, except, Al says, you are meant to say "Native American". Al doesn't have a lot of time for them. He says they are spongers and they are lazy, lying around all day, drinking the money which the state gives them as a way of saying sorry for stealing the land from their ancestors, not so long ago. There is a Flathead Indian Reservation not far from Missoula, to the north. Consequently, Al says, a lot of them come into town, head for the bars and get drunk, on *his* taxes.

Now, I have to confess I am an Indian lover. Ever since I saw *Hiawatha* at Banff Picture House, probably when I was about my seventh year to heaven, I have been in love with Indian culture, especially that of the Plains Indians. I love their dress, from their full-feathered headdress to the soles of their moccasins. I love their beadwork and the strange cabalistic signs on their tepees. I love their canoes, their skill with horses and their bows. I love their tepees and their beds made of buffalo hides. I love their outdoor way of existence, their apparent harmony with nature and Mother Earth, their respect for their ancestors and the animals they kill and use for food, the thanks they give them for the donation of their lives, so they may live.

They believe in the Great Spirit in the sky, and I, who regard all religions as a kind of superstition, regard with abhorrence how the Catholic–Protestant hate is carried on in the name of Christianity where I live, but thankfully is alien to the north east of Scotland from whence I come. And I have even less patience with the so-called "charismatic" religions with their arrogant belief that only *they* are God's chosen ones.

No, I can't accept conventional Christianity, but I *can* believe in a Great Spirit in the sky, where fundamentalists don't argue the toss between a word here and a phrase there and then concoct a whole separate religion around it so they can despise and even hate those who happen to disagree with them, condemning them to purgatory on the strength of the interpretation of a word which is itself a translation of a translation of the original source. Who's to know the precise meaning of the original in those days a couple of millennia or more ago? And anyway, have these people never heard of figurative language, of imagery, of symbolism?

And that's another thing I love most about the Indians – the sheer poetry in their names: Black Hawk, Red Cloud, Sitting Bull, Laughing Water, Running Deer. Who would not be proud to be called such a name instead of Maida Smellie or Joe McGrotty or even David Addison, for that matter? No kidding, the first two really do exist, I can assure you, not to mention the third. And then there are all those names like Longbotham, pronounced "bottom" or Campbell, which, on the face of it, sounds respectable enough but actually means "twisted mouth", or Cameron, which means "twisted nose".

I am disappointed that my first meeting with a Red Indian in real life, I mean Native American, should be a slobbering youth with long hair who is wearing jeans and other conventional clothing of the young. He is a million light years from Hiawatha.

I wince as he's dragged into the car by the hair, and Al and his partner give him a pretty rough talking to, then he's chucked out again. He's probably heading for Arlee, the nearest and main settlement on the Reservation. I don't know how he's going to get there and Al and partner couldn't care less. I don't suppose they can go around providing a taxi service to every drunk in town but I would call the way they have manhandled him "assault" and I'm a bit shocked at the treatment he has received. I feel pretty uncomfortable. I wonder if they treat all drunks like this, or whether, because he's an Indian, their prejudice is showing.

"Damned Native Americans!" Al growls as we leave the drunk Indian no doubt considerably sobered up after his brush with the law. The headache he'll have tomorrow won't just be due to the alcohol.

Next is a call to the scene of a road accident. It's not serious, just a scrape with a parked car, pretty routine stuff and Al is the epitome of civility in a brusque sort of way. Then another traffic incident, this time between a car and a motorbike, again not serious.

Then an announcement over the radio. Some youths have been reported as speeding across the bridge on Higgins.

"Ten four," says Al, switching on his lights and his siren and screeching his tyres as he executes a U-turn to the alarm of the oncoming traffic.

Now, this *is* exciting, as we speed off in pursuit, but the chase is short-lived as by the time we get there, our quarry is gone. Al switches off his flashing lights and siren and we patrol the streets, not far from Lincoln, looking for likely suspects. Al thinks he sees one and pulling up to within a foot of the car, he flashes the driver to pull over.

Al is really surly with the youth as he asks him where he's been, where he's going and so on. The youth has what sounds to me like plausible answers and he doesn't have the demeanour of a joyrider. I'd be surprised if this were one of the speedsters and I don't think Al thinks he is either, but he tells the youth to "Cool it!" anyway and we both go our separate ways after Al follows him for a block or two. If I'd been the youth, I would have been wishing I'd been wearing my brown trousers, terrified of making the slightest traffic infringement and feeling pretty aggrieved at being treated as guilty when all I was doing was going about my lawful, peaceful business.

Time is wearing on and Al says, "Anybody like a hamburger?" It's time for a break and nothing much is happening anyway. We go to a drive-thru hamburger place. It's my first experience of the drive-thru culture. I am convinced that eventually Americans will be born with only one leg. They wouldn't even be born with that if they had the brake pedal and the throttle on the steering wheel. Al's mate is not partaking of anything so Al tells the metal pole just abreast his window: "Two whoppers, two French fries an' two chocolate milk shakes."

The disembodied metallic voice of the pole repeats the order and we head towards an illuminated window at the side of the establishment. The idea is supposed to be that by the time you get to the window, your order is ready. Only, because there are no customers before us, we get to the window long before they have time to process the food. I mean, we have to wait at least a couple of minutes. I offer to pay, hoping I have enough cash with me as I was not expecting this nocturnal adventure. I need not have worried. I can't get over how cheap the food is here. This little lot only costs $1:98. And the food is really good. All this excitement has given me an appetite.

As we are munching our way through this, the radio crackles instructions again. It seems a shopper has been injured in a supermarket. I look at my watch, incredulous. It's after 1 am. I am informed that some stores are open 24 hours. If Marnie has been used to late-night shopping in Missoula, she'd better think again in Falkirk, where she'd be lucky to find a shop open after eight.

Al switches on his flashing lights and sirens as we speed off. Whenever I see this back home, I am half-tempted to follow to see what the cause of all the excitement is but I never do and the annoying thing is you never usually find out. The best you can do is scour the local newspaper and conjecture if such and such might have been it. It is intensely infuriating, but tonight I have a ringside seat. Ha, ha! you poor members of the public, you don't know that we're rushing off to see a shopper in Safeway who has pulled a glass bottle onto her foot and cut an artery. Come to think of it, maybe not knowing is better than knowing as this sounds a bit on the mundane side – but I hadn't seen the blood then.

I am aghast at the river of dark red blood spreading up the aisle and the spectators of staff and shoppers hanging around, looking on helplessly. I can see what Macbeth meant now when, in his nightmares, he recalled the sight of King Duncan whom he had so viciously murdered and remarked: *Who would have thought he had so much blood in him?*

Someone is trying to staunch the blood, not very successfully, by the amount of it relentlessly fanning out over the tiles in a thick red tide. There's not much we can do either until the ambulance comes, which it does shortly afterwards, and the lady is whisked away. I hope she has good health insurance. Which reminds me...

Al takes the car out of the built-up area and as we climb, the houses become sparser until, eventually, we come to the top of a rise and from this viewpoint, we can see the whole of Missoula shimmering in a myriad of orange lights, whilst the strip as it is called, Route 89, is a Technicolor kaleidoscope of flashing neon. As we are admiring the view, the radio crackles into life and tells us we have to be on the lookout for an escaped convict who has gone AWOL from hospital.

Our next call is to a suspected heart attack victim. I had thought Al would have had the lights and siren on for this one, but not only does he not, but he stops at every traffic light and doesn't appear to be in the slightest hurry. I'm glad it's not me who's having the heart attack and I think it's just as well that the victim's family can't see the leisurely pace at which we are driving to the scene or they'd all have had one too. But maybe there's nothing the police can do anyway. They are not paramedics, after all. In fact, I wonder why they had called the police at all and when we get to the address, the patient has already been removed to hospital.

The next call promises to be exciting. We get a request for backup from a crew who are at The Top Hat on West Front, a trendy venue, where youths tend to hang out. There's been a fight and someone has been pushed through a window. But by the time we arrive, there is no sign of any action, only splinters of glass reflecting the flashing red and blue lights of the police car already there and masses of bikers thronging the street outside. They look like Hell's Angels and I see now why Al needs his mighty muscles. If it had been me investigating, they would just have laughed at me. I wouldn't like to get on the wrong side of any of these guys. They have biceps easily the equal of Al's, if not bigger, giants whose tattoos and long hair make them look really intimidating. Against them, and vastly outnumbered, Al must rely on his uniform (and gun) for protection, to save him from being torn limb from limb. But how can he be sure it would? And how could he shoot unarmed men? If he did, he'd be in real trouble, so in the end, it all comes down to the thin blue material after all.

Whilst Al and his mate leave the car to sort things out, I decide to stay where I am on this occasion, just in case things start to turn ugly and watch proceedings from the shelter of this little tin can, though I am nervously aware that should any one of these bikers take it into his head to open the can with his bare hands, a tin opener not being to hand, he could rip me apart like a rag doll.

The sight of one of the bikes distracts me from this unpleasant prospect: a gleaming monster of chrome and black steel with handlebars set at a rakish angle like something out of *Easy Rider*, and so wide apart it must be exceedingly uncomfortable to steer, practically like being crucified, but more amazing than all of that is it is not a motorbike at all, but a tricycle!

"Didn't your mommy never teach you how to ride a bike, son? Or are you so brain-retarded that you need three wheels?"

Is that what Al is saying from behind the shelter of his thin, navy-blue shirt with all the badges? But of course I can't hear a thing inside the cocoon of my little tin can.

Whatever he says, it looks as if the bikers are about to leave as they are mounting their chromium steeds. As they move off, we follow in the wake of the throaty roar of their exhausts and Al switches on his loudhailer, telling them not to rev. They are heading for the Interstate and we follow them like a dog shepherding sheep until they are out of town, going we know not where, but they are someone else's problem now.

It is our last action of the night: the shift is drawing to a close and for Al the most distasteful part of his shift looms. He has to write up his "goddamn report". He sits there, in front of the typewriter, stabbing the keys with two thick stubby forefingers, as if he is taking it out on them personally, cursing each time he makes a mistake, which is often.

But at last his torment is over and we head for home and Lincoln. I thank him profusely for this insight into the nightlife of Missoula. Perhaps next time, I could return the favour by writing his report for him.

It is 3.30 am and I creep to bed as quiet as a mouse so as not to disturb Iona. It has been another interesting day. In fact, every day in Missoula has been an interesting one and as I settle down to sleep, I congratulate myself on my decision to apply for the exchange.

But I haven't been to school yet and maybe I am counting my chickens...

Chapter Twenty

In which we help celebrate a wedding anniversary and discover more about the American way of marriage.

No rest for the wicked: I have to be up, showered, dressed and breakfasted to take the car to K-Mart for the alignment and suspension. That's what the torsion bar is all about apparently. We leave the car there and make the trip on foot to Safeway, the same one where the drama of last night occurred and where shoppers now walk up and down that same aisle and over the very spot, totally unaware that a major drama had occurred there not many hours before, since not a spot of blood remains.

Iona is interested in boring items such as Betty Crocker food mixes and pancake syrups so I wend my way to the aisle of necessities where there is a vast array of beers and wines. There are no spirits though. You have to go to a liquor store for that and in Montana, you have to be 21. Just as well, because you can have a driver's license at 15, as long as you take what they call "Driver Ed" at high school. Imagine all those neo-pubescents driving around, let alone driving around drunk. It's not an uncommon sight in Missoula to see drivers nursing a can of beer in one hand, their elbow resting on the open window and of course, a cowboy hat on their head.

Some of this Californian wine looks quite interesting and you can buy it by the gallon for about the same price as you would pay for a bottle of Cyprus plonk at home. It's a lot of wine if it turns out to be as bad as that is, so I decide to play safe and just get some beer instead. Budweiser – "the king of beers", seems to be the market leader and seems to me a fraction dearer than the rivals such as Schlitz, Rainier, Coors, Millers and Pabst, which is a bit cheaper still. But here is one called Brown Derby that, for some reason best known to the manufacturers, has a picture of a bowler hat on the front. Why anyone would call a beer after a hat and why not call it "Brown Bowler"? At least it would be alliterative.

But it's not the name that attracts me: it's the price. It's only $1.25. That works out about 10 pence a can, except their cans only hold 12 ounces, whereas ours have 16. The other beers work out at about 13 to 16 p a can. I can save nearly a whole dollar if I buy this instead of the Bud, so I buy a six-pack. After all, I reason, I may as well try them all, and if I like the cheapest, well, I may just stick with it. By the end of the year, I could save quite a few dollars.

When we get back to K-Mart, there is bad news waiting for me. The car has not been done. And why not? Because they don't have the tools for my car. I look at the bearer of this news sceptically but he doesn't seem to be joking, or at least, he can convey the news with a straight face, so I don't argue the point and when we get back to Lincoln, I go over to report to Al.

Of course I should have known better, or perhaps, subliminally, that's why I went there instead of phoning, because no sooner do I arrive than Al offers me a drink. Since he's drinking anyway, I say I'll have what he's having. It's a Canadian whiskey liqueur called Yukon Jack and it's 100% proof. It's warming and sweet, a kind of rye Drambuie and, I think wryly, a pale imitation of that, but perhaps an acquired taste. By the size of the measure Al pours, I am going to acquire a taste for it quite quickly.

Time passes in convivial conversation but I realise that my short visit to consult my friend is appearing more like an abandonment of my wife and I start to make noises about getting back. They are not blabbering noises, but if I have any more Yukon Jack, they soon will be. At the moment, they are still intelligible phrases, such as: "Well, I suppose I should really be getting along home" and "It's about time I was thinking of leaving" and "Iona is home alone with the kids." But Al won't hear of it. He produces a phone with the longest extension cord I have ever seen. It can stretch from the back of the kitchen where it is anchored, right to the front door, and maybe even beyond.

Al hands me the instrument but I'm too scared to phone. Too scared to let my new friend hear me say in his presence: "I'm just with Al. Just having a couple of drinks... Yes, dear... I'm just coming. I'll be right over."

Al is so obviously the boss in his house, a godfather in fact, and I am ashamed to let him see what a wimp I am. He may never want to drink with an underling like me again.

"Why don't *you* call her instead? It might sound a bit better coming from you," I suggest.

"Eeona! This is Al. We're just havin' a few drinks here. You gotta come over and join us. Yeah, that's right. Right now." He hangs up. "She'll be right over."

"Eeona!" Al greets her a few moments later with the affection and the bear hug of one long-lost and just rediscovered relative. "You gotta try this Yukon Jack Dave and I are drinkin'. It's really smooth."

Before she can stop him, he pours her a big slug. Iona doesn't list drinking amongst one of her pastimes and the smell of the whiskey doesn't thrill her at all, to put it mildly. In fact, had Al presented her with a big, fat, black slug and said to pop that in her mouth and chew on it, the revulsion on her face could hardly have been any less.

"No... well, really... I don't *really* like whiskey."

"Aw, c'mon, Eeona! You really gotta try this. This is Canadian whiskey. It's so smooooth."

Al will not be deflected from his hospitality. There is nothing else for it. Iona screws up her courage to the sticking place, blocks off her nose so at least she doesn't have to smell the atrocious medicine, and takes the merest sip.

"Ugh! It's horrible! Give me some water! Quick!"

She is flapping her hands agitatedly, her tongue sticking out, her face red and contorted as if invisible hands were strangling the life out of her.

Al is dumbfounded, his mouth gaping in disbelief. I don't think he can ever have seen such a display of distaste for the elixir of life before. And this from a Scotswoman too! It wouldn't surprise me if Al assumed all Scots had whisky mixed with their mother's milk. He is still in a state of semi-paralysis, so it befalls me to come to Iona's rescue with the lifesaving mouthwash.

After she recovers and Al a bit later than that, he finally finds something that Iona *will* drink, a glass of white wine. Which means I have to drink her Yukon Jack as it would be a shame to waste it.

We come home laden with so many gifts that it practically rendered our trip to the supermarket unnecessary. We have all the vegetables we can carry (plus George), plus some trout that Al had caught. And when we get to the doorstep, we find a bulging brown paper bag full of sweet corn waiting for us. A note says it's from Millie Fergusson, the school librarian, and her husband. It's very kind of them, but we are snowed under with vegetables. We can't eat them half as fast as people give them to us. We still haven't touched the ones Grandpa gave us.

The trouble with Al's trout is they still have their heads and tails on, but I'm pleased to say that their innards have been left behind somewhere. All the same, for us, who are used to having our food presented in such a way that any resemblance to any animal, living or dead, is entirely coincidental, the de-heading and the de-tailing of these creatures fills us with a certain amount of hypocritical and squeamish distaste. When they finally make it to our plates after their grilling, I am sure that they would have been much more tasty had I not seen them *au naturel* first.

Amazingly, I have not had time to look at the mail yet. There are three letters. One from Iona's mother, one from her sister, and one has an American stamp and a Missoula postmark. From whom could this possibly be? The only way to find out is to open it. It turns out it's from Matt Olsen. It is on green Banda paper which does a pretty good job of making the indistinct blue characters hard to read.

We are invited to his house for a fish fry as he has had a "very good season this year". It seems everyone in Missoula goes fishing. He's also going to provide the "vegtables". We have to bring along something as well, a dessert or something savoury. The last line has one of my eyebrows arching: "We plan to eat at 6.29."

I'd better make a dry run past his house so I know where I'm going to ensure I don't get lost and arrive at 6.30.

* * *

It's a lovely sunny day and I spend the morning in the garden just sitting there with the children, watching the grass grow.

I'm going to have to do something about that sooner or later. I don't want to have to buy a lawnmower. It can't be much of a priority for Marnie, since she didn't leave any instructions and Lindy's husband hasn't obviously done anything about it. But since, according to Sam White, all he consists of is a rectum and a sphincter muscle, he wouldn't have the arms to push it.

Whilst I wrestle with this weighty problem, Iona is taking advantage of this bright sunshine penetrating, as much as it can, the branches of the fir outside the kitchen window. She is baking some scones and pancakes that we can give to people in return for trying to bury us alive under a mountain of vegetables.

Iona interrupts this thinking (which has brought a sweat to my brow) to tell me that Terri has just phoned. It seems that today is their wedding anniversary and we are invited round for the celebrations. Of course this is a happy occasion, but Iona's face does not seem to share this sentiment.

"What's the problem?"

"Nothing. It just means that's another day you'll be over there, drinking all day."

I don't see this as a problem, but clearly Iona thinks that I have begun a slide into alcoholism since if we go, it means I'll have been drinking over there two days in a row. Besides, as I point out, we can hardly refuse, can we?

But, methinks, the lady doth protest too much: two or three hours at the most, yesterday, hardly amounts to *all day*. Still, it does mark a departure from my habits back home where I hardly drink anything at all but that, I have to admit, has probably more to do with my not being able to afford it, rather than abstemiousness. In fact, we are so impecunious that I hardly buy any alcohol at all, except at Christmas and New Year. Instead, I make my own wine. Gallons and gallons of it: bramble, elderflower, elderberry, peapods, oak leaves, coltsfoot, rose petal. My brother-in-law, who is a bit retarded as far as his taste in home-made wines is concerned, on tasting the latter, pronounced that the label should have read "Rose and Dettol", rushed to the sink and spat it out. At least he had that much refinement.

Yes, I think for that insult, when I get back, the Deadly Nightshade 1974, should be nicely matured. As far I was concerned, if it grew and it was free, I picked it and turned it into alcohol so that whatever the season of the year, (a wine for every season) our house resonated with the sound of bubbling airlocks releasing carbon dioxide like some mad scientist's laboratory. As a matter of fact, the health visitor was rather astounded at the number of demijohns she had to step over in order to reach Hélène, the newborn baby, surrounded in her Moses basket like a pioneer wagon encircled by Indians on the warpath.

"It's the warmest room in the house," I felt in necessary to explain. Apparently the health visitor was rich enough to buy her own alcohol – or she might be teetotal which might explain the way her nose wrinkled as she entered the room. I didn't do chemistry at school, but didn't she know that carbon dioxide increases a child's intelligence? It stands to reason: oxygen does and twice as much must mean that the child will turn out to be very intelligent indeed.

Now I merely wave Iona's words away airily, like some irritating insect: "Oh, don't worry! It's not going to happen every day! This is a special occasion."

"Any time is a special occasion as far as Al is concerned."

When we get there, Al is doing something to a fish with a sharp knife which reminds me of what happened to the teacher he told me about in the Heidelhaus and naturally, he needs a glass of Yukon Jack at his elbow to support him through this operation.

As we watch him, suppressing our desire to vomit, Terri asks, "Do you flay fish?"

"Em... em... do I *flay* fish?" I place particular emphasis on the mystery word. I know that to "flay" means to skin, normally when the person is alive. It seems an uncharitable thing to do to a fish, even a dead one. But since I never do anything to a fish except, once in a while, eat a dead one, I feel it's safe to say that I have never flayed a fish in my life.

It's only when Al puts a gleaming white skeleton in the bin that I realise that Terri has been saying "fillet" but she's given it a bit more of a French pronunciation than even the French would. Which is odd, since they have a Catholic college in the town called "Notre Dame" but which they pronounce in such a way as to give any Frenchman an apoplectic seizure on the spot. They say "Noter" and "Dame" like the one you get in a pantomime. And to me, "dame" carries connotations of disrespect, tantamount to calling the Virgin a "broad".

And while I'm on the subject of pronunciation, there is one word which the Americans say which really amuses me – they drop the "h" when they are talking about herbs, so they say things like: "Do you grow 'erbs?" which makes me think of Dorothy Dolittle in *Pygmalion*, a few elocution lessons short of RP from Professor Higgins.

Al dexterously "flays" his last fish and holds up the fingers of his right hand under my nose. "Here, smell my new girlfriend, Dave!" he says, throwing back his head and laughing uproariously.

If there is anything more calculated to persuade Iona that Al is not a suitable companion for me, this is it. I am compromised. If Iona had not been there, I would have laughed uproariously too, in a manly sort of way, like buddies sharing a joke. But I can't do that with Iona here and I can't show her the disapproval she would like to see either, so I just give a weak sort of laugh and end up pleasing neither. Terri, however, affects to be embarrassed, chuckles in that infectious way she has and gives him a playful punch on the shoulder before recharging our glasses. She doesn't seem to mind Al's lewd humour, or maybe she is just in a good mood. It is their anniversary after all.

But things are not all they seem. We get to talking, not unnaturally, considering the occasion, of marriage, in which institution Iona and I are only beginners. Al and Terri, despite not being a huge deal older than us, have, amazingly, been married for twenty years, even if you don't count the years they were separated.

To my credit, even if I say so myself, I don't turn a hair at this revelation and take it completely in my stride. I have not been in this country long, but by now I am perfectly acclimatised to the idea that over here, you separate or get a divorce at the drop of a hat.

Terri tells us that before they were separated, she went to counselling and she'd be happy to recommend her counsellor to anyone. I hope she doesn't have Iona in mind. I bet that sort of advice doesn't come cheap. Imagine paying a fortune to hear that your husband is an incipient alcoholic and she should take the kids and get on the first plane back to Scotland. I don't mind being called an "incipient alcoholic" but I do object to having to pay through the nose to be told something I can work out perfectly well for myself. In any case, since they ended up separated anyway, the counselling didn't seem to have worked. But here's the amazing thing: here they are living happily together again, apparently.

Terri says that it wasn't easy for Marnie because she and Perry talked after the divorce was filed, but by then it was too late. The thing that really made it intolerable for Marnie was Perry set up home just a block away with Karen and her brood, (for, not surprisingly, she was already married with kids) and she saw him practically every day, leaving for his new home after a cosy chat. But was it just a cosy chat?

It's as if Al has been reading my mind.

"Perry is an asshole," Al cuts in. "You can't have your cake an' eat it."

From the fervour of his tone, it sounds as if he really means it. But doth he protest too much? From what I had seen so far, he seems very popular with the ladies, could possibly have his pick of all the women in Missoula, apart from Iona. Never having received any offers, it is difficult for me to know what I would do should such a temptation arise, but I would hope to be as resistant to it as Al sounds as if he is. And he is a very strong man.

What would really get to me would be taking on someone else's kids as well as my own, not to mention all that maintenance and alimony. That sounds like three very convincing antidotes to lust as far as I am concerned. I am sure I am destined to be monogamous: all I want is the simple life and above all, avoid unnecessary expense.

We are going to Grandpa's house now so he can wish his son and his daughter-in-law many more years of happy marriage. His house is a small wooden affair, painted green and, as you might expect, full of antique furniture. (Eat your heart out, Marnie.) His yard is huge and given over entirely to the garden where the "prodoos" comes from, so it is really a garden in the English sense. He shows me round and presses zucchini and corn on me but I manage to persuade him just to let me have what feels like a stone of potatoes instead.

We can't leave Grandpa's without having a drink, so it's more of the Yukon Jack for Al and me and also a Green Stinger for me. The Green Stinger was actually for Iona, whom Al is finding it increasingly difficult to introduce to the evils of drink. I don't think he has met a woman like her in his life and he is finding her resistance to alcohol rather bewildering, to put it mildly. We don't know each other well enough yet for me to reveal that she has had a Methodist upbringing. She can't help it. It's not her fault, yet I hope there may be time for her salvation and if Al has anything to do with it, she might yet be saved from a lifetime of temperance before we leave Missoula.

The concoction of brandy and crème de menthe doesn't seem to add up to the Holy Grail either. Iona takes small, polite sips without looking as if she were drinking arsenic and when Al and Terri's backs are turned, I do my duty. Glug. Hic! No-one expresses surprise at the way that glass has suddenly emptied, so presumably they didn't notice.

Maybe it was the Yukon Jack talking, maybe it was the Green Stinger, but anyway, I heard my voice saying: "Come back to the house from *Psycho* for a Scotch." I didn't really say that did I? Of course I didn't. What I really said was: "Why don't you come back to our house for some of Iona's excellent Scottish home baking?"

Of course you can't have a scone without a dram to wash it down, so that is what we do, especially when there is an anniversary to be celebrated. Terri is just revealing that her counselling guru had extracted the information from her that she had been abused as a child when the doorbell rings. Damn! Just like the person who interrupted Coleridge's dream and so all we have of *Kubla Khan* is an intriguing fragment. Our unexpected guest is none other than Chris Mendez who has seen Al's Thunderbird parked outside our house and made the intuitive leap that Al and Terri must be with us.

He has come to celebrate Al's anniversary. Well, maybe not just that. Maybe he's come to celebrate *his* anniversary. It turns out that he also got married on this day. He's brought his wife with him so they can enjoy the festivities together, which is very interesting because, as it turns out, he and his wife are not actually married at all. They are divorced, but have made a point of meeting up today so they can all celebrate their anniversaries together. Well, why not? What could be more natural?

When Chris says he'd rather have a beer than Scotch and when Al says he'll have a beer too, my heart sinks. All I've got is that six-pack of Brown Derby and they are lucky I have got that. I hadn't intended that anyone else should drink it except me. Fearing the worst, but with an outward show of nonchalance, I bring a couple of cans through from the fridge. Before my guests can say anything, I say with a naïve air, of someone who has just arrived on the continent: "I thought this was an interesting logo. Tell me, is this a really good beer?"

I've missed my vocation. If I could be guaranteed a response like this on the stage, that's where I ought to be, for Al and Chris's laughter is loud enough to be heard in heaven. I pretend to look on in puzzlement. I would rather be thought a fool than a miser, so when Al tells me that I should buy Bud from now on, I nod and thank him for his expert advice.

Perhaps I gild the lily when I explain I didn't know anything about beer and I just picked this up by random as it happened to be the first one I saw.

Al and Chris manage to down them though, but it does have the effect of their making a hasty exit to pursue their celebrations where there is better beer, amongst other refreshments. To Iona's relief, we are not invited, but earlier, at Grandpa's, I had been invited to go fishing the next day to Placid Lake with them. The Plymouth has a tow bar and the Thunderbird doesn't. BIG AL is undergoing intensive surgery and Al is suffering from fishing-withdrawal symptoms.

"It would be really neat," said Al, "if we could go fishin' tomorrow."

I'm not remotely interested in fishing, not since when, aged about ten, I was taken sea fishing by some friends of my parents and a poor unfortunate cod or something of that ilk was dragged on board. Many boring hours later, when I was happily convinced that the poor panting creature must have met its demise by drowning after all this time, I was horrified to see when one of the men, having had no more luck that day (fortunately), picked up the cod and it wriggled with a great deal of life.

But the worst horror was to follow, the horror which was to make me a non-fisher forever more. The fish was placed on one of the seats and its head sawed off with what seemed an exceedingly blunt knife. The tail threshed, gallons of blood flowed under my Wellingtons and I was revolted. I've never forgotten the sight.

So, when Al said we'd go fishing, like it was a big treat, it was actually the reverse. But I couldn't possibly refuse: Al was looking forward to it so much and perhaps, so was Grandpa, though it's hard to tell what he's thinking and he's so mild-mannered and quiet you get the feeling that if Al said he should help him rob a bank, the old man would just nod and drive the getaway car, though very slowly. Perhaps because of his deafness, he didn't even know he was going to enjoy himself fishing tomorrow.

For your friends, you have to make sacrifices. Had Al not shown me Missoula by night and poured Yukon Jack down my throat like he had shares in it and shown me lots of other kindnesses besides? And didn't I say that I wouldn't refuse any invitation? But worst of all, the *coup de grâce,* was when Al said I'd have to pick him up at 6.30.

If only I had known not to buy a car with a tow bar.

Chapter Twenty-one

In which I have to confront an antidote to a romantic ideal, go fishin' and embark on a little nature study.

Sometime later the doorbell rings again. This time it is Art Moore. He was just going round to Sam White's and wondered if I would like to join him. I reckon that any invitation to socialise with my colleagues is a thing I've got to do, so I breathe Yukon Jack fumes over Iona and the children as I kiss them goodbye and set off in Art's big beige station wagon to Sam's house on Central. It is a white wooden house with what I would call a veranda out the front, but what they call the "deck".

Sam is pickling cucumber and dill and slugging Budweiser out of a can. His mother is also there: slim, white-haired, bespectacled, and smoking. As we get to talking, it doesn't take me long to form the opinion that she is a really nice old lady and I wonder if she would approve of her son's description of everyone as an asshole or even a dildo. Or maybe she is sorry for him – that he has not been luckier with the people he has met in his life. And maybe that will include me, once he gets to know me a bit better.

Naturally, Art and I have some beer too: it's the equivalent of having a cup of tea in England. But I come from Scotland where the fermented juice of the home-grown grain, the barley brew, either in its distilled form or less potent frothy form, I regard as eminently more quaffable than tea, which, you may remember, Iona can't bear. In fact, she detests both beverages: the one that inebriates and the one that does not. You might conclude she is a bit picky, and you would be right. But her taste is not all in her mouth, for after all, did she not pick me?

So, while I have not had a drop of tea for the past six years, or to put it another way, since I got married, I can't say I have missed it, having been indoctrinated into the coffee culture instead. I have not however, abandoned my national drink whenever I could afford it, which as I have already said, is not often. But I could never have lasted six months, let alone six years without a drop of the wee nectar.

Budweiser has a mid-European pedigree to justify its claim to being the "king of beers" and seems to be the leading brand here, but to me, it is just a lager and Brown Derby would have done just as well. I prefer real beer, but they don't seem to do that over here, only varieties of lager, which in appearance always reminds me of a urine sample. But you never see what you are drinking over here unless you buy a pitcher as they drink it straight out of the can or bottle. What the eye doesn't see...

And the Americans have had another good idea as far as beer is concerned. Unlike our cans, which are 16 ounces, theirs are only 12 which means the beer is still cold, in its original chilled container, by the time you get to the last drop. And then you think: *I could have another beer as it doesn't look that big.* Is it any wonder that this nation (or their German scientists) has put a man on the moon and we haven't?

But there is another nation in this country. I am regaling Sam and Art about my trip with Al in the police car, except I only get as far as the drunk Indian when Sam interrupts: "Asshole. Those Indians are all assholes!"

"No, really they are, David," he goes on, seeing the shock on my face. "D'you know that if they live on the Reservation, they don't pay any taxes, but they can come into the town and use any facility they want?"

"And," says Art, "they get an allowance from the government, just for bein' Indian. And it isn't just purebred Indians that get it. If you've got any Indian blood in you at all, you get an allowance – out of *our* taxes," he adds for good measure, stabbing the air with nicotine-stained fingers in which a cigarette is clamped so tightly I almost feel sorry for it, though I have to confess, I have no liking for the pernicious weed myself.

"No wonder they're always drunk," says Sam. "And they don't have to work for a livin'. They can just lie in their tepees all day smokin' dope... Hey, David, wouldn't you just *love* to be an Indian an' drink beer an' smoke dope all day instead of havin' to teach kids?" The gurgling laughter at his own joke apparently shows no resentment at this happy state of affairs, conjuring up Ira Gershwin's immortal words: *Nice work if you can get it.*

Now that's a sentiment I would find it hard to disagree with, but it is rather at odds with my idealist preconception of "Native Americans" as they apparently prefer to be called, or what we are told we *should* call them for the sake of political correctness.

"You know what makes me really, really angry?" Art poses the rhetorical question, shaking his head as if to rid himself of the unwelcome thought, like a dog with fleas.

I shake mine, somewhat bemused by this double-pronged attack on my beloved Indians.

"It's that Indian Studies course."

"Oh, God! Gee! That Indian Studies course!" chimes in Sam. "What a loada bullshit that is! I mean to say... " Words fail him, allowing me to ponder the horrors for myself.

"You see, Dave, under federal law, we've all got to take a course in Indian Studies, so we can understand our red-skinned brethren better. And *we've* got to pay for it too!"

"God, yes," agrees Sam. "Hey, Art, wasn't that just the *worst* course you ever took? I mean, really, just the *worst!*"

Sam and Art obviously feel very strongly about the subject. Personally, I would adore to go on this course if I could. I would even *gladly* pay to go on it. But what sticks in Art and Sam's craw is that they see it as an imposition, an attempt to foist Indian culture upon them, something which they don't recognise as contributing the slightest iota to making them better teachers.

If the Government's plan had been an attempt to atone to the Indians for the conquering of their land, for their removal from their homeland, and moving them on again if they later found they were sitting on top of a mineral they wanted; for the imposition of the white man's culture; for past treacheries and atrocities, then it was failing badly. Instead, with the best of intentions, they were in fact, creating prejudice. The whole thing had backfired very badly.

Somehow, I don't think this is the right time to ask Art and Sam where I can find out about enrolling for the Indian Studies course.

* * *

When I eventually left Sam's, I was well on the way to being as pickled as one of his cucumbers. The really, really annoying thing is I could have gone rafting with him today about noon, as he said the forecast was for a high of 90 degrees. But here I am instead, trying to persuade the Plymouth to start. It is in empathy with me, reluctant to get going this cold and dewy morning. It is 6.30 am and I am feeling less than 100%. I was not able to leave as soon as I would have liked, being dependent on Art for a lift. And those pickles are strong if you have a few of them. But maybe they don't mix with Yukon Jack and six Buds.

The boat is parked at Grandpa's so we head there first. Al hitches up the boat and fetches a bag of ice from the freezer. This is for the beer. The cooler, whose acquaintance I had first met in the Thunderbird, is now in the back of the Plymouth, filled with beer. You can't go fishing without beer, naturally. In fact, Al can't go anywhere without beer apparently, for even at this early hour of the morning, he removes one of the cans and swigs from it as he steers us round the serpentine twists of the road as it follows the Blackfoot river. I had thought it prudent to let him drive as he knew where we were headed. Nothing at all to do with the state of my head.

A mist is evaporating from the surface of the river and pine-clad mountains shoulder their way into the sky. As the road suddenly dips to reveal Salmon Lake, ethereal in the morning slanting sun, and with the warmth from the great car's heater on my toes, I begin to thaw out, gradually come awake, and I am glad now that I made the sacrifice to leave my warm nest at that ungodly hour as the scenery is so splendid it can't fail to lift my spirits.

Salmon Lake is not our destination however. Presently, we cut off the main road and follow a dirt track through the trees until we come to another lake. This is Placid Lake, named after, or "for" as they say here, Placid Albert, an early settler. And here's the amazing thing – a relation of Al's! Placid Albert is Grandpa's grandfather's brother, no less. The placid genes descended to Grandpa all right but how did they then get so incredibly lost?

It is a beautiful setting. The lake is ringed with trees and log cabins are dotted round the shore. Towering in the distance is the Bob Marshall wilderness with snowy, craggy peaks serrating the cloudless blue sky. Now that's more like it! That's what I would call Rockies, not those humps in Missoula that look like Rip Van Winkle elephants gone to sleep and been covered by vegetation during their slumber.

The last of the mist is evaporating into the warming air as we unhitch the boat and launch it into the water. We chug out into the lake, disturbing its mirror-like surface. We are going to be trawling apparently, which means that we keep moving, dragging our lines behind us – at least Al and Grandpa's lines, for I am in charge of driving the boat. I am very happy to do this and know that Al would dump me overboard if he knew what I was thinking: *Please don't let them catch anything.*

Apart from the threat of death lurking for those unsuspecting denizens beneath the water, it is an idyllic setting. As I take photos of my companions, it crosses my mind that it's like something out of *National Geographic*, especially Grandpa with his battered and faded green baseball hat, his checked shirt, intent on his line, oblivious to the soaring mountains behind him as he has seen their splendour so many times they have become so commonplace he isn't aware of them any more.

"C'mon you goddamned fish!" Al curses his invisible prey.

And so it continues, hour after hour, beer after beer, Al's curses practically the only conversation until even I begin to think that maybe just one fish, just to relieve the tedium, would be welcome. Al's mood is not improving.

"I can't understand it, Dave. I've never had such bad luck as this before. Let's get the hell outta here!"

Grandpa, as usual, says nothing. Nor do I, but I heartily agree. You can only take so many beers without wanting to go somewhere else without polluting the waters. And however astounding the scenery may be, you can only look at the mountains so long because no matter how often you look, they are still as beautiful as they were before. For me that was every two minutes. I had seen pictures like this before of course, but I had never actually *been* in a landscape so beautiful before.

Fish one – Hertz nil – for the first time ever, if Al is to be believed. But then the little fishes didn't have their protector, Saint David of Banff with them before.

But Al hasn't quite admitted defeat yet. On the way home, we park by a creek. He is going to try his luck here. The creek flows through a meadow of long grass and before Al starts fishing, we have to catch grasshoppers as bait. I watch as Al puts the hook right through the tiny body of one poor unfortunate. While Al fishes and Grandpa sits in lonely contemplation in the car, it is my job to catch grasshoppers as fresh bait, a task in which I am incredibly incompetent. Well, actually, they were pretty easy to catch, but I looked them in the eye and thought: *How can I condemn you to be skewered alive or drowned or eaten by a horrible fishy mouth?* so I let them go. My jinx on Al and the protection of the fishes continues. He catches nothing, but I catch sight of a beaver.

"Hey, Al, look! There's a beaver!" I shout excitedly. The creature has scurried into the water and is ploughing its way upstream, leaving a V-shaped wake in its trail. And since Al is looking at me with a rather a curious expression, I feel it necessary to explain, "I've never seen a beaver before!"

Al produces one of his outrageous, megaphone laughs. The very mountains seem to resound to the sound. He manages to get out, "What! Ain't you never seen a beaver before?" before he is overcome by another gale of laughter.

I can't see what's so funny. "Well, we don't have them in Scotland, you know. They are not an indigenous species," I add, a bit miffed.

But this only increases Al's mirth more.

"What you got in Scotland, then? Pussy?"

I may be naïve, but I'm not that slow on the uptake, especially knowing the way Al's mind works and the reason for his laughter becomes amazingly obvious in an instant. I can't imagine how I had not cottoned on earlier. Of course they do things bigger over here.

"Oh, I see what you mean! No, no, we don't have any beavers, but we've got plenty of pussies!"

Al is pleased with his joke and my rejoinder. It seems to have lightened his mood a little – probably because I've taken his mind off his failure, a failure which does not sit lightly on his shoulders, and they are pretty broad. I have created a diversion: perhaps he's now thinking of beavers instead of fish. Instead of past fishing expeditions, perhaps he's now thinking of past beaver-trapping expeditions in which he had a bit more success than he's had today. I can't be sure what he's thinking, but at least I can see his scowl has been replaced with a broad grin and I console myself with the thought that if I were partly responsible for his misery by providing the vehicle for it in the shape of the Plymouth, I was also the vehicle for his recovery.

But this first sight ever, for me, of a beaver, and in the wild too, is such an exciting sight that in my recently acquired role as Protector of Fishes, I somehow manage to prevail upon Al to abandon the fishing and follow the beaver upstream to see if we could see any of its relations. We don't have far to go until we come to its lodge, a huge, untidy pile of sticks that must have taken many a weary gnaw and nibble for such little creatures. There are no signs of the builders though.

We head back to the car and for home, completely fishless. I join Al in yet another beer in the front seat with Grandpa semi-comatose in the back. As Al drives us effortlessly along the wide, uncrowded roads, with only two fingers on the wheel, I reflect that for me at least, the trip had been a success, even if the fishing interludes had tended to - no - *remained* firmly rooted in the boring.

I also knew that if I could not enjoy fishing amongst such splendid scenery, in such warm sunshine and amidst the peace and the tranquillity I'd experienced today, I never could. If that is fishing at its best, for the life of me, I can't see what possesses people to spend countless hours in the rain, as they do in Scotland, sometimes immersed up to their waists in water. To reinvent Oscar Wilde's aphorism on fox hunting, I would describe fishing as the unspeakably boring in pursuit of the edible.

Al seems immensely more cheerful as we wend our beery, fishless, seventy or so miles back to Missoula and after we have unhitched the boat and decanted Grandpa, he has recovered his good humour sufficiently to press me to stay for a Yukon Jack. After his disappointments of the day, I don't have the heart to refuse.

"Hey, Terri, Dave didn't know what a beaver was!" he tells her the moment she appears, unable it seems, to control another gale of laughter which wells up from the depths of his barrel-like chest. I am the very antidote to a wasted day in piscatorial pursuit. Which is only fair really as I am also the jinx.

"Oh well!" she says, smiling good-naturedly, as she always does, then shrugs her shoulders as if to say: "What can you do with him?"

"Yeah, so I showed him one! Didn't I, Dave?" and he produces another of his most gravelly laughs.

After a few more Yukon Jacks and some more ribald humour, the hour approaches when I must prepare to meet the wrath of the abandoned wife. I've had a pretty good day really, since no death was involved (apart from a few grasshoppers). On the other hand, had I gone rafting with Sam, I might well be in the morgue at the moment as I am not the strongest of swimmers, being self-taught. Better to have lived boringly than died prematurely enjoying yourself. It almost sounds like another of Oscar Wilde's aphorisms. But it was another Montanan experience.

I am not sure what my reception will be when I return to the house from *Psycho,* especially if I breathe Yukon Jack fumes over the most dearly beloved, but saying no to Al when he is offering a drink is like King Canute trying to hold back the waves. Having said that, poor Canute has been much maligned as a madman when, in actual fact, his purpose was to show how he was a mere king, subservient to the King in Heaven. He knew perfectly well he was not going to turn back the tide. That was his point and that is mine.

But will I be able to make my point convincingly to Iona that I have had a perfectly boring day and how glad I am that it is all over at last?

The kids, at least, seem pleased to see me and even Iona, amazingly, seems in a relatively good mood for someone who has been housebound with two small kids all day while her husband took the car away and left her to her own devices.

It has been a long day. I'm tired and I want to get to bed early. But it's not just because of my weariness. There is another special reason.

That was my last day of freedom. Tomorrow I have to do what I came over here to do – work. But it could be worse. There will not be any children.

School without children rules OK.

Chapter Twenty-two

In which I learn something about deaf education, meet some more of my colleagues and make a blunder – but not half as big as someone else's.

I have to go to an orientation meeting at the admin building which is quite ironic really as I am disorientated and can't find it. By the time I get there it is long past the 8.30 start, but that doesn't matter really as it is a form-filling session for new teachers and doesn't apply to me.

I happen to sit beside a person called Mike Wynne. Of all the people in the room to sit beside, I am beginning to wonder if, after all, there is a hand of destiny guiding my fate in a benign sort of way, for who should Mike be, but the new audiologist! When I tell him about George, he gives me his phone number and says I should get in touch with him and he'd give George a hearing test sometime. He introduces me to a man called Paul Rollo who is in charge of deaf education.

"I firmly believe in total communication," says Paul. "We must see what we can do to help you and your wife help the little feller. I'll speak to Kathy Kuhn and Matt and see if we can arrange something."

"What's total communication?"

This is my first introduction to the world of deaf education. Paul explains that total communicators believe in signing as well as speaking to the deaf. They are mortal enemies of the oralists who believe that in a speaking world, the deaf should lip-read and be taught to speak as far as possible. They say that in an aural/oral word that people won't take the trouble to learn sign language and that to sign means condemning them forever to the deaf world.

Total communicators, on the other hand, believe that what is important is getting the message through by whatever means you can. It's important, they insist, that if the child is to maintain his development with his hearing peers, to use any method you can to get across vocabulary, concepts and ideas. Since the ears don't work, they see no problem with using sight as a means to include the deaf person in what's going on. Too often the deaf person is excluded from the family and from society in general because they can't hear what's going on and therefore can't take part in the social intercourse around them.

What's more, people tend not to have the patience to speak to the deaf and in any case, it's impossible for the deaf person to keep up with the conversation in a group situation. Not many realise it, but deafness is much more of a social exclusion than blindness. Blind people can be, and are included in conversation quite readily, while the deaf sit on the fringes, ignored and left wondering what's going on.

It all makes sense to me, but I can see the oralists do have a point too. The hearing have to *want* to learn signing, actively seek it out and why should they, unless there is a deaf person in their family or someone they know who is deaf?

I remembered Matt saying he'd see if there could be some help for George, but with him being so young, still in diapers, as they say here, I thought that would be dead in the water, but now I am beginning to believe that something may be possible after all.

Talking to Dan Gunn, he too has good news for me, or so he thinks. Blue Cross will give me a reduced rate. He doesn't know how much yet but however much it is, it is still likely to be too much as it's my view I should not have to pay anything at all since I am replacing Marnie whom they know will definitely not be making a claim this year. So unless it is really, really cheap, I think I'll risk it, make do with the $2000 free cover I get from the Bureau and just buy insurance for Iona and the kids.

The meeting is over and now, at school, I haven't a clue what I'm meant to be doing. I guddle about, making it look as if I am doing something, but feeling the panic beginning to mount as I realise that the kids will be here this time next week and I'm no nearer being any the wiser as to what exactly I'm meant to be doing with them. Unless it is just what it seems: endless exercises from that book that has the answers for the teachers. It's not even as if they are in the least bit challenging, for God's sake! I wonder if the teachers feel rather insulted to think that the publishers think they need the answers.

It did surprise me to learn that the other 7th and 8th grade teachers also have to teach grammar to their form classes, or "homeroom" even although English is not their subject. But all that seems to consist of is handing out "dittoed sheets" to the kids, getting them to fill in the blanks, taking them in again, putting ticks and crosses against their answers, as appropriate, and handing them back. Simple really. But I wonder why you would need a degree to do that. Where's the teaching?

Art had the kids in my homeroom last year and he gives me the lowdown on them, which is pretty useful as I can't even tell from their names which sex they are. Since there are not even as many as twenty of them, learning their names shouldn't present any difficulty. Apparently a lot of them come from broken homes, which I could have easily predicted. They come mostly from North Missoula and live in "trailer homes" – residential caravans, to me. North Missoula is out the Interstate a few miles and considered to be a poorer sort of area. Well, that's fine with me as it's the sort of thing I'm used to in Abbotsgrange. The Bureau had made a good match in that respect at least.

Art says he will pick us up at 6 and take us to the Olsens' barbecue, which will give us plenty of time to get there for 6.29. Iona has made some shortbread to take as our offering to the proceedings, but when we see the enormous salad that Art has prepared, it makes our offering look very meagre indeed. If everyone else brings something like his, it's going to make us look like Scottish scrooges. I had no idea that the contributions would be so elaborate and I express these concerns to Art but he says not to worry. Of course, it's easy for him to say that. He's not the one who is going to look like a miser, so I am not feeling in any way reassured when we pull into the drive and see other people carrying in platters big enough to serve up Samson's head.

Matt's wife, Patty, receives us and if she is insulted by our humble offering, she doesn't let it show and when Iona explains that it is a Scottish delicacy, she is effusive.

"Oh, how neat! That's really neat!" she coos, but it does little to assuage our worries.

Patty puts our tribute on a table covered with so many huge dishes that, by contrast, our little plate looks small, drab and apologetic. To make matters worse, there is another table where the desserts are, where the shortbread should really be, but I don't have the courage to point this out to Patty. I wonder what the guests will make of it when they put it on their plate with the salad and the fish.

There is another table which holds the drinks, but I notice there is no sign of any beer, to which anomaly I draw Art's attention.

"Matt doesn't drink," he explains.

"Yes, but, I mean, that doesn't stop everyone else, does it?"

"Yep, it does." We are talking in whispers. "Matt is a Christian."

I nod as if that explained everything. "You see," Art goes on, "he belongs to the Church of God."

Oh well, *that* does explain it then. Another thing I had been aware of in Missoula was the plethora of churches with unconventional names, like Matt's, and of all of them, his sounds the best. You can't get much higher than that. But if He, through His son, turned water into wine at the wedding feast in Cana, what reason could Matt possibly have for banning beers to help wash down the feast?

And at this feast in Missoula, it looks as if Jesus has been reprising another of His miracles to judge by the number of fish. Matt is tossing what looks as if it might be his entire year's catch in oatmeal and then popping it into a black potbellied stove which is hottering on a wood fire. (If only Al could see all this fish! And if only he could be here without a can of beer in sight!) The fish is salmon and trout, but I get trout each time. Or maybe I can't tell the difference.

We are at a table in the yard with Art and the two "custodians" or janitors, Danny Lukska and Jimmy Wood and their wives. Jimmy's wife, Pat, is a nurse at the Community hospital. They are on strike just now. I remember seeing the pickets as I passed once. What amazes me is that she tells me that she has been on strike now for two months and her employers don't seem to be in any hurry to settle because they have drafted in other nurses from somewhere else.

Apparently that is quite the thing here. When baseball umpires went on strike recently, Art tells me, they got amateurs to do the job. I think how easy it would be to get people off the street to be teachers, if they ever went on strike. And as if reading my mind, Art informs me that if teachers were to go on strike, they would have to make the days up as they must teach a regulation number of days every year. If, for example, the school were closed because of snow, the summer holidays would be delayed until the shortfall was made up. I am crestfallen. There doesn't seem much point in praying for heavy snowfalls this winter as that would delay when we took off on our travels.

I meet some members of staff and there are too many to remember all at once, but I do get talking to a tall man with short fair hair and light blue eyes which look out of a tanned face with an almost hypnotic intensity. He introduces himself as Blake Schulz and I think that with a Christian name like that, he should have been an English teacher. He is in fact, the science man and his room is next to mine. I ask him how he feels about teaching Reading and he says it's not a problem as he is elementary trained. It still seems strange to me though, for a science specialist to be teaching my speciality as well as his own. Just as well it's not the other way about but maybe I could, if I had a book of answers and dittoed sheets.

Inside Matt's house, an enormous stuffed salmon hangs over the fireplace and on the wall next to it, a duck has been captured in flight, but not like the china variety favoured in many British homes, usually three staggered across the wall. This one looks as if it could be real. Closer inspection reveals that it is and it's really dead. At the other side of the room, a deer's head is staring impassively at the salmon. Fish, bird and mammal: all trophies that have fallen to Matt's gun. His church doesn't hold with obeying the sixth commandment obviously. He stuffed them himself Matt tells me, for another of his hobbies is taxidermy. I now recall seeing several signs around town advertising the services of the stuffer's art, something I've never come across in Scotland.

A case of his killing instruments is on display in the room too, containing no less than five rifles. Why would anyone need *five* of these things? Can you not kill enough with one? Not for the first time, I marvel at how extensive the gun culture is here. There are shops and shops selling guns and rifles along the Strip. Maybe these aren't even the ones he uses. Maybe he just likes looking at them, like ornaments, like the stuffed creatures on the wall.

The party is beginning to break up, although it is very early. Perhaps it has got something to do with the absence of beer, or maybe it's because they don't really want to be here at all. I am getting the idea that this get-together of the whole staff is meant to make us bond, be part of a team, but without the beer to make people more sociable, they seem somewhat lost with perhaps the only thing they have in common the school, which, they don't need reminding, they will be at all too soon. And perhaps they are there only because it would be noticed if they didn't go, like Sam for example, but of course I have no idea who else hasn't turned up.

Art goes to retrieve what's left of his salad. Apparently this is permitted by the etiquette. I notice that Iona's shortbread has not been touched. Probably no-one knew what it was. What do we do? It is our right to remove it, but anyone who catches us smuggling it out will know who brought it. Better to leave it. Maybe Patty and Matt will try it later, or not knowing how they should eat it, will consign it to the bin, or "trash" as they call it.

Art is persuaded to come in for a beer and tells us a bit more about Matt. He has two grown-up children and his daughter was married just last week. But he also has two adopted children because he thinks it's his Christian duty to do so.

"Did you notice that someone actually brought along some beer?" Art asks.

"No," I say, astonished.

"That's the first time that's ever happened, an' boy, was Matt not pleased!" Art chuckles.

Could it have been taken along in perfect innocence, like I might have done? Or was it a deliberate act of sabotage by someone who wished, in no uncertain terms, to express his opinion of Matt's beer ban? If so, as a taxidermist, Matt could not have failed to get the message.

Chapter Twenty-three

In which I express an opinion on American education but keep others to myself. I experience a shock when the shape of my school day becomes clear but I still am not on what to do with my students.

It's another orientation day, this time at another school in District 7, the Lewis and Clark school. Lewis and Clark were two explorers who had passed this way in the early 19th century, after Thomas Jefferson had made the Louisiana Purchase from France and wanted to know what he'd bought. Imagine that! Buying a pig in a poke like that! It turned out to be a pretty good bargain in the end, though.

We begin with the pledge. Everyone stands and puts their hand on their heart and pledges allegiance to America. After that there are speeches. The first one is by someone on the school board. It seems to be a good speech as lots of people are laughing but it goes completely over my head as he's mentioning names that don't mean anything to me.

The main speaker is Charlotte Brookes from American University in Washington, where we had had our briefing. She deplores the way that Language Arts is currently being taught in the USA. She says the students don't read enough, write enough, think enough or use their imaginations enough. I prick up my ears. I think she could have a point.

When we meet later in the library as a smaller group, she encounters objections from a number of teachers that the implication of her proposals would result in their having an increased marking load. She counters by saying that no one needs *all* of their written work corrected every time. Privately

I think: *What have you to be worried about with class sizes of 18? It's a Scottish teacher's dream.* But I do chirp up and say I agree with her and tell her that's what I do – that I don't mark every single thing, that it's not necessary, that the important thing is to get them to write and keep writing, not be discouraged by red marks all over the page.

However, I think it is a step too far to add that I also wholeheartedly agree with what she was saying in her lecture on the methodology of the teaching of Reading and it's high time it was due for an overhaul. For one thing, I have some reservations about my understanding of the way it works, and just in case I've got it wrong, I don't want to make a fool of myself by betraying my ignorance. I prefer to think of myself as a diplomat, but I know I am really a wimp, for I know that Charlotte will be jetting back off to Washington leaving her unpopular recommendations behind and it's not my job to come over here before I've even had any classes and criticise the system. I'm here to observe it, not change it.

When it's over, Tammy Kinsella, the Reading director, thanks me for my contribution. It wasn't much but I reckon she would like to see some changes too and it's nice for her to have some support and for people to realise that there is another way. A much better way.

In the afternoon, I go back to the school, hoping I might find some inspiration, but I don't. I don't know what I'm going to do with the kids but I've got nearly a week yet and I hope, like Mr Micawber, that something will turn up. Down in his office, I hope Matt assumes I am preparing lessons instead of worrying what I'm going to teach.

In the evening, Steve Knight turns up. He is the Social Studies teacher and is going to be across the corridor from me, only they call it the "hall". He's the sort of person you can't help liking instantly. He has a walrus moustache and makes himself at home in the Viking chair which suits him very well and he seems very taken with Hélène, calling her "Miss Hélène". He's bouncing with enthusiasm, can't wait to get back to school. I used to feel like that too, once upon a time.

He's very keen on sport and he takes the kids for football (the American variety of course – our type is hardly known at all, which they call soccer) and basketball. He is paid an extra $500 for that and I form the impression that that is what Steve likes most about his job. He takes them in his lunchtime, to the park. That's what I call dedication. In Scotland, I come home, just to get a break from kids.

* * *

School, without kids, is not such a bad place, but I don't really care to see it at 8.30 in the morning, especially since I have nothing to do when I get there except try to make myself look busy. I'm sure I should be busy, like I expect everyone else is. But busy doing what?

I have a meeting with my colleagues, Steve, Blake, and Nat Paxman whom I have not met before. Nat is the Math teacher. Another American idiosyncrasy. It sounds odd to me, as if it has been devised for people who can't say their esses.

Nat is new to this school, but not the district, having been drafted in, compulsorily transferred from another school because the previous Math teacher had moved to Washington State. Nat doesn't seem over the moon about it. The main purpose of our meeting is to discuss the timetable. We are autonomous in a way, in charge of the upper school, we four. And Blake, perhaps because of his grey hair, seems to be the ex-officio leader. His modest proposal (and you can expect this sort of logic from a scientist) is that the students will travel clockwise, and who could disagree with that? So my timetable works out as 7S, followed by 8P, followed by 8K, followed by 7A. I don't know what we would have called the classes if two of us had happened to have surnames beginning with the same letter. More importantly, I don't know how it works out for the others, but it doesn't turn out to be the ideal arrangement for me as it means I will have my homeroom class all afternoon, having just had them before lunch as well. I hope we are going to get along as we are going to be seeing a lot of each other. Such a long period of contact may be the norm in the elementary system, but not for me. And does it work out the same way for the others? I would have to ask Nat to work that out for me, but I'll just wait and see.

I also learn that all classes will get PE three times a week. Great! That's when I'll do my correction, such as it is, but I am soon disillusioned when Blake says *we* have to take the classes.

"What! Me? But I don't know the first thing about teaching PE! What do I do?"

I am horrified. The General Teaching Council in Scotland would have a hairy fit at the idea of me teaching a subject I am not qualified to teach. Besides, you would only have to look at me for a moment to see I was supremely unfitted to teach personal fitness. You only have to look at Nat, Steve and Blake's flat stomachs and biceps (they all seem to favour short-sleeved shirts) to see they look like finely-honed athletes compared to me.

Blake tells me not to worry, he'll take care of it but I tell him I can't let him do that, take my PE class, so it's agreed, to my huge relief, that we'll do it together.

"We usually play scatterball," he says.

"What's that?"

"Well, someone throws a ball an' the rest have to scatter," says Blake with a deadpan expression. He must think I am a moron.

"But what about the PE?"

Blake looks at me closely. He's no longer in any doubt that I *am* a moron.

"Well, that's it, Dave. That's what we usually do."

I nod sagely, trying not to look as stupid as I feel, but thinking my private thoughts about the standard of physical education in this country. And yet they win all those gold medals at the Olympics!

From 1 to 1.40 they have silent reading.

"It's good for them to read," says Blake. I certainly can't argue with that – but for 40 minutes, when they could be getting the benefit of my pearls of wisdom! "And it's good for them to see us reading too," he continues.

I can't argue with that either, but somehow I can't get the idea out of my head that it's a bit of a skive and I can't see it going down too well with Her Majesty's Inspectors back home either. But if that's the system, well, so be it: I'll read my correction. I can already see that I'll never have to take any marking home, unlike poor Marnie who will have to take mountains of it back if she is to keep her head above water.

There will also be Music once a week and Art too. That will be putting on a record I suppose and drawing something a bit more advanced than a doodle. Perhaps they have to colour it in afterwards. But actually my cynicism is unfounded – they do have specialists for these.

Later, we have a whole staff meeting in the library and Matt catches me off guard when, after he has introduced me he says: "Is there anythin' you'd like to share with us, Dave?"

My mind races along facetious lines, being unaccustomed, as I am, to American-speak. Well, I have a cheese sandwich, but that wouldn't go round everybody and there is the bill for the car – I'd certainly like to share that. Instead I say that I am looking forward to starting school (what a liar) and how helpful and friendly everyone has been, especially Matt (what a crawler) and how I'm looking forward to meeting everyone and getting to know them in the course of the year which I am sure is going to be a great year for me. (Liar again. I am not sure of this at all, but I sincerely hope it.)

Matt is pleased with my few words of flattery and moves on to the day's business. He hands out a sheet of instructions amongst which I notice there are directions on what to do with "absent" notes. I recall the "vegtable" of the invitation and I wonder if this is another slip or another idiosyncratic Americanism, like Math.

At lunch, all the new teachers are invited to the Holiday Inn. There is only one new teacher to Emerson apart from me – Judith Johnston who is a Title One teacher. It makes her sound like a really good teacher, and maybe she is, but actually it means that she teaches remedial, except you are not allowed to call it that any more. The Holiday Inn is pretty near the school so Judith and I walk along there together. There is no such thing as a free lunch however and we have to listen to a boring speaker who chunters on about how little is wrong with American education. After all, haven't they put a man on the moon?

"Excuse me, ma'm, but would it not be more accurate to say that it was the Germans who came to the USA after the war, like Werner Von Braun, and who took with them the rocket technology they were developing under Hitler, who are *really* responsible for putting a man on the moon?" Pausing for breath, while I let that fundamental truth sink in, I add, "And what's more, obviously you were not listening, nor present at Charlotte Brookes' lecture this morning when she said one thing *was* definitely wrong with American education – the teaching of Reading. And I'll tell you another thing – I couldn't agree more."

But of course, I only thought it. The lunch was as good as the speaker was bad, so they got that the right way round at least. To my astonishment, this less than momentous occasion is being covered by the television cameras. Had I voiced my question, I reckon I could have been watching my TV debut tonight. I might even have hit the headlines. All I do however, after it is over and as we walk back to school, is to tell Judith how surprised I was to find the cameras there.

"Oh, no," she says, "I wasn't. In fact, I've been told that there is a strong likelihood of them coming to film one of my classes. And I'm up to high doh about it," she adds confidentially. I can see the strain already appearing on her face now that I've reminded her of the ordeal.

"I shouldn't worry about it," I try to reassure her. "It'll probably never happen."

"Yes, but it *might*," Judith responds, looking more worried than ever. After all, she must be thinking, what does a Scotsman know about local American TV?

A lot more than she thinks actually, thanks to what Marnie had confided in me. So, should I pass this on to Judith? But Marnie had made me swear not to let on that I knew about this very amusing trick, so despite Judith's worries, I do not put her out of her misery.

Back at school to my own form of stress, for some more fiddling about until Art sticks his head in the door and asks me if I'd like to go to The Depot. I don't know what The Depot is, but I want to go there because I want to leave here.

As I suspected, it is a pub, and Sam is there too and so is a friend of Art's, Chuck Paterson, who teaches in one of the other schools. He is pleased to meet me as he says he's interested in going on exchange. I tell him that I can probably put him in contact with someone from my school who might like an exchange with him. The Bureau doesn't mind this arrangement. I suppose it cuts their work down, trying to find suitable matches. It could be good for me too: which one of the monstrous regiment of women in my school would I most like to get rid of?

We have three pitchers of beer and amongst other things, discuss Matt's handout. It is 7 pm by the time I get back. Iona is not amused, even when I explain that it was work; that Art and Sam were going over the information that Matt had given out to us, for my benefit. She has had to feed, bath and put the kids to bed all by herself. That's work. And she is right. That I can't deny.

* * *

Bliss was it this morn to lie abed and not to have to get up at 7.45 in order to get to school by 8.30. I stagger in by 11 instead. I could have got there sooner, but decide to walk as Iona is going to take the car to The Dairy so she can get used to the car, especially the brakes. She says me watching her makes her nervous and I reckon it's better for my nerves too if I don't, so everyone is happy.

I sit at my desk and try to read Marnie's notes again, but they may as well be Egyptian hieroglyphs. I can't make head or tail of them and I decide I'm not going to bother trying to follow them any more. I don't like those books anyway, with their one-word answers. I'm just going to have to do my own thing. The question is – what?

Having decided that, there is not much more I can do, so I decide to go home again and think about it there. Iona got back from The Dairy all right, though she says she has a sore head from the concentration. There is a crossroads that has to be negotiated. There are no traffic lights: instead you take it in turns to go. I can imagine if two excessively polite drivers should arrive together, you could stay there forever: "No, after you... No please, after you... No, I insist... Not at all... " Then you both decide to go at the same time. But actually it seems to work, in the main, pretty well, she is assured.

Steve Knight comes round and introduces his wife, Jackie, to us, but before we let them across the threshold, we charge them a vegetable fee. They have to give us a big bag of corn on the cob. Earlier, I had told Steve about the compression test I had done on the car and Steve said he had a tame mechanic who could do the job, so we leave the women to talk and the mechanic tells me he can do the valves for $150 perhaps even less, but since he only works in the evenings, it would take a week to do. I don't mind that at all as I will be saving $100 at least on Al's pal.

Steve takes me back to his house which has a pleasing prospect on a hill commanding a view over the sprawl of Missoula. In the drive are three vehicles, a car, a jeep and a truck. His house, by my standards, looks large too and of course it is detached. We have had quite a job explaining the concept of semi-detached to people. Even when we show them a picture of our house, they find it inconceivable that anyone could live in such a rabbit hutch. They ask if it's a duplex. I've never heard the word before but it seems to make sense to them so I say, yes, that's what it is and they nod in understanding.

"I don't go for all that materialistic bullshit," Steve says when I tell him he has a nice house. "That's why we got such a high divorce rate an' I'm gonna make sure that doesn't happen to me."

Chapter Twenty-four

In which we go on our first expedition with some embarrassing results.

It is Labor Day weekend and we are off on our first expedition. Steve has suggested we visit the Lewis and Clark caves on the other side of Butte which wittily rejoices under the soubriquet of "The Butt of the Nation". This is a round trip of 340 miles, which would be like driving to see my mother in Thurso and back, all in the same day, something I would only contemplate if I were suffering from a severe bout of insanity. But here the roads are so empty you can divide the distance by 55 mph, which is the ridiculously low speed limit in this state for such wide and empty roads, not to mention such powerful cars, and that will tell you how long it will take you to get to your destination – precisely.

So, just after 9 am, we hit the I 90 Interstate and head east for Butte, and I set the cruise control at 55, at least to begin with. But driving at that speed along such a straight road narrowing to the horizon miles ahead, with scarcely another vehicle behind us or in front of us or coming towards us, makes it seem as if are hardly moving at all and I up the cruise control to 60, which still seems painfully slow but a speed I can just about tolerate. All I need is one hand on the wheel to keep us pointed in the right direction, though I scarcely need that, and eyes to appreciate the scenery.

Our journey takes as at first through forest-clad mountains and as we reach the continental divide and begin to climb, sweeping effortlessly round vast bends, the terrain becomes increasingly more rocky, until the road cuts a swathe through massive boulders the size of elephants. At 6,392 feet, we are at the summit and begin the descent towards Butte. We have crossed The Rockies, and a lot more easily than Lewis and Clark.

It is a gorgeous day. According to the radio it is 91º and it certainly feels like it. Another reminder of how I was far too hasty to dismiss Sam's invitation to go rafting when it got hot enough. I obviously don't know much about the climate, but there *is* something else I do know for certain – that yet another thing is wrong with the car.

It's the air conditioning and although we have all the windows open and a draught is blowing through the open windows and out the back, Iona, who is not much good in the heat, is turning decidedly lobsterish. Just before the caves, and not a moment too soon as far as Iona is concerned, we stop to have a picnic and find a cool site in a wood. What a civilised country! Picnic tables and litterbins have been thoughtfully provided for our convenience and by the time we have finished, Iona has reverted to a more normal and paler shade of pink.

The caves are further up the mountain, but when we get there we are greeted by bad news. Apparently great minds think alike and a lot of people have had the same idea as us and it's going to be an hour and a half before we can get in. It's getting even hotter and I am basking in the heat, lapping up this complete contrast to what I would expect the weather to be like in Scotland at this moment, while Iona and the kids, despite being in the deepest shade they can find, are beginning to wilt.

There is not a great deal to do apart from visit a tacky gift shop whose wares we find eminently resistible. Time hangs heavy, the heat becomes increasingly oppressive, but at last it is our turn to go and we set off up a path towards the entrance. It must be a 20º incline and the kids and Iona are struggling in the heat, whilst I, carrying the camera and the bag with the jumpers (sweaters) because it is going to be cold in the caves, am beginning to sweat. Not half as much as I am about to though, because it soon becomes plain that the kids are not going to make it. I have to carry Hélène and Iona carries George plus the camera to lighten my load since Hélène seems to be made of solid lead.

We make it to the top and put our burdens down, only to discover that we must pick them up again to go through the caves if we are to keep up with the guide and negotiate the steps and stairs. At least it is not such warm work in the cool of the cavern, and though the steps are steep at times, there is the distraction of the stalactites and stalagmites, their wondrous weird shapes and the myriads of crystals twinkling in the artificial illumination. Sometimes we have to duck down very low and once we even have to slide down a chute. I recall the limestone caves we had visited in Lourdes five years ago and for my money this is better, even although it seems a bit like an assault course with, for good measure, a two-ton infant hanging round my neck.

Out again into the light of day and into the shimmering heat. We carry the kids to the car, all of us desperate for a drink, but although we have a cooler, courtesy of Marnie, we are still innocents when it comes to the business of travelling in the west in summer heat and have not any ice, trusting apparently to divine intervention to keep the contents of the cooler, cool, though had I not seen Al's cooler a third full of ice countless times and should have learned from his example?

Well, a cooler should cool, shouldn't it? Why else would it be called a cooler?

Although we have done all the carrying and most of the perspiring, it is the kids who devour most of the Coke kept lukewarm in the so-called "cooler". The car by now has been baking in the sun for almost three hours. With all the windows open and the warm air whipping our faces, we retrace our steps to the butt of the nation.

Never was there a place so well named. It is a copper-mining town and like all mining towns, the excavations are a bit of an eyesore. Copper has to come from somewhere, otherwise how would you get copper-bottomed anything, from boats to pans, never mind its metaphorical meaning, so it might as well come from the butt of the nation. Having said that, Butte seems particularly seedy. I consider myself very lucky indeed to have been placed in The Garden City, considering some of the places I could have been sent to.

I stop for gas, (I'm beginning to pick up the lingo) but when I go to pay, I encounter a problem. It is the first cheque I have written on the beautifully scenic cheques from the First Bank of Missoula. You can choose to have your cheques in a range of designs and we had chosen scenic views of the Rockies and mountain lakes so beautiful it seems almost like desecration to write on them.

"You got any photographic ID?" the attendant wants to know, though I was not to know it was really a rhetorical question and she was merely hinting that I should produce it and the quicker the better.

"Em... no."

"Like a driver's license?" she hints, helpfully.

I have, at home, I mean in Missoula, but in any case, even if I had brought it with me, it would not have been any use as it does not have a photograph. My passport has, but who would have thought that I would have needed it here in the middle of the American continent? Well actually, more left of centre than that.

"Don't matter anyhow," says the girl, having had time to study the cheque while I am doing my goldfish-gasping act at these unexpected questions. "I couldn't cash this."

"Why not?"

She sighs heavily as if explaining to a child who is rather slow on the uptake, "'Cos this cheque's from a Missoula bank."

"Yes, I know. I live there. What's the problem with that?" And thank God that I do instead of this hell hole I wanted to add, irritated by what appears to me to be the attendant's whimsical fastidiousness.

"I just told you," she sighs, even more heavily than before. "This cheque's from Missoula."

"So, what you are saying is that because this cheque is from a bank in Missoula, you can't accept it? Is that right?"

"Yep."

"But why not?" I keep my voice low and even but want to shout in exasperation. "What's wrong with cashing a cheque from Missoula?"

"Can't be done."

"What? Do you mean to tell me that my cheques are only good if they are cashed in Missoula?"

The girl looks relieved and nods. Thank God, the moron has finally got the message.

Shaking my head, I walk back to the car, hoping that Iona has enough money to pay. I tend not to carry any cash when she is with me as I never had enough money to consider it worthwhile investing in a wallet. Thankfully she has. What would have happened if she hadn't? The attendant would have had to call the cops. And then what would have happened? Would my accent have been enough to persuade them that it was a genuine mistake or would we, God forbid, have had to spend the night in the cells in the butt of the nation?

Wending our way home by the scenic Pintler Route, this unexpected turn of events has rendered us seriously short of cash. By the time we get to Anaconda, still with many, many miles before us before we get home, the kids let us know they are desperate for food and drink in that particular brain-piercing way they have that means you must either give in to their demands and the sooner the better or you will be driven insane. The warm Coke was finished long ago, and when I see the neon lights of a fast-food place in the distance, I think there must be angels lighting the way to heaven and bless and praise this country for the ubiquity of its fast-food industry and I pull in to what I imagine is going to be my saviour.

It's the sort of place where you don't lose any calories by getting out of the car to consume the calorie-laden food. Instead it comes to you.

Before we have time to count our cash, a face materialises at the car window. It is a waitress who wants to know what we want, and expects us to answer instantly, without the benefit of studying a menu, as if we had done this every day of our lives, at least since we were fifteen and able to drive. I am shocked into an automatic response and thankfully I remember what Al had ordered on our night out, and tailor it to our particular requirements.

"Em... four burgers and four chocolate milk shakes, please."

"I'll be right back!" she says cheerily and she is, with a tray which she clips to the door. George is maddened by the sight of the drink and holds out both chubby arms and makes gimme-that-drink-now-before-I-die-of-thirst sort of noises. His hair, as usual in these conditions, is plastered to his head with sweat. I let him have a milk shake so I can hear myself think. Hélène lets up a howl of protest. The only way to shut her up is to give her one of her own too.

In the sudden, blessed, silence, I study the bill whilst Iona rakes in her purse for the money. There must be some mistake! These are not like Missoula prices. But then Anaconda is no Missoula either, just a two-horse town stuck between the metropolises of Butte and Missoula, where there is little or no competition to drive prices down.

"How much have we got?" I ask, trying to quell a rising tide of panic.

It's as I feared. We have not enough. The waitress is waiting, not so patiently now, for payment. It's not just the food that is expected to be fast.

"Em. I'm afraid we don't seem to have enough money." Somehow I manage to get the words out because my throat has suddenly gone drier than ever.

The waitress says nothing. She's probably a high school kid and has not met a situation like this before. As for me, this confusion and embarrassment does nothing to help my mental arithmetic, a skill which I freely admit I am severely lacking in at the best of times.

"Em... let me see... " I study the tab as I try to work out what we can afford and what we'll have to send back. For a start, we will have to pay for two milk shakes which George and Hélène will have probably entirely demolished by now.

"Em... if you take back these two milk shakes and one of the burgers, I think you'll find that this will be enough."

I smile apologetically as I take three burgers from the tray and pour a cascade of coins on it in their place. It sounds a lot, as if one of those one-armed bandits was coughing up its guts, but actually it is in such small denominations, made up of quarters, dimes and cents, it is going to take the waitress a lot of time to count it all, before she is sweetened up by the discovery that, impecunious though I appear to be, not only have I paid in full, but included the customary 10% tip, if not more, if my calculations are to be trusted.

Apparently our waitress does trust me. Saying nothing and without counting the money, she unhooks the tray. She'll have been trained to treat all customers with respect, however crazy they may seem, but her parting look leaves me in no doubt that that is what she thinks I am. Once the tray has been removed, I consider us out of bondage and gun the car out of there as fast as I can.

I've lost all feelings of hunger and the kids have indeed practically finished their milkshakes, so my throat will just have to stay like sandpaper till we get home and I can have a Bud. Anyway, George's grip round his drink is like an anaconda's, appropriately enough, and if I wrested it from him, just for a sip, he would get his revenge on my superior strength by using the superior sound of his lungs.

It is 9.30 and dark by the time we get back. Had we not had to wait that 90 minutes to get into the caves, we would have been back in daylight and long before the kids' stomachs thought their throats were cut. But after they have been bathed and put to bed, and I have jugged a Bud, and thus refreshed and revived, I reflect that despite the little hiatuses we had encountered, it had been a successful day overall. It showed us we could cover vast distances quite easily as long as we were prepared for it, which boded well for our lengthy travelling plans in the summer. And it was just as well that we had discovered our cheques didn't work outside Missoula.

But the very next day was to show that apart from that, we hadn't learned a thing.

Chapter Twenty-five

In which we undertake a second expedition and I host a surprise party.

The National Bison Range is a mere 40 miles up the road and after yesterday's trek, this seems a trifling amount, so in the morning we laze about in the sunshine and I watch the grass grow even longer in the yard and try not to think about what I *should* be thinking about – what I'm going to do with the students in two days' time – and in the afternoon, we head off for the Range to see the buffalo roam.

Like all the best things in life, it is free. There is a compound near the entrance where some bison have been penned in. Seeing us, one fellow comes over and rolls in the dust just in front of us as if he's inviting us to come and tickle his tummy. He looks as if he has thrown a matted and flea-ridden blanket over his massive shoulders. It is my first ever real-life bison and it's great to see him at such close range. He looks at us with tiny little eyes in a head which seems disproportionately huge and I shoot him with nothing more harmful that my camera.

Because others, but most notoriously, Buffalo Bill, (though he should really have been know as Bison Bill) were not so discriminating in their choice of weapon, this is why the National Bison Range had to be created, to restock the population after the massacres of the Indian Wars of the 19th century had driven them to the point of extinction, a policy calculated to do the same to the Indians by starving them to death.

The trail through the range is 19 miles long and since it is not tarred, we are stirring up a dust storm behind us. Pretty soon the car is covered in a layer of dust, so the original colour is only barely discernible beneath. It's another sweltering day, so the widows are wide open which means we are soon covered in a film of dust ourselves. The kids are finding it hot in the back without the air conditioning and the dust is mingling with the sweat that is pouring in rivulets down their faces. George has rubbed his face with his grimy hands and could easily be mistaken for an orphan urchin from the back streets of Naples.

We stop on the crest of a hill to admire the distant snow-covered Mission Range whose jagged peaks are sawing a rent in the cloudless blue sky. It's good to get out of the car, but George is girning. He's thirsty, and despite our experience of yesterday, we have not brought any drinks with us. Who needs drinks for a mere 40 miles?

"Would she like some pop?" The speaker is an elderly woman who has also been admiring the view.

"Well, thanks very much, that's very kind of you." It seems churlish to point out that she has the wrong gender, and anyway George doesn't care. He has the can in both hands and is draining it for all he is worth. He sets up a howl of protest when Iona wrests it off him to let Hélène have a slug. But once he's got it back and glugged it dry, he's no longer girning. We really must carry drinks and a cooler full of ice in future, especially since the air conditioning is not working.

Meanwhile I get talking to our benefactress who wants to know what someone with an accent like mine is doing in deepest, darkest Montana. Her granddaughter is with her and it turns out that she is going to be in Art's class. Further conversation reveals she is a Mormon and when I tell her that I'm interested in genealogy, she invites me to her church and says she'll show me how to access their records. If all my parents are going to be as friendly as this girl's grandmother, I am going to have nothing to fear.

Further along the drive, we see some elk and deer and I pick up a baseball hat which must have blown off someone's head. Now I can look a proper American!

When we get back to Lincoln, Hélène makes a beeline for the Hertz household. She's wearing a bikini only and Terri tells her how cute she is. But we have clearly walked into some sort of family row. The air is thick with tension. Al is waving a piece of paper about and doesn't seem to be aware of our presence, or doesn't care.

"$900!" he is shouting. "900 goddamn dollars! That goddamn Cassie!"

I notice it is a bit quieter in the house when Al has stopped his ranting, and the silence has crept softly back on tiptoe. That's partly because there is no sign of Cain raising blue murder with Abel, his brother, nor is their mother languishing on the sofa as she usually is, not that she contributes anything to the degree of decibels in the house. Has she been thrown out? More probably she has just gone to join her husband who has come back on furlough. From where and what I wasn't told and didn't ask. I had met him briefly however.

When I was a teenager, I watched, I have to admit, a kid's cartoon series on TV called *Top Cat* who was known to his friends as *TC*. Like him, Cassie's husband is known by his initials too but in his case by the less fortuitous combination of

"W" and "C". Tall and lean, he had long hair and an earring which gave him a distinctly hippy-like appearance. One thing for sure, he was not on leave from the armed forces.

"Goddamn hangers on!" Al is off again. Terri doesn't seem to be affected one way or the other; she is making a fuss of the children. "An' what the hell is that Ben doin' here? He practically lives here, goddamn it!" Ben is Debbie's pale and vapid boyfriend who works down the sewers. "This whole goddamn family thinks when I have a shit, silver dollars drop out my ass!"

Al's bank statement is not making pleasant reading apparently. I wonder if Terri had seen the statement first and advised Cassie it was time she moved back home to Seattle before the you-know-what-hit the fan. I have no idea how long she and her brood had been staying here before our arrival.

Still muttering at his misfortunes, Al says I'm to have a drink and pours us some whisky. Because he is wearing shorts, I can't help but notice, to my fascination, that on the calf of one leg, he has a tattoo of a half-naked woman. Could Terri have modelled for this? Was this what she was like when they first met? Was this a symbol of his undying love?

"What d'ya want Eeona?"

As usual, Iona demurs and says she'll just have a soft drink.

"Aw, c'mon Eeona, you gotta have a proper drink!"

He is finding Iona a severe trial. Unable to tempt her with anything alcoholic, finally the long-suffering Al suggests she has a raspberry juice and anisette and steps back to watch her reaction. Could it be that he has finally hit upon something that she does like?

"Aaargh! That's foul!" Iona cannot contain her displeasure. Politeness and decorum go out the window as she rushes to the sink and spits it out. "Something to take away the taste! Quick!" she gasps.

As on the previous occasion when this happened, Al is powerless to act so I pour her some raspberry juice and I park the one with the anisette next to my whisky so it won't be wasted, though I wouldn't have drunk it by choice. I think I'll need at least one other whisky to get rid of taste.

"Well, goddamnit!" says Al, practically at a loss for words. "Ain't there *any* drink you like, Eeona?"

"No, I don't think so."

Al's moustache quivers in disbelief. He slowly shakes his head as if he can't believe what he has just seen and heard, before turning a bemused look at me which I interpret as: "How come you married a broad like this?"

Terri apologises for not having seen us for a while, though it has only been a week. We tell them all that we have been doing and after that we are pressed to stay for a meal. Al rustles up a steak and the kids have baked potatoes. Iona's anisette drink is finished and so is the whisky after that and that turns out to be the end of the whisky altogether. The cupboard is bare and Al is not amused.

"Where's the rest of that goddamned whisky?" he wants to know.

Terri shrugs like she hasn't a clue what happened to it and doesn't care. Nothing seems to worry her.

"Did that goddamned Cassie take it?"

No answer.

"I bet she took it! Goddamnit!" Al grits his teeth in rage. Coming on top of the bank statement, he is not having a good day and when your friends are not having a good day, there is only one thing you can do.

"Why don't you come on over to us and we can finish the Dewar's?"

I am not looking in Iona's direction, just in case her look kills me. But after all, we had enjoyed their hospitality so often in the past, to say nothing of the meal we have just had, how could I not refuse my friend in his hour of need?

So while Iona gets the kids ready for bed, I ply Al with the rapidly shrinking Dewar's. Then, without any announcement, in walks Terri and Grandpa, plus the woman who lives on the other side of the Hertz house from us. She is introduced to me as Dolly.

"Well, hello, Dolly" I quip, the whisky having made me exceedingly witty, and covering up, I hope, my surprise at seeing her, not to mention Grandpa. I wasn't expecting a party. Thank God I had got rid of the Brown Derby and had replaced it with some Budweiser, though not in party quantities.

Dolly is leaving Missoula so she has been celebrating or rather drowning her sorrows. She seems more sad than glad to be leaving.

Maybe Dolly's gloom is rubbing off on us because Terri suggests it would be a good idea to light a fire, not because it is cold, but because it would cheer the place up. She's right of course. We're in the room with the Viking chair and the rat's jaw and *Yoke on the Wall* and all the other junk, so it's gloomy all right. Mind you, it's no wonder Terri is feeling rather chilly. She is wobbling out of a black shirt with a plunging neckline while on her other side, a pair of globes are peeking out from a pair of tight navy shorts. It's a long time since Terri had the figure for such garments, since she looked like the tattoo on Al's leg (if it is her) and which just goes to show how the mighty have fallen.

Al seems to have got over his earlier bad mood. Indeed he is getting more convivial by the minute but whether it is due to the Dewar's or the treasures Terri is putting on display or a combination of both, I couldn't say for sure, but anyway, he tries to grope her and makes lewd comments at which Terri laughs coquettishly and pushes him off. Grandpa sits nursing a whisky and looks sad. Is he wondering if Al really is his son, or is he thinking of his dear, departed wife, or is he thinking of something quite different, years in the past?

Iona is not really a party person and I can see her glowering at Al, with his tattoo and his moustache (she can't stand moustaches) and his raucous laughter and his hand on Terri's bum whenever he gets the chance and I can tell he is not her favourite person, especially since he seems to want to poison her every time he sees her. I know she's mad at me for inviting him in the first place and now we are ending up with half the neighbourhood getting drunk on my whisky. It doesn't look good for me when they decide to go, whenever that is, and the longer they stay will be in direct proportion to the depth of the trouble I'll find myself in.

Since he seems a bit out of it, not to say as depressed as Dolly, I ask Grandpa if he'd like to have a look at the light in the kitchen. We're still operating with the Anglepoise lamp which he had fixed. While he does that, Al and I get some logs from where they are stacked in the basement. Actually, they are made of compressed sawdust which maybe explains why Terri has such a hard job getting them to light. Grandpa juggles his whisky and the light switch, which to my alarm, showers him with sparks but which doesn't seem to bother him in the slightest. I'm afraid he has had too much whisky to know what he's doing but maybe he wants to join his dear departed in heaven and doesn't care. If that's the case, I wish he wouldn't do it here: "Old man electrocuted in house from Psycho" I can just see the *Missoulian* headlines screaming tomorrow.

A bit of a meagre flame is going at last when the door opens again to admit what appear to be Beauty and the Beast. If there is any truth in the saying opposites attract, then surely this must be it. She is small and petite, whilst he is huge and fat as if he carries all the beer in Missoula around in his belly. He looks a lot older than her and tattoos spiral their way through the undergrowth of his meaty forearms. Like WC, he sports an earring. It wouldn't surprise me in the least if he had a big chromium steed with wide-apart handles and maybe three wheels. To be honest, I find him a bit of a scary character, especially the way he just walked in unannounced. And he looks in a bit of an ugly mood.

He has come to dig Dolly out, mad at her because she is over here, drinking, enjoying herself while he does all the work. In fact, he points out, she has been doing nothing *but* drinking all day; he's fed up of doing all the packing; she's the one that's leaving, not him "for Chris' sake."

He is, however mollified when I offer him a whisky and once I get speaking to him, he doesn't seem nearly so intimidating and actually appears quite friendly, the sort of friend that you would like on your side if someone told you they were going to rip your arms and legs off and eat your liver for breakfast.

He volunteers the information that he lives with Beauty some sixty miles from here in a cabin in the woods with no running water, toilets or other basic facilities. I have to admit that this revelation doesn't altogether surprise me.

He looks like a Hippy if ever I saw one, and I never have till now, unless you count WC. And the reason for Dolly's despondency becomes apparent when he tells me that the deal she had made to buy her new house had fallen through and she was going to be staying with them.

At last Dolly drains her glass and gets unsteadily to her feet. "It's been real neat meetin' you," she says and with that takes her leave escorted by the Beast and Beauty. She looks rather like someone being put under arrest.

There's not much of a party atmosphere now, but the flames, bright now, do lighten our dim and dark living room, even if they do not succeed in lightening our mood very much.

"We're gonna go loggin' tomorrow, Dave. You oughta come and get some logs for this here fire. Keep you goin' through the winter." He breaks off to yell at Grandpa who is still occupied with the light switch. "Ain't that right, Pops? We gonna go loggin' tomorrow."

The old man hasn't heard. Al sighs and shakes his head like he did when Iona admitted she didn't care too much for alcohol. "Geeez," he says and raises his voice a dozen more decibels. It is a severe trial being surrounded by pathetic people like this. "We're gonna go loggin' tomorrow!"

Grandpa nods but doesn't say anything. I've a feeling he still hasn't heard. Or maybe he thinks Al has said: "Is it true I am adopted?" and doesn't want to answer the question. In any case, his face has an ineffable sadness about it as he wrestles with the switch.

"Yeah," Al goes on. "We got an old Ford tractor engine an' we run a saw off of that and saw those logs up good. Come round at nine tomorrow."

Chapter Twenty-six

In which I find out the meaning of hard work before I even begin it properly.

We take BIG Al, now out of hospital, to Grandpa's where we hitch up the trailer but we have to come all the way back to Lincoln as Al has spotted my footwear.

"Aw, geez, Dave, those ain't no good. Ain't you got no other footwear?"

My sandals are the first indication that the day is not going to be a restful one.

We take the highway to Lolo and after a few miles, turn off onto a forest track. It seems we drive for miles, climbing steadily through densely forested hillside until, without warning, we arrive in a clearing. The view is breathtaking. As far as the eye can see, on every side, there is the lush green of the forest. There must be millions of trees spread out below us and pointed peaks with a topping of snow poke their heads above the seemingly impenetrable carpet of green. What a fiendishly difficult but beautiful jigsaw it would make!

Our clearing is due to fire damage. Pines, stripped of all foliage and most of their branches, point forlornly at the sky. In between, others are lying on their sides where they have collapsed or have been felled by the forestry workers. Al tells me that this was a lightning fire, that it happens from time to time and that anyone can take as much wood as they want for free. Piles of trunks, blackened by the fire, are piled up by the side of the track and it is these that we have come to salvage.

First Al ties a chain round as many trunks as he can which means climbing the log pile, passing the chain round some charred trunks and then passing the other end somehow through any chinks between them. Once this is done, Al hitches the end of the chain to the tow bar of the truck and pulls the whole lot out onto the track. This creates an avalanche of falling logs and a whirlwind of black dust. The chain is untied and Al gets out the chainsaw and begins to cut the trunks up into eight-foot lengths. It is my job and Grandpa's to put these logs in the back of the truck. These logs are a good bit thicker than my thighs and at eight-foot long, not lightweight.

As the pile builds up in the back of the truck, we have to lift these logs higher and higher and my heart sinks when Al puts iron stanchions into slots in the side of the truck, so we can pile the logs up and up. I am stronger than Grandpa and if I am soon wishing I had never been born, God knows how Grandpa is feeling and no wonder he was looking glum yesterday. Now it is taking the two of us together to lift the logs up into the truck while Al saws on and on, giving us no respite. The sun doesn't make it any easier, beating us to death out of a cloudless sky. I would have sweated anyway, but thanks to this heat I am perspiring freely and I hope to God Grandpa isn't going to have a heart attack.

Eventually Al has to suspend his cutting and help us lift the logs onto the truck as it must be ten feet high by now. Then it is time to chain up the next batch of logs which I foolishly volunteer to do. Leaping like a gazelle onto the first log, I climb the pile only to slip and graze my arm on the rough bark even through my shirt. It hurts like hell and blood wells to the surface and mingles with the sweat and the soot. I curse and think that if I don't get blood poisoning, then it will be a miracle.

I think a miracle may have happened when the chain saw won't start again. Wouldn't it be a shame if we had to give up and go home! Seems to me that we have quite enough logs anyway to last all winter. But after a few curses from Al, the saw, intimidated, finally growls into life and soon the air is rent with its whine as it chews through the wood and spews out sawdust. It is a procedure which is repeated several times, each breakdown giving me fresh hope that it is broken for good, only to be dashed as after a good few "goddamns" from Al, it bursts into life again.

Now, however, it has been silenced deliberately because it is lunchtime and I take advantage of this rest to get some sunshine on my body. Sunshine in September in Scotland is as rare as hens' teeth and when it does happen it is definitely never this hot. Not even at the height of summer does it get this hot. Not withstanding my labours, reason enough to make me feel hot anyway, I reckon the external temperature must be at least in the mid-eighties. Al agrees.

I bless the foresight I had to grab a six-pack of beer from the Grizzly Grocery convenience store before I went over to Al's. This I did since I had consumed so many of his brews in the past, although it felt a bit like carrying coals to Newcastle, or more fittingly here, trees to the forest. And just as well I did, for to my amazement, it turns out Al is travelling beerless for once. I, however, have learned that you never travel anywhere in Montana without something to drink, just as you wouldn't if you were crossing the Sahara.

The cooler, which would normally have resided in the back of the truck, could not of course, occupy that space today and there being no room in the inside, this is what has given rise to the present drought. When you bear in mind that Al must have known that our labours would be thirsty work, it is all the more astonishing that he chose not to bring any at all, not even a six-pack. He must think that unless a beer is ice-cold it is not worth drinking at all. That's because the only beers he knows are lager beers, not ales and dark beers that need to be drunk at room temperature. But far be it from me to teach Al anything about beer or alcohol in general.

It is by no means as cold as it should be – not too surprising after all, since although I had picked it up ready to drink out of the chiller cabinet, (that itself another of the little culture shocks I was being gradually acclimatized to) it had been baked in the truck for four hours, but from my point of view at least, was still cool enough and at least wet enough, to wash the black dust down my throat.

Our sandwiches are black too, where we have touched them. This is as close I am going to get to being a miner I reflect, here in these wide-open, tree-clad spaces, with the sun beaming fit to burst and now that the chainsaw has stopped, the silence has crept back, apart from the sounds of the birds celebrating another splendid sunny day. It's all right for them: they can afford to be happy – they don't have to lump bloody big logs about. When I contemplate the trailer and the amount of wood that it can hold, double or even treble the amount the truck can take, I feel like telling Al that I am just going into the forest for a pee and in view of the beer I have drunk, like Titus Oates, I may be some time. I should imagine you could hide in this forest and never be found again, even if you wanted to be.

When, after lunch, the slave master curses the chainsaw into life again, I reckon I am so black and scratched anyway, I may as well work with my shirt off. May as well get a tan, if the sun can penetrate the black dust, which should be good protection from the UV rays and, besides, living in Scotland, I reckon I have got a lot of UV rays to catch up on.

I trust my hair won't be so contaminated as I am wearing the baseball cap I found at the Bison Range. My Levis, (from K-Mart, naturally) are filthy where I have been letting my thighs take the weight off the logs before I hoisted them into the truck, and I hope that my lungs don't look that colour, though I don't see why they should escape this all-pervading blackness. I reckon this logging expedition, whatever it does for my winter warmth, is seriously bad for my health, although it might be many years from now before it finally takes its toll, when the words on my death certificate bear the mortal words: *Death by carbon inhalation.*

At last it is all over. Both the truck and the trailer are piled high with eight-foot lengths of blackened logs. There is not room for a single extra log. I can't believe that Al would ever burn all that wood in a winter, but he says we'll need to make another four or five trips. If I could bottle the heat I've expended today, I wouldn't need any fire and although a log fire would be nice, I seriously wonder if all the effort is worth it. And this is before we get back to Lincoln! We still have to saw the logs up into fire-width pieces, but that can't be so bad as what we have just done, can it?

Yes it certainly can because all that wood has to be unloaded, one by one, and fed into the circular saw run by the old tractor engine that Al was talking about. Eight-foot lengths have to be reduced to one-foot lengths and once that is done, they all have to be stacked in a neat pile along Al's garage. The circular saw makes quick work of the logs. It is

Al's job to feed it and although I wouldn't mind betting he has twice the strength of both of us put together, it's Grandpa and I who have to bring the logs to the saw as well as picking up the fallen pieces and then carrying them and stacking them until I think my back is going to break.

There is something else wrong with my back. I can't see, but it feels red hot and I know that it is red from sunburn. Apart from that self-inflicted injury, Grandpa, the little of his little strength remaining, accidentally drops a log on my foot which causes Al a great deal of merriment as I leap about cursing. It continues to throb as the stack mounts higher and higher but it does serve the purpose of transferring the awareness of pain from my back to my foot. Fundamentally, that's about all that could be said in favour of it.

For once I do not stay and have a booze-up with Al, (although naturally we had one or two beers to slake our thirst as we toiled with the wood) but I make my excuses, firstly because I am far too filthy, and secondly, I am totally shattered.

Back home, I have to have a lukewarm shower because my back is so sunburnt and as I watch the black water gurgle down the drain, I think I have never worked so hard in my life before, nor has my back ever been so sore, not even when I picked potatoes as a boy.

Work! I have been so busy I have not had time to think about tomorrow. This has been Labor Day weekend in more ways than one. It has also marked the end of the holidays. Tomorrow is the first day of school with the students, and I haven't a clue what I'm going to do with them.

Thanks to Al I hadn't been worrying about that all day. But I don't think I'm exactly in peak condition to meet whatever tomorrow is going to bring either.

Chapter Twenty-seven

In which I meet my classes for the first time.

I get to school by 8.15, thinking that is tons in time for a 9 o'clock start.

"Well, *hello*, Mr A," says Steve.

"So you finally made it, huh?" says Blake.

I am astonished two times over. What time am I meant to get there, for heaven's sake? I've never been so early for anything in my life and here they are telling me I am late and although they don't say so, twice as well-dressed as them. Both are wearing slacks and short-sleeved shirts open at the neck. I am wearing my normal working clothes – a suit and tie. I feel conspicuously overdressed as well as under-prepared. Nat is busy writing his cabalistic signs on the blackboard, but he is new to this school and needs to initiate his students. Steve and Blake, like me, don't seem to have anything much to do. So why did they arrive so early? They've done it all before, but for all that, look like greyhounds eager to be let out of the traps. Maybe they hope some students will turn up early and they can start teaching. I have to remind myself that this is mid-September and they haven't seen a student in a professional sense since early June. No wonder they have withdrawal symptoms.

I skulk off to my room feeling desperately alone and despite the proximity of my colleagues, terribly isolated. What am I going to do? I am going to meet my students in half an hour or less. It would be far better if they came in now as thirty minutes is not going to make any difference to me except it would reduce my torture. There is nothing I can do but sit and wait.

They come straggling in, dressed as if they had already gone home and changed into their leisure wear. Most of them are in jeans, which would mean being sent home right away if they appeared like this in Abbotsgrange. They wear some sort of baseball or football top (American football, naturally) to complement this, which in Scotland is an even greater crime than the jeans since it can inflame sectarian passions if the top belongs to either Rangers or Celtic. The girls are dressed precisely the same, except you can tell the difference because some of them have a gap in the middle so you can see their belly button, while all the boys, without exception, have theirs covered up as their shirts are worn outside their jeans. They don't have schoolbags; they just carry their stationery. Textbooks are provided but stationery isn't. I like this idea. In fact, I would also make them buy their textbooks if I had my way, then perhaps they might take better care of them.

They seem to be a friendly enough bunch, if a bit noisy. Some even say "Hi!" like I am one of *them*. Some of them are chewing gum. That will have to stop. I don't know what the school rules are, but there is one rule in my class and that is that they don't chew gum. I can't bear the sight of the jaws endlessly moving like cows chewing cud and the mess under the desks and the mess on the streets where they spit it out if it doesn't stick to the soles of your shoes first. I'd ban it from the planet if I could, never mind my room.

So they are settled and are waiting for me to start. Educate me, or even better, from their point of view, entertain me. That's a good sign as with some classes that is the hardest thing to do of all: to get them to stop talking to each other and listen. No doubt I am benefiting from a certain novelty and curiosity value.

I begin by writing my name on the board and show them on the map of Scotland I had pinned up where I come from as well as pointing out some other geographical details. That takes about two minutes. I've still got the best part of an hour to go. At least no-one has laughed at my accent, but no-one has any questions and I prefer to think they are still weighing me up rather than completely disinterested. Art has told me that I come with a reputation as Mr Strict. They expect this, not from any personal information which has preceded me, but because I come from Scotland. This is no bad thing. I may as well cash in.

I tell them my class rules, of the sort of behaviour I expect, like not shouting out and putting their hand up if they want to speak and not eating gum or anything else. They are starting to look a little anxious now, turning round to look at their neighbours as if to say: "Who is this jerk? So it's true what they say about Scottish teachers. Boy, are we in for a tough time from this meanie!"

I start off with a timid-looking blonde in the front row, offering her the wastepaper bin to spit her gum in. She doesn't let me down: she spits, and so do the rest, or some of the rest. I know there will be some who have concealed it, but I'll be on the lookout for masticating mandibles. And if they tell me it helps them concentrate, I'll tell them to concentrate on what I've just said.

"Now that your mouths are empty," I tell them, "I'll be able to make out what you say. We've got to get to know each other, so tell me about yourself – names, hobbies, family details, like if you are married and so on."

They look at me unblinkingly. The joke has fallen flat. Perhaps they hadn't understood it because they couldn't understand my accent or, more likely it wasn't very funny in the first place. Too late, it occurs to me that possibly most of their parents are not even married – at least not to each other any more.

"All right," I say, "I'll begin. I'll tell you something about me, to show you the sort of thing I have in mind." They listen, politely enough. "Any questions?" I say hopefully, when I've finished.

No-one says a thing and all studiously avoid eye contact with me, though they are shooting nervous glances at each other. Aren't American kids meant to be much less inhibited than Scottish kids? Since there are no volunteers, I'm going to have to volunteer someone. It's not fair to pick on the fair one again, so I pick on someone who looks as if he will do it without demur. Fortunately he does. He doesn't say much and when the others see that it's not such an ordeal and I ask who'd like to be next, hallelujah, there is a proper volunteer and then we are off. But with only eighteen kids in the room, this is not going to take very long – and it doesn't.

"All right," I say, "that wasn't so bad was it? Now you are a little less nervous, maybe now there are some questions you'd like to ask, either about Scotland or me, so fire away."

To my relief, a fair-haired boy at the back raises his hand.

"Yes?"

"Do you know my ancestor, Lord Sample?"

Is this a wind-up? It doesn't sound too likely a name to me, more like a test or trick question. On the other hand, the boy looks innocent enough and he is not looking around at his peers for approval. So does he really have a relative who is a peer? Is this a sample of the sort of subtle indiscipline I might have to watch out for?

"Are you sure that that is the right name? I mean, it wouldn't be Semple, by any chance would it?"

He doesn't know, but he doesn't think so. And he can't give me any more clues, but I know I don't know him anyway. I have tended not to mingle with any of the aristocracy. The accident of their birth doesn't necessarily make them bad people, it's just a bit harder for them to be a member of the human race and I tend to sympathise with them, if anything. If my erstwhile student had been trying to wind me up, it hadn't worked as no-one in the class is tittering or even smiling. I conclude he must have asked the question in total innocence, though God knows how he thought he was distantly connected to a member of the British aristocracy, I have as much idea as he has.

No-one else seems to be able to think of anything else to ask at the moment, so I tell them to get out their pencils and think of some questions and write them down. While they are doing that, I watch the clock on the wall and think about what I am *really* going to do with them. But writing, or thinking, or doing both together, seems to be incredibly taxing for them and it's a great relief to us all when the big hand on the clock finally creeps round to the time when they can be released from their labours.

Before lunch I have the other classes but for only thirty minutes which is a whole lot easier to spin out. By the time I have introduced myself and told them the class rules, it is practically time to move on to the next lot. They seem all right, if a bit informal and don't seem to be in awe of me at all. They seem to take me in their stride as if they are used to having a teacher from a foreign land every day of the week.

But of course, I have been exposed to this sort of thing already at the Hertz household.

One thing that does irritate me is when they don't understand something, they say "Huh?" in a tone of voice which suggests I am some sort of snail with a particularly low IQ but I don't challenge them like I would have done in Scotland as I reckon they don't mean to be impertinent; it is just the way they are, part of this more informal culture that I had been warned about. Nevertheless, it's still a bit of a shock and I can already see it's going to take some getting used to.

After lunch, my homeroom is privileged to experience some foreign culture. I recite what is probably the premiere in Missoula, if not Montana, of *Tam O' Shanter*. Not, I tell myself, because it is long and will take up some time but because, as I tell them, it is probably our national poet's best-known poem. And maybe I am kidding myself, but it seems to me that they understand the gist of it, especially after I have explained it to them. Anyway, nobody piped up and said what a load of rubbish it was, like they would do in Scotland, but perhaps they were just bemused into a trance by the strange-sounding words. After that, I give them a spelling test from the book I don't like the look of and feel that if Matt were to walk in now, he would see me doing something he would approve of and what I am supposed to be doing.

After that, Blake and I take them down to what I would call the hall, (really a multipurpose room that serves as gym, music room and dining hall) for my first PE lesson, the aforementioned scatterball, which basically consists of throwing a basketball at each other as hard as they can or trying to dodge it. By way of a change, they play pinball. I don't see what difference there is actually, except that in pinball, they place two pins, actually two pyramids of wood about three feet high, on the floor. The object of the game is supposedly to knock the opposing team's pin over, but they don't give two pins for that: they still throw the ball at each other, pretending they were aiming for the pin.

They all seem to enjoy it and it does make them run around, hopefully making some, at least, a little less-fat Americans. They still wear the same clothes as they did for English, however. There is no such thing as changing into PE kit, so that solves the problem at a stroke, the problem that plagues PE teachers everywhere in Scotland, the perennial excuse of the reluctant exerciser: "I forgot my kit". There is no attempt to treat this like a serious subject worthy of a place in the curriculum like Math and English; it's just a run around for the kids, but for Blake and me, there's nothing much to do but sit on the bleachers and watch. It's quite easy being a PE teacher really.

Finally the bell goes for the end of the day and they pile into long yellow buses and are whisked away, some even wishing me farewell and saying they will see me tomorrow, as if it were some sort of social occasion.

I now know for certain that I am in a strange land where they do things differently. Such informality would never happen in a Scottish school. I am left to ponder on the gulf that exists between teacher and pupil in Scotland and the little or no distance that exists between the students and the teachers here. My training, in fact, had instilled the notion that this divide must be maintained at all costs: become too friendly with your pupils and discipline first, and then learning goes out the window.

It seems to me that the opposite prevails here – these kids imagine themselves to be the equal of their teachers, despite their lack of knowledge and years, showing no deference, no hint of shyness, even a certain cockiness. Having said that, they look like nice, friendly kids. I mustn't of course allow them to overstep the mark, and once I've sorted out what I'm meant to be doing, I think I'm going to enjoy it here.

And so, with a certain amount of relief, thus endeth the first day at school. Tomorrow is another day and I can't do the same again...

Chapter Twenty-eight

In which I get some views from the Other Side, foresee an alternative mode of transport, Iona meets a friend and I see a solution to my problems at school.

Next day, Art brings me a letter from Marnie which he lets me read and which I do with difficulty. I find myself described as a "sensitive, imaginative, beautiful person". "To see oursel's as ithers see us" Burns wrote in *To a Louse,* but his purpose was to prevent us from becoming too vain and this is in danger of turning me the other way. So this is what I'm really like is it? I had absolutely no idea! And neither, I bet, does Iona. But then she has had the benefit of knowing me for longer.

Iona, however, is "not really a person at all". This is going to go down well when I pass it on and I also wonder what possessed Art to let me read this letter with this kind of comment in it. Perhaps he hadn't noticed it or perhaps he'd forgotten or even worse, hadn't realised it was an insult. Marnie continues that Iona is "more interested in becoming a wife and a mother than a person". And there you have it! No wonder they have all these divorces! It seems being a wife and mother is just about the worst thing you can be, a sort of pariah with a stunted personality. Instead of staying at home looking after your kids, you should be out there being somebody or something. That seems to be the American way.

Also to my surprise, they seem to be settling in well. Not a word about the shock it must have been to come to such a small house, what it was like living on top of each other. Or perhaps that was in an earlier letter. As for school, in one not noted for the good manners of the majority of its pupils, I am amazed to read that Marnie thinks the kids are "so polite". Well, maybe she would, I reflect, because on my second day, I am finding them the complete opposite and it's beginning to annoy me the way they are constantly getting up to sharpen pencils or go to the toilet and want to have an explanation for everything I ask them to, instead of just doing it. She is also astounded that the kids can write 200 – 300 words without blinking an eye and thinks they work really hard.

She can't get used to there not being a clock in the room. Of course you don't need one there because a bell announces the end of the period, but here you have to keep an eye on the clock so you can send them on to their next class in time. There are also no breaks and that is why they are allowed to go to the toilet whenever they want, though they are encouraged to obey the call of nature between 10 and 10.30. Another thing is they are allowed to phone home whenever they want. There is a rectangular block of wood with the shape of a phone carved on it that they take to the phone at the end of the hall to show they have the teacher's permission. Of course the call is free, being a local one, but I can see that this could be a possible source of friction when some kid decides to phone home, for example, when I am in the middle of a fascinating and riveting lesson on English grammar.

Today I stay at school for lunch. You don't get very much but at least it's free. I don't care to eat much at lunchtime anyway as it makes me sleepy. I can have a free lunch every day if I want, as long as I supervise the kids during their lunch hour, not just during lunch. It seems there are two free lunches every day and I can always have a free one as the other teachers bring their lunches in paper bags which they call sacks. It amuses me how the American word for the same thing as ours is always so much bigger; just as "bags" become "sacks", "stones" become "rocks", "pupils" become "students" but curiously, when they go to university, they go to "school".

What I think is a good idea is that the students are issued with a meal planner for not just the week, but the month. The idea is that mothers can avoid duplication at home but a side effect is it stops students becoming inattentive as lunchtime draws near, wondering what's on the menu. Instead they can anticipate their "sloppy joes" or "burritos", culinary delights which I also look forward to becoming acquainted with in the near future.

After lunch, Blake, Steve and I take the kids to a nearby public park where they play American football. It seems a stupid sort of game to me, always stopping to discuss tactics for the next "play" they are going to make. None of the end-to-end play that you get in proper football, but a bit of action for about 15 seconds if you are lucky, then they stop, have a discussion, regroup, then there is a bit more action again, and so it goes on. It seems boring and tedious to me in the extreme, but then I don't have the faintest clue what is meant to be going on, though it has been explained to me.

"What *are* they talking about?" I ask as the players go into yet another huddle.

"Well, you see, Dave," says Blake, his face poker-straight. "That's when they tell jokes."

I could well believe it. You'd have to do *something* to make this game more interesting, somehow.

* * *

That evening Perry phones, apologising for not having been in touch due to pressure of work and asks how I am finding school. When I say that I think the students are a bit too familiar, impertinent even and they give up a bit too easily, he roars with laughter.

"Too damn right, Dave!" he says. "They are and they do!"

I tell him I've seen an old bike in the basement where Norman Bates keeps his mother and I wonder if it would be OK to use it as that would mean Iona would have the use of the car during the day when I am at school and if I cycled to school, instead of walking, I would not have to get up so early. Also, Iona could find the car useful as we have had a package from The Welcome Wagon, an organisation composed of all sorts of businesses who give discounts and freebees to newcomers – such as free hamburgers, coffees, cakes and so on. The kids even get something on their birthdays from some toyshop or other! What an amazing town!

Anyway, today there was a coffee morning for newcomers which is why Iona needed the car and I needed to get up even earlier than usual. This coffee morning, which was held in someone's house, was attended by so many people that Iona thought to begin with it must be a proper café, or "regular" café, as they say here. There she had met a person whom she rather took to. Carolyn Snively by name, her husband, John, is setting up a dental practice. They used to live in Lame Deer which is a long way to the east and on a reservation too, the lucky people. Iona thinks that the thing that drew them to each other was that they were the only women in the gathering who were wearing skirts and somehow, they just seemed to gravitate to each other. It is good that Iona has found a friend and it's good for me too, because it will enlarge our circle of friends and acquaintants outside the teaching fraternity and thus enhance our experience even more.

"Yeah, sure!" says Perry. "You're welcome to use the bike. It hasn't been used for a while, so you may need to do it up."

"I didn't want to use it if it was an antique or something." In this house where old, never mind decrepit, is synonymous with a revered and treasured object, you can never be sure what is meant to be functional or an antique left to gather dust and cobwebs to enhance its attractiveness.

* * *

My students are writing about themselves. They don't have a lot to say because they are not used to writing extended answers and this is a bit of a shock to their systems. Tammy Kinsella blows in briefly, unannounced, to see how I am getting on and I arrange to see her at the end of the school day. I want to be reassured that what I perceive as what the kids are expected to do *really* is that little.

"How much did you say we gotta write?" The speaker, a fat boy with a lugubrious expression, cannot hide his dismay.

"I told you," I say patiently. "Between 300 and 500 words. That's probably about a page and a half, depending on your writing and the size of your paper." Because they all provide their own paper, no two pages are alike.

"Geez! That's a lot!" This from someone else.

"What we gotta say?" chimes in another.

"Like I said, just write the sort of thing that you told me when you introduced yourself the other day."

"That'll never take 300 words."

"Just try it and see."

Heads are bowed, bodies are slumped over desks as they begin writing. Some even have their head on the desks. I'd like to tell them to sit up properly, at least *look* as if they were going to put some sort of effort into their work, but I realise that that would be a step too far. Their burden is already heavy enough.

"I'm finished." A boy has just come out with his paper. It's about ten lines long and at a rough estimate, it must be about 100 words at the most.

"That's not finished," I tell him.

"Yes it is. I can't think of anything else to write." His tone is insolent, challenging. The rest are watching and listening.

I read the curiously curvy script that the Americans have which makes one person's handwriting an imitation of everyone else's. I ignore the spelling and punctuation errors. He's told me about his Mom and his Dad and where he lives and the names of his siblings and what his hobbies are, in the manner of a shopping list, without any attempt at elaboration or an attempt to make it sound interesting.

"That's fine," I say, but you've got to put in more detail. "Take a new paragraph and tell me why you like your hobby so much. Then you can tell me about North Missoula, where you live. Describe the neighbourhood to me. I'm new here. Tell me about it. Do you like living there? Tell me why. If you don't, tell me why not."

He goes back to his seat, unhappy, grumbling, disconsolate.

A few moments later, from someone else: "How much we gotta write?"

My name isn't Job and this isn't the second time I've been asked this question; it isn't even the third or the fourth. They think their ears have deceived them; they can't believe that they have actually been asked to write this much. Surely I meant 30 or 50 words, not hundreds.

"You know perfectly well," I snap. "300 to 500 words." I write it on the board. "Nobody need ask again. Just look at the blackboard next time you forget!"

"That's not a blackboard. That's a chalkboard," he points out insolently.

"What colour is it?" I snap back.

"Black."

"Well then, it's a blackboard isn't it?"

There is an atmosphere in the room now. It has gone very quiet. No one dares ask another question or openly complain. Their heads are down. Most are laboriously counting the number of words they have done and audibly sighing, despairing at the number still to do.

At last it is lunchtime and there is a collective sigh of relief. I ask them to leave their papers behind for marking and there is a rasping noise as they rip pages from their spiral notepads. It sounds like machine gun fire and if they could shoot me with their notebooks, they would do it gladly.

* * *

It is too wet to go to the park today, so games are to be played in the hall. This means first of all we have to wipe the tables and clear them away. In an ingenious arrangement, the tables with little round seats attached, fold in the middle and have wheels on them so they can be wheeled away for stacking in the hall outside. It is therefore, just a matter of minutes before the decks are cleared – but not quite. To my amazement, Blake gets a mop from Danny, the custodian, and wipes the floor whilst the latter looks on. Then, a few minutes later, when some kids are slipping because the floor is wet, Blake asks him for a towel. Danny fetches and Blake dries. Just what does a custodian *really* do I wonder?

Lunch hour becomes another PE period as they play scatterball and put behind them the ghastly English period they have just endured. I don't know if I can go on like this every day, with wall-to-wall children. There *really* is no such thing as a free lunch and although it's not hard work watching the kids play scatterball, hardly work at all, I'd prefer to have a break from them, even if it is just for a little while and skip the free lunch.

* * *

After school, I have a heart-to-heart with Tammy and tell her my worries: how I can't seem to get the kids to do the simplest of tasks without them asking innumerable questions and after I have explained it, they still need to have it explained to them personally. And as for getting them to write more than a hundred words, you'd think I'd asked them to undertake one of the labours of Hercules. I tell her that at this rate, I'm going to be completely bald by the end of the year with ripping my hair out in frustration.

She has the graciousness to laugh and then I tell her what I'm really worried about – the curriculum. I do not express my concerns in tones of scathing disapproval, more a sort of - as I understand it - is this *really* what you want me to do? It's just that, what I do in Scotland is this – and at this point, I show her the samples of the work I have brought with me, as I'd been advised to do by the Bureau, in the more than likely eventuality that I would be asked to give a talk on the Scottish educational system.

There is silence whilst she peruses the type-written sheets, a silence so deep and long that I have time to contemplate the enormity of what I have done. I have probably committed the biggest faux-pas in the history of cultural exchanges: tantamount to telling her that I think this curriculum (for which she is responsible) is doing the kids no favours, they are under-achieving, they are not being stretched at all, and, even worse, should be doing it my way.

The silence is palpable as Tammy reads on... and on. No skim-reading this – she is giving it her full and undivided attention. It's impossible to read from her expression what she is making of it. She appears to be neither horrified nor impressed. Perhaps she's a poker player. At last she is finished.

"That's pretty interesting, Dave. So this is what you do with your kids, right?"

"Yes, that's right."

"And do you get any complaints?"

"No, not really. They don't know any different. It's what they have to do, so they just do it. In fact, some of them actually *enjoy* some of the writing assignments."

"No, I meant from the parents."

"The parents?" I am puzzled. "No, never. Why should they? They don't have to do it – it's their kids!" I add, injecting what I hope is a light-hearted tone into an atmosphere which has been too heavily-charged for too long.

"This looks pretty interesting stuff, Dave," she says again.

I try not to show my relief, but I feel as if I am soaring to heaven from the slough of despondency I felt I was in while she was reading my material. From those brief words, I am almost tempted to hear in them tones of ringing endorsement. I can now see more clearly that probably it was Tammy herself who had invited that speaker from Washington University and my worksheets were exactly the sort of thing she had in mind for encouraging the students to write more, think more and be more imaginative.

"Em... so you wouldn't mind me using this material with the kids then?"

"No, why not? Why not give it a whirl?"

It sounds so light-hearted, so off the cuff, it doesn't sound a big deal. But in fact, to tell the truth, it makes me feel a great deal better. It means I can do what I am accustomed to doing, but with half the number of students. Who knows what results I may be able to get these pupils to achieve? And, in a sudden flight of fancy, I wonder what hymns may be sung to me in the future about how, as a humble exchange teacher, I came to Missoula, Montana, and unwittingly, at first changed the course of English teaching there, then Montana, then the Western States and finally, my ideas spread over the entire country.

Of course I knew that was a dream. What I did not know was that the nightmare was just about to begin.

Chapter Twenty-nine

*In which I spend an evening with my new colleagues
and discover some more cultural differences between
our two nations.*

It is Friday evening and we are invited to the Schulz house. I had thought to begin with that it was just us and had intended taking the kids with us, but when I later realised that it was for the whole "faculty" that is to say, it included Steve and Nat and their spouses, I thought it better to get a baby-sitter, of which we have a ready supply from the Hertz household. And on the subject of baby-sitting, I have already discovered another cultural difference. Back home, this service is normally rendered by fond grandparents, normally delighted to have close contact with their genes, but happier still to hand them back at the end of the evening. Not for Iona and me, however, whose parents live far away, especially my mother, in Thurso, who Hélène, with the unwitting wisdom and insight of the young, describes as being at "the far end of the North".

For us, baby-sitting normally means a tit-for-tat arrangement with our good friends and neighbours, Pete and Izzy, whom we had known from our university days, with whom we had lost contact and ended up, completely by accident, rediscovering each other as neighbours and whom we had nominated as our equivalent of the Hertzes.

I hope Marnie does not find them too boring compared with Al and Terri. In our relationship with Pete and Izzy, there was more "tit" than "tat" which is to say that we were the ones who were usually going out and it was Izzy who normally provided the baby-sitting service. All it cost was a bottle or so of my delicious bramble wine which we imbibed on our return. It was always a pleasant prospect to sustain us if we were not particularly enjoying ourselves wherever we were and where our get-out clause: "We have to get back for the baby-sitter" was true but ambiguous, for we would often stay up drinking and chatting till the early hours on our return.

In the United States, you can always be certain of a baby-sitter, in fact it is a regular industry among high school students with rates laid down according to the Baby-sitter's Union. Normally we have the services of Debbie for this, so I give her a call as they say here, but tonight she cannot oblige, getting down and dirty with Ben I presume. She's says Rob could probably do it, but he's not in at the moment and she'll get him to give me a call when he gets in.

It so happens that Iona's friend, Carolyn, arrives when I'm on the phone and when I report to Iona that we may have a possible problem, Carolyn immediately volunteers and with such obvious enthusiasm, that it is impossible to refuse. Unfortunately, she and John can't have children and are considering adoption. Now she sees this as a chance to get a bit of practice in. Looking after our children would be good for her CV – unless it puts her off altogether, of course. It will give her some hands-on practice, a five-star service for us and it's going to be free, though of course that does not enter into the equation much. In fact, I get the feeling I could actually get Carolyn to pay *us* to let her baby-sit. So that's arranged then. In the event, Rob doesn't phone. Maybe Debbie forgot to ask him, but it saves us having to explain that we no longer need him.

Blake has given instructions as to how to get to his house. It is out of town, up in the hills and it is the last house in Missoula, at least in this direction, at the end of a dirt road. He needs a four-wheel drive to get out in the winter. We had better leave plenty of time in case we get lost, but before we do that, I must buy some gas. I know now how to fill the tank of course, since that embarrassing first time when I couldn't.

Fourteen gallons gurgle their way into the tank. They are American gallons and therefore smaller than ours, but it still seems to be taking forever and I am feeling increasingly uncomfortable. I am very conscious of people staring at me. It's making me feel embarrassed and I want to get under cover, into the car and even better, get out of here as fast as possible. Instead, I have to hang up the hose and draw more attention to myself as I walk across the forecourt, enter the brightly-lit store and take my place in the queue.

I should have got the gas on the way back from school. I know exactly why people are looking at me in this odd way. When I was giving my classes their introduction to Scottish culture, one question they had asked me was if I wore one of those funny plaid (pronounced "plad") skirts. I should have surmised from that it was perhaps not a good idea, but I had thought it might be a treat for my colleagues to see their exotic visitor in his national dress. Now I have the impression that people think that I look like something on the way to the transvestites' ball.

Amazingly, we find our way to our hosts without mishap. We park beside a couple of trucks, a tractor and a car. Once upon a time I might have supposed from the number of vehicles parked outside, and at five minutes later than our arranged time of 6.30, that we were the last to arrive, but now I know better and rightly suppose, as it turns out, that the two trucks and the car outside belong to Blake and Diane. And there you have two cultural differences in one. Two-car families are not uncommon in Scotland, but there is no-one I know, or have heard of in Scotland, who comes from a three-car family. Perhaps I don't move in elevated enough circles. In fact, I know I do not – I find it a struggle to pay the mortgage every month, let alone keep my car, now removed for the year to a shed on one of my cousin's farms. But even they, my rich bucolic cousins, don't have three vehicles per family, tractors not withstanding.

The other cultural difference is just how early entertaining starts over here. Nothing later than 6.30 and usually you are tucked up in bed with your cocoa by 10.30 at the latest. At that time, in Scotland, we are just getting into the swing of things and by 1.30 am or so, you might begin to be thinking of staggering home, "staggering" being the operative word.

If Blake and Diane and their guests think that tonight's the night that I have chosen to "come out" in Missoula, they don't show it and certainly don't ask, though I think they might have shown just a little more interest. In fact, the absence of any comments, either comical or critical, makes me think that I have made a grave error of judgement and I vow I will not wear my kilt again and certainly not at school, as I had been thinking of doing one day.

We have been invited to a barbecue, the usual form of entertaining here. And there you have yet another cultural difference. All I have is a small Hitachi on which I occasionally barbecue a couple of lamb chops. You could only cook for half a dozen people on that, like we are tonight, if you were to offer your guests their food two by two, like the animals entering the ark.

And supposing I did have the proper equipment, at least in the primitive-barbecuing Scottish definition of the term, where you must light the charcoal and wait until it gets white hot, (if you can get it to light in the first place) before you can begin cooking, there is still one major difficulty which you must overcome – the vagaries of the Scottish climate where you can get all seasons in a day. It's no good assuming that just because it was a bright sunny day when you lit the coals that it will be the same by the time they are ready to begin cooking. Here on the other hand, you can invite your friends to a barbecue weeks ahead and be assured that the weather will be conducive to such an arrangement. And instead of laboriously trying to ignite stubborn pieces of charcoal, all you have to do is press a button, quaff a beer, and by the time that is finished, your gas barbecue is ready to cook.

Spread out on one wall is the pelt of a black bear complete with head, the teeth bared, ironically, in a grin, as if to say, not only does it not mind being dead, but it looks perfectly happy to be in that state of grace. It is certainly the focus of the room, but the eye having had its fill of that, has its attention drawn to a lamp standard composed of antlers.

"I shot them myself," says Blake, following my gaze.

"And what were they?" I ask ingenuously, and not altogether approvingly, for although, hypocritically, I am not a vegetarian, I would be if it meant killing anything with my own hands. The lamp is such a crisscross maze that it is impossible to count how many antlers there are, but obviously a great many animals had lost their crowning glory for the sake of this lamp. And I definitely disapprove of the bear.

"Elk."

"Wapiti," adds Steve, confusingly.

"And the bear?"

"Yeah, I shot that too. Wanna come an' see my bows?"

"Your bows?"

"Come on."

And taking my interest for granted, he leads me down to the basement. Of course, I should have realised. When he said "shot" I imagined guns. I was brought up on a diet of Robin Hood and Cowboys and Indians and to me, a bow is a piece of string stretched between a slender pliable branch from a tree. Things have moved on, obviously, since I wore short trousers and indulged my imagination in the wood behind my boyhood home. This is a killing machine constructed out of fibreglass and as tall as me, but what surprises me most are the strings and the pulleys. Well, I suppose it is just one string, only it is threaded through so many pulleys it looks as if it goes on and on. What mortal force there must be when that string is pulled back and released!

It is easy to be impressed by it, but I am more impressed still when Blake tells me he made it himself. "I send them all over the world," he adds modestly but the pride in his voice is unmistakeable.

He also makes the arrows. These are vicious-looking things, the point made by four razor blades set into the shaft. I am horrified at the sight of them. I can't conceive how anyone could possibly shoot something like that into any animal. I know I certainly couldn't and the very thought of it makes me feel queasy.

"Do you make these too?" I hope I am keeping the disapproval out of my voice.

"Yep."

"And where do you shoot them?" And before he has time to make a smart-aleck remark line "in the forest" or wherever he does the ghastly deed, I add hastily, "The animals I mean. In the heart?"

I don't know why I am asking these questions. I really don't want to know – unless it is to cover up my horror or that I was hoping it would be the heart and it would be over, if not instantly, at least very quickly.

"In the lungs."

"The lungs?" I wasn't expecting that. The lungs sound more painful and much, much slower. I really wished I hadn't asked.

"So they bleed to death, right?" There I go again.

"Right."

He says it completely without sentiment and I can't think of anything else to say so I hurriedly look away in case my face says it all.

"You would never know that this wasn't beef would you?" Blake asks later as we sit round the table eating a rich, dark stew.

Plainly, an answer in the negative is required, but I can truthfully say that I wouldn't.

"What is it actually?"

"Elk."

"Is it really! I would never have guessed!"

Blake is pleased. It is not just the "joy" of the hunt – it is a money-saving exercise. In this country, in this cattle-rearing state, meat is abundant and cheap (and you should see the size of the steaks) but it is cheaper still ($5 for a permit) to go and hunt your own.

"And did you eat the bear too?" I ask with a nod in the direction of the pelt in the wall.

Blake nods. I'm glad about that in a way. It did not die in vain.

"Maybe I'll get one before you leave. Maybe you'd like to come along?"

There's nothing I'd hate more – but didn't I say I'd turn nothing down? The way I hear it, it's not even a rhetorical question, but an offer – an offer it never crosses Blake's mind that I would dream of refusing.

"How many do you kill in a year?"

I don't really want to know, but I feel I have to say something to avoid a direct answer.

"One's all I can eat," Blake says with a deadpan expression. "But I'm hoping to get a moose permit this year."

"I've heard some really hungry people say they could eat a horse, but I've never heard them say they could eat a moose before!"

Once everyone has recovered from my extremely witty remark, Blake explains that moose are protected (to a limited extent) and only a certain amount are allowed to be hunted every year and you have to enter your name in a draw. He's been trying for years now and never been lucky. The moose, I reflect, never gets lucky. If Blake doesn't get it, someone else will.

"What does bear taste like?" I want to know.

Human flesh is said to taste like pig and perhaps we are more closely related than some would like to admit. I have even been called one occasionally. And do they not use pig hearts or parts thereof in transplants? I know they are more intelligent than dogs and that worries me when they go to slaughter, because they might realise what's going on.

"It depends what they've been eatin'," says Blake. "Usually it is blueberries, so that is what they taste like."

He says it with that deadpan expression again, so I don't know whether to take him seriously or not. I am beginning to cotton on to the idea that Blake has a very dry sense of humour and what he's told me could be a bear-faced lie, so to speak. Since I don't know how to handle it, I just nod and smile in what I hope might be interpreted in an ambiguous manner, in acknowledgement of the information and if it *were* a joke, that I was amused, but only faintly. He might have said it tasted like bear, and *that* I would have believed, though it would not have made me any the wiser.

Blake's not the only killer. Steve, it transpires, shoots birds. He's training a new retriever at the moment and invites me to come along. I am aghast. He's not to know that feathers are my phobia since a time before memory, when I was in my pram, some pervert tickled my face with a feather (so my mother said) and then the fear was exacerbated by a hen who flew off her perch into my face when I was "helping" my aunt to collect eggs or stealing her embryonic children, as she would see it. No prizes for guessing *The Birds* is the scariest film I have ever seen, and Steve's invitation fills me with fresh horror. Apart from the death I would have to witness, the combination of feathers and blood is a combination, like liver and onions, which is guaranteed to turn my stomach.

Nat's hobby is furniture restoring. What a gentle, positive pastime! Imagine that! He doesn't kill anything, but brings back to its former glory, a table, a chair, a cabinet, a chest of drawers perhaps.

Only it's not just a hobby. Nat's furniture restoring is not just for relaxation, but to provide extra income. Steve, who is sports mad, gets an extra income from coaching students in football and basketball, as I already said. Blake, apart from filling his larder, also has a fencing business – which explains the tractor. He uses that to drive the posts in. He's quite a handyman, Blake, built most of his house himself.

I do not approve of his hunting, but I have to remember this is the West and that is the way they do things here. In fact, Blake is actually a Californian and moved here precisely because of the outdoor life. In any case, my objection is pure hypocrisy, which I realise all too well. I eat meat. I just prefer someone to kill it for me, cut it up for me, put it on a plate for me and even cook it for me.

In the unlikely event that if I were ever to be stranded on a desert island with anyone, should I be given the choice of a companion, I reckon I would choose Blake. However, if that were not possible, I'd fall back on the likes of Raquel Welch. And if she were not available either, if there is one thing I'd really like to fall back on, it would be a really pneumatic mattress.

The same thing actually, now I come to think of it.

Chapter Thirty

In which I experience some Native American culture and am treated like a celebrity.

What a great weekend this has been! And it is not over yet, for it is only Sunday morning. Iona is off to church; I am baby-sitting and reading the *Missoulian*. It's no great hardship for me to miss this religious experience. In the first instance, I am a heathen, and secondly, they are my children after all (Hélène at least is undeniable as she looks so like me) and has not Iona looked after them whilst I have been out enjoying myself, predominantly with Al, even if the operative word should sometimes have been enclosed in inverted commas? If that is what she regards as fun, so be it.

My attention is drawn to an advertisement. There is to be a memorial service at St Mary's Mission in Stevensville, in memory of Mary Combs and after the service, there is to be a potluck lunch and a powwow. For a moment, I think there must be some mistake, that it is I, not poor Mary who has transcended into heaven, for this is my chance to experience some Indian culture at first hand.

When Iona gets back from church, though not half so much an Indian lover as me, she gets down to concocting a salad for the potluck. What a simple and brilliant idea a potluck is! Since our embarrassing experience at Matt's, we now know how it works. Everyone brings a bit of something and the result is a feast that can feed a multitude and you need not hesitate to invite hundreds of guests since they will all bring something to the feast and take potluck with the rest. If there is one thing I will take back with me from this cultural exchange, it will be the potluck concept. Too poor to throw parties, let alone invite guests to dinner, weekends in Scotland might not be so dull and boring in future.

Meanwhile, in the present, I answer the phone. It's John Snively, ringing to say that he's got our stroller in his car (how did that happen?) and he'll bring it round later. I tell him what we're intending to do this afternoon and he says that Carolyn would love to go with us if that's all right. She's at Mass at the moment, but he'll tell her when she comes in and he's sure Carolyn will want to string along, if we don't mind, as she is a bit of an Indian fan too. He can't accompany us unfortunately, as he's going kayaking. I tell him that we'd love her to come along and I'd appreciate her insight into the proceedings.

By the time Carolyn is released from Mass, there is no time for her to prepare something to take to the potluck. But that's all right too. You don't *have* to provide anything; no one is going to grudge you a bite just because you're too poor, which of course, is not the case with Carolyn – she was merely caught unawares.

Although it's 30 miles to Stevensville, it takes rather less than that in minutes to drive there, difficult to keep to the ridiculously slow 55 mph speed limit, especially with a wagon train of horses under the bonnet as I have. The highway is broad, broader even than our motorways as it follows the Bitterroot River which is flanked on both sides by cottonwood trees. It is as empty of traffic as I imagine the traffic was in my own faraway land half a century ago and about as far away from our present day traffic-congested arteries as it is possible to imagine.

The bitterroot is the state flower, *Lewisia Rediviva*, named after Lewis, of Lewis and Clark fame, who "discovered" what the natives called "spetlum" and which formed an important part of their diet. This knowledge, courtesy of a book I found in Marnie's library, almost as extensive as my own.

When we arrive, the service is still in progress. Through the open door of the church, we can hear the sounds of a hymn being sung followed by people standing up to give a testimony on the deceased. The church is packed and it seems as if this could go on for some time yet as person after person gets to his feet to describe a memory or extol the virtues of the dear departed. We drift away. This service is not for us. It's a bit like eavesdropping. We did not know her, but she must have been extremely well liked. If I could muster up a tenth as much as this for my sending-off, I'd be more than happy to set off for the Happy Hunting Ground.

Whilst we are waiting for the proceedings to end, I have a chance to take in my surroundings. The church is the most prominent building amongst a cluster of others, set in an incredibly green sward, with the Bitterroot mountains forming a dramatic backdrop as they rise steeply, straight up from the valley floor, with one soaring head and shoulders above the others. The church itself is a very attractive building, the façade painted a pristine white with a shallow porch supporting a square tower with a simple dome and a cross the crowning glory, if that's the right word for such a simple building. It's that very simplicity that appeals to me. The church, I'm intrigued to see, is constructed from logs, like a pioneer's cabin. For the first time since I came to Montana, I have a sense of the past.

At last the service is breaking up. To my astonishment, not one priest emerges, but no fewer than six, dressed in robes as snowy as the church, their stoles resplendent in magnificent and multicoloured beadwork. These are the Black Robes, Indian style, or perhaps they are in white because that is the colour of funerals here. And this is the congregation, unmistakeably Indian, but some more Indian than others, depending on how pure the blood, and they are not noticeably dressed in black either.

It's the mauve headscarf clashing violently with the bright orange shawl that I notice first. They belong to an old woman, so stooped she can hardly walk, yet who manages to shuffle along without the aid of a stick or any human support either. Her face is as brown and as heavily scored with deep lines as a walnut, testimony to a long life on which a multitude of experiences have been etched. What stories could she tell if I had the courage to ask? But alas I haven't.

They appear to be taking communion now, two priests officiating, the other priests partaking along with the congregation. Naturally, not being of the Faith, apart from Carolyn, (who has already partaken) we hang back at the outer fringes of the gathering. However, to my horror, the senior priest, (or so I take him to be, since he has the most flamboyant beadwork on his stole) invites us to join in.

"I see you are from Scotland," he says before I have even had a chance to open my mouth. I suspect this is because in honour of this cultural event, I have donned the kilt, despite my experience of last night, and Hélène too is wearing a tartan skirt that Iona has made.

I explain why I am such a long way from home, introduce the rest of the family and Carolyn, then go on tell him I am an admirer of Indian culture, particularly the Plains Indians.

"We're very honoured that you have chosen to visit us today. You must have your photograph taken with us."

And there and then he clusters his flock around him and we all stand in front of the church while someone who looks as if he might be from the *Stevensville Squeak* or even the mighty *Missoulian,* takes our photograph with us given a position of prominence right at the front, in the middle, beside the chief priest.

"Excuse me," says a young man as we break up, "but I couldn't help overhearing what you said just now – that you are an exchange teacher from Scotland."

"That's right."

"Well, actually, I'm a teacher too. I wonder if you would mind tellin' me how you went about it. I'd be interested in doin' an exchange myself."

"Certainly." So Addison the ambassador tells him all about it and answers all his questions besides, while Iona, the kids, and Carolyn drift off.

Whilst I have been regaling the prospective exchange with all this information, I couldn't help but notice a semi-circle of Indian children gathering, hovering on the fringe, eyeing me with curiosity, perhaps, even, in awe or wonder.

"Hello."

They seem too timid to speak, which, for American children, is extremely unusual as they are not backward in coming forward as my limited experience has already discovered. That I should address them in this way instead of with the more familiar and colloquial "Hi", not to mention with such an outlandish accent, and above all, peculiar attire, must certainly confer upon me the status of a sight to behold and the like of which they have never seen before. Which no doubt accounts for their reluctance to speak to The Strange Object lest it is provoked into biting their heads off.

"Are you from Scotland?" one hazards eventually.

"Yes, that's right."

"Why do you wear that funny plad skirt?"

"It's not a skirt. It's called a "kilt" and I wear it because it is my national dress and it's not "plaid", it's tartan."

They seem to be in the mood for further information, so I tell them about the clan system and how you could tell a person's name from the kilt he wore and elaborate about the scores of different tartans, how one tartan can have variations on a theme, the hunting, the dress, and the ancient for example.

"Are there any questions you'd like to ask me? Anything else you'd like to know about Scotland?" After all, even if I have had them enthralled for five minutes or more, there is so much more I could tell them, if only they would give me half a chance. It's good fun being an ambassador, the resident expert. Just as long as they don't ask me what is worn under the kilt.

"That's pretty neat," says one.

"Yes. But I think your national dress is pretty neat too. I love your beads and feathers."

They don't quite know what to make of that, smile a bit self-consciously but say nothing. I take it that the interview is at an end.

"Well, I'll see you around," I tell them and stroll off in search of the others.

I've not gone very far and still not found them, when I bump into a middle-aged lady. Well, actually, I think the meeting was rather contrived and she had singled me out.

There is nothing like a kilt to make you look like a curiosity - at least in deepest remotest Montana, especially when everyone else looks like an Indian or partly Indian.

"You're a long way from home," she says.

I explain again why I'm in Montana. It's getting to be quite a habit.

"And so what brought you here today?"

I tell her I'd seen the advertisement in the paper and how I am fascinated by Indian culture. I spare her the details of its genesis. Don't tell her how in the films I watched as a boy, I was always on the side of the "no-good Injuns", partly, I suspect, because their clothes were better, but mainly because they were the underdogs, the downtrodden, but to me possessing a nobility much greater than the alleged savagery attributed to them, such as their fondness for scalping their victims, a practice which in fact, was not universal amongst all tribes and not unknown to the whites who had been known to pay a bounty on Indian scalps.

She introduces herself as Lucylle Evans, spelling this unusual first name out for me.

It turns out she is a local historian and is only too happy to tell me more about the history of this place. She's even written a book about it.

"This is where the State of Montana began," Lucylle explains. "The Mission was founded after the local Salish tribe and neighbouring Nez Perce heard tales from Iroquois trappers about how the Black Robes possessed the secret of life after death and invited them to talk to them."

This is news to me. I had assumed they had been reluctant converts who had been weaned off their own religion by missionary zealots. Not a bit of it. In fact, Lucylle goes on to say they were so desperate to hear the message that they sent off no less than four delegations to St Louis, begging a Black Robe to come and deliver the secret of everlasting life.

That puts an entirely different complexion on it - if they did voluntarily adopt Christianity and abandoned their own faith and beliefs. That promise of life after death must have sounded pretty good but why did they think it was better than going to the Happy Hunting Ground? The Bible does contain some wonderful stories, but to me, the Indian myths are much more fascinating with their wonderful imagery and close affinity with nature. If I were to adopt any religion, I am sure it would be one of the Indian ones - just as long as I did not have to do The Sun Dance and hang from hooks skewered through my flesh. That's taking things a bit far - but then the crucifixion wasn't very pleasant either. At least the Sun Dance sufferers were volunteers and survived this ordeal of the mortification of the flesh - which is more than could be said for poor Jesus.

In the course of this fascinating conversation, I am reunited with my entourage.

"Would you like me to show you around?" Lucylle offers, after the introductions have been made.

There's nothing we'd like better and Carolyn can't believe her luck. I wonder if she has any idea that this is entirely due to the kilt. I'd heard before that it was a sort of "Open Sesame" and this is the proof.

Although Father de Smet was the Black Robe who kicked the whole thing off in 1841, it was his recruit, Father Antonio Ravalli, who was the prime mover in this place, Lucylle tells. Originally hailing from Italy as one may have guessed, he arrived in St Mary's in 1845. He was a real *lad o' pairts* as we say in Scotland, able to turn his hand to anything. Not only did he minister to the spiritual needs of his congregation, he was their teacher, doctor and pharmacist as well. He also built the first grist mill and saw mill.

Nor were his talents confined to matters of a practical nature: he was also an architect, artist and sculptor. Well, woodcarver would be more accurate, furnishing the chapel with the trappings of the Catholic Church, such as statues of Mary and St Ignatius (though that was made of metal and canvas), a pair of candlesticks, and a cross. (Well, that at least would be comparatively easy. Even I could do that. When I was about ten, I made one myself for the grave of my beloved collie, Rex.) Father de Smet also painted the chapel, basing the design and colours on his church back home. Some man! No wonder they named a county after him. It's a wonder it wasn't the entire state!

Looking at it straight on, you would never have realised just how extensive the church is. It may be narrow but it seems to extend back forever. It's actually four buildings in one. Apart from the church or "chapel" as Lucylle calls it, there is the Father Superior's residence, then the dining room, then the kitchens, each descending in height like a line of Matryoshka dolls.

Set apart from that are a couple of cabins. One belonged to Father Ravalli, the other to Chief Victor and his wife, Agnes. Agnes! *Agnes*, for God's sake! Victor is just about acceptable as a name for an Indian chief, especially if he had won lots of battles, or even if he hadn't, to inspire the troops. But Agnes! How in the name of the Great Spirit in the Sky did he end up with a wife with a name like that? It's hard to respect an Indian chief who has a wife whom he calls "Nessie" for short. It makes her sound a bit of a monster in fact. But of course I'm only bringing my Scottish culture to the name. It is extremely unlikely that Victor and his tribe had ever heard of Loch Ness's most famous resident. And perhaps to their ears, "Agnes" sounded as exotic and romantic as "Laughing Water" or "Running Deer" does to me.

"Victor died in 1870 but Agnes lived here till her death in 1884," Lucylle volunteers and I have a feeling we are meant to be impressed by the extreme antiquity of these dates, but I remember the old woman I had seen and reckon it's possible that Agnes knew her and what's more, Father Ravalli could actually have baptised her! He died the same year as Agnes.

The season is over, Father Ravalli's cabin is closed and unfortunately someone has had the foresight to draw curtains over the windows so it is impossible to have a peek in. It looks as if it is in need of some restoration, and as if reading my mind, Lucylle explains that they are restoring and preserving the site, bit by bit, as far as funds allow.

Next on our tour is an apple tree, the oldest apple tree in the state and planted by Father Ravalli himself and so ancient that its branches need artificial support, like many human beings do at half that age. Finally, we come to where Father Ravalli himself is planted. The spot is marked by a large stone cross and the grave fenced off with a chain. I am very happy to pay my respects here for I have a peculiar hobby - visiting the graves of famous people, especially literary figures. I had never heard of Father Ravalli before until a few minutes ago, but clearly he is a man of some fame and distinction here and it's easy to admire and respect him for all his talents. No wonder he was revered by his flock and still is, deservedly, today.

I tell Lucylle how much I appreciate her insight into St Mary's and she says it was a pleasure, and I am sure it was. And although Lucylle has nothing of his intensity or glittering eye, I think of the Ancient Mariner for it seems to me that

Lucylle is so passionate about this place, that she will tell anyone about it who will listen.

It's time to get our food now and we queue at a hatch in a wooden structure where you help yourself to paper plates and plastic utensils and where there is enough food to feed an army. I find myself behind a huge man, his raven-black hair pleated in two strands hanging over his shoulders and reaching to his waist. He is wearing jeans and a shirt stretched so tightly over his vast stomach, I might have been forgiven for thinking he was a member of the Gros Ventre tribe rather than the Salish, or Flathead, as they are popularly known, not due to any deformity of the cranium, as some tribes practice by binding the heads of their infants, but apparently from their gesture of striking the forehead with the flat of the palm as a greeting. He is also wearing a cowboy hat.

From the rear, apart from the plaited hair, he might easily have been mistaken for an overweight cowboy. But when he turns round and I see him face to face, his features mark him out as indisputably Indian as Hélène is my daughter. I am pleased to see, in deference to his origins, the feather from a bald eagle, or so I deem it to be, with its distinctive black-and-white markings, is tucked into the broad band that runs round the crown. All the same, it's a bit disappointing to see how Indian culture has been influenced so much by the headgear of the white man. That's progress I suppose, and in all fairness, I can't expect my heroes to remain in a time warp just for my delectation, going about all the time looking like Red Cloud in full regalia, including war bonnet or more prosaically, like Tonto from *The Lone Ranger* who wore a fetching set of buckskins and his hair in plaits.

Interestingly, *tonto,* in some European languages, notably Spanish, which in certain parts of the south is more dominant than English, means "stupid". And here's the joke: Tonto's constant addressing of the Lone Ranger as *kemo sabe* or "great scout" could, to Spanish ears, sound like *qui no sabe* or "he who knows nothing". Touché. And, as anyone who is as old as me knows and who watched the TV show religiously at 5 o'clock every Saturday (and who didn't?) Tonto was by no means as stupid as his name might have suggested to Spanish-speaking audiences.

After the meal there are signs that the real Indian experience is about to begin. Some people are now attired in their costumes, resplendent in feathers and beads. This is more like it. Little girls are looking charming in shawls, moccasins and beaded headbands. I think it's about time Hélène had a cultural exchange of her own. It would be nice if she could meet a little Salish girl.

The area where the entertainment is to be held has been roped off and standing looking at the performers beginning to gather is a little girl, who, by her height, I imagine must be approximately the same age as Hélène. Too shy to speak, they eye each other with undisguised interest as only small children can, with a complete lack of embarrassment. They must look so strange to each other, they could not possibly imagine they had any language in common, even if the little girl's first language should turn out to be English. In any case, they are so young they are only taking their first hesitant steps in learning language themselves and certainly don't have enough to strike up a conversation on their own.

"And what's your name?" I bend down to ask the little girl, hoping I will get something like Laughing Water (how disappointed I would have been if she had said "Jane") but all I get by way of an answer is an embarrassed sort of smile and she moves away. No doubt her mummy told her not to talk to strange men, especially if they are wearing skirts.

Suddenly, an unearthly sound rents the air. It is the rhythmic sound of a drumbeat, but it's not that which causes the hair to rise on the back of my neck and my heart to beat in syncopation - it is the sound of the human accompaniment. I can only describe it as unearthly, a sort of cross between a chant and an ululation, the sort that the women of some cultures make when they are in a paroxysm of grief. These are the singers. They are also the drummers. There appear to be half a dozen of them sitting round a drum as big as a tympanum which they appear to strike at random, but perhaps it is all carefully choreographed. You would think it would have to be with so many people bashing away at the same instrument and "bashing" seems to me to be the precise word for what they are doing, rather than "playing". If that is what passes for playing an instrument here, then I, who am completely and utterly tone deaf and have no sense of rhythm, (thus making me quite probably the most unmusical person on the planet) could play this drum. And, if that is the singing, why, I could do that too. I could caterwaul like that with the best of them.

The beat is insistent, making the pulse race, seeming to penetrate to the heart's core and then, just as suddenly as it started, it stops without any crescendo or diminuendo or any other hint that it was about to end, like a sudden death. That was the first song and the curious thing is that after the third and the fourth, they all sounded exactly the same to me. No-one could possibly call it harmonious or even musical, but I think it one of the most stirring sounds and experiences I have ever witnessed.

But the singing and the drumbeat are only the backcloth to the dancers who are now dancing in a circle round the drummers. And if that is dancing, then I could do that too. It requires, or so it seems to me, no more taxing steps than a shuffle interspersed with the odd skip and jump and a little stomping thrown in for a bit of variety. My maternal grandmother was a Crow and if Victor could be married to an Agnes, is it not within the bounds of possibility that I might have some Indian blood in me since I apparently possess all these Native American skills?

The chief priest must be some sort of honorary tribal member, for he has joined the dance, now dressed in black apart from a jazzy waistcoat with a geometric design and a scarlet streamer at his waist which, against the black of his trousers, looks like a river of blood. With his high-crowned hat with an enormous feather (a turkey's I think) stuck in the band, he has a vaguely sinister air, reminding me of Indian Joe in *Tom Sawyer*. He slouches, shuffles, and skips round the circle with, in one hand, what looks like a wing of some grouse-sized bird stuck on the end of a stick, and a rattle of some sort in the other. I can't help but get the feeling if he were to point those feathers at me that it would be very bad news indeed - that it meant I had been selected for some sort of ritual sacrifice, for he looks primitive and pagan, more shaman than priest, and it's hard to reconcile this image with the Roman Catholic priest who officiated earlier. I can scarcely imagine any Church of Scotland minister of my acquaintance indulging in such "heathen" pursuits.

As for the other dancers, although there are some ladies, as is so often the case in nature, they are dull and dowdy compared with the finery exhibited by the males. These so-called "fancy dancers" are a modern concept Carolyn says. While it may have nothing to do with tradition, it certainly is eye-catching, particularly the display of feathers on their backs, great fans of brightly-coloured plumage that any peacock would be proud to display, one centred between the shoulder blades like angels' wings and another at the waist - to say nothing of the magnificent headdresses. And they shall have music wherever they go for they have bells strapped just below their knees above a pair of furry acrylic gaiters whose hues, like those of the plumage, do not occur in nature either. It may not be traditional Indian culture but it is as Indian as tartan and shortbread is to Scotland, and as iconic. I could scarcely have hoped for more and when you combine that with the music and dancing, I am more than well pleased with my first exposure to Indian culture.

* * *

Back home, a brown paper bag is sitting on the porch. It turns out to contain some corn from Mary Mason, one of the teachers from the lower school. It seems as if corn, like the Triffids, is taking over Missoula, if not the entire state. How fortunate that we happen to be here to help dispose of the glut.

I phone Mary to thank her.

"Have you ever eaten corn on the cob before?"

"Just a little," I reply, instinctively feeling my other ear to check that a little yellow grain is not coming out of it.

I get the kids something to eat and cook the corn, while Iona jumps into the car and heads for Brownies, a hamburger joint, as we have a voucher from the Welcome Wagon for two Big Buns. They are not kidding. They are so packed with salad, tomatoes, onions, cheese and other trimmings, not to mention the burger which is itself an inch thick, I stare stunned at these skyscrapers and wonder how I can possibly go about attacking it as I can't possibly open my jaws that wide. Impossible to eat with any dignity, Iona and I tactfully avert our eyes from each other as we start to demolish this mountain of a meal. We could have done without the starter.

And if it's a lot of food, it's food for thought too. Not too bad a move, this freebee from Brownies. We will certainly come back for more, and with a whole year here, we will probably go back there many, many times. And not too bad a move on my part either, to come here. I've had a pretty interesting weekend, a welcome change to the dull routine back home where nothing interesting ever seemed to happen. So interesting has it been in fact, that it is has flown past and now, all too soon I am facing a whole week in school.

I realise I must be getting over the culture shock if I'm now starting to feel that I'm glad I made the move. And I don't have to worry about giving the kids boring, meaningless, pointless, language exercises once I start using my own material and begin to stretch their imaginations.

Or so I thought.

Chapter Thirty-one

In which I learn more about the American way of education, do some homework and learn some worrying news.

I am feeling more of a primary school teacher than ever. The students are going to be taking a course in shop (wood and metal work) and home economics, but since only half the class goes at one time, I must fill in the time doing something else.

"What can you offer the students, Dave?" Matt wants to know.

"Well, how about I teach a lesson then teach the same lesson to the other half?"

Matt appears stunned by this suggestion. He studies my face closely as if to see if I could possibly be making a joke. I was never more serious. Teachers in Scotland would give their eyeteeth for classes of eighteen - but think of the progress you might possibly be able to make with only nine! What a golden opportunity!

"No, you see Dave, it's got to be a mini-course. Somethin' completely different."

"But I'm not qualified to teach anything else - except history and I only taught that for one year, in my first year of teaching."

The GTC (General Teaching Council) had recently been formed in Scotland, our own professional organisation to regulate the profession, to ensure high standards of professionalism, by amongst other measures, eradicating uncertificated teaching and ensuring that teachers actually held a qualification in the subject they were teaching ⁃ for example not teaching Maths with only an 'O' Grade certificate, and that at the second attempt, in my particular case. I can hardly see my students being enthused by the prospect of learning Scottish history. Besides I haven't any materials.

Matt considers this objection. He swallows nervously, clears his throat and asks tentatively: "Have you got any skills, Dave? Any hobbies or interests?"

Skills I have none, apart from wine making I suppose. Interests I have quite a few. At least two. I like beer and bare ladies.

"I could teach them soccer, I suppose."

Matt looks so relieved to hear it, it's as if he had been reading my mind before I came up with this much more modest proposal.

"That would be great, Dave!" he says, putting his arm round my shoulders. "I want you to know how lucky we all feel to have you here with us, Dave. I'm sure the students ⁃ all of us, will benefit from havin' you with us this year."

And with that he departs, leaving me feeling under a great deal of pressure to live up to this expectation. Coming from Scotland, and from the north east at that, where overly enthusiastic displays of enthusiasm on anyone's success or talents is regarded as unnecessary and likely to turn their heads, I am unaccustomed to praise, even had I been worthy of any. But I have been here long enough now to realise that Americans frequently dole it out, and by the shovelful, so that all but the most vain must question the sincerity of it. And even people who don't know you from Adam, such as bank tellers and supermarket girls relieving you of your money at the check-out, treat you as if you had been friends for years, so that you feel valued as an individual, not just another faceless customer. Except they treat everyone exactly the same.

So I suspect that this is Matt merely doing his PR stuff. Whenever he speaks to me, he seems rather nervous and I think he must regard me as a bit of a loose cannon. Not for the first time, I am surprised he ever agreed to this exchange, unless Marnie was a thorn in his side that he wanted shot of for a year. Maybe to utter the name of the enemy is seen as sacrilegious in the Church of God, but surely he had heard of the aphorism "The devil you know… ?

* * *

After school, I find myself in court. I have not committed any crimes, misdemeanours or even traffic violations. I am there because the District Court is where I have to get the license plates for the car. It costs $16 plus taxes, but that's only for the remainder of the year - till May. Despite it sounding like a song to me, I am a bit offended to see that it includes a charge of $2 for "Junk Vehicles".

"Hey, what's that?" I ask the clerk, offended, but astonishing myself at my readiness to challenge officialdom. Perhaps I am learning from my students.

"It's to pay for the machine that crushes junk vehicles."

"Oh is it? That's all right then." I am somewhat mollified. I'm not in love with the Plymouth exactly but I resent the idea that it's ready for the scrapheap.

So now I am the proud possessor of my very own number plates depicting the outline of the state (mainly a rectangle apart from a wiggly bit on the west and south west) and bearing the legend "Big Sky Country". The number is prefixed with a 4 which designates it as coming from Missoula. Since the plates belong to the driver, not the car, when I sell it at the end of the year I'll be able to take them with me as a souvenir.

***

In the evening, Millie, the librarian, and her husband, Lee, arrive bearing gifts. A brown paper sack is full of vegetables: zucchini (courgettes), carrots, cucumber and beetroot. If we didn't mind eating vegetables all the time, we could just about eat here for free, what with these donations and those from the Welcome Wagon. Nestling at the bottom of the bag, the obligatory corn on the cob. They had me worried for a minute - I thought there wasn't going to be any.

***

It's a cold, miserable day as I set off for school the next morning. The worst weather we've had since we arrived, but there is snow on the mountains which makes them even more appealing. I relish the coming winter, snow deep on the ground but us cosy and warm in front of a roaring log fire - when Al gets around to bringing over my share of the logs.

Although we are only just back, Steve and Blake are already grumbling about the teachers' conference in a month's time. From what they say about it, it appears to be the universally accepted nadir of the whole school year.

"You don't want to listen to all that bullshit," says Steve, who knows I have relatives in Vancouver. With the schools being closed from Wednesday to the following Monday, it would be a perfect opportunity for me to drive the 2000 miles or so round trip to meet these relatives I've never met before. "You should fix it with Matt that you don't have to go."

"That's right, Dave," agrees Blake. "We usually go huntin'."

As usual, his face is expressionless and I can't tell if he's joking or not. I had intended to go at Christmas, but now this seems like a good opportunity to go while there was still a chance that the 8,000 foot high pass over the Rockies would be passable.

Sam and Art agree that the conference is a total waste of time. A handpicked bunch of teachers are selected to tell their colleagues about the exciting and innovative methods they have introduced into their classrooms, which, it is hoped, other teachers will emulate. Both Sam and Art regard it as a brain-numbing form of torture and would far rather have their kids in front of them, getting on with the job, inspiring the kids in their own way, resenting this interference, this suggestion that they need some new ideas to add sparkle to their lessons. They are predisposed to reject it from the start. Like the proverbial horse which can be taken to the water but not made to drink, you can make teachers attend the conference but making them adopt new methods is an entirely different matter. In fact, if Blake is to be believed, it sounds as if they may not even be able to do that...

For me to attend such a meeting, I feel, would be rather like Ruth standing among the alien corn. It's hard to see how I could glean much that I could usefully transfer to the Scottish situation to improve my teaching. And yet, I am meant to be here to experience the American educational system, whether for good or ill...

"Matt will let you off, for sure," Steve says.

But Matt rubs his chin as he listens to my request and even before he speaks, I know that Steve was wrong to be so confident. "Em… ahrrum… I don't know about that, Dave. I think you know… em… ahrrum… that you should attend."

A silence descends which grows increasingly uncomfortable.

"Oh." I had been so psyched up by Steve and the others that they had me almost convinced that Matt would overcome his natural caution and allow me to go, so the tone in the single word conveys not only disappointment but shock.

"I tell you what, Dave. I'll make some enquiries an' get back to you. How does that sound?"

"That sounds just great, Matt. Thanks a lot."

That, at least, gets us both out of an embarrassing situation. I have a suspicion that Matt will come back to me in a couple of days and tell me that the answer is no.

***

Millie has shown me the mysteries of the copying machine and I have made copies of the worksheets I intend to use with my classes so they can go for printing later. Out of courtesy, I decide to show them to Matt and let him know that I've cleared it with Tammy.

His face is serious as he looks them over. I wouldn't say they're the most exciting documents he's ever read, but on the other hand, his face is not turning purple with apoplexy either. I have a feeling he doesn't quite know what to make of them, that he's never seen anything quite like them in his life before.

"That looks like a lotta work, Dave," he says at last.

I explain that it represents a year's work for all the classes.

"That looks mighty fine, Dave."

"So you've got no objections to me using them with my classes then?"

Matt swallows hard. I'd say he was looking even more nervous as if I'd just asked him a trick question which might have serious repercussions if he got it wrong. He picks up the documents again and scans them as if looking for mantraps.

"See this here, Dave - 'Write about your most daring school prank.'" There is an awkward silence while he seems to be searching for the right words to say next. "Well, I'm not very sure about that one."

"Well, you see, it is to tie in with the stimulus we are going to be reading. (If I can find one. Naturally, I had one back home.) I don't ask them to write in a vacuum. The idea is that they are meant to be stimulated by what they have read and then to try their own hand at writing in a similar vein. And in any case, they don't *have* to do that one. It's a choice of one of three - as you can see."

Matt doesn't appear to be persuaded, and although he can't apparently tell me what's wrong with it, he feels instinctively it's not right. "It's just I'm not very happy about it. I think it would be better if you took that one out, Dave." He's looking at the offending paper in his hand rather than me.

I'm rather shocked. I'm not accustomed to this - my lesson plans being criticised, vetoed even, at least not since my student days, some seven years ago. I had only shown him this out of courtesy, after all, to keep him informed, but now the opinion I had been gradually forming of Matt - that he is a bit too conservative by half, was beginning to take more concrete form.

"It's not going to incite a revolution, you know," I respond in a light-hearted tone meant to convey the preposterous nature of such a notion.

Matt doesn't want to fall out with me: I'm sure that's why he is so nervous, worried that we're going to have an argument over this and he's going to have to put his foot down. Maybe I have put my finger on it - he really *is* dreading an outbreak of bad behaviour, kids getting up to all sorts of mischief as they find material for their essays. His Adam's apple is a yo-yo and he looks distinctly uncomfortable as he looks at me at last.

"I think, Dave, it just would be better if we left that one out. But the rest is neat, really neat."

"OK."

The relief on his face is unmistakeable as I leave the room.

* * *

Iona hasn't seen Terri in ages and decides she'd better go over and invite them to dinner some time. When she comes back, she reports that Debbie was having trouble with her English homework and I decide I'd better go over and see if I can help. Naturally, Al offers me a beer.

It's a précis sort of exercise and Debbie is having a bit of a problem grasping the concept, so in the end, to save time, I just do it for her. What the heck! Debbie is just marking time until she can leave school and go to beauty school. She doesn't need any lessons in looking beautiful, being the most comely of Al's daughters in my opinion, and after she has finished her course, she has been promised a job by Al's best friend, Chris Mendez, the hair bender.

"What are those scratches on your hand?" I ask Debbie as she begins to write to my dictation. They are quite deep and look as if they had bled quite a lot.

"Oh those!" she says as if she had forgotten all about them. "I was in a wreck."

"A wreck? What happened?" I know that a "wreck" is what we call a "car crash". I wonder what they call it when a ship comes to grief, but I'm more interested in the details of Debbie's crash and surprised, not only by her matter-of-fact attitude, but that Al had not mentioned it when I was over yesterday.

"I was in my boyfriend's truck an' he rolled it over. Three times!"

"Three times! Good God! What happened?"

"Well, he passed out an' lost control an' it just flipped over."

"Passed out? How did he pass out? Is he epileptic or something?"

"Naw, he was drunk," she says without drama.

"And what about Ben? Was he hurt much?" I ask when I have recovered the power of speech.

"Ben?"

"Your boyfriend. The one who works down the sewers."

"Naw. I'm over with him. Naw, he didn't even have a scratch."

"You're both very lucky," I tell her and think that the new boyfriend was probably lucky to escape with his life, not so much from the accident, but when Al found out he was drink driving. Perhaps he was even the officer called to the scene. I'd love to ask, but I've a feeling that Al and Terri would prefer I did not know about this event, so instead I change the subject.

"Who's your English teacher?"

"Bill Kennedy."

"For God's sake, don't tell him I did your homework!" Of all the English teachers in Hellgate High School, it would have to be the only one I know, the one who was on exchange to England. I wish I hadn't done such a good job on it. I wouldn't mind betting that this is the best piece of English homework that Debbie has ever produced and I'm worried that Bill becomes suspicious.

As I leave however, I discover that Terri is annoyed about something. She has written an amazing five times and not had a single reply from Marnie. I tell her I am not surprised, that we have had a letter from Iona's mother who had been to visit her and found her in a terrible muddle over making an apple pie, but in an even bigger mess over the work at school, really struggling to keep up with all the correction and saying she had never worked so hard before in all her life. Under the circumstances, I tell Terri not to expect a letter until Christmas at the earliest and I don't mention that Art has had at least one letter.

That same letter reports the toaster as broken and I'm not sure if I should replace it or not. I suppose I should really, but I'd like to know how it came to be broken in the first place. But what is really worrying me is that Lindy has apparently paid Marnie the money for the phone calls. Why did she do that when I'm the one who is going to have to pay the bill? She has not, however, paid the utilities. The instruction from Marnie is I am to contact Lindy and ask her for the money.

It's just too embarrassing. Could Marnie not have instructed Lindy to pay me instead? It wouldn't matter if I were as rich as Croesus but I'm not and not for the first time, I have an uneasy feeling about the financial arrangements...

Chapter Thirty-two

In which I experience a number of shocks, George meets his future teacher and I benefit from the kindness of Missoulians.

The rest of the week begins with a couple of shocks and I'm not just referring to those I get as I walk across the nylon carpet then touch the metal frame of the windows to let in some air, for the weather has turned fine again, the snow has disappeared off the mountains and it seems as if the inclement weather of the past few days was merely a blip and it does look indeed as if we might be heading for an Indian summer as Al had reassuringly predicted yesterday.

Nor am I referring, to one day, seeing Matt - dressed in a long white apron with a white cap perched on top of his head, the kind that I associate with corporals in the US army, only smaller, and merely tipping a wink in the direction of any possible hygienic use - dishing out ice cream in the dining hall. It's the sort of thing that would never happen in Scotland, the headmaster losing his status, not to mention his authority and dignity, by indulging in such a menial task. But plainly Matt has no such worries. In fact, the only reason I can think of for such eccentric behaviour is that Matt imagines, rightly or wrongly, that he gets Brownie points for appearing to be a man of the people and not too high and mighty to serve the students, whereas in Scotland, nothing could be more calculated to have the opposite effect.

It was also a shock to the system to find that if it is Thursday, it must be staff meeting day and this is the real shock, it begins *before* school - at 8 o'clock. Never having been any good at getting up at the best of times, Thursday is naturally my least favourite day of the week and I see little point in having a staff meeting just for the sake of it. In Scotland, we have the good sense to have them after school, and only then on an ad hoc basis.

And it was a shock at the time, but of course I am used to it by now, to learn that once the children are released from school, that we teachers are not free to go home right away. It's not even as if there is any correction I could be doing.

"It creates a bad impression," says Matt.

And so we must sit in thrall to our desks for another half hour. Of course teachers in Scotland are accustomed to this practice and many stay on for a lot longer than that, but at the same time it is not compulsory and if you prefer to cart your correction home or do your preparation there, then you are perfectly entitled to do so. Here, my correction is so slight I can dash it off, more or less on the spot, and now that my materials have gone to the office for reproduction, it's just a question of waiting for them to arrive, so I have no need for any preparation either.

Accordingly, I am in Steve's room, chatting away when the next shock comes. Incredibly, a parent has arrived, looking for me. That's only the first shock, for we are not accustomed to parents just strolling in and seeking an audience. We have parents' evenings and in the rare event that a parent should wish to see us outwith that time, it is by appointment only.

The second shock is that she has come to enquire about homework. I had been told that the parents in our catchment area had very little interest in their children's education. Now it transpires I would have been better, in the matter of homework, to have attended to my own, rather than

Debbie's, or more precisely, to the matter of giving out homework to my students, for this person's daughter is off school with some mild illness or other and she would like to have the homework she has missed.

"Well... actually... as a matter of fact... she hasn't missed any." My hesitancy is born from a realisation that there is an exception to every rule and this is it. I'm worried about how this keen parent is going to react, for not only has she made a pointless journey at what cost and inconvenience to herself, I couldn't possibly guess, but what I do know is she is going to go away disappointed at best, and at worst, furious at the kind of inadequate teacher this exchange program has produced.

Fortunately, she is a parent of the most reasonable kind and I reassure her that plans are afoot and her daughter will have homework in spades and there is no need to worry. I take her into my room, show her the *Murder Mystery Magazine* project, explain that it is being printed and explain that the concept is that the students have to imagine that they have to write a mystery magazine featuring a ghost story, a murder story, a horror story, letters to the editor, readers' supposedly true accounts of weird events and a horrorscope [[sic]].

"Hey, this looks really neat," says my parent. "In fact, I wish I was at school doin' this. Cindy's really gonna enjoy usin' her imagination."

"That's the idea." I tell her, and then add, "If you'd like to write the essays, I'd be happy to grade them for you!"

She laughs and departs and I go back to Steve's room and report that I have just sent one happy customer on her way, but modestly refrain from telling him that I suspect I am just about to take the teaching of English in Missoula by storm, if not by the scruff of the neck and give it a much needed shake-up.

All the same, to defray any other possible complaints, I print off a boring exercise on the period (full stop) and the comma, and issue it as homework.

* * *

It is George's first day at school. He and Iona meet Kathy Kuhn, the Hearing Impaired teacher. I had met her earlier in the week and was impressed with her easy, friendly manner. Now, as she meets George and Iona for the first time, if she feels any sense of trepidation about taking on such a young pupil, her youngest ever, and still in diapers, she certainly does not show it as she squats down in front of him, and touches him to get his attention.

"Look at my lips," she says - and, interested in this new face right in front of him, he does. "Hi! You're a little cutie aren't you?"

As she speaks, Kathy is signing and carefully making the shape of the words with her lips. This is total communication in action - any and all methods to get the message through the ears that don't work, so he can be included in the hearing world and not excluded from it. To see Kathy in action like this fills Iona and me with a great sense of hope and excitement.

Kathy explains that she'll teach George signs for everyday household objects, colours, animals and so on, and of course, Iona will learn them too and pass them on to me. Later on, she will be running a class at the university which I can attend. Not only that, but the audiologist, Mike Wynne, will test him soon.

I am not religious, but had I been, I might well have seen The Hand of God in this, that it had been ordained that I would end up in Missoula and in Central School in particular, the only one in the District to have deaf kids, though we should call them "hearing impaired" as that is meant to make them feel more included, to make people realise that they are not handicapped, that they are as "normal" as anyone else. It's just that their ears don't work as well as other peoples'.

Compare this to Scotland. We found out that George was deaf when he was eight months old, alerted by Iona's mother who had become suspicious, despite his having passed his hearing test. Our point of view was that the sooner we could get some sound, any sound, into his head the better, but we had to fight tooth and nail to get him a hearing aid.

"He'll never keep it in," we were told, but we persisted and George became the youngest ever to be issued with a National Health hearing aid in our district, and perhaps the youngest in the country for all we know.

If I have not been too impressed with the standard of English teaching as I was expected to deliver it, I am more than impressed with the standard of deaf education. It may not be as good as this over the state, where each school district in the city is autonomous, but from where I'm standing, I could not have asked, nor expected more. In the matter of provision for the deaf, School District # 7 is light years ahead of Scotland.

And not only does the future look good for George; it looks good for Hélène too. She will be going for a couple of hours a week to a nursery class at the university since Iona must come with George, partly to learn the signs, but more importantly, from Kathy's point of view, to change his nappies. "I don't do diapers," she says, laughing. "That's mom's job!"

Conscious of Matt's part in this, for getting the ball rolling, and detecting what I perceive as a slight awkwardness in our relationship and knowing the fondness Americans have for a pat on the back, for boosting the ego, I see an opportunity for a more positive meeting with Matt and go to express my thanks to him personally as well as my appreciation of what is being done for George, extolling the virtues of deaf education in Missoula.

"That's just fine, Dave. You're welcome. Glad we could help you out!" Even in this situation Matt gulps like a frog and looks highly embarrassed, but I go away happy with the feeling that I've done the right thing.

* * *

Sam takes me to Mincoff's after school to buy the brake parts I need for the car, saying that if I need any help, he'll help me. I say thanks anyway, but Perry is going to help me. Actually that means I'll stand and watch as I haven't a clue how to start. However, when I phone Perry to tell him I have got the parts, he tells me he hasn't eaten yet and then he has to go to a meeting so it will have to be postponed till another time. I tell him not to worry, that someone else will do it and thus Sam finds himself propelled into the position of honour, leaving me to reflect that back in Scotland I would never have found such a band of willing helpers in a month of Sundays.

But right from the start, fitting the brakes turns out to be more problematic than Sam had anticipated. It turned out that it needed discs, not shoes, at the front so we had to go and change them, then there was difficulty in getting a clip off, then on its release, it sprang out with such velocity that it was never seen again.

Leaving Sam to start on another brake, I take his truck to Devlin Frey's, a Plymouth dealership, to get another clip - only to find that the parts department is closed.

"Where y'all from?" asks a bloke behind the desk who has overheard my request.

"Scotland."

"That so? What d'you say you was lookin' for?"

I tell him the story of the escaping clip, at this moment probably somewhere in orbit.

"Let me see if I can help you," and he picks up the phone and talks into it. "Yeah, they got one. Just grab a cup of coffee over there an' I'll be right back," he announces a moment later. And with that he is off, leaving me with my lower jaw hanging somewhere about my navel.

Whilst my new benefactor is away, I am left in salesmen-infested waters. Apart from being an object of some curiosity, I could be a potential customer, so I am engaged in polite conversation to which my every response is met with "Gee, that's great!" or "Wow!" or "That's really neat!" until I begin to feel slightly nauseous. Then, what I have felt all along this has been leading up to comes out: "We got a really neat car that would be just right for you. Why don't you come an' have a look?"

"I've already got a car." I would have said "wreck" but I knew that would just encourage him. Earlier this week I had had the wheel alignment done; the water pump had been done before that; the brakes are being done and the valves still need to be done. I know *who* was done, good and proper. Sam had noticed that the drums were pretty badly scored, but I decided that they would last me and I'd save some money at least, by not replacing them.

Having said that, it was difficult to persuade this sleazy salesman, without being rude, that I really did not want to buy another car, especially from him. It was a relief when my friend returned with the clip, and there was another act of kindness in store for me. Because he was in the trade, he got a discount and it only cost me 90 cents instead of $1.19. Now that's what I call service, the like of which I would never expect to see in Scotland. But, had it not have been for my Scottish accent, I might never have been accorded this first class service in the first place. I am mildly surprised in fact, when he doesn't offer to come back with me and put it on. He probably assumed I knew what I was doing.

In the end it turns out to be a waste of a whole 90 cents, as Sam, being the mother of invention, had found a washer, sawn it in half and used that instead.

* * *

One thing that they *were* right about in Scotland was when they said that George would never keep his hearing aid in. He's forever pulling it out but we keep stuffing it back in. This time however, it seems to be really lost. After a search in the house fails to uncover it, I stroll over to the Hertz house, keeping my eye fixed to the ground and fortunately I spot it nestling in the grass on their front lawn.

Since I am over there, I decide I might as well see if Debbie is at home and find out how the homework went - if I had got off with it.

She is on the phone to the new boyfriend. Ah well, it's still on then. She has not held the crash against him nor have

Terri and Al banned her from seeing him as I suspect I would have done had she been my daughter, but then maybe Terri and Al are wiser than me and know that is the very thing which would make her even more determined to see him.

I have to have a beer with Al while I wait for her to come off the phone.

"How did the homework go?" I am able to ask eventually.

Debbie barely pauses in her passage through the kitchen to park the phone where it is tethered by twenty yards of cord.

"Oh Kennedy gave me the wrong stuff. He said I didn't need to do it."

* * *

The next morning I do buy another car. It is in immaculate condition, which it should be, considering it is brand new ⁄ and exceedingly cheap. Not only that, but it is extremely economical to run. That's because it is a plastic pedal car, a Formula One racing car and very flashy it looks too, white, with all sorts of stickers on it and best of all, with a stabilising bar on the rear. Even when it is standing still, it looks dead fast. I always wanted a pedal car as a boy, ever since I saw a photograph of Prince Charles, who is about my age, in one. But my parents, not quite being in the same financial bracket, could not afford to buy me one. His was only an Austin though, not nearly as classy as this. Here, they are so cheap that, impecunious though I am, even I can afford one.

He may be deaf and not able to speak yet, but there is no doubting George's delight as he gets in behind the steering wheel and his little legs are like pistons as he roars out of the pits. It's a bit unequal I know, but we buy Hélène a book. But she can always pedal the car too - if we can persuade George to let her have a go as he has a grip like a gorilla's when we try to prise him out of the seat.

*　*　*

If George is disgruntled because it's Hélène's turn to have a ride in the car and he can't go anywhere, I am feeling down in the dumps because I am not going anywhere either. For the first weekend since we came here, we have not been invited anywhere nor have anything to do. Could it be that the novelty of my arrival is beginning to wear off amongst my colleagues and our minders, the Hertz?

Iona suggests we go round and visit the Kennedys. I don't know why she suggested them instead of John and Carolyn unless it because they happen to live nearer and because she has seen quite a lot of Carolyn this week, including going with her to the Newcomers' Club where they went to a potter's in Lolo. They will visit one of the Arts each month. Iona's suggestion would be an idea I'd greet with more enthusiasm, if only I could be sure that Debbie hadn't blown the whistle on me, but to be honest, I'm not too sure that I can trust her not to have put her foot in it, despite what she said earlier.

To Iona's dismay, they serve us tea, not coffee, as you expect in the USA, where there are more types of coffee than I would ever have thought possible - at least as many ways as they have as cooking eggs. Perhaps we have just as many ways too, but when you go into a café in Scotland you know exactly what you're going to get - either something so overcooked it is so solid and rubbery you leave it at the side of your plate (and never dream of complaining) or done to perfection, where the yolk runs out like yellow blood as soon as you stab it. But when you go into a diner over here, the waitress reels off a confusing list of cooked eggs amongst which are some arcane varieties such as "over easy" which leave you feeling even more helpless and less capable than ever of making a decision.

But Bill was born in England and probably it is his English genes coming out, just like it is Al's Italian ones that are responsible for his drinking and love of hot food - I don't think. It's a pity that we hadn't taken with us the massive German chocolate cake we cashed in for another of the Welcome Wagon coupons as that would have made it more like an English afternoon tea.

Unsurprisingly, the conversation turns to our exchanges. We had received letters from their exchanges, the Browns, who had been advised that we were coming to Missoula and had been requested by the Bureau to pass on any tips to us. Mrs Brown, says Mrs Kennedy, was very bossy. Somehow, I had reached that conclusion myself when I read her notes. What a writer, to convey her personality like that, in mere notes! What I had not picked up on though, was they were Buddhists. It does, however, explain why there were so many references to where we could get good vegetables but not a single word about the best hamburger joints in town.

We leave laden with winter clothes for the kids and I am left marvelling again at the generosity and kindness of Americans. We have been so lucky to have landed amongst such nice people I reflect - little realising how my opinion was soon about to undergo a radical change.

Chapter Thirty-three

In which we undertake another expedition, I am rendered practically speechless, Iona finds a potential new hobby and I reflect on the shocking nature of American TV.

It's Sunday morning. Where shall we go and what shall we do today? The trouble is that although there is so much to see, Montana is so vast that you can't avoid a long drive to get there. There has been a chill in the air recently and the radio confirms that winter is on the way, forecasting snow on the passes, so we decide we had better not venture too far and decide to follow in the footsteps of Father De Smet and visit the St Ignatius Mission, his second project after St Mary's in Stevensville. It's on the Flathead Indian Reservation, a mere 50 miles away, a skip and a jump in Montana terms. It's in the Mission valley on Highway 93, with the magnificent Mission mountains as a backdrop, so whatever the attractions of the Mission and St Ignatius may be, it promises to be a very scenic drive as we head towards what I consider to be "real" Rockies.

That was the plan at least, until I discovered that I was out of film, so we head for K-Mart. The photos I've had back from there seem perfectly satisfactory and represent a great saving over the well-known brands. In fact, K-Mart is my favourite store, but when I vouchsafed this information to the kids at school, they laughed and said "K-Mart Fall Apart" and told me it would be more than their life was worth to be caught wearing anything from there.

The snag is it is so far out of town that it is almost an expedition in itself to get there and in entirely the opposite direction to St Ignatius, so we decide we'll just keep going to Lolo Hot Springs and then, after that, we'll go to Idaho because it is not very much further. There is a well-known song in Scotland which contains the lines: "I don't want to go to Idaho/I'd rather stay here in Kirkcaldy" - a young lady's response to her boyfriend who had gone on ahead, like Jesus, to prepare a place for her. Presumably, in his absence, she had found another. Poor sod.

In fact, it would even be possible to go to Washington, the state that is, since Idaho is only a narrow panhandle at this point. And, at the other end of Washington, it gives me a frisson of excitement to realise, lies the Pacific Ocean. I could see it today, if I wanted to, though it would take a good matter of hours to drive there. I would, however, gain an hour as Idaho marks the start of the Pacific Time Zone.

Lewis and Clark stopped here at Lolo on *their* way to the Pacific. I imagine they must have been pretty pleased to have had a hot bath, whether they thought they needed it or not. The water feels comfortably warm, but I am just dabbling my hand in a running stream. They have made a swimming pool and there are even swimming costumes for hire ($2 for the day) but unfortunately we only noticed this on the way back, one hour before closing time, otherwise our journey may well have ended there. It's hard to shake off the influences of a lifetime and no self-respecting inhabitant of north east Scotland would dream of paying $8 for an hour when you could get a whole day for the same price - even force yourself to get up early to make the most of it. I am only kidding of course. Since it is an open-air pool, it would be much nicer to come in the winter, with snow on the ground and preferably snowing too and have a swim or just laze about soaking in the hot water and in our own cozzies.

It's a beautiful drive to Idaho through massive amounts of trees, though the last part of the journey - 16 miles of it - is on an unpaved road. The car bucks like a bronco as we hit potholes and are bounced out of them, despite the fact that I have slowed down to not much more than a walking pace. Lewis and Clark themselves could not have had it much rougher than this and if I had entertained any ideas of seeing the Pacific today, I certainly would not have, not at this rate, on this road.

A sign announces that we are at the top of the pass and also informs us that we are at 5,235 feet. There is a visitor centre as well, but of course it is closed - the tourist season is well and truly over - if there are any tourists to Idaho, or Montana for that matter. I suspect this is more for local consumption. It's hard to imagine hordes of tourists from around the globe beating a path to this remote spot to see a vista of trees - and more trees, unless it is history buffs following in the footsteps of Lewis and Clark.

We head down a ravine and then branch up a little path where we find a patch in the sun to have our picnic. Other people, most people I suspect, prefer a shady nook for such pastoral activities, if anything I've read in literature, especially children's, is anything to go by. But when you come from Scotland, you grab as much sunshine as you can, and we have been lapping it up ever since we got here.

It's idyllic. So peaceful and quiet. It is easy to imagine we could be the only people for miles around. Certainly no-one had followed us here, at least by car. Just the thrumming of invisible grasshoppers to let us know they are there, and no other sign of life apart from the occasional fly-past of alien and exotic birds - one in particular, about the size of a pigeon with a black crest and brilliant turquoise plumage, reminds me, if I needed any such reminder, that we are on another continent.

After lunch, and venturing further and deeper into Idaho, we are presented with another sight which it is impossible to see in Scotland. We have arrived at the Bernard de Voto cedar grove. These are the kings of trees, mightiest of the mighty, broad, tapering, reaching tall and straight for the sky and so high that it hurts your neck to look at their slender tips, swaying in the breeze and blocking out the sky. It's impossible to look at them for long, and apart from the danger of doing serious damage to your neck, the sight of these massive trees swaying like that gives me a horrible sense of vertigo as if those towering cones which had been firmly anchored in the soil for centuries were about to topple over upon my puny cranium. Bernard de Voto, a small notice informs us, for whom this cedar grove was named, as they say here, was a celebrated naturalist. So now I know.

If Idaho does big trees, Montana does huge boulders. You cannot help but be impressed with these massive hunks of rock as we stop at Lolo Hot Springs again on our homeward journey. These are the largest boulders I have ever seen short of a mountain. But how could so many, such massive lumps of rock just happen to be gathered here by the side of the highway? One good thing about being married to a geography teacher is I know someone I can ask.

"They could be glacial erratics," she says, "but they probably just fell down the mountain."

Some glacier to have moved boulders that size! And the mountains here are not the craggy, stony type, but soft, rounded velvety-type things like Mt Sentinel in Missoula. I can't imagine those spawning these monsters - unless, in a time very long ago, they were huge craggy peaks and have been eroded to their present state and these massive splinters were sent tumbling down to the valley floor.

"Just so," says Iona.

And that's not all I learn today either, for after Lolo there is a Historic Marker by the side of the road. A word in praise of these Historic Markers. Rustic in appearance, rustic-red in colour, the message they convey is painted in yellow letters on a huge board slung in a pine frame. To my mind, the message and the presentation are in a perfect state of equilibrium and harmony with the surroundings. And from this marker, I learn something interesting: that near this site was Fort Fizzle.

Fizzle, of course, must have been a name bestowed later, after the event. It all harks back to when, after the discovery of gold, not to mention land being required for ranchers, the whites decided that the Nez Perce in Washington and Oregon must squash onto a reservation in Idaho - an 80% reduction of their territory. Some agreed but Chief Joseph and his tribe of refusniks, including the more poetically named subchiefs, Looking Glass and White Bird, refused (quite rightly) to kowtow to the whites. After a skirmish in Clearwater, Idaho, the Nez Perce were pursued eastwards. At this spot, in 1877, they were meant to be halted in their tracks by a detachment from Fort Missoula who hastily erected a barricade in the narrow neck of the Lolo canyon before it broadened out into the Bitterroot valley. In a manoeuvre which foreshadowed the Nazi's circumnavigation of the Maginot Line, Chief Joseph and his troops merely went round it by climbing a crest and continued their long trek, with some battles on the way, until it ended tragically in the

Bear Paw mountains, a mere handful of miles short of Canada
- and safety.

***

The minute we get back, there is a phone call from Al.

"Hey, Dave, you gotta come over here an' see the fish I caught today."

Is it coincidence or has he been waiting and watching out for me? As ever, it is an imperial summons. You can't say: "Em, thanks Al, but I'm not evenly remotely interested in fish, especially dead ones with their horrid dead eyes staring at you and their horrible smell. In fact, I'd have been quite happy if they had all gotten away." (I think I am getting quite Americanised in my imaginary speech, at least.)

Like the wimp I am, I hang up the phone and tell Iona, like the masterful husband I am not: "I'm just going over to see Al's fish."

I leave her to her own thoughts but leave Al's a few hours later with a shoal of fish and enough beer inside me, not enough to feel dead drunk, but happy with the world and Montana in particular. It has been another good day.

***

"Hey, Iona, you gotta come an' see this!"

Iona is worried that I am learning too many bad habits from Al, especially drinking habits, and she could be right, because even as I speak, I have a can of Bud by my side, though I did not feel particularly thirsty. I don't bother to pour it into a glass any more, just drink it straight from the can in the American fashion. Now I am even beginning to speak like him.

I have found an advert in the *Missoulian* for the Sweet Adelines, the female equivalent of Barber Shop. If there is one thing Iona likes, it is to let her tonsils have a jolly good warble. Back home, she is an enthusiastic member of the Gilbert and Sullivan Society - and not just as a member of the chorus either. Now she has the chance to participate in a real American singing experience - if she would like to.

And it seems she would. She seems quite excited by the prospect and if I have to attend her show, as I must if she is in it, I will be happy to do so, for I love the harmonies, and in any event, it will be a million miles preferable to the G&S show. I am sure they do it very well and I know it is meant to be very satirical and amusing, but somehow I never get the jokes, probably because they date from an era before my time and I am not an expert in Victorian politics. And with only one good tune on average per show, I find them tedious in the extreme.

They are holding the auditions for the Adelines that very evening.

* * *

The phone rings again. I answer it.

"Hi, Dave. Hope you don't mind, but it's Pauline Morrison here. I'm a friend of Marnie's and I wonder if you would mind talking to my son - he's never talked to a Scotsman before."

"No, not at all. Put him on."

I am trying to sound casual as if I'm not at all fazed by the request, as if I were used to being treated as some sort of extra-terrestrial every day. I have to hand it to the woman, there's no beating about the bush - she got straight down to it. I like that in a woman. She didn't even tell me her son's name.

"Thanks. Here you go, son."

There are some fumbling noises during which I imagine the receiver being exchanged, then silence.

"Hello?"

"Hi."

"Hi. What's your name?"

"Loren."

Thank God I knew I was talking to a boy or I would never have guessed from the name - or the voice.

"Hi, Loren. How you doin'?"

"Fine."

"That's good." I am racking my brains to think what I can say next and thinking I have not exactly fulfilled my remit in Scots-speak so far. Then inspiration strikes. "What school do you go to?"

"Adams."

"That's great... Do you like it there?"

"It's OK."

"That's great! What grade are you in?"

"Fourth."

Fourth. I am trying to do the arithmetic. That means he must be about 9. I have never talked to anyone that age since I was that age myself. I am struggling. For the life of me I can't think what to say next.

"Gee, that's great! Who's your teacher?"

"Mr Martin."

"That's great!"

Silence.

"Em... What do you like to do best?"

"What d'you mean?"

"Well, after school, how do you like to spend your time?"

"Just kickin' around."

"Do you play football?"

"Sometimes."

"What else?"

"What d'you mean?"

"Do you do anything else, apart from football?"

"Yeh, sometimes."

"Like what?"

"I dunno."

I'm sure the dampness that I can feel on my forehead must be the blood I've sweated. I can imagine Mrs Morrison standing by making encouraging faces to open out his answers a bit.

"Do you like reading?"

"No."

"No?"... The silence between us hangs heavy on the air. No matter how hard I grope in the dark recesses of my mind for something else to say, I can think of nothing. "Well it's been nice talking to you... Bye."

"Bye."

I can hear the line go dead before I have the chance to hang up. I get the feeling that talking to a Scotsman was a bit of an extra-curricular activity devised for him by his mother which he was particularly reluctant to undertake. He sounded quite a shy boy, perhaps as a reaction to his mother constantly pushing him forward. If so, I am glad I let him off the hook so soon, but I have a feeling of failure: that whatever Mrs Morrison expected from this outcome, neither of us has achieved it and both of us have let her down very badly.

If I ever give another talk over here, I don't imagine they'll come much harder than this.

* * *

In the evening, I light a fire built from the compressed sawdust logs. They don't burn too badly, once you manage to get them lit, and at the moment are glowing a cheery red, but the trouble is they don't last very long. It'll be good when I get my share of the dearly-wrought logs that I mined with Al and Grandpa, and we can have a roaring fire to dispel the winter blues and the depressing dark reds of the family room.

According to *The Entertainer*, that film tribute to Vincent Van Gogh, *The Agony and the Ecstasy* should be on TV. Being a bit of a Vincent fan, I decide to watch it on Marnie's TV through the usual amount of snow. But without any announcement to explain why, it seems the programme has been replaced with *The Flight of the Phoenix,* a war film about a group of British soldiers (and a German) stranded in the desert and their only hope of salvation is to escape by repairing, more accurately rebuilding, their crashed aeroplane with the vital help of the German, he being the most technologically-minded in the group.

It's quite gripping actually, full of suspense, though the advertisers do their best to ruin it and suspend your disbelief by interrupting it every fifteen minutes, again without any warning. One minute you are watching dirty, sweaty men in the desert in need of a good bath, and the next you are watching a lady in a bath in a luxurious bathroom with soap suds up to her neck (unfortunately) and just as suddenly, when you've spent nearly as many minutes watching adverts as you have the film, you are transported from the image of a cooler, cans of beer nestling on a bed of ice and perspiring with condensation, to the desert again, just like that, so for a second or two, you wonder if the protagonists in the film are seeing a mirage. Just as well they couldn't see the adverts. It was bad enough for me.

At 8 o'clock, the programme abruptly stops in mid-speech, and before I have time to gather breath to ask myself what all that is about, the opening credits announce the start of a *Lassie* film. I am too dumbstruck at first to be angry, but then the enormity of what has happened penetrates the fog of disbelief. I have watched an hour of this film, (well probably half an hour, if you discount the adverts) dedicated an hour of my life to this programme and they leave me in suspense like this, without the slightest warning or the merest hint of an explanation - for a *Lassie* film of all things! Ye gods!

Now I'll never know if they managed to build the plane, and if they did, if it took off and if it did, whether they made it to safety and if the German could really be trusted. I have a feeling that in the end all will be well. Perhaps the title gives it away - but it would be nice to know for sure!

* * *

In the evening, Iona comes back from the Adelines, having really enjoyed it but she doesn't know if she's in or not. She doesn't anticipate a problem though as she can read music while many of the others can't. It's not just a question of having the requisite amount of musical talent - each prospective member must be voted in by a written secret ballot. Whether that is based on their perception of your musical ability or just whether they like the cut of your jib or not, she doesn't know, but I tell her I am sure the Scottish factor alone would be enough to get her in, even if like me, she sang like a crow.

Chapter Thirty-four

In which the park turns out to be a very dangerous place in more ways than one and I end up in court, in more ways than one.

The following morning I am in the park with my soccer class.

"This is how the goalkeeper takes a kick out of goal, boys. The idea is to get the ball as far up the field as possible. If you are lucky it will go to one of your side, but you don't need to worry about that. It is the player's job to try and get it. You just concentrate on getting it as high and as long as possible."

I hope I am lucky and can do what I have just said, without making a fool of myself and at least make contact with the ball. If I'd had any sense, I should have kicked it first and whatever resulted, should have said, just as long as it wasn't patently pathetically obvious that it was a duff kick: "Just like that." After all, I have not done this for the best part of 20 years.

I take a short run and drop the ball from a height of a safe six inches onto my right foot. Well, that was the idea. Only I did not quite drop it on my foot and had to stretch for it. My satisfaction and relief at seeing the ball rise into the air, though not as quite as high as I would have liked, is tempered by an agonising pain shooting up my thigh. No one seems to notice my injury as the boys hare off after the ball, but all I can do is hirple off to the sidelines.

"You go on ahead boys," I tell them when it is time to go. I can walk, but only very slowly and with a great deal of discomfort. I am late getting back for my class. It's an uphill struggle climbing the stairs and I wonder how I will manage to get back home on the bike. Iona can't come and get me as the car is with Dennis, getting the valves reground.

"You ought to go to the Court House," says Blake when I tell him about my injury later and after he has stopped laughing at my funny new way of walking.

"Why? What have I done?"

"Pulled a muscle by the looks of it."

"Is that a crime in the United States?"

"Some time in the jack oozy should sort you out."

He makes it sound like the jug, the jail, like Cockney rhyming slang, if I could only think what it could possibly rhyme with.

"What's the "jack oozy"?"

"It's where you take off all your clothes an' naked women massage the damaged part until you jack off."

Now I know he has to be joking, but since he hasn't told me what this mysterious "jack oozy" is, I reckon the only way to find out is to go there and find out in person.

"I'm goin' there myself tonight. Care to come along?"

Am I not the person who said when I was over here, I would try anything at least once?

I get directions, but fortunately, when I am just on the point of setting off by bike, (funnily enough, cycling is much less painful than walking) Terri arrives. I had reported to her more than a week ago, that we had some water lying in the basement and I was a bit worried that Mrs Bates might find herself up to her ankles if something was not done about it soon - except I didn't actually mention the bit about Mrs Bates.

It seems as if the water is seeping up through the floor. That's Terri's department. As well as being our friend and mentor, she is responsible for dealing with any household problems, just like Pete and Izzy are for Marnie. Even now I have given instructions for Pete to check if there is something minor wrong with the toaster, such as a fuse or something and if not, for Iona's mother to buy a new one. But Terri seems to regard this much more serious problem with a laid-back attitude bordering on the horizontal. I had thought this is what she had (finally) come to see me about, but I am disappointed. She has merely come, like a good neighbour, to see if we want anything from The Dairy. I remind her about the basement and point out that the water is still coming up the drain.

"That's bad. We had that problem a while back."

"Would you like to see it?"

"Nah, it's OK. I believe you. Don't worry about it," she adds with that characteristic flap of her hands which she fondly seems to imagine will wave problems away, "I'll get Little Al to have a look at it."

"Little" Al is built like his father - a human tank - but curiously, he is as fair as his father is dark and as pale as he is swarthy, which is odd as Terri is dark too. He's the oldest son and works for a company known as The Sewer Arranger, which is pretty lucky for us as he may do it as a homer and any awkwardness between Marnie and me as to who should foot the bill may be avoided.

While that sounds hopeful and encouraging, I wonder when this glorious state of affairs might come about; Mrs Bates could be up to her neck down there by then. Just as well there's nothing down there that could be ruined though it's just as well Marnie was not here to witness Terri's reaction as

I'm sure she must love the dusty old junk down there with a passion.

"And you know somethin'?"

"What?"

"That monkey still hasn't written to me!"

Another real worry is that Iona's mother *has* written to us. No surprise in that. She could keep the Royal Mail going single-handed. She loves writing letters to such an extent that I have known her write to Iona: "It was so nice talking to you on the phone just now, I just thought I'd write you a letter… " But this time she has written to say that she had had a bit of a job getting Marnie to sign the inventory that our solicitor had advised (and what a pain it was drawing it up - how would *you* like to itemise the contents of your house?) and get her to hand over the deposit which would be returned in full if an inspection of the premises proved satisfactory.

Terri says she'll take me to the Court House as she is going that way, but first we must go to Skaggs as Al needs another bait box. Maybe since I've stopped accompanying him, the jinx has been broken and he thinks he's going to need a lot more fish food.

But at Skaggs, to my increasing alarm, Terri finds she is down to her last cheque so back we come to Lincoln - by which time I should have been meeting Blake at the Court House. It's for members only and he had said that he'd meet me at 8 and would sign me in. I don't want to keep him waiting. If I had set off walking, even at my snail's pace, I could have been there by now. It takes me right back to when she and Al met us at the airport and I am reminded that as far as they are concerned, time is made of elastic.

Likewise Blake, apparently, for when we arrive, what should I see rolling up, but his truck. Pretty neat timing. I couldn't have timed it better. Thanks Terri.

The Court House, of course, is a sporting venue. What else would you call a place that is full of courts: basketball courts, racquetball courts, handball courts, badminton courts and squash courts to name but a few, not to mention a swimming pool and the mysterious "jack oozy"? It is not just a house though, not even a mansion, but a palace devoted to sport. I can just see the Romans having such a dedicated place. As soon as you enter the building, set foot on the thick red carpet, see the padded leather armchairs and the bar with rows of bottles reflected in the mirrored shelves - the utter luxury of the place impresses. Just like my cousin's club in London - without the snobbishness I imagine.

At last it is time to meet the mysterious "jack oozy". It turns out to be a whirlpool bath and it is spelled "Jacuzzi". It's been all the rage here for some time.

"Lotta people have them on their decks," Blake informs me.

His face, as usual, betrays no clues. No twinkle in those eyes which might hint that he is joking, but even when I know he is, those eyes remain as cool as chips of blue ice.

"Their deck?" I ask, knowing that I must sound like an idiot. A surreal image springs to mind of affluent Montanans relaxing in Jacuzzis while, presumably, someone steers the yacht up and down Flathead Lake.

"Decking. It's a wooden terrace."

"Ah, I see!" That makes more sense. And how pleasant, I think, in the winter, instead of travelling all the way to Lolo, to merely step out your back door and sit in the hot tub with the snow settling in the garden around you and melting on your shoulders; or on a boiling hot summer's day, to slip into the cold tub for a refreshing cool down.

The Jacuzzi continues the theme of Roman grandeur and luxury, for this one at least, is made of marble ⁄ and communal, as the Romans preferred. You sit upon a ledge so only your head and shoulders protrude while the bubbles eddy and froth up about you. The temperature is 105°. It's a pity it's not hotter but it's a bigger pity still that the only massaging has to be done by myself and the water when I manage to manoeuvre the affected part directly into the jet. Still, unless it is my imagination, after only ten minutes or so of the treatment, my thigh does feel a lot better. I could barely touch it before, but now I can massage it without looking as if I were giving birth.

It is a bit boring, though, sitting in the pool, stroking my own thigh. There is no-one to talk to as Blake has gone to play a game of handball with Steve. Handball, I gather, is like squash, only you don't need to go to the expense of buying a racquet, only a glove, which slips over your palm.

Some instinct tells me that stroking my thigh, even if it is under water, is not a pursuit in which I should engage in the presence of people to whom I have not been introduced, so when some people get in, I get out. Instead I go to the steam room where the temperature suits me better and where I hope I am losing weight without the tedious trouble of having to run about working up a sweat.

Steve gives me a lift home and delivers some bad news which he has kept from me till now. Dennis, his tame mechanic, and to whom I have entrusted the Plymouth, has found a cracked cylinder head and has had to replace it. That's going to cost me another $30 at least and is the reason, apparently, why the water pump went. Not only that, but when Dennis removed the head, he discovered that two of the pistons had already been replaced and that too was due to the same problem.

Buying a car, when you are as clueless as I am about matters mechanical, is a bit of a lottery and I rely upon the advice of friends and trust to the honesty of car salesmen not to rip me off. Ruefully, I give a sardonic little laugh as I think of the collective nouns I had to learn in school such as "a herd of cows" but more poetically, the rarer examples which I have yet to come across outwith *The First Aid in English* such as "a murder of crows" and "an exultation of larks". I used to love learning such esoteric linguistic eccentricities, despite their totally impracticable use, just for the joy of the words and I now reflect that had I been taught "a mendaciousness of used-car salesmen" or "an honesty" of the blighters, just as long as I was aware of oxymoron, that would have been a practical use indeed.

If I had been reluctant to admit it before, I have to face the fact now. I should have listened to my compatriot from Elgin.

* * *

The next day, at lunchtime, I accompany Steve to the park for tag football with the girls. If you pull the tag from the belt of your opponent, that is deemed to be a successful challenge and you don't have to wrestle your opponents to the ground which is not considered to be very ladylike. Steve is refereeing and I am watching from the sidelines when a woman approaches me. Actually "marches" would be a more apt description.

"I want a word with you."

"Oh yes?"

"I'm Ray Taylor's mom."

As soon as she says the name, my heart hits my boots where it starts to throb so fast it feels like it's been run over by a truck. This can only mean trouble because in the past couple of days especially, I've fallen out with her son. In my experience, the chances of the mother coming up to apologise for her son's behaviour is about as remote a possibility as my winning the pools, especially in my case since I don't do them. In any case, the hostile tone of her voice leaves me in little doubt that she's not come to ask me out on a date.

Her son had always been a bit on the forward side, and although I had relaxed the rules far more than I would have in Scotland, his degree of forwardness, even by American standards, was going a few more degrees further than I was prepared to tolerate and his behaviour had resulted in some admonishments to moderate his behaviour.

On Monday, Taylor had shouted out in class and out of turn, and when I told him to stop doing that, the bold boy retorted: "Why? I'm not doing anything wrong." What the bald words fail to convey is the insolent tone with which they were delivered and if there is anything more calculated to ignite my (short) fuse than that, then I have yet to learn what it is, so before he knew what was happening, I ran him out the room into the hall. I got him with his back up against the wall and laid it on the line: "Now, just you listen to me, son. In that classroom, *I'm* the boss, not you. If I tell you to do something you do it. Right? Have you got that? If I say jump, you jump. Right?"

By the shocked look on his face, I imagine no-one had talked to him like that before, ever. His eyes started to fill up and before he could get himself under control again, I ushered him back into the class *pour encourager les autres* as Voltaire put it.

But the next day, yesterday, he was no better - worse in fact. So much for the shock tactics. He had not done his homework which was to write a piece which was intended he should deliver to the class the following day. My classroom was well-suited to this purpose, having a dais at the front reached by three steps.

"Why didn't you do your homework last night, Ray?" I began, adopting a friendly, reasonable tone, trying to keep my voice pleasant and my temper under control as if we had had no previous run-ins at all and I liked him just as much as all the other kids when, in actual fact, I thought him the most annoying little tick on the planet. After all, I tried to persuade myself, he may not be deliberately trying to test my authority again - he might have a perfectly good reason, such as being overcome with grief at the death of his pet rat - that universally detested, yet intelligent species of lowlife - which, in my mind, I could not help but associate with Ray on account of his recent behaviour, except of the two, the rat would have the higher IQ.

A shrug of the shoulders. Laconic you may say, but dumb insolence is how I saw it and that *was* the way he said it.

"Right, go to the back of the class, turn your desk round and get on with it. By the time the others have finished, I'll expect you to have done what they did at home while you were doing whatever you were doing last night instead."

I have to win this one. Disciplining a class is largely a matter of kidology and all you need is one kid to call your bluff and after that you are struggling to keep pandemonium and chaos out of the classroom as the less daring realise your bite has no teeth and join in the fun of teacher-baiting. Meanwhile, education disappears down the tubes.

He does not protest as I lead him to the back of the room, manhandle a desk to face the scenic view, Mount Sentinel with the M carved on its flank, and tell him to get writing. Whilst the rest of the class produce their pieces, I keep him under close observation. Because his back is towards me, I cannot see, but assume he is writing - nothing. It would be nice if the class should end before the others have finished their talks and I could tell him, without looking at his non-progress: "Right, get that finished for tomorrow" and we could both save face, which, as I understand it, Kennedy realised he had to do with Khrushchev during the Cuban crisis if he were to avoid a nuclear holocaust. Bigger bottle, same drink.

No such chance. The contributions from the class were so short that to my utter disappointment, it was not long before Taylor had to be called to the rostrum. He could easily have written as much as they had, if he had put his mind to it - which he clearly hadn't, since I could see without making an obvious attempt to look, his paper was blank. Ever the diplomat, I pretended not to notice and pointing to the steps, indicated that he was to take his position at the top. Even at this eleventh hour, all might have been saved if he could pretend that he had written and I could pretend not to realise that he hadn't.

But then he made it impossible. He sat down on the middle step, bold as a brass monkey.

"What do you think you're doing?"

"I'm gonna read it from here."

I blinked to clear the red mist from my eyes and when it cleared, I could see him there, as arrogant as whatever *The First Aid in English* said an arrogant person was compared to and I knew that our conversation of yesterday had had absolutely no effect, and this was an open declaration of hostilities. I knew he was doing it precisely to see what I'd do next and if I said "OK" he'd know he'd won, for I wouldn't mind betting he could muster up two or three sentences off the top of his head and make it look as if he'd written them down. Anybody could do that, seeing how short the contributions from his classmates were, measured in seconds rather than the couple of minutes they were intended to last and would have, in the Abbotsgrange.

"*What* did you say?" I said, as if giving him the benefit of the doubt, as if my ears had deceived me - his last (and very last) chance, to extricate himself from the mess he had got himself into, and so loaded with power and incredulity that he had defied me that he ought to shrivel up like a weed dosed by some powerful weed-killer.

There was a deadly hush in the classroom. Time seemed suspended as everyone waited to see what would happen next - no-one more keenly than me.

"I'm gonna read it from here."

Twang! That was the sound of my patience snapping.

"Get outta here!"

Even he could not mistake the fire in my eyes, the fury in my face and the imperiousness of my finger as I pointed to the door.

To my relief, he went, and not even arrogantly. He had got the impression that if he hadn't, I'd have strangled him on the spot. That was his big mistake, for if he had not moved, I don't know what I would have done and he would have won.

It would have been utterly humiliating. As I said, in the matter of discipline, it's all a big bluff. Now we were alone in the hall I could willingly have kicked two tons of shit out of him, but he knew I couldn't and I knew I mustn't. As for him, he could refuse to do what he was told, disrupt as many lessons as he liked, challenge my authority as often as he liked, prevent others from benefiting from my expertise (call that arrogance if you like, but that's what I was trained to do and what I am paid for) and yet I was not allowed to do the slightest thing to *him*. In other words, he held all the cards and could get off scot-free. Well, this Scot was definitely not having *that*. No way José, as they say here.

"Look here, you little brat, what gives you the God Almighty arrogance to think that you are so much better than your classmates, that you don't have to do what they have to do? What makes you think you are so almighty superior, eh? Eh?"

No answer.

"Well then, if you don't want to tell me - why don't you tell them, eh?"

With that, I opened the door and sent him back to the fold like the sheep who had gone astray.

"Ray has something to tell you, class... Well, Ray?"

Silence.

"Ray wants to explain to you why he's different and doesn't need to do the same work as the rest of you, class. Well, Ray?"

It seemed he had nothing to say but at least he had the grace to hang his head and keep his eyes fixed firmly on the floor.

"Right, get to your seat."

It was not the time to pursue the point about the homework. My point was, or so I hoped, that I had shown him and the class who was boss in the classroom. And if I had come out on top in this skirmish, I didn't imagine for a minute that the war was over. If the next battle were to be avoided, Ray would have to produce his homework the next day. If he didn't, I'd have to call in Matt for support. That's what he's paid for: to back the teachers.

But now it seems events had moved faster than I had anticipated. Ray has called the big guns into action. This is serious: for if there is one thing worse than a bad pupil, it is one who is aided and abetted by an adoring and gullible mother, in whose eyes the teachers are the bad guys and their offspring can do no wrong.

Chapter Thirty-five

In which I clash with a parent, clash with a student and clash with the culture again.

"I'm very concerned about the way you're treatin' Ray."

"Oh, yes? In what way exactly?"

"He came home in tears yesterday an' said he was frightened to go to school."

"Really? And why should that be?"

"You shouted at him an' he's frightened of you. He says you're pickin' on him."

"Really?"

"An' he said you called him a little rat."

"No I didn't. I called him a "brat". I called him "a little brat". Not rat." (Did I? Since he reminds me of one so strongly, maybe I had made a little slip of the tongue).

"I've got witnesses."

"Impossible. He didn't hear me right. I called him a "brat" and I did so in private out in the corr - hall - so I don't see how there could be any witnesses." I know my face was about six inches away from his when I called him that and I hadn't shouted at him then, not out in the hall.

"Well he says he has."

"And did Ray tell you why I had him out in the hall to speak to him?"

"He says you're always pickin' on him. You don't like him an' he's worried that you're going to hit him."

"Hit him!"

"Yes."

"And picking on him?"

"Yes."

"Now why would I'd be picking on him, do you think?"

"Dunno. You just don't like him, I suppose. I dunno why. But I want you to lay off of him."

"Oh really? Did he tell you why I was "picking" on him yesterday?"

"He said it was somethin' to do with his homework."

"That's right. He hadn't done it."

"He said he'd do it, right there and then."

"That's not the point. It was supposed to be a written exercise, done at *home*. Your son did not do what he was asked to do. Why should he be treated differently from the others?"

"That *is* the point. You *are* treatin' him differently from the others."

"Let me tell *you* something, Mrs Taylor. Maybe I do pick on your boy, - " I notice the shocked expression on her face before I plough on - "and I'll tell you why. Maybe it's because the others do what they're told - unlike your son. He doesn't do anything the first time I ask him to do it. He's always asking *why* he's got to do whatever I ask him to do and, may I say, in an extremely impertinent manner. If he wants me to stop "picking" on him, then maybe *you* should tell him that I will - just as soon as he starts doing what I tell him to do."

At this juncture, like a referee intervening between two boxers, Steve appears between us.

"What's the problem?"

"He's pickin' on my son." To my ears, the hostility in her tone has deteriorated into hate. I bristle but say nothing.

"You gotta understand," says Steve, "that where he comes from, it's a lot stricter. That's the way he's used to doin' it and Ray's just gonna have to get used to it."

"But *he* keeps pickin' on him." A nod in my direction and a look as you might bestow upon a slug. It's weird being talked about as if I weren't there.

"It's not just him. We're all having trouble with Ray. Boy, but he's got some mouth on him! I just tell him to button his lip and he zips it. But with him, he's just tryin' it on, 'cos he's new, see?"

"Right. Right!" and with that Mrs Taylor leaves the field of battle without so much as another glance at me.

As we watch her retreating figure, I thank Steve for his timely intervention, for the blood which he had just averted being spilled on the sporting field.

"Boy, I thought I had better get over here right away the way you two were eye ballin' each other!" He chuckles. He's obviously enjoyed the drama he's just witnessed, but I have a feeling that that was only round one.

***

The class, not Taylor's, is filing out and as usual, I am standing by the door to make sure that they do so in an orderly manner.

One boy stops in front of me, looks me straight in the eyes, though he has to look slightly down at me to do so.

"You've got short legs, haven't you?"

I can't believe what I've just heard.

"What did you just say?"

Apparently the boy is unaware that he has said anything wrong, for he repeats it again.

"Just you stay behind." I wait until the last one has gone and to the class lining up to come in, I say, "Just wait there a moment," and for effect, I slam the door. I'm not really angry, but I've got to show these kids once and for all, that this is inappropriate behaviour: they can't talk to me like this.

"Right, you. What did you mean by that personal remark?"

The boy looks crestfallen. He's got none of the arrogance of Taylor.

"I didn't mean nothin'. I was just sayin' that you've got short legs."

"And what has that got to do with anything?"

The boy shakes his head. Apart from being an impossible question to answer, the boy looks plainly perplexed at this turn of events.

"How would you like it if I said you've got a spotty face?" It's nothing less than the truth after all.

He hangs his head and remains silent.

"Well?"

"Not much," he has to admit, quietly.

"Right. Just you remember that. I'm your teacher, not one of your friends, so don't talk to me as if you were. Got it?"

"Yes."

"OK. You can go now."

"Sorry. I didn't mean nothin'."

That's another one sorted I think smugly, as I let in the next class.

* * *

"Dave, can I have a word with you?"

This sounds ominous. I have a certain *déjà vu* about this.

"Sure."

It is the end of the school day and Matt has just materialised in my room.

He swallows hard. "How's it goin' Dave?" He's looking distinctly nervous, even more than usual.

"Fine." I get the feeling that this is merely a preamble and wait for him to continue, for him to tell me what I've done wrong. I guess he has come to tell me to lay off Taylor. If that's the case, I'm happy to report to him that this afternoon I'd had no trouble with him. I'd ignored him and thankfully, he had ignored me. From his sulky expression, I had formed the conclusion that her unsuccessful mission must have been conveyed to him by his ever-lovin' mom. I did not pursue the matter of the homework. It just wasn't important enough. What's more important is that in future he does what I tell him to do without making a big song and dance about it.

"That's good. Em... ahrrum. I just wanted to say... ahrrum," he clears his throat nervously, "... at lunch today... you went to the front of the line."

That's right. Nothing new in that. I do that every day. By the time I get down there, there is an enormous queue and as a teacher, naturally, I go straight to the head of it. Nat, Steve and Blake don't need to queue as they bring their own sandwiches.

"Em... well, the fact is, Dave... it would show the students more respect if you got into the line."

I can scarcely believe my ears. Is this not the very thing I had been going on about? Respect. But *me* show the students respect? What about some respect for the teachers? Teachers deserve some privileges, considering their advanced years and status, surely? I can't believe he's not asking me about the Taylor incident - that this, my jumping to the head of the queue, is what seems to be the most pressing problem of the moment.

"So you want me to queue up with the kids?"

"Well... yeah... It would be more... em... respectful."

"Well... if that's the way you do things here... "

"That would be just grand, Dave."

Giving me a warm smile, he turns to leave. I can practically see him floating with relief that his mission has been accomplished so easily. At the door he stops, arrested apparently, by a sudden thought.

"Say, Dave, did you see Mrs Taylor? She was here lookin' for you."

"Yes, I saw her."

He looks at me, as if waiting for me to go on, but nothing being volunteered, he swallows hard. I expect he's just about to ask what had transpired, but to my surprise, he merely gives me a weak smile and a nod and leaves me sitting alone and bemused. Had Mrs Taylor told him the nature of her complaint? Surely she must have! And what had he said - apart from where she could find me? And why didn't he ask me what the outcome was? Or had Mrs Taylor already reported back to him? If so, surely it must have been to appeal to him to sort me out - but all he'd done was to ask me not to jump the dinner queue!

Sam thinks that Matt just bottled out. He has given me a lift home, slinging the bike in the back of his station wagon. How convenient to have a car big enough you can just do that without having to take it to bits. He comes in for a beer and naturally, the talk has turned to the Taylor incident.

"God, y'know, David, he's such a dildo." I love the way Sam drawls. "It could be he's too scared of Mrs Taylor to tell *her* to get her son in order an' he's too scared to admit to *you* that he's told her he's gonna tell you to back off. Anyway, he should never have let you see her on your own."

"I was glad Steve was there, that's for sure."

"Yeah, he was just duckin' out," by which he means Matt. "He'll hope it'll all blow over an' he'll not need to do anythin'." He takes a deep pull on his beer. "An' I'll tell you another thing. That son of hers is an asshole. Just ask Art. He had him last year an' I had him the year before. We used to knock him about."

I almost choke on my beer. "And did Mrs Taylor complain?"

Sam seems to regard this as almost an irrelevance. "She might ha' done. Might ha' told Matt, but if she did, we never gotta hear of it. God, but he was such an asshole!" Sam reminisces, shaking his head, but whether in sadness or disbelief, I couldn't say, but certainly requiring another large swig of beer.

"Well, anyway, it didn't work. Steve and Blake say he's a pain in the butt too."

"Too right he is!"

"You know Sam, talking of Art, it's a funny thing. I thought I'd see a lot more of him than I have done. Marnie said he was her special friend but so far I've seen much more of you and Steve and Blake than him… "

* * *

Life is full of coincidences. Would you believe it, but the very next day, Art issues an invitation.

"Say, I was wonderin', Dave. Chuck Paterson an' me are goin' to the ball game an' then we're goin' for a beer after. I was wonderin' if you'd like to string along?"

"Gee, that would be great, Art. Thanks."

To tell the truth, I'm not that impressed with the ball game, but it's the sort of thing the staff do here, go after school and watch the 7th and 8th graders play games, even if they don't teach them any more. There's nothing I would like less, after a hard day's work at the chalk face, to watch a game of kids playing football, but here they don't seem to mind - positively enjoy it in fact. I could do with missing that stage out and getting straight down to the beers.

"An' I was wonderin' if you an' Iona would like to come round for dinner tomorrow?"

This sounds more like it! "We'd be delighted! Thanks a lot!"

Nothing of Art, practically, since Matt's fish fry, and now two invitations in a row! Art is doing his duty. But I'm not totally naïve; I smell the hand of Sam in this. But maybe Art has been motivated too, not only by the hand of Sam, but by the possibility that Marnie and I might write to each other (how annoying would Terri find that!) and she would discover that we have not been seeing too much of each other. And this is not beyond the limits of possibility, for unbelievably, Marnie has found the time to send an epistle to the entire school! I would no more think of doing that than taking a long jump off a short pier. She writes that she'd been to the Edinburgh Tattoo and once again restates how impressed she is by how polite the children are.

Although it is on my doorstep, only half an hour away on the train, I have never been to the Edinburgh Tattoo. You always think, when it's on your doorstep, you can go anytime. We had to make a special trip back to Dumfries from Falkirk to visit Burns' house as we never did all the time we lived near there and even parked the car in the car park opposite. I'm glad that Marnie is making the most of the experience and it's not all just hard work.

I assume she is not having any problems with pupils, since they are so polite, or parents. That's another one to you, Marnie!

Chapter Thirty-six

In which I have a pedagogical discussion, further differences between our cultures begin to surface, and I have a feeling of foreboding.

If there is one thing more calculated to raise a comment from your pupils other than abandoning your wife and running off with the glamorous young twenty-something French *assistante* (as one of my English teachers did, most excitingly, in the late Fifties and even more astonishingly, in *his* early fifties) - it is to make the slightest change to your appearance, or wear a new item of apparel such as a tie or socks even, such is the attention paid to minutiae by the young to anything other than what they *should* be paying attention to. Less likely to happen here where none of the teachers wears a tie and where casual dress is the norm, apart from Matt and me, who wear a suit and a tie. Thus, back home, a boisterous pupil bounding into the classroom ahead of the others, so desperate his thirst for knowledge, might say, (and often did):

"You've had your hair cut!"

"No, you're kidding me! (Suddenly slapping my head.) How did that happen? I had no idea!"

Blake's hair, at the best of times, amounts to little more than stubble, but apparently he has a sudden brainstorm and has decided that he desperately needed a haircut. Accordingly, he has had an appointment with the shears at lunchtime and emerges as bald as a billiard ball. You can scarcely not notice his new image, but of course we are too polite to mention it and if Blake feels self-conscious about it, he gives no hint of it.

We are walking down to the park, Blake and I, plus a couple of dozen assorted kids to the scene of my encounter yesterday. It is his turn to be bodyguard.

Suddenly a tall, gangling youth runs past us. He's one of ours, in Blake's homeroom.

"Hi, Bald Eagle!" he shouts, laughing over his shoulder at Blake.

"Hi, Ichabod Crane!" Blake responds without missing a beat.

The boy laughs in return and runs on.

Once again I'm culture shocked. I can't help but reflect on the difference between Blake's reaction to this familiarity and mine yesterday. On the other hand, the loose, lax, free-for-all, and total lack of control in the way we "walk" the kids to the park, has long since ceased to shock me. In Scotland, if ever we are out and about with our charges, they are made to walk down the street two-by-two like the animals entering the ark. Or at least we try to keep them like that. And we're nothing like such a litigious society as they are…

"And where were you Mr Addison, when Ichabod Crane was run over by the truck?"

"I was behind him, your Honour."

"How far behind, Mr Addison?"

"I'm not very good at judging distances, your Honour."

"Come off it, Mr Addison. Was Ichabod Crane under your control at the time of the tragic accident or was he not?"

"Em… um. Well, he had run on ahead, your Honour."

"In other words, totally outwith your control at the time of this tragic accident. You were *in loco parentis*, Mr Addison and you had a duty of care towards poor Ichabod.

Fined $1 million. Have you any last words, Mr Addison? I trust you are insured?"

"I'm afraid not your Honour. Just put me in the Pen and throw away the key. I would like to say sorry to Mr and Mrs Crane, but if it is any consolation, he died happy. He had just made a very good joke and we were still laughing at it when the truck flattened him."

* * *

I think I am beginning to understand the rules of football a little. It's a bit like rugby, only not like that either, with the field divided into grids ten yards apart. You get four attempts to make ten yards, then the other side get a go. If you make it to the last line, you are awarded 6 points. It seems you are allowed to tackle people who don't have the ball - at least the way that it is played here.

I find it impossible to get as passionate as Art and Chuck about their respective teams: "Go! Go, Mullan!" shouts Chuck till he is red in the face. "Go! Go, Emerson!" roars Art. It's not just that I haven't any particular interest in the outcome, though naturally I hope that Emerson win - it's just the way that the game keeps stopping. You are lucky if you get 30 seconds of play before they stop. They have to stop each time the ball touches the ground or each time someone is tackled and they have to measure how much ground has been gained (if any) after each play. It's much more stop than start. The game is divided into four quarters of ten minutes each, and you would be lucky to get that amount of action in an entire game. I find it extremely irritating and cannot understand why soccer with its free-flowing movement has never caught on here - or rugby, even, though I suppose it is too similar to have any chance of ousting football as the nation's favourite sport.

I can't see it ever catching on with me either. Another cultural gap.

I am glad when it is over and we can head off to the pub. We go to the Gay Nineties. Like many of the bars here, it is very dark, and very busy. It soon becomes clear why the place is packed - Friday night is Happy Hour which means that you get half-price beer, and not only that but a girl wanders about with a tray, tempting you with all sorts of snacks, hot and cold. They are free and you can eat as much as you like.

"What a country!" I enthuse, helping myself to another slice of pizza from the tray.

If Art were a cat, you'd hear him purring, but instead he goes on to tell me what I already know, that the Happy Hour lasts two hours in some places and when that closes, if you want to, you can move on to another bar which has just begun its Happy Hour. And no doubt that is the precise word to describe how the customers leaving their third Happy Hour bar for the fourth are feeling as they clamber into their trucks.

"What a country!" I repeat, mainly for Art's benefit as he seems to bask in praise of his native land.

"They don't all have the same standard of food," he cautions.

"Still, as long as you have the price of a beer, you could always eat the cremated remains of what your wife had made for you when you got home!" I say in jest, knowing perfectly well Art is a bachelor. "And you know the most amazing thing, Art?" I add confidentially, having another long pull at my glass.

"No, what?"

"The beer here is so cheap in the first place, I can't believe that they can cut the price in half - and give you food into the bargain!"

Art chuckles as if it were a personal compliment.

Warming to my task, I add, "Gee, if you were too poor to eat, you could just buy a beer and eat to your heart's content, by just moving from bar to bar! What a place!"

So, with beer at half the price, it seems a saving and silly not to have as many as we can before the price goes up and as we drink, *getting' fou an' unco happy*, Art and Chuck quiz me about the price of beer in Scotland and various other aspects of Scottish cultural life, by the end of which time I hope I have convinced them how lucky they are to live here and how much I appreciate being sent to Missoula, Montana. I think my new role as a diplomat is going pretty well. We are getting on like a house on fire, quaffing the beers, agreeing about everything and I am thinking how lucky I am to have all these new friends and lucky too, to have a wife like Iona who stays at home looking after the kids whilst I engage in this extra-curricular cultural ambassadorial activity. Though, it is fair to say, she's doing all right on that score with her Newcomers Club and soon, I fully expect, the Adelines.

I have to confess, in response to Art's query, that I have found the ball game less than inspiring, but he understands that I am new to it and can't be expected to pick it up just like that. He is confident that when I understand it, I will love it. I do not disabuse him of his mistaken confidence.

Whenever teachers get together, you can be sure that before long, the conversation will turn to shop talk. With a teacher from the other side of the Atlantic, it is guaranteed to be sooner rather than later. I comment on Marnie's letter and express the opinion that although I couldn't agree with her on how polite the children in Grangemouth were, I could well see how she might reach that conclusion compared with the kids in Emerson.

"Of course maybe it's just Emerson. Maybe I should go to some other schools and see what the kids are like there. Maybe I could visit your school, Chuck?"

"Sure. I could ask my principal."

"And of course, I'd have to ask Matt."

And that would be the problem. He'd have to get a substitute to take my classes and I can't see him agreeing to do that somehow. But more than that, I have a sneaky suspicion that Matt would worry that I might tell tales out of school or make unfavourable comparisons.

Art is frowning. "What makes you think our students are impolite, Dave?"

"They're more than more impolite, Art - they are downright rude. Look at the way they talk to me. Take Taylor, for instance, he's openly defiant but he's not the only one - merely the worst. Why, just yesterday, one of them had the cheek to say I had short legs!"

"Who said that?"

"Tony Zweig."

"Tony?" Art puffs a whole engine-load of smoke into the air. "Oh, he's a swell kid. He wouldn't have meant any harm. He was just being friendly."

"Some way of being friendly, insulting your teacher by calling him names to his face."

"He wasn't insulting you, Dave!"

"Oh yes he was!"

"You're wrong, Dave. I know Tony. He's a really neat kid."

"Well, maybe he is, but that doesn't give him the right to speak to me as if I were one of his friends - as if we were equals even."

"But he *is* your equal, Dave."

I practically choke on my beer. I can't believe I'm hearing this. I feel myself getting hot under the collar.

"My equal! Don't be ridiculous! How could he possibly be my equal?"

I can see Art is struggling to keep calm and his voice has a hardened edge to it and his eye has lost all the earlier bonhomie as he repeats: "Because he is, Dave."

"Nonsense! How could he be? I am older than him for a start. And I know a damned sight more than him for another. It's my job to teach *him* and *his* job to learn - not for us to become bosom buddies."

Art shakes his head vigorously. Chuck is staying out of it.

"No, Dave, just because he's your student doesn't make him a lesser person than you."

"Who said anything about a "lesser person"? All I said was I am his superior in the classroom. That's what a teacher should be, any teacher - if he's worth his salt. You've got to keep a distance between you and them."

"No, you don't, Dave," Art says firmly.

"Yes you do. If you're their friend they won't respect you. They'll take advantage of you - think that they can get off with murder because you won't want to fall out with them."

"You're wrong, Dave."

"How am I wrong?" I can feel myself bristling.

"You should create a fun, relaxed atmosphere in the classroom so the students feel they can approach you an' not be afraid to ask you for help."

His use of the word "relaxed" reminds me of the first time that I gave my homeroom silent reading. Blake had said it was a good idea to let the kids see their teachers reading, and if they didn't get the habit in school, where would they get it? From what I had heard of the majority of their backgrounds, if there happened to be a book in the house, its only use would be as a doorstopper. So, on the face of it, it seems a good idea, but I could only watch in astonishment as they took their books to the back of the room and sprawled on the floor where they adopted postures more appropriate to slumber than reading. I took a relaxed attitude to that myself. They were so clearly conditioned to doing that that there was no point in trying to undo the habit of a lifetime. Besides, if that is what it takes to get them reading, so be it.

But to me this seemed time misspent when there were so many more pressing things that needed to be done, so I cancelled the silent reading in my homeroom and gave them the benefit of my voice instead. We should be teaching, not watching students reading; anybody could do that, and I couldn't imagine me ever trying to justify that strategy to Her Majesty's Inspectors of Schools. Not unless I had a desire to be drummed out of the profession pdq.

"And would "anything" include questions on your private life?" I ask, coming back to present differences.

Art exhales smoke and shrugs his shoulders and his tone makes it sound like a fatuous question as he answers: "Sure, why not? You don't have to tell them if you don't want to."

My turn now to shake my head in disbelief. "Don't you think that's impertinence - none of their business? " I can't keep the incredulity out of my voice.

"No. It's just their way of showing they find you approachable."

"But you *shouldn't* be too approachable, that's my point. There should be a distance between you and your pupils, just as there should be between the headmaster, or principal, and the staff. And above all, there should be a distance between him and the pupils - I mean students. If you are friends with everyone, how are you ever going to come to a decision when you have to choose between friends?"

Art looks as if I'd uttered the solecism of the century, whereas I think I've made a pretty salient point. But instead of answering my question, he asks me another. Grinding his cigarette into the ashtray he ripostes with: "Why do you think that, Dave?" The tone, in contrast to the abuse meted out to the poor, defenceless cancer stick, is measured and reasonable.

I should have insisted he answered my question first, but like the innocent I am, I swallow the bait. "You need someone at the top who's strong, who runs a tight ship, who backs up the teachers." I put my beer down and lean forward, locking eyes. "See my school in Scotland - we don't have that because the headmaster is more scared of the parents than he is of us. If we give a kid a punishment exercise for example and the kid complains to the parents, he always supports the parents and it ends up with the kid winning and us having to back down. It's so bad, the worst kids sometimes go straight to him without even complaining to the parents first. They don't hesitate to do that; never think twice about it. That's because he's too *friendly* with them. And can't you see, when he supports *them*, it undermines *our* authority and makes the job much harder? Multiply that throughout the school and pretty soon you'll find the lunatics have taken over the asylum - unless you are a pretty strong teacher and can maintain discipline in your own classroom while the rest of the building crumbles around you." I pause to let Art chew over that, then hammer home the final nail in my argument. "You know, Art, a school is only as good as the man at the top."

After this rant, if there are any lunatics going about, Art clearly thinks he is talking to one now. He takes a gulp of his beer and puts the bottle back on the table with more force than he probably intended. "No it's not, Dave."

"But it is, Art. It's like a tree. If the top of the tree is healthy, then so will the rest be."

"Lotta good things go on in my classroom, an' lotta good things go on in other classes too, an' it's got nothing to do with Matt."

"I'm not saying there aren't. In fact, I am sure there are, but I'm talking about the school as a whole, the ethos of the place. That's got to come from the top. Whether the staff feel valued and supported or not, whether they feel they are pulling together in the same direction or not or whether they feel they are struggling along on their own."

Art shakes his head, bemused. An uncomfortable silence descends, getting heavier by the second. I wish I could think of something light-hearted to say, anything really, to change the subject, to defuse the oppressive atmosphere. Just as well I hadn't told Art that I also thought the Emerson students were lazy and not very bright, but mercifully I hadn't, or hadn't had time to. It may only have started as a clash of pedagogical cultures, but I feel it has substantially undermined our relationship.

After what seems an eternal silence, Art and Chuck start talking about people I don't know and whilst it does relieve the tension, I can only contemplate gloomily on tomorrow evening and worry what we'll talk about. It had better not be about school or education anyway: it would be like a carnivore asking a vegetarian whom he'd invited to dinner: "How would you like your steak?"

Fortunately, Sam and his friend Chris, the lawyer, and his wife, Mary-Jo, arrive and since there is no room at the table, we have to move across the street to The Squires which happens to be the very first pub I ever patronised in Missoula with my ex-neighbour, Colin. Thinking about it now, it makes me realise how insecure I must have been feeling to have picked an English pub for the christening. Nothing wrong with English pubs, but you might have thought I would have been a bit more adventurous.

As with the Gay Nineties, it is hoaching with people, alive with the buzz of conversation and just as dimly lit. And I didn't need to worry about the beer being dearer, for in The Squires, the Happy Hour still has an hour of reduced-price drinking left. With so many people and such a lively atmosphere, it is easy for Art and me not to have to speak to each other.

A girl, overhearing my accent, wants to know where I'm from and reveals that she has just been to Edinburgh. She's at college in Avignon of all places. Then I'm recognised by one of the salesmen from H.O. Bell's. Telling him all about the problems I've had with the car takes up quite a bit of time, and by the end of the saga, if I had been expecting any apology or words of sympathy or an earnest request as to how he could make things up to me, I would have been sadly disappointed, for all he has to say is: "If it was workin' OK, you shouldn't ha' fixed it."

"The point is, it wasn't," I try to tell him over the hubbub of conversation, but by coincidence, he has spotted someone he wants to talk to rather urgently at the other side of the room.

Art takes me back to Lincoln, and to my immense relief, agrees to come in for a few minutes. To his surprise, I guide him through to the left, to the lounge and dining room.

"We live mainly through here now," I tell him. "The family room is so dull and gloomy," adds the beer.

"Do you really think so? I always think of it as such a warm, friendly room."

"Oh it is! It is!" I agree wholeheartedly. "We just love to go through there in the evenings and light the fire. No, I mean during the day, we use this room and go to the family room in the evening."

It sounds unconvincing, even to me. To bolster up the deceit I add, "Besides the TV is through there - though why I bother with it, I just don't know." The beer will insist on having the final word.

"Why, Dave?"

I had envisaged diverting attention from my faux pas to a hearty discussion on the shortcomings of American television, but it appears I have made another gaffe and find myself having to defend my stance.

"All those adverts! They get on my nerves!" And, by way of setting the seal on it, I tell him about my misadventures with *The Flight of the Phoenix* followed by an exposition of the virtues of the BBC (but not too much) which has no adverts at all. I have enough sense and tact not to add that my dim view of American TV is compounded by having to watch it through John Logie Baird's prototype, though if I had, I could have revealed that it was in my home town of Falkirk that he first began his experiments and which might have provided something of a diversion - for I feel I have not been entirely successful in convincing Art that I am right, again. Another diversion seems required, and fast.

"Say, would you like to see my slides of the powwow? They just arrived today and I haven't had a chance to see them myself yet."

I might just as well have asked him if he fancied having his fingernails torn out with pliers, for to my complete astonishment, he extends both arms, palms towards me, as if to ward off an attack from something unspeakably evil and backing towards the door as he does so.

"No! No! I'd rather not today, if you don't mind, Dave."

But his emollient tone cannot cover up the horror of the proposal which, caught off guard, he'd instinctively recoiled from. I realise not everyone has such an interest in Indians, especially Art, as I should have known from our earlier discussion about the Indian Studies course. All the same, I feel strangely insulted by the vigour of his refusal.

"No, no, that's all right… See you tomorrow then."

"See you tomorrow, Dave. Bye."

"Bye," and as I watch him climb into his station wagon, I can't say I'm exactly looking forward to it.

Chapter Thirty-seven

In which we dine out, I make another mistake and the day ends mysteriously.

In the land of the free and the automobile, it is frustrating not to have a car and not be free to go anywhere, having to hang about the house, especially with this self-appointed mission I have to go somewhere, do something every single weekend, otherwise, what was the point of the exchange? Ironically, I remind myself, I *am* doing something tonight and for the first time since I arrived on this continent, I am almost wishing that I was back home having another boring weekend. In the end, I can't stand hanging around any longer just thinking, so I cycle to Dennis's workshop to see how he is getting on with fixing the car from hell.

He's not there, which adds to the feeling of anxiety which has been gnawing away at my intestines since I woke up - if you can wake up after a sleepless night. Now I am worrying he has found something else wrong and has gone to get a new part - like a new engine.

There is nothing else for it but to head back and confront problem number two, feeling as if a huge big black cloud is hanging over me. But, I reflect, it's not so surprising after all. Just as I was beginning to feel that I was getting on top of the culture shock, recent events have shown me that I am as innocent as ever about the way of life over here. They may talk English, of a sort, but I couldn't feel more in an alien culture if they had been talking double Dutch.

I've been putting off a trip to the basement, not because I'm afraid of Mrs Bates but because I'm worried about how deep the water is going to be down there. To my relief, it is no worse but water is still welling up from the drain like - well, a well. I suspect the villain of the piece is the washing machine, for it is not fully plumbed in - the waste water pipe dangles over the drain down which most of the water does disappear, but it would be a pretty handy device if you just wanted to shower your feet, as long as you didn't mind the water being a revolting shade of grey.

Once more I put my hand in the murky mixture, right up to the elbow, and fish about in it, and finding nothing again, strip to the waist and try again. This time I do feel something. I get a finger hold on it and withdraw a disgustingly sodden object which turns out to be one of my socks. Aha! This is more promising! This could be the answer to my problem - no need to call in the Sewer Arranger, and better still, avoid any possible wrangling over the bill, especially if it turns out that it was our washing that was the cause of the blockage. I could argue that it was the machine's fault for disgorging it into the drain, but I've always suspected that machines have personalities of their own - in fact, I reckon they take a perverse delight in deliberately malfunctioning just to drive me crazy. In defence of Marnie's machine however, I can well understand its desire to spew out my socks rather than wash them. I wonder if my underpants could be down there?

Lying at full stretch on the wet floor, I try again. Yes, I can definitely feel something, my fingers frustratingly brushing against whatever it is, but failing to catch anything. Oh, for longer arms, never mind legs. At least I am in proportion. Small, but perfectly formed.

At last my patience and endurance is rewarded. I get a nail's grip on whatever it is and withdraw my trophy. It's another sock, but only one of Hélène's. Still, you never know, if a little boy's finger in Holland could hold back a flood by sticking it in a dyke, perhaps this little sock could cause a flood by stuffing up a drain. But it doesn't. The water seems to retreat, and my heart lifts up, but within less than a minute it's back to how it was before.

I wander over to see Terri to see if she can give me any idea when we can expect Little Al but only Rob is at home, which is quite useful really, to remind him that he's baby-sitting for us tonight. He was remembering, or so he says, but on the question of sewers, he has absolutely no idea if his brother even knows about the job next door.

It's only when I get back that I realise that I haven't the foggiest clue where Art stays, nor do I know his telephone number. No problem, I'll just look it up in the phone book. Damn! He must be ex-directory. Not to worry, I'll phone Sam. Margaret answers and tells me Sam is not at home and won't be back till late. Although she knows how to get there, she hasn't the vaguest idea what the name of the street is, let alone the number. She suggests I phone Mo Momoko, another 6th grade teacher. Mo is in the book, the only one thankfully, but she is not at home. I know. I'll look up Chuck's number. Hopefully there will not be hundreds of Patersons listed. Not hundreds perhaps, but certainly scores, and dozens of C Patersons. That's no use.

What can I do now? Apart from waiting till later and hoping that Mo will return before we need to leave, I can't think of anything. On a Saturday night it's quite possible that neither will. I imagine what this is going to do to my relationship with Art if we arrive really late or - even worse, don't turn up at all, and feel my brow break into a sweat. I curse myself for being such an idiot. I can't sit still. I pace about in my anxiety, racking my brains. How can I get myself out of this fine mess I've got myself into?

Finally my eye alights upon an old phone book in the bookcase. Please God! Please God! My fingers are trembling as I look for the Moores. Ma, Mac, Mc - so many Scots - Me, Mi - so many M's - Mo at last. Moore. Even if he is listed, it might only be by his initial. What do I do if there are 20 A. Moores? Start at the top until I get the right one? I think this might be the only solution and I sweat even harder as I imagine the ensuing embarrassing conversation: "Is that you, Art? - What is it to you, buddy?" and my toes curl as I imagine having to go into the explanation. Knowing my luck, my Art would be the last "A" in the book, but I would consider myself fortunate indeed and would consider the agony well worth it if I could present myself on Art's doorstep. Even late would be far better than never.

Oh, thank you, God! There it is - Art Moore. The only Art Moore in the book. But, wait a minute, that doesn't mean that all the other A. Moores are not Arts too so it doesn't necessarily mean anything, but this Art Moore lives on Eddy and Eddy is within cycling distance. To think is to act, and in less than the time it takes to tell Iona of my plan, I am painlessly pedalling my way, thanks to the Jacuzzi, to a certain address on Eddy and hoping there will be a car parked outside that I recognise.

There is and I do. Thank you, God. Hang in there. I might believe in You yet.

When Rob arrives, we are not ready for him - or rather, we have not quite got the kids ready for bed yet, thinking he was early, but Rob shows us his watch and we discover that Iona's is slow. And I still have to go to the Grizzly Grocery to pick up a six-pack. Earlier, the cake that Iona was baking to take as a tribute turned out to be a burnt offering, so she had to quickly rustle up some little cakes instead. It all adds up, or so it seems to me, that nothing is going right ⁄ all these difficulties seem to be pointing to one thing ⁄ omens of a difficult evening ahead. Naturally, I have informed Iona of this and I warn her that I am going to praise all things American up to the skies and I would advise her to do likewise and especially to say nothing derogatory about the house from *Psycho*.

It is with a heightened sense of trepidation therefore that we set off for Art's house, and fortunate that it's within walking distance. Even after all these difficulties, having found the street, it's quite hard to locate Art's house. Like us, the Americans do have an odd and even side, but the numbers seem to jump illogically from, say, 425 to 433, to 447 to 451, which makes it difficult to predict how much further we have to go. This apparently bizarre numbering system is based on the size of the lot or yard and since many of the numbers are so small and set so far back from the road, it's easier just to keep a lookout for Art's car than to strive to read the numbers on the houses.

Ah, there it is... Right here we go. Slightly breathless, but amazingly, in spite of everything, bang on time.

"Come right in, Dave, Iona." Art is extremely welcoming. "This is Joe, a good friend of mine. Joe, this is Dave and Iona."

I hadn't realised that anyone else was going to be there. Perhaps Art had drafted him in for the occasion at short notice. He tells us Joe is a retired bookbinder. I've no idea how long he has been retired, but I would guess it has been for some time. To tell the truth, I'm a bit shocked at how old he looks, surprised that Art has a friend as old as this. It's as if you included your parents in your circle of closest friends.

"Dave, I hope you don't mind me not lookin' at your slides yesterday."

Clearly he had seen through my act of indifference and is obviously doing his best to defrost the atmosphere of yesterday, but like the best-laid schemes, all it does is increase my embarrassment, especially as he comes right out with it, before we even have had time to sit down.

"Slides? Oh, those? Oh for God's sake, no, of course not! I hadn't given it another thought. There's no reason why you should be interested in my slides."

"No, no. It was rude of me."

"Not at all. In fact they weren't very good at all. A lot were very dark." I speak nothing less than the truth, though of course I did not know that at the time.

"Just as long as you don't mind. Care for a Scotch?"

"No, it's OK thanks, I'll just have one of these," and I hand over the six-pack of Budweiser which, in these parts is the equivalent of a bottle of wine at home, the traditional tribute borne by guests invited to dinner.

"Right. Thanks." As he takes the beer from me I can see that he's taken aback. What else would a Scotsman drink, naturally? Maybe he had bought it in especially. Have I made another faux pas?

"A Scotch for you, Iona?"

When it comes to the matter of drinking, as Al has already discovered, Iona is a bit of a problem.

"A beer then?"

All the women I've met here drink beer like men, swigging it out of bottles or cans with the best of them; not many I know in Scotland do that. Perhaps Scottish females are deterred from beer drinking because they perceive the swigging of beer out of pint glasses, or even half-pints, a trifle unladylike. Anyway, whatever the vessel, Iona regards the barley bree as being almost as poisonous as its more potent cousin.

There's beer galore and whisky enough for four, but not a drop for Iona to drink. No gin, no vodka, no Bacardi, no Martini. Art is effusive in his apologies, flustered and embarrassed at being caught out as less than the perfect host. There is some wine however, but I gather it was specially bought for the meal, so Iona must be even more abstemious than ever, as what is hers, is ours also.

It's not been the best of starts. Art invites us to sit down at last and we settle down in his small and cluttered living room. I'm pleased to see that he has not gone to a lot of trouble to tidy up for our visit - or even better, hopefully he has, and this is his idea of tidiness. We are not tidy people either, having better things to do with our time than waste it on housework. It gives me hope that Art and I have finally got something in common.

"By the way, Dave, there's a rumour goin' around that KPAX are comin' to film you teachin' a lesson to your homeroom."

"KPAX?"

"Yeah, one of the local TV stations."

"Really? Hey, that would be really great! We were told in DC that might happen but I didn't think it would happen to me. Just arrived and already a celebrity, eh?"

"Yeah, well, like I said it's only a rumour… " Art looks so crestfallen that I realise that I've done it again. It would have been so easy to have produced the desired reaction by pretending panic.

Cunningly, the meal consists of a meat fondue, so we do our own cooking. What a great entertaining idea for a bachelor, unless you enjoy cooking of course - and know how to do it. If ever I am reduced to widowerhood, to coin a word, or bachelorhood again, this is another thing, along with the potluck, that I could take back from this educational cultural exchange.

And so the evening passes amiably enough. Perhaps it has also got something to do with the shrinking level of whisky in the bottle, (nothing to do with me) the Bud which Joe and Art drink to keep it company, and the wine with the meal. The subject of school is hardly mentioned apart from Matt and I'm surprised at the strength of Art's feelings. Perhaps that has something to do with the whisky too.

"You know, Dave, the trouble with Matt is - he may be a nice guy - but he's got no balls. He's too scared to make a decision, let alone go out on a limb. He's too scared of offendin' people or gettin' his knuckles rapped. He just sits on the fence."

(Wasn't that just the point I was trying to make about my boss yesterday?)

"Yes, but," I point out, "there must be times when he can't avoid offending someone. He can't sit on the fence *all* the time. You know what Abe said: "You can't please all of the people all of the time". If it comes down to a one-to-one, he's got to choose one or the other, hasn't he? So what does he do then?"

"He does everythin' by the book. If you don't like his decision, he can quote the rule book at you. So, in the end, he can say it's not his decision, it's someone else's. Take this

MEA bullshit. If you had been at any other school in the District, you know what would ha' happened?"

I have a pretty shrewd idea, but I shrug my shoulders anyway.

"You would ha' been allowed to go to Vancouver for sure." He lets that sink in, before adding, "Know what you should do, Dave?"

"No, what?"

"Just sign in, stay a couple of hours, then breeze off."

I look at him to see if he's serious. I'd say he is. He's not looking at me, but at the table and I can see a muscle twitching in his cheek.

"Yeah, why not?" he goes on. "Lotta people do it. Steve an' Blake go huntin'. Why shouldn't you go to Vancouver?"

"Hmm. Maybe I will."

I say it as if I mean it. But I'm not so sure. It might be all right for Steve and Blake ⁃ they might not be noticed by their absence, but an exchange teacher from Scotland is too conspicuous by half. I have to remember that I am here to learn about American education and it is part of my duties. Apart from that, Matt might ask my opinion on the courses I'd been on, what I'd made of them from an exchange teacher's point of view. And so might other people, like Tammy Kinsella for example.

After the meal, we have a laugh as I try on a Stetson which Art sometimes wears and Iona, a Mexican hat which I assume he never does, at least only on Mexican Independence Day, whenever that is, and Art takes a Polaroid of us wearing them. This evening is going much better than I could ever have hoped. And it's taught me another thing ⁃ apart from the experiences which I'm going to take back inside my head, I'm going to take back a cowboy hat as the crowning glory.

We've been there for five hours and it's nearly midnight, far beyond the normal Montana breaking-up time, at least in our experience so far. Time to relieve the baby-sitter. He's maybe on double time by now for all I know. (Worry! Worry!) Art insists on walking back home with us.

"Thanks for a great evening. Won't you come in and have a drink for a minute?"

"No thanks, Dave."

"Are you sure?"

"Yes."

"Ah, come on, why not?" It was meant to sound like I was disappointed that the evening was over, that I felt we had got on so well that I wanted to prolong being in his company. But from Art's reaction I am horrified to see that he has treated it more like an inquisition. He spreads his hands out flat, stretching the fingers and stroking the air as if smoothing out a tablecloth. I get the message even before he speaks.

"Thanks, Dave. It's just I don't want to - if you don't mind."

I can feel myself blushing. "Yes, yes, of course not, that's perfectly fine. See you tomorrow."

Curses, curses, curses! Why couldn't I keep my big mouth shut? Why should he want to come in after a night of carousing? I was mad to suggest it. He had probably come to clear his head after all that whisky, not get it fugged up again by the remains of the Dewar's.

In any case, I had no need to strive to keep in his good company: he had volunteered to take me to North Missoula tomorrow to let me see where our students come from, perhaps thinking that that would help me understand them better. Perhaps it might, perhaps not, but it would certainly be interesting and in any case, he would not have asked me to come if he had thought it would end up in another embarrassing disagreement.

I had been getting on so well with Art, despite my earlier fears, and now, at a stroke, I had ruined it again. Dejectedly, I turn to go into the house and watch as Art's lanky figure strides off. Is that the walk of an angry man?

I'm getting ready for bed some time later when the phone rings. I tend to potter about at bedtime. If I'm reluctant to get out of bed in the morning, I'm just as reluctant to get into it at night. Who could it be at this time? It can never be good news at this late hour. It could be an early morning call from Scotland, but still likely to be bad news, as phone calls from that side of the Atlantic have been very few on account of the expense. On the other hand, it is unlikely to be a local call as someone, I can't remember who, but I think it might have been Nat's wife, Mae, who said that you never phoned anyone after 10 pm, except in the direst emergency.

"Hello?"

"Hi, beautiful!"

What? Did I hear right? It must be Art playing a joke, making light of our latest, slightly embarrassing leave-taking. After all, he is the only person, apart from Rob, who would know we were still up, or at least that I was. Maybe he's phoning to apologise for not coming in for a drink, having thought about it on the way home and decided he'd been a bit too emphatic in his refusal. Or perhaps it was merely to fix up a time for tomorrow as we hadn't done that.

But surely to God he wouldn't address me like that, not even in a slightly inebriated state. But however unlikely that seems, I can't think of anyone else who would be likely to call me at this time when all decent citizens of Missoula are safely tucked up in bed, so that is why I reply, "Is that you, Art?"

The line goes suddenly dead.

How very curious. Have I got a secret admirer? I hope not. It's definitely a man's voice. My soft Highland accent is often mistaken for a woman's on the phone, with embarrassing results. If it is someone we know, they're embarrassed at mistaking me for Iona and if it's someone we don't, like companies trying to sell us something, they blame it on a bad line, are covered in confusion and put on the back foot which is rather a good thing. Could that be what has happened now - the anonymous caller thought it was Iona who had picked up the phone?

"Who was that?" Too tired to lift her head, Iona's feeble tones come from the pillow.

"Dunno. Sounded like your boyfriend. Wanted to talk to you."

"What did he say?" It's more of a mumble than recognisable speech.

I tell her but she makes no response. I can tell from her breathing she is already asleep. If she does have a secret admirer, she doesn't seem all that excited about it.

Or perhaps she's merely pretending to be asleep. If not, she's a quick worker. We've not been here a month yet.

Chapter Thirty-eight

*In which we undertake another expedition
and get into difficulties.*

It's a beautiful Sunday morning and I am sitting in the sunshine with four pounds of newspaper when the phone goes. It's Dennis to say that the car is ready. I am on my bike before you can say "ground valves" and a few minutes later and $167.65 the poorer, I have the freedom of the roads again.

North Missoula can wait. It's a beautiful day for a picnic, so while Iona attends to that, I phone Art and say how much we enjoyed last night and ask him if he'd mind postponing the North Missoula trip. It's not so much that I don't want to go but it's such a lovely day, I'd prefer to go for a run in the car.

"It's all right, Dave. I've got an appointment with Joe this afternoon anyway."

This comes as a bit of a shock. When was that arranged then? Had it anything to do with my gaffe of last night? I hang up with an uncomfortable feeling that my relationship with Art has suffered another setback.

This is the plan. We are going to go down the Bitterroot Valley past Hamilton on Highway 93 then we will take a road off the left to see the Skalkaho Falls. It's a scenic run but it's nice to have a destination too and the Falls should be a nice place for a picnic. After that, instead of returning the same way, we can take the road over the pass of the same name and come out at Philipsburg, then take Highway 1 to

Drummond then the I 90 back to Missoula. A nice little circular tour of about 150 miles for a Sunday afternoon. I calculate four hours for the driving, allowing for the road over the pass which is bound to be slower, plus however long we decide to stay at the Falls and I reckon we have plenty of time to get back before it gets dark. All the same, we had better get weaving. We have film to buy, and gas.

It's at K-Mart that Iona notices that George is not wearing his hearing aid. It has not been handed in at the customer services desk, nor does a search of the car bring it to light. There is nothing else for it but to go back to the house. Eventually Iona finds it in a drawer where she had found it once before. That's useful to know. I don't know where he got his tidiness from but next time it goes missing, we could save ourselves a lot of time looking - until the little turkey works out we've twigged his hiding place and finds somewhere else.

We don't have seats for the kids, unless you call Iona's lap a seat. She sits in the back with them and keeps them under control. It's so roomy back there they have plenty room for manoeuvres, and they do, especially George who, totally fearless, is desperate to conquer the ascent of the precipitous north face of the front seat by the foolhardy method of launching himself at it from the edge of the back seat. He hangs there, his chubby little legs squirming and wriggling like two fat worms, searching vainly for a toehold until at last sheer determination and willpower results in his making it to the summit, when a pair of mighty hands pluck him back just as he is about to launch himself over the other side.

Because of the Great Hearing Aid Hunt, we are behind schedule and have to make an enforced stop to have our picnic before we reach the Falls since the natives in the back are getting ever more restless, squirming about beyond the limit of their mother's patience. We draw off the road and drive a short distance up a track. It may be second best, but it's not a bad place for a picnic. No shady nook for us: we want to make the most of the deliciously warm autumn sunshine, even Iona, who is ordinarily no sun-worshipper. The leaves are just beginning to turn and once again it is easy to believe there is not another human being within miles. We luxuriate in the sense of space and the sense of freedom it brings.

I should not have been surprised by now to find that the paved road suddenly stops and becomes a dirt track. It's not too bad though: wide, compacted hard and relatively smooth, but with a covering of small stones which force me to slow down, the sound of the stones as they ricochet off the undercarriage sounding like bullets. Still, it is not difficult driving, and if this is the worst we have to endure, it won't make a huge amount of difference, only make our trip a bit longer than I had anticipated.

There is plenty of room to park amongst the handful of other cars at the base of the Falls, white water tumbling down in a single unbroken cascade. As waterfalls go, it's no Niagara: not so high, nor so wide, nor so vertical but impressive enough in its own way as it tumbles down between the trees and the gash it has carved in the rock. There is a path of sorts at the side, and I clamber up to have a look at it from the top, and it is from that vantage point that it looks the most impressive. It looks a long way down - the Plymouth station wagon, big and wide and long, now looking like one of the Matchbox models I used to collect as a boy. There is something mesmerising in watching that water just as it reaches the edge, then following its tumultuous progress as it is launched over the edge. The scary thing is it doesn't take a minute for that unstoppable force to plummet down and smash itself to smithereens on the rocks below. Resisting that hypnotic urge to take the wet and shorter way down, I return the way I came, using hands and feet to negotiate the boulders at the side.

We've reached the end of our journey in the sense that we've seen what we came to see. It would have been simple then to have just turned round and gone back the way we came. But I have always had an aversion to returning the same way as the outward journey. Many years ago, I remember, in an exam, writing an essay about a day out. I had only just got to the destination, (where we had a picnic) when we were told, much to my surprise and alarm, that it was time to stop. I had just enough time to scrawl: "We returned by a different route." before I handed in my paper, despondent at how badly I had done. In actual fact, when the results came out, much to my surprise, I had done rather well. Thus I learned (but did not always remember to employ) the benefits of brevity, but never abandoned the notion of a circular journey whenever possible. We decide to take the long way back, the way over the pass.

The road, after the Falls, is only a little more rutted, only a little rougher as we head up towards the pass but then we come to a dividing of the ways. One way, the sign says, will take us to Phillipsburg, the other, a shorter route, back to Missoula. The problem is that what passes for a road stops at this point and what I would describe as a track begins. With each track looking as bad as the other, and not at all as "good" a surface as the one we are on at present, it seems unwise to choose the longer way back. Besides, the shorter one still allows me to be true to my principles. It is still home by another route.

Before very long, the track becomes even rougher than before and dust swirls into the car, despite all the windows being closed. I can feel it in my throat and in the mirror, see the motes floating in the air so that Iona and the kids appear indistinct through the haze, rather like the figures in one of those snowstorm scenes which you shake to create a blizzard, only here of course the "snow" is brown, nor does it settle and allow the scene to become clear. Indeed, it is becoming thicker and thicker by the minute and, I dare say, if it goes on like this much longer, I soon won't be able to see my passengers at all.

Eventually the track comes to an end, but to my dismay, in what appears to be the middle of nowhere. We have come to a clearing in the forest, a pasture, enclosed entirely by trees. The grass has been flattened by vehicles passing across it and, at the far end, I can see where the track picks up again through the trees. May as well go and have a look.

I don't like the look of it at all. If the way we have come might be defined as a road in the 18th century British sense of the term, the way ahead is the sort of track where you would abandon your carriage and get out and walk. Narrower, the earth on the track less compacted, the trees seem to crowd in and the forest ahead seems to have a darker, more sinister air. It looks like the perfect habitat for wolves and it would not surprise me in the slightest, should we go this way, if we came across Little Red Riding Hood hitching a lift to Grandma's. On the other hand, we have come so many miles and it has taken so long with nothing to see on either side but trees and yet more trees, that the heart is despondent at the thought of reprising all those slow and tedious miles, the ruts, the potholes, the stones like bullets. Like Macbeth, it seems as tedious to return as to proceed.

"What do you think?" I ask Iona, nodding at the way ahead.

"It's up to you."

I prefer not to make these decisions alone. I am indecisive at the best of times and would prefer she made the important ones. Yet I know why she leaves them up to me: if it turns out to be the wrong decision, there is no-one I can blame but myself. Feeling the weight and burden of the world on my shoulders, I put the gearshift into Drive and we continue, deeper into the forest.

It's a slow and painful journey, trying to avoid the deepest of the ruts. In the back, my passengers are being thrown about, even if I am travelling not much faster than the proverbial snail. Then a fork in the road appears. Not another one! And this time there isn't a sign. Which to take?

As before, one looks just as uninviting as the other. Nothing to choose between them. Nothing to suggest which might be the one to Missoula, which might just take us deeper into the forest and end up nowhere.

"Which way?" I ask Iona, and with the car no longer in motion, I can see her a bit more clearly now as the dust begins to settle. She has a pretty good sense of direction and whatever she says will be good enough for me.

"I don't know. You decide."

That answer strikes a chill into my heart, not just because she doesn't know the answer, but because of the tone in which it is expressed. To me it has too much of suppressed panic in it. If she has no idea, then I certainly don't. How could anyone tell the right direction, winding our way through these trees as we have been, without a landmark in sight, which, even if we had been able to recognise it, might have given us a clue in which direction we were, or should be, going? The only sense of direction we have is upward, for we have been climbing, not steeply, but steadily upwards. One feeling I am unable to suppress however, is the horrible feeling that we are lost, or if we are not already in that unhappy state, we will be very soon, depending on the decision I'm just about to make.

I take the right fork. Right seems right. Left is sinister. I trust in the right, hope it is the right thing to do and the right way to go.

We make our painstaking way on and on, even crossing fords. The track is getting worse and worse and the thought that I might be heading in entirely the wrong direction makes the sweat burst out on my forehead and my throat turn dry, even if there is no dust now. We are driving far too slowly.

And with every yard, nagging worries gnaw away at my mind as relentlessly and as insistently as a dentist's drill, the one I remember from my boyhood that felt as if it was going right through my jaw. What if I am on the wrong road? How will I know? Where am I going? Where will I end up? When will I find out?

There was a trail off to the left a while back, but it was narrower than this and, if anything, in an even worse state than this. It's not much of a dilemma; I had no hesitation in not choosing that one, but what if that *was* the way we were supposed to take and every jolt, every pothole, every rut, every creek, is taking us further away from our destination - and we might have to come back all this way? I keep my nightmarish thoughts to myself, but my tenseness seems to have made its way to the back seat where the kids have fallen silent. Their silence only adds to my fears, communicates that even they realise we are in a very serious difficulties.

Then, relief! Unexpectedly, we meet a jeep coming the other way, the first vehicle we have seen since we left the Falls, seemingly hours ago. It must mean the road must be open ahead and even if we are on the wrong road, it must lead somewhere and anywhere would be better than this. Even if I had to make a hundred-mile detour, I wouldn't mind. As long as it was on a proper road again, I would willingly trade it for a mile of this.

Because of the narrowness of the track, as we draw abreast, I could literally touch him, so it is easy to conduct a conversation.

"Is this the way to Missoula?"

His eyes scan me like an x-ray machine.

"Yip."

He shifts a toothpick to the other side of his mouth by the use of his tongue only, conveying a casualness which is in stark contrast to my mounting sense of panic.

I have always regarded with some scepticism the idea that Mary received the news that she was pregnant with great tidings of great joy, since she wasn't married in the first place, and secondly, the way the news was broken to her would have scared any self-respecting virgin half to death - in fact, enough to make her miscarry on the spot. But this news, delivered by the occupant of the jeep, I receive with an overwhelming sense of joy and regard him as no less than an angel, though his tattooed biceps depicting a buxom, naked lady might have had me fooled.

"Do you think I can make it?"

The suspense is breathtaking as he removes his gaze from my face and his languorous eyes study the Plymouth from end to end before they settle back, unnervingly, on my eyes.

"You ain't got four-wheel drive in that thing, right?"
"Right."

His eyes rake the Plymouth again, then come back to rest on mine, studying me, making me feel very uncomfortable, as if I am some sort of weird or alien specimen being studied under a microscope.

"I reckon jus' about."

A cold hand seizes my heart. There is a lump in my throat but my mouth is too dry to swallow it. Maybe it's to do with all that dust, but I think it is sheer, naked fear. All I can do is nod. This is hardly reassuring news, especially since he had thought so carefully before giving me my answer.

"Em... um... how far do you reckon it is before we hit the road?"

"Twenty somep'n miles - maybe more."

Twenty miles! At least twenty! If it's possible to hear more depressing news on top of already bad news, then I don't know what it is, unless it is you've just come back from holiday to receive the news that your house has burned down and that your grown-up children are missing. You always wished that they would leave the nest, but not like that.

We must have come more than twenty miles already I imagine, so to go on perhaps does seem the better option. But I didn't like the way he called the Plymouth a "thing", nor could his opinion that we could make it be called a ringing endorsement.

"Just watch out for the crik," he says, shifting his toothpick to the other side of his mouth, putting the jeep into gear and lurching on his way.

He said something else, but over the whine of his engine and the increasing distance between us, I couldn't make out what it was. I thought I could detect the word "right" but couldn't be sure. It only serves to add to my anxiety. I want to yell after him: "What did you say?" but more than that, what I really want to do is beg him to stop, to let us follow him. To return would be a nightmare, but if we did get into difficulties, unlikely angel though he may appear to be, he would surely help us out or go for help. Furthermore, with regard to the "road", the devil you know is better than the one you don't. After all, we had managed to get this far and God knows what lies ahead.

But the *cri de coeur* dies in my throat as I realise how pathetic it would sound, and anyway, he'd never be able to hear me now. Even if he had, it would take a thirty-point turn to turn around a vehicle as long as this and the patience of even a saint would not stretch that far while I completed the manoeuvre. What would I have given for a jeep like his: short, with a high wheelbase and four-wheel drive!

But there is another reason why I don't call after him, or more than that, suppress an overwhelming desire to dash out and run after him - I don't want Iona to know how scared I am. But the truth is I am very, very scared.

There is nothing else for it but to continue. I put the car into the D1 position and edge forward into the unknown. It feels like the start of an adventure, the very thing which had made me apply for this exchange, to get out of the rut. The only thing is I had never expected to exchange those metaphorical ruts for the literal ones I now find myself in. God has a mysterious way of answering your prayers, even if, like me, you don't believe in Him in the first place and never prayed to get you out of Grangemouth.

But now, come to think of it, in this dire situation, it would be nice to believe in God. In fact I think I do now. I don't appreciate Your sense of humour though, if You don't mind me saying so. I get the message, but if it's all right with You, would You mind showing me the way, and get me out of here? Please. Pretty please.

    Amen.

Chapter Thirty-nine

In which the journey from hell continues.

Twice we have come to a creek and successfully negotiated them, climbing successfully up the other side and at each one I asked myself: Is this it? Is this the "crik" which the man in the jeep had referred to? But now I have stopped and am contemplating the way ahead with despair and a fresh bout of panic. I have little doubt that I have now arrived at the "crik" in question. It looks like an insurmountable barrier - far steeper than any of the others. I don't know if I can do it, but should I attempt it and fail, to reverse out of the situation would seem hopeless. We'd be stuck. And then what?

There is however, an alternative route. The road, or rather track, continues ahead, while the creek forks off to the right. Was this the "right" turn that I thought I had heard the man mention? There are no signs, nothing to tell me where to go. Once again the thought of taking the wrong road and getting lost in this forest turns my guts to water but here the decision is not too hard to make, for if the choice of the creek looks bad, the other track ahead looks even worse. The ruts there are so deep I can't see me making it up that road without tearing the undercarriage out of the car. If that's the right road, it's an impossible road for us.

But there is another, a third choice - I could, before it is too late, turn the car around. If it were to be done, though perish the thought, it would be best to do so now, for should I make it over the creek, I wouldn't care to have to risk it again. But what if I am forced to? What if the man in the jeep was wrong and I can't make it through whatever obstacles lie further ahead?

I don't how long I sat looking at that ravine, weighing up the possibilities. But once again the prospect of returning all that way proved too horrible a prospect and whatever the future holds, I deem it preferable to the certain knowledge of the miles and miles of barely passable track we have already covered.

I edge the Plymouth over the abyss. The nose seems to point vertically down as we descend. At last the front wheels touch the water and we begin the climb up the other side. Bang! What was that? Before I have time to work it out, bang! there it goes again. It's the tail of the wagon hitting the bank on the downward side as the front begins the ascent for, to my horror, I realise the car is longer than the creek is wide - and I, in the front of the car, have already crossed, while Iona and the kids, in the back, are still on the other side. For a nightmarish moment, I have an image of us stranded there with the car bridging the gap, but by the time I have begun worrying about that, the second bang means the tail has followed the front and we have at least all made it down and I can begin the new worry - are we going to make it up the other side?

The sweat is standing out on my forehead as I nudge the big blue beast up the slope. I know there are plenty of horses to make it up that incline but what worries me is I get stuck in a rut or the tyres fail to grip on the loose gravel. Plenty of revs - it would be fatal to stall now. Time seems suspended. But we are getting there, inch by inch. *Come on! Come on! Just a little bit more. That's it. Don't stop now.*

Keep going! Keep going! If will power alone could make that car reach the top, it would have done so. And who's to say it didn't help - for we have finally made it.

I stop the car and become aware that I have started breathing again. Well, I've done it now. Crossed the Rubicon. Only one way now - forward. The track looks no worse than anything else I've tackled so far. But what lies around the first bend? I can only guess and fear. The only way to find out is to go there - and go there I must. I am not tackling that ravine again. No, sir!

To add to my problems, although we have been climbing steadily since we left the Falls behind a century ago, the incline seems steeper now. Somehow I have to get down to the valley and my brow springs a fresh leak as I realise that we still have not reached the pass. We have a long way to go yet and that's assuming we are on the right "road" in the first place. That we may end up in a dead end is a nightmare thought. No matter how hard I try to so suppress it, it still insists in dominating my thoughts every inch of the way.

Then, taking me be surprise, the trees on the left thin out and like a pilot who has only been taught to fly by landmarks on the ground and bursts out of cloud, I can see where we are. It's a sight that reveals to me the enormity of the situation we find ourselves in. Like The Ancient Mariner, who could see nothing but *water, water everywhere,* all I can see around me are trees. As far as the eye can see, from horizon to horizon - nothing but rank upon rank of trees. And this is miles and miles away from the vista of trees I saw when I went logging with Al. Montana, it seems, is disappearing under one dark-green blanket of trees.

Another time it might be a sight to behold, one of beauty and wonder, but looking at it now it only has the power to strike fear into the depths of my being. When I see the enormous extent of this forest, I realise we could be lost up here for days, weeks even, before anyone found us. If we were to break an axle, or burst the sump, as seems eminently possible, or take a wrong turning, we could be in a right old mess. Thank God that I got the water pump sorted. Imagine if that had happened while we were up here! I don't fancy walking down this track in my sandals, especially in the dark, to go in search of help.

Is that what I would do if, God forbid, the unthinkable happened and the car broke down? Or would I wait in the car with Iona and the kids until first light? The thought of an endless night stuck up here, without food, without blankets or even warm clothes as I am dressed only in shorts and a T-shirt, with coyotes singing to the moon out there somewhere, fills me with dread. But at least that would give me a rough idea of where they were. The prospect of going to the toilet with the possibility of bears and mountain lions padding silently about somewhere in the vicinity is enough to make me have an accident in my trousers right now. No, I think I would stay in the car after all.

We've reached a watershed, literally. That was the summit. We are on the way down now, but my troubles are not nearly over yet. We come across a sign: "Rock Creek Road and I 90 13 miles". It's a good sign and it is a bad sign. It tells us that we are at least, on the right road. But if that knowledge, the lifting of uncertainty, was like a huge weight being lifted off my shoulders so that I felt as if I were practically floating, the number of miles that we have to go before we even reach the Rock Creek Road was like a chain binding me firmly to earth. And how many miles of the Rock Creek Road would there before we finally hit the Interstate?

I grit my teeth and grip the wheel tighter. We're not yet out of the woods I tell myself, cynically smiling at the appropriateness of my pun. I am not laughing a minute later. Another sign: "Caution. Engage low gear". That's a laugh, I've been in nothing but low gear all this way, for what seems hundreds of miles. I can see the reason - or think I do. The track is starting to descend more steeply and is covered with what seem to be ball bearings, but which in fact, is loose gravel. But then I see the real reason for the caution. On my left-hand side, the trees suddenly stop - and so does my heart. We're on the edge of a precipice and it's a long, long way down.

"Oh, my God!"

In the back, Iona has turned white and instinctively moved over to the other side of the car so she doesn't catch a glimpse of the depths below. She has even less of a head for heights than I have and my knees knock when I am six feet up a ladder. She has Hélène and George under a tight rein as if a sudden movement by either of them might be sufficient to disturb the equilibrium of the vehicle and tip us over the edge, for we are perilously near the verge. God forbid that we should meet anything coming up and I would have to squeeze over to the very edge...

The effort of concentration is physically painful. I have an ache between my shoulder blades as if someone had planted a dagger there and the sensation has radiated up my neck into the base of my skull from whence it creates a pulsing throb behind my eyes. Thank God I have just had the brakes done because my foot is either on the pedal or hovering over it. They must be red hot but what worries me is not so much that they burn out but the wheels lock, we skid on the gravel and we drift inexorably over the edge. Already in my mind's eye, I can see it happening in slow motion.

"Do you want to get out and walk?" I manage to croak.

There is a moment's thought as Iona weighs up the alternatives. God knows how far she would have to walk with two children before the crevasse ends, only to find herself a widow at the end of it with me and the car at the bottom.

"No, no, it's OK. Just for God's sake, be careful!"

"I will." My nerves are as taut as a violin string and I want to yell at her: "I am! What do you think I've been doing for the past six hours?"

In fact, it would be quicker to walk, the speed I am driving. It would be nice if a great pair of hands were to descend from the heavens, scoop us up and deliver us safely at the end of the trail, like Iona pulled George back from the brink before he tumbled into the front seat. But God is not my mummy and it's entirely up to me to get us all down there in one piece.

So slowly we go down and slowly at last the endless, nightmare descent into hell comes to an end. When the road eventually twists away from the edge of the canyon and levels out and we embark upon a rocky, rutted track, full of potholes and other possible axle-breaking, sump-shattering, tyre-shredding hazards, I want to stop the car and shout for joy. We've made it! The rest will be easy. The worst is surely behind us now.

I celebrate by flexing my shoulders to ease the pain in my muscles and shift my bum on the seat to unglue my thighs where the sweat has bonded them to the plastic. They are released with a sound that had you been unlucky enough to have been with us on this nightmare, you would have recognised as like that of Elastoplast, or Band-Aid as they say here, being ripped off a hairy leg, followed by, if you had ears sharp enough to hear, not a cry of agony as you might expect, but a sigh of relief as I feel the cool air circulating where it had not been for hours.

And so, with the light beginning to fail, we come at last to Rock Creek Road, a veritable motorway of a road in comparison to all that we had endured up till now, and emerge, finally, at a place we recognise as having seen on the way to Butte - The Snake Pit, surely the most unusual attraction in the whole of Montana, where, in exchange for a few of your dollars, you can have the (dubious) pleasure of spending your leisure time in the company of snakes. A snake pit and an attraction sound like an oxymoron to me. And if it does not tempt me at all, it would never tempt Iona in a month of Sundays.

Having said that, given the choice of how to spend some other Sunday afternoon, I'd rather be in a pit filled to the brim with boa constrictors, pythons and rattlesnakes and any other snakes you'd care to mention, than do again what we did today.

Chapter Forty

In which I get into hot water again.

"Is your name Addison?"

I look up in surprise to see a stout woman whom I estimate to be in her late thirties, with dyed blonde hair, towering over my desk. This is not a social visit as I can tell straight away from her tone, not to mention her body language.

It is the end of the school day, that time of day when the kids are free to go home, but where we teachers must stay behind to leave lesson plans for the substitute (pronounced "substitoot") teacher in the event we are struck down by an incurable illness during the night or abducted by aliens or just don't feel like coming in to school the next morning.

"What's your philosophy of this?" she snaps, slapping down the *Murder Mystery Magazine* worksheets on my desk.

"My philosophy?" I'm not sure if I'm more shocked by her attitude or the question. I've never been asked to explain my philosophy before. Come to think of it, I'm not even sure if I have one.

"You heard me. What's the meaning of *that?*" The way she put the emphasis on the last word made it sound like something extremely nasty and filthy and the best thing that could be said for it was there was no smell.

Being addressed in this hostile way makes me want to respond in kind but I instinctively feel that would not be the best policy. I don't even know my enemy's name so she has the advantage over me there for a start. Calming the savage breast, (and there are two of them of not insubstantial proportions) seems the right thing to do.

"It's merely a worksheet to inspire different kinds of creative writing."

"Oh, yeah, is that right? And does that include inciting kids to murder?"

"What? Murder!"

"Murder. You can't deny it! This *thing* is full of murder."

Far from being calmed, the savage breasts seem to positively quiver with righteous indignation, presaging an incipient eruption. I can't deny it *is* full of murder - it is a *Murder Mystery Magazine* after all. I also can't prevent eruptions from volcanoes that are determined to erupt. She lets me have it from both barrels.

"And the other perversions and obscenities."

"Perversions? Obscenities?" I am becoming more and more stunned by the minute. What is this mad woman *havering* about?

"And, what's more, do you deny in *that,* you require the students to write about the supernatural?" Her finger is pointing imperiously at the flimsy pieces of paper on my desk like it was Martin Luther's papal bull and she were a morally outraged arch-Catholic.

"The supernatural?" I find myself struggling for words of my own as if I've been smitten by a sudden bout of echolalia.

"These ghost stories! You can't deny it!"

"Ghost stories?"

"Do you deny in *that,* that you instruct the students to write a ghost story?"

"Well, no, but -"

"Follow me!" she snaps, turning on her heel. "We need to see Mr Olsen about this."

What would have happened, I wonder, had I not jumped up with alacrity and followed her like an obedient little puppy dog as she marched down the hall?

It would only have been a stay of execution, I reflect, as I follow the straining buttocks in the blue jeans which are too small by half. This woman means business, means to have my guts for garters and if Mohammed had not gone to the mountain, then the mountain would have come to Mohammed. Besides, I prefer to deal with unpleasant prospects right away, not have them hanging over me like the sword of Damocles.

She marches past a startled Judy, the school secretary, and enters the open door into Matt's office like a galleon in full sail.

Behind his desk, Matt appears as astonished as I was a few moments before, behind mine. In his green suit, he appears more toad-like than ever as he swallows nervously making his Adam's apple seem to pulse like a bullfrog's.

"Mrs De Bone! How can I help you?" (Gulp. Gulp).

Mrs De Bone? What kind of a name is that? None of my students has a name remotely like that. Who is this woman who is so angry with me? Whoever she is, I had already come to the conclusion that she must be some sort of religious nut and it was the reference to "ghosts" that had really rattled her cage. I have met some religious nuts in my time, especially an esoteric sect in Dundee, and in the so-called "Bible Belt" of the southern United States I would have not have been surprised to stumble across one sooner rather than later, but not here in the north west, though it's true, I had seen a lot of churches with names I'd never heard the like of before, including Matt's.

"This," says the protesting Mrs De Bone, taking the bull by the horns and waving the offending document at Matt. "Have you seen *this*?" she demands.

"Ahrrum!" And whether it is to give himself some time to think or to prevent Judy and the rest of the school hearing any more, Matt comes from behind the relative safety of his desk and closes the door. Having done that however, he resumes his seat leaving me and the enemy side by side on the other side of the barricade.

"And *what* did you think of it?"

The tone of voice leaves no doubt as to what Matt *should* think about it but he is on the horns of a dilemma. After all, he had sanctioned it had he not? Matt, his face colouring, squirms in his seat and gulps for air. When you haven't got an answer, ask a question.

"What is your point, Mrs De Bone?"

"Ronda brought this back yesterday, practically in tears. Just look at it! Just look at the sort of things *he* is asking them to write about. And just *look* at how much she is expected to do!"

Ronda? I have only one Ronda. Ronda Lewis. In this land of the multiple divorce, it is not unusual for mothers to have different names from their children if they have married again. Blonde and not unattractive, Ronda Lewis is what I would call a "little madam", fourteen going on twenty-four and with an exaggerated opinion of her attractiveness and for whom school holds no attraction whatsoever. The only career she'd be interested in would be ensnaring an eligible (and preferably rich) bachelor so she wouldn't have to go out to work.

"It doesn't have to be done all at once," I point out. "This represents a whole term's work."

"As I said to you before, explain your philosophy." Then turning back to Matt she says, "Just listen to this," and there is no mistaking the note of incipient triumph in her voice, as if she had just caught me in flagrante delicto.

Matt, clasping his hands before him on the desk, nods at me. "Go ahead, Dave."

"Well, as I explained earlier," I begin, looking at Matt, "the idea is to provide some opportunities for writing all based around a central core idea. In these worksheets for example, the students will chose to write a horror story *or* a mystery story *or* a murder story. They won't be doing *all* three," I remark pointedly, looking at the enemy. "In addition to that, they will write an interview with a famous actor of the genre, a review of a book *or* a film and letters to the editor. It's all in the sheets. The idea, as I said, is just to give the students practice in various types of extended writing. There will also be a chance to use their imaginations by doing some artwork, such as designing a book cover or film poster for example. The students particularly like doing that."

Matt nods then swallows hard. "Thank you, Dave."

"Well, I think it is rubbish."

I am thunderstruck. For a moment, despite her aggression, I wonder if my ears had deceived me. "I beg your pardon?" I hear myself saying as if from a long way away.

"I said it is rubbish. And I'm not the only one either. There are plenty of other parents who think it is rubbish too."

Keeping a grip on my temper and instead of saying: "And who are *you,* or *they,* to pass judgement on something they know absolutely nothing about?" I swallow the words and merely come out with: "I can assure you that I have tried and tested this in Scotland and I've achieved very good results with it. The kids really enjoy doing it."

"Well, *I* think it's appalling! And so does everyone I have shown it to - and so does my attorney," she adds ominously, looking at Matt who turns a more sickly shade of green. "She thinks it promotes unhealthy thinking and is likely to encourage immoral behaviour."

"Are you serious?" It's all I can do not to snort in derision. "Are you seriously suggesting that this document is likely to incite the students to murder?"

"Or worse. If one of these students commits a crime, I will hold you personally responsible."

It is just too much. I have been insulted quite long enough and I can restrain myself no longer, but I do it through Matt as the arbiter of voice of sanity and reason as this woman is clearly as mad as a hatter.

"Just who does this woman think she is, to come off the streets like this, and tell *me* my work is rubbish? What does *she* know? What are *her* qualifications? How *dare* she - to tell *me*, a professional, that my work is rubbish?"

Finishing my rant, I look at her, then back to Matt who has his head in his hands, his fingers knotted in anguish through what remains of his hair. I can't see his face, only his ears which have turned very red. I imagine he thinks now might be a rich time to meet his Maker.

"Right," says Mrs De Bone, her nostrils flaring and throwing her shoulders back so that her bosoms jut out even more indignantly. "We'll see about that. Expect a letter from my attorney!" And with that she sweeps out, slamming the door and leaving a dreadful silence between Matt and me.

Oh, God what have I done? Whatever happened to my diplomatic skills?

After what seems a palpable and endless silence, Matt slowly unknots his fingers from the top of his head and still too humbled to raise his head fully, casts his eyes up in my direction.

"You oughtn't to have done that, Dave. Lost your temper with her."

"I know. I know. I'm sorry, but she pushed me too far. I tried to be patient but insulting my work like that was just too much. And as for inciting the students to *murder*... Well!"

There is a pregnant pause before at last Matt speaks again. "You see, Dave, Mrs De Bone is an influential member of the appropriations committee."

"Appropriations committee?"

"Yeah, you see the appropriation committee votes on the level of teachers' salaries. How much of a pay increase we get. Even if we get any increase at all."

"Oh, I see."

And in that instant, I *do* see lots of things. Once again I see that they have a different way of doing things here. There is no national pay agreement, let alone a state one, one of the things we had been told (and now I remember) in Washington - that a teacher in one town or city could be paid a lot less (or a lot more) than another teacher doing precisely the same job in the next town. Despite its vast size and being the most technologically advanced nation on earth, with the possible exception of Japan, the United States is, I realise, an incredibly parochial society. Just look at that business I had with the cheque and the sort of stuff they deem worthy of putting on TV.

Imagine not knowing if your salary will match this year's inflation or not. Imagine trying to get a pay increase when your employers, the parents, in their various walks of life, perhaps are not ⁄ or even worse, have been made redundant. Imagine them looking at your long holidays and short hours and voting to pass a pay increase for teachers. Is it any surprise they should conclude: "Huh! That'll be right! Far too much money for too little work! Time they had a *pay cut* in fact." Imagine parents ⁄ butchers, bakers and candlestick makers, especially butchers, like Mrs De Bone, having so much power over teachers!

No wonder Matt looks worried. He is studying the worksheets again.

"Maybe if you called it *The Mystery of Felstead,* Dave?" he suggests tentatively.

I can't believe he is seriously suggesting that. As if changing "Horror" to "Mystery" would change anything; as if Mrs De Bone would be appeased by that; as if I would. Poor Matt. He is in an impossible position. He has to support me, having given the work his blessing but he daren't offend Mrs De Bone either. Now we'll see which side of the fence he's on. I have given him the devil of a dilemma, the headache from hell.

He clears his throat nervously. "Say, why don't you leave this with me, Dave? Maybe we can tweak it somehow, make it you know… less… ahrrum… ?"

"No." I shake my head emphatically. "No, it's no use. You can't do that. You can't have a horror magazine without any horror and you can't write a murder story without a murder."

"How about if we just concentrated on the mystery?"

"That would leave hardly anything. And," I add pointedly, "there couldn't be anything to do with murder, or ghosts, or the supernatural in the mystery story either. What kind of mystery does that leave, for God's - I mean, heaven's sake! The whole thing would be pointless. No, I'd rather she didn't do it all than have it emasculated like that." And I feel my gorge starting to rise again at the gall of that woman, the nerve and effrontery of her to insult my work like this and not on any pedagogical grounds but simply as result her pathetic, petty prejudices. And if my *Murder Mystery Magazine* appals her, it appals me even more to think of the enormity of the power she wields - or was allowed to wield.

"Maybe that would be the best thing, Dave."

I realise that in my indignation, I have said too much. Matt has seized on this like a lifebelt thrown to a drowning man. I've made it too easy for him to wriggle off the hook.

But I also remember too well how Matt made me withdraw the school prank essay and also how Tammy had asked if there had been any objections from parents when she first saw the *Magazine*. For some reason or other, she must have felt that it might provoke just the sort of response we had just witnessed. And had it, amongst Mrs De Bone's friends, provoked the same sort of disgust and revulsion, just as she had claimed? And had she *really* consulted her lawyer about it, or was she just bluffing?

Matt comes round to the front of his desk and puts an arm round my shoulder.

"Yeah, you know I really think that's the best thing, Dave," he says squeezing my upper arm. "She's a very influential woman - an' a very dangerous one," he adds, dropping his voice confidentially.

"Yes, right."

"There's just one other thing, Dave… I think it might be a good idea if you wrote Mrs De Bone a letter of apology, huh?" He gives my arm another encouraging squeeze.

He's right of course. I should never have lost my temper, but it sticks in my craw. Game set and match to Mrs De Bone. I feel my temper rising again and break away from Matt's embrace to look him squarely in the face.

"I'll apologise for losing my temper, but I'm not going to apologise for anything else."

"That'll be just grand, Dave."

As I take my leave, my back bristling like a porcupine's with resentment, I can imagine Matt breathing a huge sigh of relief. He thinks he has got off lightly. Does he think his salary is worth all this hassle I wonder? This exchange teacher, this cuckoo in his nest, has been a potential problem right from the start. But at least the cuckoo turned out to be tame and I can imagine him thanking God for answering his prayers.

But little did he know - I didn't even know it myself - this cuckoo was about to do what all birds do, usually from a great height, only I was going to do it in the nest…

Chapter Forty-one

In which the De Bone incident escalates and so does my blood pressure.

"You should go an' see Tamaras, the Director of Curriculum," Sam advises.

I have told him the whole incident and he is mad with Matt for being such a wimp. Whilst it is good to have his support, it has refuelled my own anger and given me an even greater sense of injustice. What's the point of taking a degree in education then undergoing teacher training if, at the end of it, someone who doesn't know one end of a piece of chalk from the other can just come in and tell you what to do?

I am grateful to Sam for his suggestion. It seems a good idea to me to appeal to an independent arbiter who could express a professional opinion. Someone whose job it is to know.

Now that Sam has mentioned it, why hadn't I thought to tell that ignorant woman that the Director of Reading didn't think it was "rubbish"? Because I was so angry I wasn't thinking straight, that's why. But now it seems blindingly obvious to me that that is what Matt *should* have done - referred the *Magazine* to an even higher authority than Tammy. Perhaps he might, had I not lost my rag, but I doubt it. And given the initiatives they seem to be trying to introduce here, from Charlotte Brookes' keynote speech, I feel reasonably confident that when she saw my *Murder Mystery Magazine,* Ms Tamaras would back it and I would derive a great deal of satisfaction from seeing Mrs De Bone being put back in her cage and told that far from being outraged, she should appreciate just how lucky her daughter was to be exposed to these exciting and innovative writing exercises.

"You should go an' talk to Art, too. He's friendly with Mrs De Bone."

"He is?"

That floors me. I find it hard to imagine any teacher being friendly with one of the parents, let alone *her*, unless of course, the friendship had been formed prior to, rather than through, the offspring. There's a pretty good chance that Art had taught Ronda not so long ago.

"Yeah," Sam drawls. "An' go and see Tamaras," he calls after me as I leave.

"Will do."

Art is as disgusted with Matt as Sam is.

"Sam said you were a friend of Mrs De Bone's," I prompt.

Art spreads his hands in that way he does when he wants to make a point forcibly, as I know only too well.

"Used to be, Dave." A pause follows during which I get the impression from the tic in his cheek that he is wrestling with a mighty dilemma - whether or not to reveal some personal secret. I hope he is going to tell me soon because if he doesn't, the curiosity is going to kill me just as surely as it did the cat. At last he appears to come to a decision. "The fact is - I loaned her some money an' well... I never got it back."

How ironic! The most influential member of the appropriations committee can't even handle her own finances and now here she is directing the English curriculum.

"You know, Dave, it won't be Mrs De Bone. It'll be Ronda who is behind all this. Trust me!"

"Actually, that had crossed my mind."

"She's spoilt. She's got her mother just so," and he holds up a crooked little finger. "You know somethin' Dave? She has everything. Her room is more like an apartment than a bedroom. Her own TV. Fridge. Even her own phone. She'll have looked at all that writing she has to do, freaked out an' decided she doesn't want to do it an' told her mother to get it stopped. And her mother knows if she didn't, there would be hell to pay at home."

Though I have never been in the bedroom of any of my students and never expect to be, I don't doubt Art's inside knowledge. I don't ask, but it wouldn't surprise me if the fridge was full of beer and her whacky baccy was just left casually lying around. With Ronda, it's all too easy to imagine the tail wagging the dog. It is not a big school in terms of the number of students and if Art was aware of the home background, it's not unreasonable to suppose that Matt has his finger on the pulse too, knows what makes this family tick and know too that Ronda, not her mother, was really behind all this stramash.

This confirmation of my suspicions makes me madder than ever - to think that a fourteen-year old girl can dictate my lessons like this. How dare she! Just who does she think she is? I tell Art how angry this makes me feel and of Sam's idea to involve the Curriculum Director.

"Good idea, Dave."

***

Troubles never come singly. Back at our temporary home, still nothing has been done about the water in the basement. That's bad enough, but now Terri has a modest proposal.

"If it's a blocked drain, maybe you'd like to pay for it?"

If she had suggested I should change the *Horror of Felstead* to the *Mystery of Felstead,* I could not have been more shocked.

"No, no. You don't understand, Terri. That's not the way it works. That's not the agreement. All I'm responsible for is the electricity we use. I shouldn't be paying for the garbage here. Marnie should have set up a pre-payment before she left. But she didn't. I'm paying for hers in Scotland, you know. It's meant to be like for like. Anything to do with house maintenance is the owner's responsibility."

While it may be that the cause of the blockage is an article of clothing, it's Marnie's fault for not having her machine properly plumbed in or fitted with a filter or something. And if it's not, why should I have to pay for defective plumbing?

Terri is her usual unflappable self. She holds up her hands, spreads her fingers, and sweeps some invisible force to the floor where she pats it down in a soothing motion. It reminds me of Art's characteristic gesture and I have another *déjà vu.* Of course it is not Terri suggesting this but Marnie, on the hotline from Scotland, or she has written a letter at last.

"Ok! Ok! It was just a suggestion!" She is all smiles. Like Matt, who is not going to fight any battles for me, she is not going to fight any for Marnie. Marnie may be her friend but she is not going to spoil our relationship by having an argument with us. I can imagine her reporting back to Marnie: "I tried to persuade him, but you know… " and she would leave a little pause, "... ah well!" And she would shrug her shoulders and although she couldn't see it across the vastness of two-thirds of the continent and the Atlantic Ocean, Marnie would be able to envisage it all too well.

* * *

"So what's it all about?"

Steve has drifted into my room and always full of energy, his eyes are shining with interest as he squeezes into one of the front desks and stretches his legs out in front of him. His walrus moustache is positively quivering with anticipation.

It is the next morning, and as usual, we are ensconced in our rooms before the onslaught of those thirsting for knowledge, and as usual, there is plenty of time to pass the time of day.

"What's what all about?"

"What's goin' on between you an' Mrs De Bone?"

"How did you know?"

"Gee, the whole school is buzzin' about it!"

"Really?"

"Yeah! Boy, you sure have got the whole place rockin'." He seems to find it very amusing and doesn't seem to realise that this is increasing my anxiety by the moment. Not exactly what someone who wanted to play the diplomat, keep a low profile, not create any waves, wants to hear.

"So, give me the low down, Mr A!"

Steve's face is a picture as I tell him the story, his eyes growing wider when I tell him what I said to Mrs De Bone. I also tell him about my visit to Art's, and Sam's suggestion. Like them, Steve agrees that's what I should do.

"How do I get Tamaras' number?"

"I'll get it for you."

He reappears a moment later with the number and since there is a phone at the end of the hall, not far from my room, it is only a matter of moments later that I am dialling the number. So unlike back home where I would have to go through the school secretary who would have to dial the number for me and would no doubt pass this on to the headmaster, or maybe she wouldn't. I have no idea how confidential she is.

I get Ms Tamaras' secretary and of course such an important person is a very busy person and it will be a couple of days before I will be able to see her, but I am pencilled in for after school on Thursday.

Well, that's that and there's nothing else I can do in the meantime. The die is cast and all I can do is wait for developments, glad that I have taken positive action. But then, like a *deus ex machina,* Blake arrives, unusually for him, rather later than usual.

Steve fills him in with the exciting developments and the latest, that I have just made an appointment with the Director of Curriculum. His face grows grave and the light behind those twinkling blue eyes seems to have gone out as he asks if I have a copy of the magazine.

I go to get one with an uneasy feeling in my bones. Why is he acting like this when everyone else has been unreservedly on my side?

"I'm just going to make a photocopy of this," he says after perusing it for a moment and heads off towards the office without saying anything else. Why doesn't he just keep that one? I could have given him another one if only he had asked.

Steve and I look at each other, not knowing what to say. Although he has no more status than the rest of us, Blake is slightly older and the grey hair on his temples gives him a certain gravitas and an air of authority, like an elder statesman. I find myself wishing that it were he, not Matt, who was dealing with Mrs De Bone.

When he comes back, Blake looks serious.

"I don't think you should do this," he pronounces.

I assume he's talking about the *Murder Mystery Magazine*. "Why? What do you think is wrong with it?"

Blake follows my gaze to where he is holding the worksheets rolled up in a tight cylinder.

"No, I don't mean that. I mean, goin' behind Matt's back to see Tamaras."

I hadn't thought of it like that and I suddenly feel the blood drain from my face.

"It's not very nice," he adds, before I have time to let that fully sink in.

"No, no, no! It's not about Matt. That's not my intention at all. I'm not trying to undermine *him*. I just want an opinion on that," I nod towards the tight white scroll. "I don't want to offend anyone but it goes down really well in Scotland. The kids really enjoy doing it and I don't see why it shouldn't work here. I just want to see what Tamaras thinks of it and whether she thinks that woman is out of order."

"It's not just Mrs De Bone, Dave."

"What?"

"There have been other complaints, from other parents."

"What?"

Blake's eyes are uncompromisingly hard.

"Complaints about what?"

"About the amounta homework you're doin' out, for instance."

I can't believe it! It was only the other day that a parent had come in *asking* for homework for her daughter and, what's more, she had praised the *Murder Mystery Magazine*. Abe was absolutely right. You just can't win with some people. We had been told at Washington University to expect culture shock. How true! Ever since I set foot on the continent, it's been one shock after another, but this is the worst. And yet perhaps I should not have been shaken quite so rigid by this news. Having been drafted in from another school, Nat had confided in me just how appalled he was by the laid-back attitude of the students here and how low were the standards expected, and accepted, in this school.

"It doesn't have to be done all at once! I explained that to Matt," I protest, the exasperation creeping into my voice. "It's meant to last for weeks and most of it would be done in class anyway."

"Well, whatever." Blake has a habit of swinging his arms so that his right fist slaps into the open palm of his left and he does it now so that the scroll passes up and down between his fingers like a piston. "It doesn't matter anyway, since it's gonna be withdrawn anyway."

"Yes, but just for Ronda Lewis."

"No, Dave, it's for the entire class."

I study Blake's face carefully to see if this is one of his famous wind-ups but his face is perfectly serious as it usually is when he makes a joke. But this is not the time for jokes. And how did he know that ⁃ unless he had just talked to Matt about it? After all, the photocopier is in Julie, the secretary's office, next to Matt's.

"I think you'd better go an' see Matt an' tell him what you've done," he advises and the thin white paper cylinder makes one final passage through his fist and stops.

"Yes, I think I better had."

I feel like the condemned man on his way to the execution as I make my way to Matt's office. If I have committed a breach of etiquette, it would be better by far for him to hear it from the guilty person's mouth personally, but it wouldn't surprise me if Blake had told him of this latest development. Maybe that was the real reason behind his photocopying mission and he had never photocopied the offending document at all. It was impossible to tell from that tight scroll.

I nod to Julie in the passing. No need to ask if the captain of the ship is at the helm. Except for matters of great moment like I had had with Mrs De Bone when it was ominously shut, the door to his stateroom is always open. I can see him now behind his desk and even although he can see me coming, I rap on the doorframe before I enter. Humility is the name of the game. Humble pie the only dish on the menu.

My throat is dry as I open my mouth to speak. A surreal image pops into my mind of Matt and me as a couple of frogs: Matt the bullfrog in his green suit behind his desk, his throat pulsing ominously and me, little baby frog, about to croak.

"Look, Matt, I think I may have made a mistake… "

I hadn't meant to stop there but my mouth has gone completely dry.

At the other side of the desk, Matt looks up, startled. Although he can only guess at what I have come to say, he prejudges it serious enough to get up and close the door, an action which makes me feel even more nervous.

"Have a seat, Dave. What can I do for you?"

I don't want to sit down, had just hoped to pop in and pop out again. But I don't suppose the confessional for Roman Catholics is that simple and quick either.

"Well, you see, the fact is, that I have... em... made an appointment to... em... see Chris Tamaras about the *Murder Mystery Magazine.*"

If he already knows, Matt shows no sign of it, shows no emotion at all, in fact, merely reaches for his diary.

"When's the appointment, Dave?"

"Em... Thursday, after school."

"That's fine, Dave," and he blinks at me reassuringly. He has taken my treachery so kindly, so calmly, so matter-of-factly, without any hint of rancour, that I feel a rat for having done the dirty on him. In fact, he seems to regard it as such a non-event that I even begin to form the impression that he hadn't been put out in the slightest.

"Em... I hope you didn't think that I was out of order arranging that meeting." Before he can respond, as that would be too embarrassing for words if it were, I plough on. "You see, I just wanted an opinion on those worksheets. You see, I've never been told before that my work is "rubbish" - especially by a member of the public who hasn't any educational qualifications. That's all I was trying to do," I add rather lamely. "I know I am a guest in this country and I don't want to step on any toes."

"I appreciate y' tellin' me this, Dave," Matt beams. "It was big o' you."

I inwardly breathe a huge sigh of relief. Right, that's all right then. Ever the diplomat. Back where we started. I get up to go.

"Em... I phoned Mrs De Bone, Dave an' told her you'd be writing her an apology an' we'd be withdrawin' that piece of work."

"Withdrawing the *Murder Mystery Magazine*? From the class, you mean? Not just Ronda?" I sit down again. In my nervousness, I had forgotten I had also come to clear up this confusion.

"Yes, Dave... You see, Dave... ahrrum... Mrs De Bone is not the only one who's been complaining."

So Blake was right. But how did he know? And why hadn't he told me?

"How many others?"

Pause. "Just a couple. I didn't want to upset you, Dave..."

"Who are they?"

"Ahrrum... I think it's probably best you don't know that, Dave," Matt says, blinking at me and clearing his throat again.

"Why not? I wouldn't take it out on the kids you know, if that's what you're thinking."

Matt colours. "No, no, Dave! It's just... ahrrum... I think it's best you don't know." He swallows hard.

"Well, can you at least tell me what the complaints are about? Is it about the *Magazine*?"

"Well, no... ahrrum... it's just that they think you're too strict." Matt lets me digest that before adding, "An' you give out too much homework."

"I see."

Mrs Taylor would be one, Mrs De Bone another. That makes two. Is there really another one? If so, I can't think who it might be as I have not fallen out with any other students particularly. I shake my head in disbelief. If these protesting parents could see what my pupils in Scotland had to do, they would have an apoplectic fit. And once they had recovered, if they are anything like Mrs De Bone, would report me at once to the equivalent of the Royal Society for the Prevention of Cruelty to Children.

"Nothin' to worry about, Dave. You're doin' a fine job." Matt smiles at me in what is meant to be a reassuring manner, but I can't help feel his words have a hollow ring.

I'd do a sight better job if I were allowed to do the *Murder Mystery Magazine* I reflect ruefully. What's more, there seems little point in seeing Chris now, for even if she were to pronounce it the most marvellous piece of work in the whole of Montana, there is no way that Matt is going to retract what he has promised Mrs De Bone.

I get up to go again. This time I make it as far as the door.

"Don't forget to write to Mrs De Bone, Dave," Matt says to my back.

That stops me in my tracks and that's what sticks in my craw. It is bad enough that this woman has deprived these kids from experiencing something new, something I am sure they would have enjoyed and which would improved their writing skills, but the reminder that I have to write her a letter of apology into the bargain makes my blood boil. What about *her* apologising to *me* for the way she had spoken to me and insulted me? That would be more like the thing.

"I'll let you see it before I send it," I respond over my shoulder.

Somehow I manage to resist the urge to slam the door shut behind me.

I don't know how confidential a secretary Julie is, how much she knows about what goes on behind the closed door of Matt's office, or how much she can't help but overhear. But one thing I do know is that, as out of politeness, as I tip her a nod as I pass out of the office, she must have seen a face suffused with anger.

Chapter Forty-two

In which Iona makes some home improvements and I address some other troubles.

I go up to my room and rip a page out of a notebook with a metal spiral spine, the sort they all use here which leaves a perforated edge. It looks very untidy, especially if you leave the little bits of paper hanging from the perforations. Next I get hold of a blunt pencil and begin my letter of apology. If I received a letter written in pencil I would not be very impressed and I trust Mrs De Bone will be similarly insulted. I dash it straight off which does nothing to improve my handwriting, never very good at the best of times.

Dear Mrs De Bone,

I am very sorry for losing my temper with you. I should never have done that. I am not used to having my work criticised by parents and can assure you that I have had very good results with the Murder Mystery Magazine *in Scotland and I am very sorry that I will not be able to use it here. No-one has ever complained about it before.*

Yours sincerely,

David Addison.

There is still time before the students arrive and I dash down to Matt's office with it. He could hardly have expected to get it so soon and his face shows it.

"Is this all right?"

Matt scans it and gulps.

"That'll do fine, Dave." Gulp. "I'll see Mrs De Bone gets it." Gulp.

"That's fine thanks. I've got a class," and I hurriedly take my leave, glad to be rid of that humiliating document.

Fortunately this is test week where the students are undergoing a barrage of SRA tests in Reading, Math, and Social Sciences. These are objective tests which require filling in the blanks of oval boxes. Easy for the kids to answer. Easy to mark. Especially for us, as incredibly, the kids mark their papers themselves. It involves five hours of testing and even better than not having to mark them, it means I won't have the eighth graders for two days.

If I hadn't opened my big mouth and offered to withdraw the *Magazine* in a way that had been misconstrued by Matt, it would have meant that before resuming normal lessons with the class that contained Ronda, I would have seen Ms Tamaras. And had she approved it, it would have been very interesting indeed to see what would have happened next. Instead I will have to suffer Ronda's smug expression as I have to announce to the class that they are no longer going to be doing the *Murder Mystery Magazine* and will they please hand back their worksheets...

And my troubles don't end there. As well as this trouble in the classroom, there is trouble in the house from *Psycho* and just to complete the trio, trouble with the car - as usual. The brakes are spongy. I didn't want to ask Sam again, especially after all the trouble he'd had the last time, so last week I had given Perry a call.

"Yeah, that's fine, Dave. Bring her round on Tuesday evenin' and we'll have a look at 'em? How does that sound?"

"That's perfect," I said.

The truth is, I was just a bit worried about him coming into the house again. Unable to stand the sight of the depressing kitchen any more, Iona had taken down the rusty pastry cutters on the woodworm boards and also the kitchen implements of unknown provenance and doubtful purpose. She had also removed the army of Coca-Cola bottles with their rusty helmets from the windowsills as well as the skull of the rat from the mantelpiece. All have been banished to the basement for the duration. I have to admit - it does make the place seem less of a torture chamber and more like a mere dungeon.

* * *

"How's it goin' at school, Dave?" Perry wants to know, and, as I tell him, he chuckles in delight, thoroughly enjoying the tale. "It doesn't take you long to get them hoppin' does it!" he remarks when I have finished.

"Alas not," I tell him. "But I never meant to stir everybody up like that. I just can't believe how little work these kids do and how little is expected of them, especially by their parents."

"That's North Missoula for you, Dave!" he says, the laughter gurgling in his throat, leaving me with the feeling that if only Marnie and others had told me how low the expectations of achievement were, I needn't have rushed in like a proselytising angel. Maybe Marnie had tried to tell me but I hadn't taken it in, hadn't understood just how seriously little was expected of them, but the most likely explanation of all was that Marnie just saw that as normal and saw no necessity to say anything.

"Poor Marnie," I tell him. "She'll be experiencing the complete opposite. She'll never believe how *much* my kids have to do ، and she'll have so much to do herself to get familiar with all the texts and keep ahead of them. It'll be a real culture shock for her too."

"Don't worry about that, Dave. It'll be good for her. Come on in an' meet Karen," he says as he puts his arm around me and steers me into the house.

So this is Karen. This is whom Perry left Marnie for. If not for Karen, I would not be here now. I have a lot to thank her for, even if I am going through a bit of a rough patch at the moment, but I find myself unable to say anything, at least anything coherent, though I hear myself stammering some sort of greeting. I just hope I am not drooling, for Karen is the most gorgeous woman I think it has ever been my pleasure to meet in the flesh. Marnie was not unattractive, but she couldn't hold a candle to this younger competitor ، few women could, apart from Helen of Troy perhaps.

She is dressed in black slacks which match her raven, shoulder-length hair, and an eye-catching bright-pink sweater. But what catches my eye more are the curvaceous contours beneath. As I shake hands, I notice the delicate fingers with the matching pink nail varnish and fervently hope she doesn't notice that my palm is leaking like a colander.

"You have a very nice place here," I manage to get out, tearing my gaze away from the depths of her hazel eyes and looking around me, hoping that neither have noticed how much I have been smitten.

Fortunately Perry doesn't show me around as that would have taken the rest of the afternoon, but he does confide that they have three full-sized bathrooms, one of which he tells me he is going to convert into a sauna. I have to admit, there can't be many better ways of spending an evening than sitting in the sauna with Karen - as long as you have a nice glass or two of chilled Chablis to take in with you of course.

I don't suppose Marnie was ever here, but she must have seen the house from the outside at least, it being within walking distance, even for Americans, and that must have increased her depression I would have thought, as she looked after the kids in the house from *Psycho* and saw this spick-and-span, modern, spacious, brick-built mansion with its double garage and trim neat lawn at the front. And yet, I reflect, Marnie is inordinately proud of her house and its ghastly contents and how upset she would be if she knew what we thought of it and like Art, how heartily she would disapprove of our migration through to the sunny room, not to mention Iona's banishment of her treasures to the basement.

"Just look at this, Dave," Perry says, leading the way to where an ancient wooden writing desk stands in splendid isolation in the middle of a wall. "Isn't that somethin'?" He could not have gazed at it more fondly than if it had been Karen for the first time.

I have to admit it is something. Something I wouldn't give houseroom to. Something big and dark and ugly. Something that is totally out of keeping with the other modern furniture in this light and airy room.

Aloud I say, "Yes," in what I hope is a tone of modest admiration. "Where did you get it?" Obviously it's not the sort of thing you pick up in your local furniture store.

It is the right question to ask. "At a rummage sale. I only paid $40 it," Perry adds proudly.

"Really!" and if I sound really surprised, it is because I am. I wouldn't have paid four cents for it.

I wonder what Karen thinks of it but it wouldn't surprise me in the least if she thought it was a piece of junk. I remember how fondly Perry sat in the Viking chair and it is certainly one thing that Perry and Marnie have in common, their love for "antique" furniture. And if Perry were to insist on bringing more stuff like this home who's to say how their relationship might not end up?

The first set of discs prove particularly troublesome and time-consuming, and after Perry has wrestled manfully with them whilst I stood helplessly looking on, they feel just as spongy as before. But Perry says not to worry, they'll be all right after I have bled them and he shows me what to do.

When I get back, it is to find that the Sewer Arranger van is parked at the Hertz house and my hopes are raised that he has called, which Iona confirms a moment later. A trip to the basement confirms that our unwelcome guest, the water, has left (even if Mrs Bates hasn't) and all it needs now is time to dry out.

"Did he say anything?"

"No." Iona says, "I was putting the kids to bed and he just came and left. It didn't take him long."

"Did he leave a bill?"

"No."

That's good I think. Coming at this time and unannounced perhaps means that he is doing it as a favour for his mother or Marnie or both. Or perhaps he has left a bill at his parents' house and that is why he is there now rather than making a social call.

Time will tell. I decide I'll say nothing about it and just wait and see if Terri mentions it first.

Chapter Forty-three

In which meetings predominate.

"Have a good teach, Daddy! I'll see you when you get home, OK?" says Hélène as I leave for school the next morning.

I'm astonished and moved, not just by the sentiments but how like an old head on young shoulders it sounds, not to mention how American, like a wife on some sitcom show saying goodbye to her husband and who you know will end up in all sorts of improbable adventures in the course of the day with which she will regale him on his return from yet another day plodding routinely away at the office.

It makes me pause and ponder how much she has understood of what she has heard of the conversation between Iona and me concerning the De Bone affair. I would have thought it far above her head, otherwise we would not have discussed it in front of her. Or has she some premonition, some sort of child-like intuition, that today was going to be rather more stressful than usual?

"I will, darling," I tell her, bending to kiss her, but this unexpected benediction has left me feeling distinctly uneasy.

It is routine, on arriving at school, to go and check your pigeonhole in the office in case you have any messages, and as usual, through the open door of his office, I can see Matt behind his desk, doing whatever Principals do behind their desks. No doubt he has been here long before us. I don't expect I'll ever find out just how long. Maybe one of the things they do is note down when the teachers arrive for work and deduce from that how keen and how good a teacher you are.

"Say, Dave."

Oh, God, what I have done now? It can't be too serious I realise straight away, otherwise he would have got up and closed the door.

"I'd like to arrange a meetin' with you sometime to discuss the amounta homework you're expectin' from the students."

"Yeah, right, whenever."

"That's grand, Dave, thanks."

Although I nod and give a brief smile, inwardly my heart is heavy. Nor is it lessened when I find in my box a message from Tammy Kinsella who wants me to attend a meeting of Reading teachers - on a Saturday! She also suggests it might be an idea for me to address a meeting of all the Reading teachers sometime. That's part and parcel of the exchange and I expected to have to do that. But on a Saturday!

Clutching these intimations of bad news and depression beginning to settle on my shoulders like a cloak, I see a figure approaching me as I walk along the hall. There is no escape. If my mind had been less concerned with problems present and future, had I been more alert, I might have clapped my hand to my head and in an elaborate show of having suddenly remembered something, might have spun on my heel and gone haring off in the other direction. But it is too late for such subterfuges, even if they were as transparent as glass to her that I was avoiding meeting her face to face again. This unavoidable meeting was imminent and not nearly far enough away to give me time to work out how I am going to deal with it other than to keep on walking and not get engaged in conversation. After all, we are not exactly bosom buddies.

"Hi."

"Hi."

"How's it goin'?"

"Much better, thanks," I lie as these words carry me past her, wondering if I might have been better to stop and talk to her, forestall her before she poured out her latest complaint to Matt but then I think, no it was better, considering our last conversation when we were eyeball to eyeball in the park and Steve had to separate us before the fur flew.

Still, it would have been nice to know why she is here. Young Taylor has been much less cocky of late and I have had no more confrontations with him, but who's to know what I might have done inadvertently to offend him? Or perhaps it is merely my paranoia. Could she possibly be here on some other business, nothing to do with me at all?

If it *is* to do with me, Matt will let me know sooner or later - at the same time he tells me about my draconian homework regime.

* * *

It is 8.10 am and we are all in the library for the weekly staff meeting.

It begins with routine matters, enough to bore anyone to tears, a meeting for the sake of a meeting but which Matt must have because that is the way they do things here, even although it seems to me a message in our pigeonholes would have sufficed just as well and we could all have had another half hour in bed. But I sense something different about this meeting. There is a tenseness in the air which I am at a loss to explain. It is not long in coming.

"Ahem!" Matt pauses to clear his throat. "There's been a lotta talkin' behind my back recently an' a lotta rumours. It's... ahrrum... not good for morale... "

I am sure that I am blushing furiously and I stare at the floor. Blake, to my right, is leaning forward, his hands clasped between his open knees. I am not aware of anyone else but I sense everyone looking at me.

"Ahrrum, we've gotta pull together, you know. If you have... ahrrum... any problems, you should come an' see me, not go talkin' behind my back."

There is a pregnant silence then Sam pipes up.

"You're right, Matt, there is a problem with morale in this school. It *is* pretty low, you know... "

Matt goes very red in the face and his Adam's apple bounces like a rubber ball on concrete.

"A lotta us feel that we're on our own, that we get no support," Sam continues after a pause, during which time the atmosphere has become increasingly awkward.

"Right," says Art, the only person brave enough to support the bravest one.

"If it comes to a showdown between us and the parents, we feel that you'll support them, not us," Sam continues.

A murmur of assent ripples round the room.

"That's right." Once again, Art is the only one to speak up.

This is just too embarrassing for words. I feel that everyone must be thinking of me and the De Bone case, perhaps even the Taylor incident as well. Far from playing the diplomat, I have stirred up a hornet's nest. I imagine Matt must be regretting more than ever having allowed the exchange to have gone through, for he would have had the right of veto, just as my headmaster had. Could it be, in far-off Scotland, that my headmaster is regretting the exchange too? Has Marnie been at his door complaining about the pressure of work and saying she just can't cope?

Matt is looking increasing uncomfortable, his face above his collar a bright red, as if it were choking him to death. "Well... ahrrum... I'm sorry you feel that way, Sam... ahrrum."

"It's not just me."

"Well... ahrrum." Matt looks at his watch. "Say, why don't you come an' talk to me about your concerns later, Sam? I'm afraid we're outta time now," and he begins gathering his papers together to indicate that the meeting is over. But by my watch, there is plenty of time to spare.

"No," Sam persists. "It's a whole school issue. It's the morale of the school we're talkin' about here an' I don't think we've discussed it properly. There's a whole lotta issues need to be aired."

"That's right," Art chips in.

Impossible to back down in the face of this onslaught, there is nothing Matt can do apart from try to maintain his composure and look as unflustered as possible.

"How about Tuesday?" His eyes sweep the sea of faces.

No-one demurs. Inwardly I am thinking: *Oh, God, see what I have started now* and not least, *Oh, no, not another early morning!* But if there is anyone who must be looking forward to it less than me then it must be Matt who looks as if he has swallowed a poisoned chalice as he says, "Right, eight am on Tuesday."

***

The day at school passes uneventfully with me trying not to think about the meeting past and meetings yet to come, consoling myself with the thought that I was merely the catalyst and there already was a general feeling of dissatisfaction amongst the staff.

As for my meeting with Chris Tamaras, there is no need for me to get uptight about that apart from wishing it wasn't taking place at all. Having said that, I can't help wishing that that is how Matt had resolved the problem - by referring it to her. Had that been the case, I would have felt really nervous about her verdict. At least I am spared the worry of that.

Then there is the meeting with Matt who wants me, I'm sure, to cut the amount of homework I am giving, kowtowing again to parents who in their turn, no doubt, are finding life at home intolerable by their offsprings' incessant whingeing. If it takes the homework to be cut to stop their heads from being nipped, what do they care? And in the light of this morning's developments, this meeting is going to be more awkward than ever...

***

When I arrive at the Education Offices, Ms Tamaras is having a meeting with someone else and I have to wait.

Tammy Kinsella is there however, seems surprised to see me and welcomes me like a long-lost relative. I suppose teachers are not normally in the habit of darkening the hallowed portals of their lords and mistresses, (more mistresses than lords it would seem in this land of sexual equality) unless of course they are in trouble - like me. Although she had given the *Murder Mystery Magazine* her blessing, when I tell her the reason for my visit, Tammy has no time to make any response apart from an arched eyebrow before I am shown into the Holy of Holies.

Chris is an elegant woman in her forties with an impeccably neat hairstyle which suggests to me an unflappable sort of efficiency, that regardless of how frustrating or irritating the problem she was called upon to deal with, not a hair would be disturbed, let alone would she ever feel the need to pull it out by the roots. She exudes warmth and friendliness as she ushers me into a chair.

"It's a pleasure to meet you, Dave. How are you enjoying Missoula and Montana?"

I tell her how beautiful the latter is and how friendly and helpful the inhabitants of the former are, with certain exceptions, which I don't bother to mention. She asks some questions about Scotland before asking, "Well, Dave, what can I do for you?"

I hand her the worksheets, filling in the background as she reads them. For all I know, Matt has already told her but there is nothing to read in her expression as she gives her undivided opinion to what she is reading, just as Tammy had done before her. When she has finished, before she speaks, it is impossible to judge what she thinks of it and although her opinion is immaterial now, I find this speechless silence a trifle unnerving.

"Well, that's very interesting, Dave. Very imaginative. Intriguing. Lots of opportunity for creative writing. I'd appreciate if you'd let me have a copy."

This is very gratifying, unless she is merely being polite, like the questions on Scotland may, or may not, have been. I tell her she can keep that one. "But what I want to know," I tell her, more relaxed now and leaning forward in my chair, "is do you think there is anything in *that* which is likely to morally corrupt or incite the students to murder?"

If, up till now, her face has been inscrutable, there is no mistaking the genuineness of her laughter as she throws her head back and gives vent to unrestrained mirth.

"Well, that's what I'm being accused of!" I reply, not a little astonished.

"That's North Missoula for you, Dave!" and she chuckles again before she suddenly becomes serious again. "Anywhere else in Missoula would be fine," she goes on, "but not North Missoula. You see, North Missoula has a lot of poor families, dysfunctional families, trailer homes… "

"I see," I tell her, as if this is news to me. She makes it sound like something out of *Deliverance* though to me it sounds just like Grangemouth, just like my parents, or a lot of them, if you substitute council houses for trailer homes. Yet none of my parents, bless them, has ever felt an overwhelming desire to march up to the school wanting firstly, to rip out my guts, followed by my scheme of work.

"Well, Dave, it's been really neat meeting you." She extends her hand. The interview is at an end.

I think I know what her decision would have been.

Chapter Forty-four

In which I reflect on further differences between Scottish and American culture.

Schools in the United States being strictly secular, even to the point of ludicrousness where His name may not be mentioned at all, let alone in vain, the mornings always begin with saluting the flag, a ceremony which is meant to inspire some sort of feeling of patriotism in the students but which, like the prayers we have in our weekly assembly in Scotland, are as meaningless as a mantra intoned in a foreign language.

Accordingly, for my benefit as much as theirs, and with the help of Millie, the librarian, who has provided the resources, my students, as part of their language lessons, have been reading about, and making notes on famous figures from American history: George Washington and other revolutionaries; Davy Crockett and other boyhood heroes; Mark Twain and other writers; Thomas Jefferson and other geniuses. And James Monroe, 5th President who, I was interested to discover, died on the 55th anniversary of the nation's birth and 116 years before mine, as America and I share the same birthday. And, in another connection, my middle name is the same as his, only he spells his differently. Furthermore, we both have a Doctrine. The difference is his was adopted and mine will never be, at least not here, not after the De Bone debacle.

To add to their misery, my homeroom students, having done the research and made the notes, (with much grumbling and protestation at the unfairness - none of the other homeroom classes have to do this) have to follow this up for the edification of their fellow students by delivering a talk on their findings to the class.

Cindy, one of the nicest and most intelligent of the students, is in full flow on the topic of Betsy Ross and the design and sewing of the first American flag when Matt suddenly appears. I can guess why he has come but a stay of execution is granted as he listens attentively to her exposition.

"That was swell, Cindy," he says when she is finished, swallowing hard with emotion.

Normally I encourage the class to ask questions, which, in the event, are normally done by me as no-one seems to be able to think of any, but it is Matt who has the burning question for me this morning.

"How did your meetin' go yesterday, Dave?"

"Fine." Then, as Matt continues to stand there like a question mark, I feel it incumbent on me to expand upon the monosyllable. "She liked the *Magazine* but thought it wasn't very appropriate here. She said it would be OK in the other schools but not here for some reason. Something about the kind of community it is."

Matt nods as if he'd expected no other outcome. "Say, why don't I pick you up tomorrow mornin' an' take you up to North Missoula an' show you around?"

"That would be great. Thanks, Matt."

"Shall we say 9 am?"

"That would be great!" My face may appear to be smiling but inwardly I am bemoaning the loss of the Saturday long-lie, small children permitting. But this is an offer I can't refuse.

True to his word he is there on time, bright-eyed and bushy-tailed but then being a teetotaller, he never suffers from a hangover. Not that I am suffering from that this morning either, but as usual on a Friday after school, I had been imbibing the beer after the game with Art and Chuck, together with Sam who, as usual, has the good sense to skip the preliminaries and just comes for the refreshment. On this occasion however, at the game, I had been promoted from role of mere disinterested spectator to a participant with real power. The amount of ground gained during a play is measured by a chain attached to two sticks and I was given the honour of holding one end.

Somehow, Matt, who does not attend the games, has heard of my "support" for the football team. As we head towards the Interstate and North Missoula in his truck, he brings the subject up.

"Say, Dave, I hear you go to all the football games. I just want you to know how much I appreciate that. I think that's neat, really neat." And to give emphasis to the point, he nods his head three or four times like those dogs some people sometimes put on the rear shelf of some cars just to infuriate you as you follow them for miles before you are able to pass them.

Credit accepted where none is due. Poor Matt, he'd have a hairy fit if he knew the real reason I was there. I might have been eaten up with embarrassment had I not been able to cover up my confusion by remarking: "I ran the chains yesterday."

"Did you, Dave?" It sounds as if he can't believe that a Scotsman could be entrusted with such a vital and responsible job. I'm amazed they gave it to me myself but then I am only the Dum part to someone else's Tweedledee. "Gee, that's really swell!" and after bestowing a beaming smile on me and adjusting his glasses, he turns his attention to the road again.

I know what Matt is doing. He's trying to make me feel welcome, wanted and appreciated. He *is* a nice guy, just like Art said. And what had I done for him in return? Landed *him* with an awkward staff meeting on Tuesday, and *me* with having to get up even earlier than necessary. In that respect, whatever our differences, we have this is common: neither of us is looking forward to it in the slightest.

It doesn't take long to arrive at our destination. The first thing I see is some sort of transport depot. A few juggernauts are parked there, their owners presumably partaking of the refreshments provided by the seedy-looking café at the far end of the parking lot, not paved but packed as hard as concrete from the tons of ton-weight trucks that had parked there for more years than I could hazard a guess. Perhaps having such a place on your doorstep might be regarded as a bit of an eyesore by most people, but not by me.

I love American trucks. Where our lorries are exceedingly boring with their flat noses and the engine hidden discreetly away beneath the driver's cab, I love the way the engines of American trucks proudly stick out in a macho, manly way. And I like the acres of gleaming chrome everywhere: on the bumpers, on the wheels, on the massive diesel tanks and especially on the twin exhaust pipes pointing to the sky, often with the ends swept back, paying some sort of lip service to streamlining. And, apart from the often imaginative and artistic paintwork, many have a row of horns or lights, or both, on top of the cab. And that's another thing I like about them - the blast of sound the horns make, like a train. You don't mess with a beast like that coming at you full pelt, especially with a driver who is protected by six feet or more of solid steel and iron sticking out in front of him like a battering ram.

We don't stop unfortunately, to look at the trucks more closely, but sweep on past. Houses, not trucks are what we have come to see. I knew to expect trailer homes mainly and there are a great many of them, so large that they were intended to make only one journey in their lives. But there are "proper" homes too, and if "shacks" would be too extreme a word to describe them, many certainly look as if they could do with a bit of urgent maintenance. As for the yards, there is not one you could say was tidy or well kept. They are merely places to abandon a vehicle, or vehicles actually, for most have two parked outside, one of which is invariably a truck. As for the homes which seem to have only one vehicle, that's only because the other is currently being used ⋅ I shouldn't be surprised to learn. The trailer homes, by contrast, though supposedly the inferior dwellings, look by far the better kept, some even with what I would call a garden in the English sense of the word.

"So what you think, Dave?"

"Em... "

"You see, Dave, what an impoverished neighbourhood this is."

I don't hear a question mark. So this is poverty American style, or should I say, the poorer face of America ⋅ at least here. And Ronda Lewis lives here somewhere, in a flat within a house or trailer home with her phone and her fridge and God knows with what other recreational comforts besides.

"Em... " I wish I could show him my pupils' neighbourhood, the flats, where people are filed like documents in a filing cabinet one on top of the other, where the idea of having your own patch of yard or garden would be a dream. Here every home is detached, and I've no way of knowing, but I would bet the majority are owner-occupied. In Scotland, my flat-dwelling parents pay a subsidised rent to the local authority and if they own a car, it would be their one and only, their pride and joy and would have many thousands of miles on the clock before they bought it. And even then I wouldn't have described them or thought of them as being particularly impoverished.

"Do all our students come from North Missoula?" I ask. We are already nearly out of the place and the curious thing is we hadn't seen a single soul and this a Saturday morning too. It was like a ghost town.

"Pretty much, Dave."

I had expected no less. Being in the downtown business area, there are very few houses near the school.

"And what do the parents do for a living?"

"That's parta the trouble, Dave. There's quite a lotta unemployment amongst our parents and a lotta our kids come from single-parent homes. A lotta the fathers work at the sawmills in Bonner. The others are mainly truckers an' on the road a lotta the time."

How marvellous I think, to have a job sitting behind the wheel of one of those magnificent beasts, driving all over the continent! We drive in silence for a while. I am aware of Matt's jutting jaw and his Adam's apple moving in his throat like an anaconda's latest meal. I'm pretty sure he is working up to say something momentous. But as time passes without him spitting out what he wants to say, I feel I have to say something to break the tension.

"I saw Mrs Taylor in school yesterday." And since Matt still says nothing, I go on, "I just wondered if she had been up to complain about me again."

"No, no, Dave. I sent for her as a matter of fact. Her daughter, in Art's class, was caught playin' hookey."

Hah! And if that doesn't tell him and Mrs Taylor something about her children and their attitude to school, then I don't know what does. She wouldn't be able to pull the too-scared-to-go-to-school trick again, especially against Art, a much-respected member of staff.

"Dave?" Out of the corner of my eye, I can see Matt swallowing hard. This looks like it and it may just be my imagination, but it seems to me he is gripping the wheel like a drowning man hanging on to a lifebelt.

"Yes?"

"Em... ahrrum... Well you know I wanted to talk to you about the amounta homework... "

"Yes?"

"Well, you know a lotta the parents... ahrrum... think you give out too much... " His eyes are fixed on the traffic as we go down Broadway. Soon we'll be passing the school.

I want to tell him what I've been giving out is only a fraction of what my kids in Scotland do; want to say "tough"; want to say that I'm the teacher and I'll decide what is best for the education of my pupils; want to say that if the students want to get out of the "poverty" into which they have apparently been unfortunate enough to have been born, that education would be their passport.

But I don't. All I do is to knock the ball back into Matt's court: "Do they?"

Matt risks a quick look at me, before turning his focus back on the road.

"You see the sorta community it is, Dave. Lotta poor families with problems. They got plenty other things to worry about other than homework, you see?"

I see all too clearly, miles further than Matt realises. If I were to cut back on the miniscule amount of homework I am issuing it would hardly amount to anything. But if that's what he wants, so be it. He's my boss after all. And if I get any parents coming to me complaining about the *lack* of homework in future, I'll direct them straight to him.

"Yeah, I see that, Matt. I'll cut the homework."

Matt beams at me from the other side of the truck. He could hardly have hoped I would roll over so easily.

"That'll be just grand, Dave."

Chapter Forty-five

In which I am forced to confront my phobia.

"Well, hello, Mr A!" The voice at the other end of the telephone unmistakably belongs to Steve Knight with his irrepressible zest for life. Besides, he is the only one who addresses me by my title. "You gonna be around for the next few minutes?"

"Well, em... Yes, I suppose..." Actually we were planning to go on another trip, this time to the ghost town of Garnet. I was particularly interested in this, having been brought up on a diet of TV westerns as a boy. You could hardly not if you watched TV in the 1950s. In the days when there were only two channels, it was no good switching over, as not just primetime, but anytime TV resounded to the sound of gun fire, the whine of ricocheting bullets, the war whoops of Red Indians and the hoof beats of stampeding cattle. Not that I minded: I was a devoted fan of *Wells Fargo, Laramie* et al and in those far-off innocent and halcyon days, ran as wild as heather in the wood beside my house, playing Cowboys and Indians with my friends. We were the cowboys and my sister and her friends were the unwitting squaws whom we stalked and mercilessly shot down with our rifles (beech tree branches) as they innocently went about their domestic duties outside their tepees. We drew the line however, at scalping them.

"I'll be right there. Say about twenty minutes."

Forty minutes later, from the window of the family room, I see Steve's truck draw up outside. There's a white hard cover on the back and I watch as Steve delves into the interior and withdraws a bundle of limp feathers. Then I remember that he is the birdman of Emerson, not because he is a bird lover, but because he kills them. I watch horror-stricken as Steve transfers his first haul to his left hand and reaches in again before making his way to the door. In another moment he will be here with a brace of dead birds in each hand, their wings and heads lolling loosely in death. Clearly they are meant for me. Poor Steve, he was not to know that he was bringing me the present from hell.

When I married Iona, she came with a pet budgie and I could just about tolerate it especially when it was safely caged up but to feel the fan of its wings near my face made my blood run cold - just as it is now at the sight of what Steve is carrying.

What am I going to do? If I hadn't answered the phone, he'd probably have dumped them on the doorstep and how traumatic would that have been to have had to step over those feathery bodies before we could get in! I might well have concluded this was some grim and portentous warning from Mrs Bates in the basement: we would be next.

"Here you are, Dave. I brought these round for you," he says, hoisting his trophies aloft, affording me a better view of them, giving me the chance to notice the blood dribbling from the beak of one poor unfortunate. It also enables me to identify the deceased as some species of duck and from the uniformly brown plumage, I would guess the female of the species.

"Oh... em... em. That's very kind of you, Steve," I say, making no effort to relieve him of his offering. "It's just... em... I wouldn't know what to do with them... "

"No problem. I'll show you what to do... Well, hello, Miss Hélène," Steve breaks off as he catches sight of her, but she is either too shy or too frightened by the sight of this man with his massive feathery hands and runs away. I'd like to do that too but I am a man and must not show my wimpiness, especially in front of a frontiersman like Steve.

"We're gonna need a sack. You got such a thing?" Steve says over his shoulder as we march through the kitchen. He is so full of energy he does nothing slowly, puts his whole life and energy into whatever he is doing at the moment. "Hi, Iona." She is, as usual, in her bailiwick, chained to the kitchen sink. I know at this precise moment, she will be praying that I have mislaid the keys to the padlock and therefore, regretfully, will be unable to join us for the disembowelment ceremony.

"Yeah, sure." I find one under the sink, happy for my hands to have something to do, glad of the excuse not to offer to relieve Steve of one of his burdens at least. I am content too, to open the back door into the yard, so I don't have to touch the feathered remains, but knowing and dreading that the moment is rapidly approaching when I won't be able to avoid that fateful, feathery contact.

"I'll do this one while you watch, then I'll watch you do the next one. Right?" He dumps them with a feathery plop on an old table that happens to be outside the back door. Steve is so pre-occupied with the task in hand that my reluctance to participate in these proceedings has not even registered the slightest tremor on the Richter scale of horror.

Producing a knife from a sheath in his belt, Steve dexterously cuts off the head and neck, followed by the wings (the worst part) then the legs, then the tail. They plop into the paper bag which I hold open, trying not to let Steve see that I am averting my eyes. And all the time I am thinking: *Oh, God. I can't bear to touch one of these things, let alone hack them to bits like this.* And then I notice the blood that has dripped onto my shoe. And I feel sick.

But worse is just about to come, for as Steve starts plucking what is left of the bird, he remarks casually: "You can make a start on the next" giving a nod in the direction of the heap of corpses, while feathers flurry around like flakes of brown snow.

My memory rewinds to another time, some seven years or so after the encounter with the hen, when my phobia began, and I can see it now as if it were yesterday. One of my parents' bucolic friends had presented them with a goose for Christmas, just as it was when it met its death. Connotations of a cosy, Christmas, Dickensian scene it was not. In fact, if I had been the boy in *A Christmas Carol* whom the re-born Scrooge had commandeered to go to the butcher's shop to buy the fat goose that was hanging there, the one intended as a gift for the Cratchits, they would never have got it. (And it was surely a sign that Scrooge was truly reborn, for it doesn't seem to have occurred to him, at this late stage before Christmas, to negotiate on the price). But the Cratchits did receive, and gratefully, although it is a fair bet that Mrs Cratchit wouldn't have had a clue what to do with it, being unaccustomed as she was, to feasts.

And although I don't know for certain how my parents felt at being presented with this goose, I am sure they did not regard it, as I would have done, as a big white elephant. Metaphor aside, to my boyish, phobic eyes, it seemed to fill the room as they sat on either side of the fireplace with the bird between them, ankle-deep in feathers.

Somehow, I don't know from where I summoned the courage, but back in the present, I put my hand out towards the feathery mound in front of me. I don't pick the bird up. I could never do that. Suppressing a shudder, I let my fingertips touch the breast of the topmost bird, trying to avoid looking at the lifeless head with its dead, closed eyes. I close my own as my fingers close upon the first feathers and pull. With surprisingly little resistance, they come away in my hand and I hurriedly let them go. There now! I've done it! That wasn't too bad was it? But I don't hurry to repeat the process, putting off as long as I can the moment when I must start the dissection.

But Steve is such a quick and experienced plucker that my delaying tactics are scarcely necessary.

"Now watch this, Dave."

Inserting his knife into the diaphragm, Steve unseams the bird's abdomen, then pulling it apart with both hands, inserts his hand into the slit and withdraws it. His fist is bulging with guts, the back of his hand red, slimy, glistening red. At the same time, the air is polluted with an awful stench and I step back, appalled. I know if I managed somehow to perform the incision, this final step would be one too far. Even to save my own life, I doubt if I could disembowel this dead thing.

"Oh! Steve!" I manage to gasp. "I... I... could never do that!" I am close to fainting.

"I could see you weren't likin' this too much," he says, light-heartedly. "Here," he continues, "take the quills outta that," and he passes me the carcass where the broken ends of feathers are lodged in the flesh.

Without the feathers, the head, the tail, the feet, the bird doesn't look or feel half so bad. Even so, the flesh, soft, yet hard and cold to the touch, gives me the shivers. I take a long time over it, letting Steve get on with the next bird, hoping he thinks it's just the disembowelling I couldn't stomach. And then I have another thought. I hope he doesn't ask us any time soon how we liked the birds because I am going to put them in the freezer and it's going to be a long, long time before we get round to eating them, maybe never. Maybe Marnie will be the one who enjoys them.

"See, when you're eatin' these, Dave, mind you don't break your teeth on the pellets!" Steve jokes, as if reading my mind. At least I *think* he is joking.

Oh, God, I hadn't thought about that. If ever I *did* get around to eating one of these poor birds, which I might force myself to do so they did not die in vain, coming across a lead pellet was just the very thing that would be enough to make me put down my knife and fork and never pick them up again. Even if I can't be sure if he's joking or not, I suppose it is possible that not all these instruments of death would have passed clean through the body or been thrown out with the guts. I suppose it might depend upon the distance the birds were from the gun when they made that awful plummet to the ground.

The last of the four bids turns out to be not a duck after all. About the size of fat pigeon, I suppose it was some sort of infant grouse and Steve has a novel method of plucking it. After chopping off the neck, wings, tails and legs as before, he makes an incision on the breast and with some deft manoeuvre of the wrists, peels the skin back, turning the bird inside out like peeling an orange.

"Pretty neat, huh?"

I have to admit it is and I'm quite impressed in spite of myself, but of course there is another incision to be made, a deeper cut so that what is in the inside can be brought to the outside. Time to look away again.

I help Steve carry the ready-for-the-oven birds (some time far in the future) into the house. I switch on the tap so Steve can wash the gore off his hands. Sometime later I will have to dispose of the sack in the yard with its grisly contents and pick up the feathers before they are strewn to the four winds. I can handle that. Feathers, as long as they are detached from their owners, hold no terrors for me. You could tickle me to death with one and I might even laugh, but I wouldn't care to pick up a wing and I certainly could never use one as a fan or a totem like the priest at Stevensville.

The bodies of the birds, Iona can deal with later. Her department to wash them, freeze them and cook them later. Perhaps.

"Care for a beer, Steve?"

It's only hospitable, after so much generosity, to make the offer. Besides, it's too late to go to Garnet now and why not spend the time in amiable company? So we troop out to the garden again where the glorious sunshine helps dispel any lingering memories of recent horrors, as long as I turn my back on the sack and ignore the pile of feathers beside the table and the blood on my shoe.

Hélène too has come out of her shell now that the man has disposed of his funny feathered mittens, or maybe she has just got more used to him as he sits there sipping his beer, obviously quite at home.

"This is my house," she tells Steve. It looks like a climbing frame to me, but if I could once see a tepee where only a bush was growing, why should she not see a house?

"Why, that is a mighty fine house, Miss Hélène. Is it OK if I come in?"

Hélène nods, pleased as punch to have her first guest and she must have very hospitable parents because she knows how to treat a visitor. "Would you like a sweetie?" she asks as soon as he is inside.

"Would I like a sweetie?" Steve is tickled pink, relishing the sound of the word in what is for him, an unusual context. "You bet I'd like a sweetie, Miss Hélène," he says, grinning from ear to ear. "In fact *you* are a little sweetie!"

But the only sweetie he got was in Hélène's imagination. Not that Steve minded that at all. He said it was very good indeed.

That's what I'll say if he asks me what I thought of the birds. I just hope he doesn't.

Chapter Forty-six

In which we visit the ghost town of Garnet and I learn a mine of information.

Sunday morn dawns bright and gay. Well, I presume it did. I couldn't possibly say as I was not up then but by the time I do manage to crawl out of bed, Iona and the kids have long since gone to church. I make my breakfast, a cup of instant coffee, though "instant" is a bit of a misnomer due to the absence of an electric kettle. I might have made some toast too, but it's too much trouble without an electric toaster.

I pick up the *Missoulian* and take it and my breakfast out into back garden where the sun is beating the grass to death, or so I hope. At least the growing season seems to be over and the leaves on the trees are beginning to turn. Soon my favourite season will be getting into its stride, when Nature puts on her motley, but I've rarely experienced this delicious warmth at this time of year before, what we would call an Indian summer but which is probably quite normal here. It is the first day of October.

Dark stains on the table remind me of something I'd rather not think about, though other signs have been removed. I remove myself to another part of the garden. After all it is big enough. Poor Marnie; she could never do that in our garden unless she sat out the front in full view of the rest of the street. But then she wouldn't want to sit in a damp so wet it is practically drizzle and a cold so chilling it freezes the marrow. So lucky to be here instead of there, I think, and with a ghost town to look forward to once the family returns from their religious indoctrination. My cup of happiness runneth over.

And so, sometime later, we find ourselves once more driving up another forest track which bears some resemblance, in its worst stretches, to the one on the infamous journey to Skalkaho Falls - on one of its better stretches. Then, I was far too scared to stop and take a photograph of what the "road" looked like, but now I do, just in case, a long time from now, in some Home for the Elderly and Confused, I should ever wish to regale my fellow residents with the tale of how, once in a place far, far away, (whose name I can't remember) I once had a near-death experience. And although, as before, we are surrounded by an endless vista of trees, there are a couple of other differences between that trip and this.

We have been in Missoula six weeks now and are finally beginning to learn at last how to go about an expedition Montanan style. We have some warm clothing with us and the cooler has been filled with some cans of soft drinks and ice from the Grizzly Grocery. In addition to that, though like the clothing, we don't expect to use them, we have a supply of dollars and have left the chequebook at home. We have food too but don't expect to have any of that left after our picnic.

In a clearing, my attention is drawn to a small area of land surrounded by a rickety wooden fence. It turns out to be a small cemetery up on the hillside, but why here, in the middle of nowhere? Too small to belong to Garnet and too far away: it needs investigating. It contains only a handful of graves, the ground rough and uneven - lumpy, as if the dead were rising again, or sunken, as if one false step and the unwary visitor might find himself crashing through the rotten lid of a coffin. But there are no clues as to why these people happen to have their bones laid to rest here, so far from any human habitation and where they could expect hardly any visitors.

It is after 1pm when we get to Garnet. We stop on the brow of a hill and look down on the town, set in a clearing below us. The serried rank upon rank of soldier conifers in their dark green uniform have retreated to the background and here the accent is more on deciduous trees. Perhaps it has something to do with the higher elevation or merely just the soil, but here they are much further on than in Missoula, providing a veritable artist's palette of autumnal splendour that is a feast for the eyes.

It is picnic time and we set about consuming our food in the strong sunshine while we sit and contemplate the sight before us. The buildings, at least those that remain, look dilapidated for the most part, as you would hope and expect, but yet in a sufficient state of preservation that the imagination is not overtaxed picturing what they must have looked like when they were first built. Not so much a town any more, but more like a collection of buildings scattered throughout the clearing, though it is obvious where the main street would have been from the presence of a couple of buildings, bigger than the rest, with the high false frontages which clearly mark them out as public buildings. The others are clearly miners' cabins, dotted here and there randomly. Some seem in a perilous state of decay with caved-in roofs, almost entirely collapsed, others seem, at least from here, not exactly habitable but at least sufficient to provide some shelter - if you could ignore the thought that the roof might suddenly give way and give you a bit of a headache.

I can hardly wait to start exploring lest this solitude is spoiled by the arrival of other people, though you would hardly expect a mass influx along such a long and unmade road with only a collection of ramshackle buildings at the end of it - yet we came here, so why might not others? The last thing anyone would want in a ghost town would be a spirited bunch of the living disturbing the peace.

The obvious place to start is what would once have been the main street. Alas, many of the buildings are gone now, while those that do remain, for the most part, look ready to crumble, the logs grey with age, riddled with minute holes. The wooden sidewalks are gone, and if there are no wagon tracks to be seen, or horses or people, then all the better to imagine Gary Cooper in *High Noon,* one of the best films ever made.

Here is the jail, not a large building, with the date - 1876. It has either been restored or hardly used because it is in a pretty good state. So too is the hotel, at least from the outside. Peering in through the grimy windows, we can see a couple of rooms, surprisingly small given the overall dimensions of the building, but all we can make out is some peeling wallpaper.

Just then I catch sight of a woman crossing the street further ahead. Not quite a ghost town then. But where did she come from? There is no designated car park and no sign of any other car, nor could she have come after us or we would have heard her arrive. By the time she has crossed the street, it is clear that she is not a visitor but heading purposefully towards a cabin, the most habitable one in the town, the most *des res*, as if she owned the place, or at least lived there. By the time she has reached the door and just before she opens it without knocking, we are within sufficient hailing distance for me not to have to raise my voice too much.

"Em, excuse me... " She stops and turns round. "Em... I wonder if you could tell me, do you have any information about this place?"

For truth to tell, there is nothing to tell us what we are looking at and pleasant though it might be to just stroll about and absorb the decaying ambience of the place, better still would it be if we knew something about its history.

"Why, yes," says she. "Where y'all from?... Scotland! Hey, Jim," she shouts into the interior, "these people are all the way from Scotland!"

It turns out that Jim, her husband, is the custodian here.

"Yeah, we're doin' the place up, or tryin' to," he says. "Gonna take a long time. But we'll get there," he adds optimistically.

It looks like a massive project to me, a race against time and where's the money going to come from? They didn't even charge us for coming in here. But I don't give Jim the benefit of my doubts. Instead I ask: "I was wondering if you could tell us a bit about the place, its history and so on."

"Sure can. Be delighted to. Just a mo," and he disappears into the cabin to emerge a few minutes later with a sheaf of typewritten sheets while in the interim, his wife makes a fuss of the kids. "It's all in there," he says, "but I can tell you some facts if you'd like."

"Yes, please, if you don't mind."

"Well, for a start, you're in Garnet, not like most people think it's called, Garnet." I can hear the difference, though you can't see it. The correct pronunciation puts the stress on the last syllable and makes it sound like the sort of thing you don't want crawling through your hair, while the other is the sort of thing you might wear to keep your coiffure in place during the night.

"It was begun in 1895 when a guy named Dr Mitchell set up a stamp mill at the head of First Chance Gulch -"

"A stamp mill?"

"Yeah. A stamp mill is an ore crusher."

Seeing the blank look on my face, Jim realises that as an ignorant Scotsman, he needs to go back to basics. Taking a deep breath he goes on, "There are two types of mines, see. Placer mines an' ore mines. Placer mines are near the surface an' you wash the gold out with water, right? You've seen Western movies ain't you, where they pan for gold?" Well that's a placer mine. That's the easy stuff. This is the hard stuff. This stuff you gotta dig outta the ground, then you gotta crush the ore, see, to get at the gold."

Yes indeed, I do see this is real mining, real hard work, and I pass these thoughts on to Jim.

"Darn right," he says. "Mosta the miners were employees of mining companies."

What! Did I hear him right? Bang goes another romantic illusion. Gone is the notion of a bewhiskered old geezer, maybe with a "pardner", seeking, and more often than not, failing, to make his fortune, or staking a claim only to find that he's been duped in some way, or if he does strike it rich, some unscrupulous character or other comes along and robs him of the biggest nugget in the west. In actual fact, the only "romantic" thing about this whole sorry saga exists in the eyes of the beholder who likes a good story, seen through the prism of time and distance, especially the latter. In real life, I imagine, if you were to come within a whisker's length of the old-timer, you would discover that personal hygiene ran a poor second to the quest for gold.

Jim proceeds to destroy the illusion even more. "Yep. They had a Union an' their own hall where, as well as meetin's, they held dances every Saturd'y night. As well as other social events durin' the week of course."

Dear oh dear. This won't do. Far too civilised, far too modern, not like the movies at all. This could be Anytown, Anywhere. The more Jim talks, the more my illusions are being shot to pieces. And yet there is a jail. Surely there must have been *something* of the Wild West in "Garnit" wasn't there?

"Well," Jim admits, "there *is* a story that it was used once. A guy named Frank Dearn shot a dog while under the influence. You know, (what did you say your name was?) Dave, most people here carried guns but that was just to shoot game. Birds an' suchlike, you know, Dave?"

Oh, I could tell him about shooting birds for game all right. I'm not quite the innocent he takes me for. But there is something that puzzles me.

"You know, Jim, you told me, didn't you, that the town was founded in 1895?"

"Sure was. By Dr Mitchell. Dr Armistead Mitchell was his full handle an' they named the town for him, but that didn't last more'n two years 'fore they called it Garnet on accounta that stone bein' pretty plentiful around these parts, see?"

I do see, but what I still fail to comprehend is why the jail should predate the town by nearly twenty years. There must be some mistake.

"Well spotted, Dave! You're quite right. There's an old-timer, one of the former residents, comes up here to do some restoration work an' he kinda got his dates muddled!"

I understand perfectly. I often get dates muddled myself, but not wanting to burden Jim with my troublesome past on taking out young ladies, I ask instead, being careful to give it the correct pronunciation: "So when did Garnet become a ghost town?"

"Oh, just about the turna the century. The gold had pretty much run out by then. Well it wasn't exactly a ghost town then. But the population had shrunk from 1,000 in its heyday to 150 by 1905. Then there was a fire in 1912 that pretty much gutted the downtown area. Then there was the war. That took men away an' it was finally abandoned in the early Twenties. People just left their stuff, or the bulk of it, behind, walked clean out."

It sounds very sad, the way Jim puts it, the gradual decline moving inexorably to the end, just like a person growing old, except Garnet would not have been much older than twenty-five. And like all premature deaths, that is extremely sad. But then, after death, there was life. Garnet was resurrected.

"Gold doubled in price in 1934 an' the miners moved right back in, but then when the war came along again, dynamite was harder to come by an' the gold was harder to get out too, so Garnet became a ghost town again."

I have to remind myself that Garnet's second period of existence is actually longer than a European might at first suppose. As they did in the First World War, the Americans also showed up late for Part Two. We had been going at it hammer and tongs for more than two years before the dates on their war memorials began to record their sacrifice on another continent, so remote from their peaceful lives.

"A few people came back after the war, built new cabins, but by 1948 it was all over for good."

Just think - Garnet became a ghost town just about the time I was born! Such a short time ago! I wanted something much, much older. But that's the trouble with the Wild West. Even in the Civilised East, you struggle to find anything older than 200 years. Garnet. Born 1895, died 1948. Not a long life, especially when you take two prolonged periods of coma into account.

"Well, thanks, Jim. That was really interesting."

"You bet! Y'all take care now. You're our first visitors from Scotland!" he calls after us.

That doesn't surprise me. Montana is hardly on the hit list of your average tourist, let alone Missoula, let alone Garnet, which I only heard about courtesy of the *Missoulian.*

And so, armed with Jim's notes, we set off on our own exploration. Amongst the interesting facts we learn from them is that there were no less than 13 saloons. Now let me see... what's 13 into 1,000? Never mind. If you allow for the fact that these rough-and-ready drinking dens were a place that no respectable lady would be seen dead in, never mind a married one, (and there were a lot in Garnet) and take the children into account (the school catered for 41 students) let me see... that must bring prospective punters down to, let's say, something in the region of 600.

It's still not an easy sum for me to do but it sounds like an awful lot of watering holes for not a lot of people, and here's another thing - there is no mention in Jim's notes of any church. Surely such an edifice must have existed, and you might have expected to find at least three, based on a conservative guesstimate of a ratio of 1:5 with the saloons. And, considering the plethora of religious institutions that exist in Missoula today, all reflecting various shades of Christianity, surely it's not too much of a stretch of the imagination to believe that some of these differences existed then, amongst the God-fearing?

But where are these churches? One would hardly expect to see something the size of a cathedral, but surely to God, they would have built something at least as large as the one surviving hotel and that one, at least, would have survived. But it seems none has. Could it possibly be that there never was even one in the first place? Could it be that Garnet is closer to the Wild West town of my imaginings and it was inhabited entirely by the ungodly?

Jim's notes are getting more interesting by the minute. It says that drunkenness was common (well, there's a surprise) and although no murders were recorded, or any shootouts (how disappointing for we latter-day tourists - they might have shown us some consideration) the suicide rate was unusually high. I wonder why. Hard work, so the aphorism would have us believe, never killed anyone, but here it seems it did. Unless it was the climate of course. The Olympic peninsula in Washington State, I happen to have read, has the dubious distinction of being the most suicidal region of the United States and, coincidentally, is also the wettest part of the country. Surely this correlation can't be a coincidence?

But you only have to look at today's cloudless skies and instantly dismiss that theory. The sun is splitting the sky, which it has been doing practically every day since we came to this continent, with the notable exception of the deluge in Washington DC. True, we have yet to experience a Montana winter, but the miners could have all the firewood they could possibly want at their back door and seen it through as snug as a bug in a rug. Unless the snow cut them off for months which meant there would be a problem bringing in essential supplies, such as whiskey, from Deer Lodge or Missoula, a three day trip. Now *that* could drive a man to suicide.

There were four stores and the one run by F.A. Davey is one of the buildings still standing today. In fact, F.A. Davey never left Garnet. After all, if the miners found it uneconomical or too much effort to take their meagre wordly possessions with them when they left, how could he ship out a whole storeful of goods - and to where and to whom could he sell them? Better to put down the anchor, weather the storm and hope for better days ahead.

He stayed on throughout the Twenties with the ghosts, and if he thought he might be able to sell his stores to them, the solitude must have made him crazy. There is no mention of a Mrs Davey, so I can just picture him gnawing his solitary way through his stores and popping off the occasional rat with his shotgun to keep them at bay, because no matter how solitary he was, he wasn't going to share his food with them.

And, sure enough, his business acumen did not let him down, (if that is what it was) for as we know, after a decade had passed, the miners came back, but not the same ones who had lived here before. And what they made of a fully-equipped store (apart from what Frank ate) and ready-to-walk-in cabins, I imagine you will only be able to experience a similar sort of feeling, when St Peter lets you pass through the Pearly Gates.

Another notable resident of Garnet was J.K.Wells. She was a lady and an entrepreneur who already owned a hotel in nearby Bearmouth and who designed the hotel that bears her name today. The hotel, one of four, and now the only survivor, was once the grandest building in Garnet, the equal, it was said, of any hotel in Helena, the state capital. It boasted a pair of very fine entrance doors with stained glass windows (no expense spared) and an elaborate wooden staircase. There was a dining room, a women's parlour, an office, and of course, the kitchen. Three storeys high, the miners who could not afford a room slept in the attic, their space marked out by lines drawn on the floor.

For the privilege of having this roof over your head, it would set you back 25 cents a night and dear at the price, I would have thought, with all those legless miners - at least the ones who had managed to stagger up the stairs, and having got there, snoring fit enough to lift the roof just above their heads.

And it would have been pretty cold in the depths of winter as there was no heating in any of the rooms apart from the dining room. When it did close, in the 1930s, it did not close its doors forever, as Davey moved into the kitchen. Some rooms were occasionally occupied by his friends on the rare occasions when they came to visit, but when the hotel finally closed for the very last time, on Davey's decease, they found mushrooms growing on the undisturbed beds in the other rooms!

Davey died in 1947 and the following year, the goods in his store were sold off by public auction. That was when Garnet *really* became a ghost town and the only people who came after that were the souvenir hunters, taking the doors, and even the staircase from the hotel would you believe, not to mention stripping the cabins of their contents.

And if the Wells hotel was the plushest building in Garnet, then the miners' cabins were the worst. Garnet had ghosts in its genes. By that I mean these cabins were never built to last. They didn't bother to give them proper foundations, just built them on the bare earth. Get gold, get out quick ⁄ rich. (Except working for a company, where do you think the money really went?) Little wonder that so many of them look as if they have been undermined by an earthquake.

But because they still exist, albeit in a pretty ruinous state, it is possible to go into them and get a feel for what it must have been like to have lived in one. There is, remarkably, still a stove in one which, for some reason, the souvenir hunters must have decided not to liberate. Apart from that, they have been stripped completely bare. Which is a pity, as the artefacts of daily life would have made it easier to connect with the ghosts.

But that is where I have the drop on most visitors, because all I have to do is think of the wall decorations in Marnie's kitchen and those on the mantlepiece and those on the windowshelf of the family room and I can picture exactly what it would have been like. (No Coca-Cola bottles, naturally).

And I know another thing too. Although there is an alternative route home through the forest along the enticingly named Bear Gulch Road, I resist the temptation, don't consider taking it, not even for a minute. Proof indeed that I am becoming Americanised, wiser by far and not half so innocent as I once was when I first set foot in this country.

Chapter Forty-seven

*In which I become reacquainted with my phobia
and am privileged to learn a family secret.*

When I get up this morning I notice there is frost on the ground, a sign that winter cannot be far behind and summer days must finally cease. Having said that, I am up extra early and I have only myself to blame for that, for this is the morning of the extraordinary staff meeting. It is so chilly that I need to wear gloves and it seems an omen for the chilly atmosphere likely to be prevalent at the meeting.

Matt seems extra nervous this morning. But as I have already discovered about life, (and me only in my thirty-first year towards heaven) things that you look forward to never turn out as well as you had anticipated, while on the other hand, those which you dread turn out to be not nearly so bad either. Which is why one should always adopt a pessimistic attitude towards life if you would like to have a happy one, and who wouldn't? All night, if I had been Matt, I would have been fretting about it just to ensure that the actual event would not be the nightmare of my dreams - had I been able to get to sleep in the first place.

If ever there was a damp squib, this was it. If anyone had been looking forward to fireworks, then they would have been severely disappointed. The tsunami of anger and resentment I was expecting turns out, to my relief, to amount to no more than the merest ripple on a pond. Matt refuses to discuss the burning issue, removes it from the agenda although it was the only one on it. He reiterates what he had said at the last meeting: that if anyone has a complaint about him, then that was a private matter and he would only discuss it in private. Far from this setting up a howl of protest, this unilateral decision is accepted without demur, much to my surprise. Perhaps everyone is too stunned.

Sam initiates another complaint, supported by Art, about the size of the classes in the Intermediate part of the school. Even I can see that this is never going anywhere. And so we are dismissed.

* * *

Today my teaching day does not stop thirty minutes after the students go home because I have agreed to take on an extra-curricular student, not I must confess, with a great deal of enthusiasm. The reason for this point of view you will readily appreciate when I tell you who my new student is. Charlie by name, he couldn't care less for any lessons in English and probably less for Scottish life and culture. In fact, he is so retarded he can't even spell his own name, let alone write it. He does have certain compensations however. He is very good-looking and has very nice silky ears, but his best feature is his nose. This olfactory organ is far superior to mine. While mine is white (well probably red after a visit to Al's) and has a tendency to spread over my face, Charlie's is black and protruding and tends to be on the wet side. But that is a good thing as it is a sign of health, whereas when mine is wet, it is a sign that I am suffering from another sanguinary cold.

Charlie is in fact, a Spaniel, and I have agreed to help Steve train him retrieve the birds he shoots. It didn't sound as if it would be too taxing. All I had to do, Steve said, was to pull a dead bird along behind me at the end of a string. That was enough to send shivers down my spine but how could I refuse to help Steve after being such a good friend to me? In any case it doesn't sound too bad. As long as I kept my eyes ahead of me, I could pretend I was a small boy pulling a toy engine behind me, couldn't I?

We drive out to some wasteland. Charlie is in the back of the truck; Steve and I are in the cab along with another. I'd rather be in the back with Charlie despite the lack of comfort because the third passenger beside us is a pheasant which has seen better days and that's not just because it is dead. Steve says it has been dead for two weeks.

"It's all right," he laughs, seeing my look of horror. "I've had it in the fridge!"

Fridge, mind you, not freezer. Imagine if I had been at his house and he hadn't told me about the feathered corpse, had just invited me to help myself to a beer from the fridge - I would have freaked out when I opened the door. I can't imagine what Jackie made of having to share the space with this disgusting object slowly decaying amongst the cold meat and cheese. It's important, Steve explains, that it should be a bit niffy so Charlie's nose has something to work on in the early days of his training. Yes I can see that and I can also see that if Steve takes any right bends too sharply, that *thing* is going to slide across the bench towards me and pin me against the door because I will be so frozen stiff with horror at the sight and feel of it nestling against my thigh that I would be powerless to touch it and put it back.

To my relief, when we get to our destination, Steve grabs the bird so I don't have to, but there is a shock in store when we get to the spot where the training is to start.

"Right, Dave. First you gotta pull some feathers out an' rub the ground with them, like this, then pull the bird along for about two hundred yards, then take the string off the bird an' hide in the bushes. OK?"

"Yeah, sure." I hope I am making my voice sound totally unconcerned. I probably am, as if Steve hadn't realised from my performance on Saturday that I have a morbid fear of feathers, then he probably never will ‑ unless it is today.

"Great. Gimme a shout when you're ready," and with that he exits stage left and I am left with the bird.

The ground is rough and uneven with tussocks of course grass and I have hardly gone any distance when I am aware that the string suddenly feels very light. To my dismay, the string has come off the bird.

I steel myself as I make a knot and place the string round the neck, just below the head. My dilemma is if I tie it back on too tightly, it means having to dig my fingers into the feathers, make contact with that sinewy lifeless neck when I have to untie it again. On the other hand, if I don't tie it on tightly enough, I'll have to go through the ghastly process again sooner than I must.

Off I go again, but more cautiously now, yet the body of the bird is bouncing off the tussocks in the most alarming of ways. Right, this should be far enough. I untie the knot and disappear into the undergrowth, where in a few minutes, along comes Charlie followed by Steve at the end of a long lead. I can see Steve pointing to Charlie, indicating the way he should go. Charlie's nose goes down and I am inclined to believe it is more by luck than good management that he eventually finds the corpse and stands over it, sniffing.

"This time don't go in a straight line, weave about a bit, huh?"

I can bob and weave about with the best of them but what I can barely bear to do is put the string round that neck again. Now I have to do an even worse thing - pull out some feathers and rub them into the ground. I'm glad Steve is not around to see how my hand trembles and knowing he can't see me, there is no need to suppress a shudder as I pull out a handful from the breast, averting my eyes as I do so.

Twice more I go through this ghastly routine. By this time, the pheasant is beginning to look rather the worse for wear. The chill has worn off and all this being dragged about by the neck and being denuded of its feathers has done little to improve its condition.

It does not surprise me unduly when the string goes slack again, only when I go back to the bird, a fresh horror greets my eyes. It is not the string that has come off at all; the head has become detached from the body. And to make matters worse, there is something red and stringy and obscene trailing out from the severed neck. As for untying the string from the decapitated head...

It's time to shout for Steve. I want to shout, "I can't do this any more. I feel sick." But instead I just shout to tell him I am ready.

To my relief, Steve examines the debris and decides Charlie's lessons for the day (and my horrors) are over. I think I must have done all right because when we go back to Steve's house he gives me a big bag of squash, potatoes, carrots and onions. I don't think Charlie did so well though. He only gets a handful of dog biscuits. Clearly he has much more to learn. I hope I am not going to be his tutor.

* * *

"Hey, Dave, where y'bin? Ain't seen you in ages. You wantin' some wood?"

It's Al's voice booming down the line. He seems incapable of speaking quietly. Given the nearness of our houses to each other, he could just have just as well have stood at his front door and spoken to me from there. But why not use the phone? After all it is free.

Well of course I want some wood. Hadn't I laboured hard and long for it, looked more like a miner than a lumberjack by the time I had dragged my weary body back for a lukewarm shower before bed, before school in the morning? A hot bath was impossible due to the sunburn. And what had I to show for all that? Not even a splinter. Now it looks as if I'm going to get my share at last, and not before time too if this morning's weather was anything to judge by. I tell him, yes I could use some wood.

"Come on over. Have some wine an' we'll talk about it."

Before I go over, however, I pick up a bill that had arrived by this morning's post. I had hoped that when the Sewer Arranger did the job and no bill had come in that that was the last I was going to hear of it.

By the time I arrive, Al, naturally, is already ensconced behind the breakfast bar with a glass of wine ready to hand. He takes a gallon flagon out of the fridge and pours out a generous measure into a large glass, taking care to top up his own before he sits down. The wine is from California, extremely tasty and so cold that condensation forms on the glass. I tell Al how much I like it, that it reminds me of my birch sap wine and Al amazes by telling me it is only $5.50 a gallon. To think I've been missing it all this time!

"So what you bin doin', Dave?"

When Sherlock Holmes was faced with a particularly knotty problem, it took two pipes before he arrived at the solution. Similarly, to bring Al up to date with my activities takes two large glasses of wine. And if his laughter is anything to judge by, by the end of the second glass they must be getting the better in the telling. The really funny thing though is I didn't think they were funny at all.

"I've found a great new place for firewood," Al says, replenishing our glasses when I have finished.

"Oh, yeah?"

"Yeah, up Pattee Canyon."

"Oh, right." I have a vague idea where Pattee Canyon is but it comes as a severe disappointment that if I want some firewood I am going to have to endure another logging expedition. Something of that must have shown on my face as Al hastens to reassure me.

"It's OK, Dave," and he gives one of his great belly laughs. "This ain't nearly such hard work. The wood's much easier to get out, an' a lot lighter."

I don't see how he can tell that as it's unlikely a balsa plantation has somehow found its way to these northern climes, but I hold my peace. However, before we get on to the details of when Grandpa and I will be pressed into slavery again, Terri drifts in to the kitchen.

"Terri, see this bill from the Sewer Arranger?"

"Yeah, hon. What about it?"

To be addressed like this makes me feel like one of the family, like I have got my feet under the table. And I have got really fond of Al and Terri and appreciate especially the alternative perspective of America Al provides outside the teaching fraternity.

"Well, em... you see, I shouldn't have to pay it."

Once more I go through the reasons why I should not have to pay. There are a few other shortcomings I'd like to have mentioned as well such as having to subsidise a whole family's electricity bill for a month but I let that go. I am, after all, talking to Marnie's best friend.

It's an invidious position to put her in, between the rock of her old friend and the hard place of the new one - me. But I can't think of anyone better placed to be in such a position. Terri takes this in her stride as usual. In a real crisis she's the one you would want to have about you with a cool, clear head that could appraise the situation rationally. Just now I can see she's thinking: *It's only a bill (as the toucan said); what the heck's the fuss about?* I ask her to send the bill on to Marnie, or let her know about it which she agrees to do with that characteristic shrug of her shoulders and the monosyllabic "sure" as if that was all the discussion such a tiny little difficulty merited.

But if I thought that was the end of the discussion about the Sewer Arranger I was much mistaken. As a sort of ex-officio member of the family, (as I now see myself) they share a family confidence with me and if I couldn't imagine Terri being worried about anything, then I was wrong, because I was, incredibly, just about to find out what it was and all because I had brought up the subject of the Sewer Arranger. As it turns out, this is a subject that had been occupying their minds a lot recently.

The Sewer Arranger business is owned by the parents of Little Al's girlfriend, or it would be more appropriate to say, as we say in Scotland, "bidie-in" which amuses Terri and Al no end and for the moment at least, lightens the mood. The burning issue of the moment is that Little Al has been offered a partnership in the business but it seems conditional on his making an honest woman of the daughter, who it seems is "great with child" as the Bible would put it. Al and Terri have invited the girl's parents round on Friday for one of Al's legendary Italian dinners, to get to know them better. Not the prospective daughter-in-law mind you, but the parents. Neither Al nor Terri are in favour of the match, but for different reasons apparently.

It's not that Terri seems to have anything against the girl as such, she just thinks Little Al shouldn't get married yet. I haven't got my feet that far under the table that she explains her reasons, so I can only deduce that at twenty-five, she must consider him too young. As it happens, that was my age when I got married (not that Terri knows that) and she must have got married a great deal younger than that, so I'm not entirely convinced that that can be the reason, unless she thinks he is incredibly immature.

Al is a bit more forthcoming. Perhaps the answer lies *in vino veritas* as Pliny put it, because he has been replenishing his glass much more frequently than ours, yet I imagine he has been quaffing wine (and other alcoholic beverages) in vast quantities for many years and perhaps the effects of this light-bodied wine have not loosened the tongue as much as one would expect from less practised drinkers.

Al has a problem with the girl's parents. *They* don't think they have a problem: they are doing just fine, thank you very much. Far too well in fact for Al's liking. He smells a rat.

"They only work at Sears for Chris' sake," he says, sloshing more wine into everyone's glass but naturally he gets the lion's share which is only right as he has the loudest roar in the house and the emptiest glass. "I bet they earn even less money than you, Dave," he says as if that proved everything. I know Blake's wife works there but it had never occurred to me to wonder what she earned, but now I wouldn't be surprised if it were just as much as me, despite my four years at university. From all I have seen, their standard of living, and I don't just mean Blake and Diane's, is much higher than ours. And yet Blake, Steve and Nat all supplement their income in various ways, not least by hunting and fishing so that their butcher's bill must be practically non-existent.

In Scotland you certainly don't go into teaching for the money and I am not in the least insulted by Al's remark though I am sure he doesn't realise just how true what he said is. He probably assumes I am earning something like Marnie and if I were to reveal that actually it's a little more than half as much, it would probably be enough to make him choke on his wine. It was a golden opportunity to reveal why I was so anal-retentive about having to pay a bill to the Sewer Arranger but the moment passed and it was lost.

However, I had just had some good news: a letter from Her Majesty's Inland Revenue Service to the effect that because I shall be non-resident in the country for a year and more, I am not liable for income tax. But even with this new tax status, the equivalent of a massive 20% pay rise, it's still not a large amount I take back at the end of the month.

There is something seriously wrong with the lavish lifestyle of the prospective in-laws which arouses Al's suspicions at least. He knows it can't be because of the Sewer Arranger business. Little Al is not that busy, to say nothing of clients like me who don't pay their bills. The source of their wealth has to come from somewhere else. Not everyone has a rich maiden aunt who has bequeathed them a legacy and it seems Al (and maybe Terri) have discounted that possibility as being too remote to be worth considering. That's why they have invited them round on Friday, to see what sort of people they are.

I don't quite know how, but somehow we get on to the subject of the Mafia after that and Al vouchsafed the opinion that it was rife in the United States, the basis of all successful businesses. Robert Kennedy he said, had managed to jail a leader of the Mafia, only for the Republican President "Tricky Dicky" Nixon grant him a free pardon. Furthermore, he alleges, with a great deal of conviction in his voice, it was the Mafia who killed Kennedy, not those "goddamned Communists".

It comes as a surprise to me, Al's vehemence against the Mafia. Does he not claim Italian heritage and what could be more Italian, apart from spaghetti, than the Mafia?

And here's the most amazing thing of all. Al in his shades, which he wears as part of his uniform, gives him a mean and sinister look which I automatically associate with the sort of people who go about mowing down people with machine guns concealed in violin cases.

I'm sure if Al remembers to wear his shades indoors on Friday, the meeting with the prospective in-laws will be a resounding success, especially if they *are* involved in anything shady.

Chapter Forty-eight

*In which we entertain the Faculty and anticipate
a great year ahead.*

The after-the-game club, Art, Chuck and me, met as usual on Friday but in The Florence for a change, where the free fare to accompany the half-price beer was spare ribs in a barbecue sauce. As usual, we were joined by Sam and his lawyer friend, Chris, and also by a friend of his called Pete who asked me if could find a mohair blanket for him. Although we don't have Angora goats in Scotland, (at least I have never seen one) we do have sheep by the score and each one with more bagfuls of wool than Baa, Baa, Black sheep.

This, no doubt, is why Pete assumes Scotland would be a good place to buy a mohair blanket. I told him I'd see what I could find out but his request makes me realise that I haven't seen a single sheep since I came to this country. Admittedly, you wouldn't expect to see them grazing the streets of Washington DC or waiting to catch a flight from Salt Lake City airport, but the area round Missoula seems like prime sheep country and I can't think why this empty landscape is not flecked with white dots safely grazing these acres and acres of hillside. Maybe that's it. There are just too many predators about like bears and mountain lions for whom hunting skills would soon become redundant. It would just be like going down to the supermarket and taking your pick. Spoiled for choice actually, unless you got tired of lamb.

It is a black sheep that eventually rolls into 419 Lincoln some time later, which turns out to be not exactly the safest environment for a sheep of that hue to be. I try to explain that I just couldn't get away as we all had to buy a pitcher and as there were six of us, it naturally took a bit longer. Besides, I couldn't leave until Art did as I was dependent upon him to give me a lift home as he stows my bike in the back of his wagon. But, for some reason, this does not go down too well.

Did I not realise, the trouble and strife wants to know, that while I have been enjoying myself she has been slaving over a hot stove and looking after two small children into the bargain? Furthermore, we have guests due to arrive any moment or had that completely escaped my tiny little mind? And what's more, there is something she has been dying to tell me all afternoon: she had taken George to the Hearing Impaired Department at the university or had I forgotten about that too and did I want to hear how my only begotten son had got on, or am I just not interested?

I apologise in chastened tones, but this broadside is insufficient to sink the feeling of bonhomie washing about inside me. "I am all ears," I tell her, putting my fingers behind them and making them flap.

To my surprise, this attempt to lighten the atmosphere seems to have the opposite effect and it is fortunate there was not one of Marnie's frying pans near to hand or my skull may have dented it. I suppose on reflection, it wasn't the most tasteful of responses under the circumstances. After I have apologised again and eaten humble pie, (which leaves me feeling rather full on top of the beers, not to mention the spare ribs) and Iona has got her temper under control again, she informs me that they tested George's hearing aid and found that it was useless. Even fully turned up, the amplification was negligible; it was actually doing more harm than good as there was so much crackling and distortion, he would be better off without it. I don't suppose however, that being left on the grass, baking in the full glare of the sun or being chucked on the floor of Albertsons is hardly conducive to the effectiveness of such sensitive equipment.

Since it is American made, Mike, the audiologist, is going to contact the makers about getting it repaired. Until then we are hiring one. Iona says that Mike tried several and with this particular aid, the one George is wearing now, the effect was instantaneous and remarkable. His face lit up as if a light had been switched on in his head and he began "speaking".

So different from the battle we had to get him one in the first place and when we finally succeeded, we were just given one off the shelf, or so it seems, as it was never tested on George while he was wearing it. In fact, one day Iona suspected it wasn't working when George pulled a pile of saucepans out of the cupboard onto the floor and showed not the slightest reaction whatsoever to the hellish clatter. She took the aid back to the audiology department of the hospital who didn't even test it, merely dismissed her with the words: "It's early days, yet." Did they take her for an over-anxious Mum? Or were they determined to prove us wrong; that they were right, that a hearing aid on one so young wouldn't be of any use? They were right about that anyway. That one certainly wouldn't.

George is going to go back for further tests and audiograms and they will monitor his progress. Meanwhile Iona is taking him to school three mornings a week where, even with his stubby little fingers, his signing is coming on, as is mine with my weekly night class. We have the same teacher, Kathy Kuhn. The difference is he is in diapers and I am not and my mummy doesn't take me there and his does. Apart from that, we are learning the same words.

We have certainly landed on our feet as far as George is concerned, and not to be outdone, on Wednesday afternoons, Hélène goes to the university too. She's been enrolled in a speech and language class as a role model for kids who have language difficulties. Hopefully, as a result of listening to her, these American kids will be cured soon and learn to talk properly - with a Scottish accent.

* * *

Naturally, when Steve, Blake and Nat arrive with their spouses, the conversation inevitably turns to school, only with a couple of nuts like Blake and Steve about, the conversation is never serious for long. They love teaching and they love the kids, but have little time for pedagogy. Which makes them a bit like me.

Earlier that day, at school, as the classes changed over, I had been moaning to Blake and Steve (Nat was already in full swing with his class) about having to give up my Saturday to attend the meeting of Reading teachers organised by Tammy Kinsella. That means all K7 - K8 teachers as we all teach Reading. I am the Language Arts specialist. That means literature, which means appreciating the written word, which a priori, assumes the students have a basic understanding of how their own language works which, regrettably, is not always the case.

I don't know about Nat's plans, but Blake and Steve are voting with their feet, but just how great a distance they were going to put between themselves and the meeting I was just about to discover.

"You shouldn't do that, Dave," Blake had remarked with his trademark serious tone and expression to match, as if he had caught me picking my nose, but in fact he meant I should not bother going to the meeting.

"Why not?" I had expected some words of wisdom, based on previous experience, that these meetings were a total waste of time.

"You should come backpackin' with us instead."

"Yeah," Steve chimed in. "He's right. You'd have a much better time with us. Have another Montanan experience instead of listenin' to all that bullshit."

I certainly can believe that, but then it's not much of a contest. Any time spent with Steve and Blake, as long as it does not involve killing and disembowelling animals has to be time well spent as they are such entertaining characters in their own right. But what's more, they are such natural foils for each other, it is as if it was in their stars that they should teach together, like some double act on the stage.

"Tell me more about it. Where are you going?"

They exchanged glances before Blake piped up. "That's a secret... we don't want anyone to find out about it... but we're gonna camp by a lake in Idaho."

My dilemma is Tammy is probably counting on my being there. She hadn't said so, but it wouldn't surprise me in the least if she intended I should address the meeting, though the message that I had retrieved from my pigeon hole seemed to suggest that a proper lecture to all Reading teachers in Missoula would be reserved for a later occasion: I was destined to bullshit later. More worryingly and more pertinently - was I not on exchange to find out more about the

American way of education? If I didn't go, wouldn't that be like a betrayal of the exchange - that I was here under false pretences?

"It's up to you, Dave," Blake said, after I had expressed these doubts and reservations, but he then added in a tone so earnest that it made a deep impression on me, "but it's an experience you'll never forget." He made it sound like the opportunity of a lifetime.

As he so often did, he was swinging his arms so the fist of his right hand slapped into the palm of his left and it seemed to me that the right hand represented the pursuit of American culture (and a good time with friends) while the other represented professional duty. Recreation or education? The choice was mine.

What was I to do? I reckoned there was nothing I could usefully gain from this meeting, but I didn't want to let Tammy down. Had she definitely signed me up to speak, then of course I would not have been faced with this dilemma. But I remember how Matt had taken me by surprise that first day when he had asked me if I had anything to "share" and I can just see Tammy saying the same thing, in which case it would be only fair to warn her that I would not be attending, if that was what I decided to do. And that, I must confess, was one of the biggest obstacles to making a decision in favour of Idaho - having the guts to tell Tammy I would not be coming. What possible excuse could I come up with that would not make it sound that I regarded her meeting as a lesser priority than backpacking in the wilds of Idaho?

Throughout my class I wrestled with the mighty problem and when lunchtime came, I decided to phone Iona. After all, if I were to be gone all Saturday and most of Sunday, Iona should have some say in this and if she said no, that would be my dilemma resolved, but good wife that she is, she said I could go if I wanted. Ball back in my court. I knew all along what I really wanted to do but how did I break the news to Tammy?

Taking a deep breath, I dialled her number and oh, the relief to find she was not in and I had to leave the bad news with her secretary and no explanations were necessary. Another instance of my philosophy of life: when you worry about things, they turn out to be not nearly as bad as you expect.

So it is all systems go for Idaho. We leave tomorrow morning at eight. Same time as the meeting, but instead of sitting in a stuffy classroom, I'll be breathing in the clean, fresh air in the wilds of Idaho. The early start, which had horrified me, does not seem nearly so bad now.

As I was saying, when teachers get together, school is always on the menu but I never expected the conversation to take the turn it did and Blake's opening gambit has me spluttering into my soup. But then, knowing him, I probably should have been better prepared, but I never was a very good Boy Scout.

"Remember that time I put the cow's vagina in your box, Steve!"

"Yeah. Boy, was that a laugh!"

While Blake and Steve relive the moment, the tears of laughter welling in their eyes, I can hardly wait to hear the details when Blake recovers the power of speech again. It sounds such a surreal scenario. I can't possibly imagine putting any part of a cow in one of my colleague's boxes, let alone the most intimate part. But then we Scots are maybe just a bit too staid for our own good and for that you can blame Calvin or John Knox or anyone else you like. But you couldn't possibly blame anyone for freaking out if you saw such a thing in your box, could you?

Steve didn't. He recognised it for what it was and who must have put it there so he merely tossed it, at random, in another box which happened to be Mo Momoko's. She, in her turn, not knowing what it was, but knowing it was nothing to do with her, and again at random, like pass-the-parcel, placed it without thinking and one imagines, rather gingerly in someone else's box. That person happened to be Mary Mason, a K3 teacher who had asked me, in all seriousness: "Do you have Coca-Cola in Scotland?"

Mary picked it up and looked at it, puzzled, as well she might.

"What's this?" she asked to no-one in particular, holding it up so all could see.

"That's a beaver pelt," Blake said, with his usual sang-froid tone and wooden expression.

"Oh, is it?" she said. "I've never seen one of those before. Thank you." And she took it off to her class to show the kids.

This episode reminds Blake of another tale of the same ilk, about the time he asked a farmer who had just dispatched a cow if he could have the entrails, giving as a reason that he wanted to use them for a biology lesson. We used to have to cut up frogs which we found revolting enough, but Byron's biology lesson seemed to me to be going a million miles too far.

But obtaining these entrails was only the start of Blake's story, shocking though that may be. No, it's what he did with them next that was the real point of his tale and I imagine he chose his victim carefully for the maximum effect. Removing everything from the poor girl's desk, he poured the entrails inside. I can just see them spreading out to fill every corner, quivering in their hideous, glutinous tubes until they settled down, lying in wait for the poor unsuspecting victim to open the lid... I thought then and wonder now, if some nights, in her smothering dreams, does her mind replay this scene and does she wake up screaming the house down? And all I wanted to do was get them to *write* a horror story!

"An' d'you know what else he does, Dave?" This is his wife, Diane, speaking. "When he breaks wind, a really smelly one, before it has time to disappear, he calls some poor kid up to the desk and makes it stand beside him while he pretends to explain something and the poor kid has to breathe in the guff and if he can, he lets off another one."

Blake throws his head back in a loud guffaw and smacks the table with the flat of his hand, not in the least embarrassed at this exposure. I suppose someone who shares his smelliest farts with other people instead of moving away or pretending he can't smell anything, like I do when one treacherously sneaks out in company, wouldn't be ashamed. I can just see him and Diane in bed together and him fluffing up the blankets after he has let one off, just to help her insomnia, so she can be gassed into unconsciousness.

After we have recovered from this latest tale, and in what seems to me to be a more serious change of tone, Blake asks, directing those piercing blue eyes at me in particular, but actually addressing everyone round the table: "You ever seen a coupla hares fightin'?"

I bet *he* has and is going to tell us. He was probably out hunting them when he came upon the scene. Aren't they supposed to box? I tell him I haven't, but once, in my very first year of teaching (not in my present school), I suspended a lesson to watch two rams, or maybe they were ewes, fighting, backing off and head-butting each other so hard that I thought I was the one getting the headache.

"No, no, Dave," Blake laughs. "Not that kind of hare. A hair, like you have on your head."

"A hair? A hair fighting?"

"Yes. If you get a saucer an' fill it with water, I'll show you."

Mystified and curious, I do as requested. It's probably something to do with electricity, I reflect, and he's the scientist amongst us so he's probably going to do some sort of conjuring trick pretending it's him, when in actual fact, it only the appliance of science. He plucks a couple of hairs from my head, his being far too short, and places the first on the surface of the water.

"Now look closely," he says as he prepares to put the second one beside its companion. But when he does, the second hair just floats about on its own and neither shows the slightest interest in the other. "It's startin' to happen," Blake reports, leaning forward, "look closer!"

Frightened that I might miss it, intrigued, I too lean closer, then - wham, the flat of Blake's hand hits the water and the next second I am screwing the water out of my eyes and everyone is laughing and I am feeling very foolish indeed but then I start laughing too at how I had been completely taken in, just like poor Mary Mason had been by the part of a cow that Blake told her was a beaver pelt. But then it was an easy mistake to make. It was a kind of beaver in a way, as I had learned on my fishing trip with Al.

It strikes me this is a lesson and a metaphor for this exchange. It reminds me I am still an innocent, however much I think I may have learned about life and living in Montana. And there were to be plenty more culture shocks in store throughout the year, beginning in fact, the very next day with the backpacking trip.

But that tale, and the others, will have to be told another time.

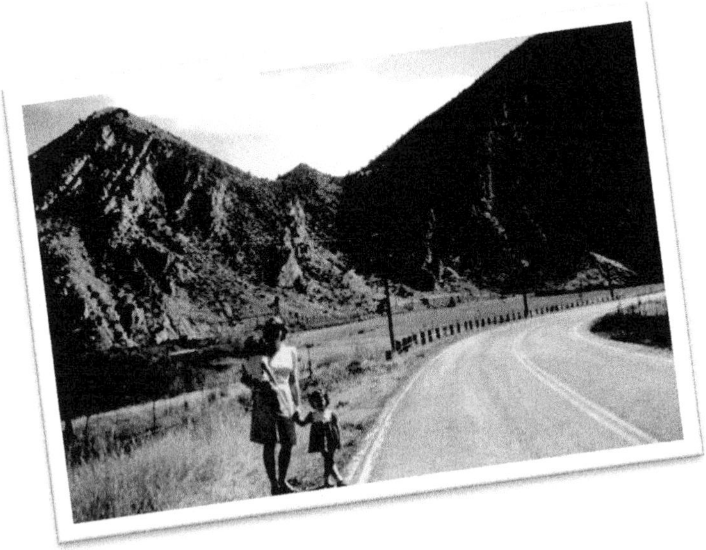

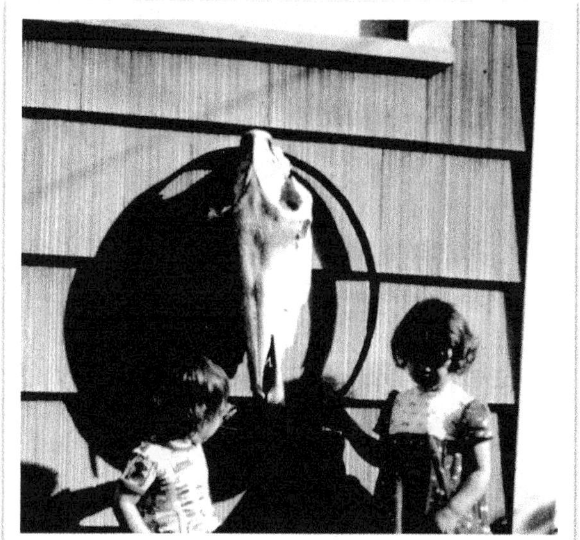

SCHOOL BUS

BACON
BUTTER
CIGARS
COFFEE
CANDLES
CHEESE
WEATHER
MONT. HAS
MILES
COURTESY ON THE
ROAD IS CONTAGIOUS
IN BEAR GULCH
JIM MALONE
BILLY MILLER
BILL HORNER
CHARLES PURISH
DICK MERCER
GEORGE TROXEL
JOHN STUART
RALPH NICES
C.M. BEST
WM. CRAMER
IRA DAY
W.S. DAY
FRED JACKSON
WEIGHED 32 OUNCES
GEORGE
W CHAPIN
JOHN J.
CHAPIN SON
COURTESY ON THE

About the Author

A native of Banff, Scotland, David M. Addison is a graduate of Aberdeen University. In addition to essays in various publications, he has written eight books, mainly about his travels.

As well as a short spell teaching English as a foreign language in Poland when the Solidarity movement at its height, he spent a year (1978-79) as an exchange teacher in Montana.

He regards his decision to apply for the exchange as one of the best things he ever did, for not only did it give him the chance to travel extensively in the US and Canada but during the course of the year he made a number of enduring friendships. His award-winning *An Innocent Abroad* is the first in a planned trilogy about this extraordinary year while the second, *Still Innocent Abroad*, will be coming soon from Extremis Publishing.

Since taking early retirement (he is not as old as he looks), he has more time but less money to indulge his unquenchable thirst for travel (and his wife would say for Cabernet Sauvignon and malt whisky). He is doing his best to spend the children's inheritance by travelling as far and wide and as often as he can.

Coming Soon from Extremis Publishing

Still Innocent Abroad

In the sequel to his award-winning *An Innocent Abroad*, Scot David M. Addison continues his account of a year spent as an exchange teacher in Missoula, Montana in the western United States.

When he embarked on the exchange, the author vowed he would embrace every experience (within reason) that came his way and mostly they *were* reasonable, though there were some he would not care to repeat.

In the course of this book, he experiences seasonal activities such as Hallowe'en (American style), Kris Kringle and Thanksgiving. He also sits his driving test in his wreck of a wagon which he not-so-fondly dubs "The Big Blue Mean Machine" and whose malfunctions continue to plague him in this book, just as they did in the last.

Nevertheless the author and his young family put their trust in it to take them, in winter, on the 1,200 mile round trip over the snow-clad Rockies to visit relations in Canada – just for a long weekend. Which just goes to show you that although he may have learned some things, this author from a small island is still very much an innocent abroad in this vast and mountainous land to even contemplate embarking on such an expedition – particularly since he set out so ill equipped.

Meanwhile, at school, he is on his best behaviour as he tries not to repeat the shocks and alarms of the first few days when he found himself up to his neck in trouble with parents out to get his guts for garters. The reader will not be disappointed to discover that he still finds some parents and students challenging. At the same time, he is also on his guard for attacks from the "enemy" within – his practical-joker colleagues who are all too keen to exploit his innocence for their own amusement.

The narrative ends with the traumatic events on Christmas Day. It would have been a memorable day whatever happened, but no-one bargained for the Addisons turning their hosts' Christmas Day into one they would not forget in a hurry.

www.extremispublishing.com

For details of new and forthcoming books
from Extremis Publishing,
please visit our official website at:

www.extremispublishing.com

or follow us on social media at:

www.facebook.com/extremispublishing

www.linkedin.com/company/extremis-publishing-ltd-/